Relational Inequalities

Relational Inequalities

An Organizational Approach

Donald Tomaskovic-Devey
Dustin Avent-Holt

Oxford University Press is a department of the University of Oxford. It furthers the University's objective of excellence in research, scholarship, and education by publishing worldwide. Oxford is a registered trade mark of Oxford University Press in the UK and certain other countries.

Published in the United States of America by Oxford University Press
198 Madison Avenue, New York, NY 10016, United States of America.

Library of Congress Cataloging-in-Publication Data
Names: Tomaskovic-Devey, Donald, 1957- author. | Avent-Holt, Dustin Robert, 1980- author.
Title: Relational inequalities : an organizational approach / Donald Tomaskovic-Devey and Dustin Avent-Holt.
Description: New York : Oxford University Press, [2019] |
Includes bibliographical references.
Identifiers: LCCN 2018015590| ISBN 9780190624422 (hard cover) |
ISBN 9780190624439 (pbk.) | ISBN 9780190624453 (epub)
Subjects: LCSH: Equality.
Classification: LCC HM821 .T64 2018 | DDC 305.5/1—dc23
LC record available at https://lccn.loc.gov/2018015590

Contents

Acknowledgments

Writing a book is a relational process, much like the general processes we discuss in the book (though less inequality exists in these relationships). This is especially true in a synthetic work like this one. As such, we are indebted to the many scholars whose work inspired us and provided the empirical and theoretical foundations on which we built this book. The most important of these is undoubtedly Charles Tilly, whose book *Durable Inequality* provided the inspiration and confidence to pursue our empirical agenda and to write a book with a big argument.

Many people have contributed to this book via their writings. There are too many of these to thank individually, other than to cite their work and name them in the text. A few were particularly influential, and we feel the need to mention them by name here: Joan Acker, Evelyn Glenn, Randy Hodson, Michael Schwalbe, and Barbara Tomaskovic-Devey. Quite a few people read our summaries of their own work as we referenced it or of specific chapters. These included Ellen Berrey, Martha Crowley, Katherine Kellogg, Alena Křížková, Carolina Muñoz, Larry King, Joya Misra, Irene Padavic, Victor Roy, Vinnie Roscigno, Leslie Salzinger, Ofer Sharone, Laurel Smith-Doerr, and Adia Harvey Wingfield. A few generous souls read the entire manuscript and provided invaluable help in clarifying our argument and presentation. These include Nancy Folbre, Tim Hallett, Ken Hou-Lin, Eunmi Mun, Jake Rosenfeld, Kevin Stainback, George Wilson, and Steven Vallas. Of course, any errors, omissions, and annoyances that remain are all of our own doing.

The project also benefited from the early research assistance of Ragini Malhotra and Nate Myers, who read many of the ethnographies we selected to include in this work and content-coded them for key analytic themes in our theoretical narrative. Peter Kent-Stoll provided careful copy editing as the book neared completion.

We report a great deal of our own research in this book, but even that was done in collaboration with others. Material on Swedish organizational inequalities was jointly developed with Martin Hällsten. Material on German workplace inequality was jointly developed with Peter Jacobebbinghaus, Silvia Melzer, and Carsten Sauer. Analyses of IT firm variation in employment diversity was jointly produced with Joo-Hee Han. The Australian-US class comparisons as well as our analysis in Chapter 8 of the influence of embeddeness on firm-to-firm exchanges were developed with Catherine Zimmer and Sandra Harding. Our past joint work with Kevin Stainback and Ken-Hou Lin directly informs the historical discussions of gender and racial desegregation of US workplaces since the Civil Rights Act and the rise of a financialized US economy, respectfully. We thank them for helping us develop a more historically, institutionally grounded approach to inequalities. Our research was supported at various times by the US National Science Foundation, the Russell Sage Foundation, the Alexander von Humboldt Foundation, and the SFB 882 Inequalities and Heterogeneities Project at Bielefeld University. Research stays at Bielefeld, Sciences Po, Utrecht University, and Stockholm University helped support this research as well.

The argument in *Relational Inequalities* was developed jointly by Avent-Holt and Tomaskovic-Devey in conversations that began in 2003. In the years that followed there were a series of five small conferences organized around the notion that we should be studying inequalities relationally and in organizational context. One of those was held in conjunction with the Eastern Sociological Society meeting, another at the Academy of Management meetings, two in conjunction with the Southern Sociological Society, and one at Northeastern University. The latter was sponsored by the American Sociological Association's Fund for the Discipline grant to Steven Vallas. These conferences attracted many of the people we cite in this work, and they were important forums for the development of a more general group of scholars with a relational inequality agenda as well as early and sound criticisms of our developing argument. Importantly, Vincent Roscigno and George Wilson edited two volumes of the *American Behavioral Scientist* featuring this work. The ideas, research, and agenda developed in this book were also presented at scores of conferences and university seminars. At this point it is impossible to say where all the influences on our thinking came from and which concepts in the book were the result of these fleeting moments of intellectual engagement. If you see your words or our conversation reflected in this book, we thank you too.

Finally, we want to thank our life-partners—Laura Avent-Holt and Barbara Tomaskovic-Devey—who were patient listeners and wise counselors over the many years we worked on this book.

Relational Inequalities

1

Generating Inequalities

How are inequalities generated? Why are economic resources increasingly concentrated in a few hands? Why do some people get paid less and others more? Why do some get better jobs, more training, and support from co-workers? Why are some people treated with respect and others as inconsequential? Who is deemed productive? Admirable? Contemptible? Expendable? Exploitable? Why are some firms profitable while others struggle to survive? Under what conditions are past inequalities eroded and replaced with new status hierarchies?

Social scientists have struggled with these types of questions for a long time. For several reasons we think that many of the past answers to these questions are deeply flawed. First, almost all prior work has ignored the actual social spaces in which income, respect, and other rewards are generated and distributed—organizations, firms, and workplaces. When social scientists do situate inequality in social space it is too often myopically focused on national markets and cultural processes, often ignoring the actual between-firm and historical variation in inequalities and their generative processes. Second, the most influential work in both sociology and economics has been misleadingly individualistic, ignoring the actual social relationships through which production is accomplished and rewards are distributed. In this sense, the theoretical model we develop in this book is an explicit alternative to the naive individualist and market explanations that dominate much political rhetoric and policy discourse in contemporary advanced economies.

We offer a general theory of inequality which foregrounds social relationships, organizations, and the intersectional complexity and fluidity that characterize social life. Our argument is that to understand the processes that generate inequalities we need to focus on relationships between people, positions, and organizations. We also believe that challenging existing inequalities requires attention to organizational variation in inequalities and to the relational processes which generate them. We reject social science approaches that rely on individual or societal explanations at the expense of interaction, social organization, and the relative power of actors to extract resources—like money and respect—through their interactions with others.

We organize our argument around three core inequality-generating mechanisms—exploitation, social closure, and claims-making—each emerging out of the social relations within and between organizations. Our strategy is to draw on multiple examples of these general processes from the social scientific literature to illustrate and illuminate each inequality mechanism. Our examples are drawn from prior research in sociology, economics, anthropology, and management sciences. Most of these examples compare organizations in order to understand and explain the variation in inequality-generating mechanisms and outcomes. Our examples span qualitative, historical, and quantitative methodologies from multiple countries and times. Some of our most exciting work is in documenting contemporary organizational variation in gender, ethnic, and class inequality across organizations in the United States, Australia, Japan, Sweden, and Germany.

We focus primarily on organizations (which we use interchangeably with the term *workplaces*) because they are the social spaces in which most of the production and distribution of income and other employment-linked resources take place. By *organizations* we mean the socially constructed spaces in which individuals' efforts are coordinated to jointly accomplish a set of tasks to fulfill some goal or set of linked goals. The organizations we use to develop our theoretical ideas are primarily private firms (corporations, partnerships, joint-stock companies, etc.), government agencies, and nonprofit organizations. We suspect our model of inequality generation is extendable to other important organizational forms and social spaces, such as families, schools, churches, and even informal or illegal organizations. We will make some of these connections in the conclusion but largely leave it to others to extend the model to these important bases of social organization.

We rely on well-recognized social processes that are found in all interactional settings as the building blocks of our approach. At the heart of our account is the fact that human beings are social animals. Because of this the generation of income and other rewards and their distribution are produced through social relationships, and the most causally significant relationships are those that exist in relatively durable social contexts. In modern societies these durable contexts are typically organizations. Moreover, in contemporary societies organizations are the income-pooling devices from which other material inequalities flow. At the level of general processes, our arguments apply to any relatively durable social network, including governments, schools, families, and churches; but we spend most of this book within the walls of workplaces.

RELATIONAL INEQUALITY THEORY

Our perspective has come to be called *relational inequality theory*, or RIT.[1] It has its roots in the social sciences with macro-level theories associated originally with Max Weber and Karl Marx and with the micro traditions of exchange theory and symbolic interactionism. From the Weberian tradition RIT takes a focus on meaningful action in cultural and historical context, as well as the basic insight that class, status, and power processes are always operating but not necessarily simple reflections of each other or equally influential. From the Marxian tradition we adopt the centrality of production as the source of resources as well as relational thinking about power and inequality as a result of claims over those resources. From symbolic interactionism we adopt the core sociological insight that people make sense of their world in interaction with others, negotiating order and change in durable social relationships and making identity and resource claims on each other. From exchange theory we adopt the idea that effective claims on resources reflect the relative status and power of actors in reciprocal or competitive exchange contexts. There are many other more proximate influences on our thinking, but that is for later. Let's begin with a brief and quite abstract outline of RIT.

Charles Tilly's *Durable Inequality* (1999) is typically referred to as the modern genesis of RIT, but there is a strong influence in the earlier work of Frank Parkin (1979) on categorically based social closure; Arne Kalleberg, Michael Wallace, and Robert P. Althauser (1981) on the multiple bases of worker power; Peter Blau (1977) on multiple socially reinforcing status distinctions; Michael Omi and Howard Winant's (2014) racial formation theory on the role of contending political projects producing racial (and other) inequality formations; and intersectional theorists, particularly Patricia Hill Collins (2000) and Evelyn Nakano Glenn (2009), on the historically embedded intersection of status-based inequalities. Relational inequality scholars share a focus on how categorical distinctions, when wed to organizational divisions of labor, become the interactional bases for moral evaluation, inclusion and exclusion from opportunities, and the exploitation of effort and value.

The starting premise of RIT is that the causally most powerful locations in social life are proximate networks of social relationships. People interact meaningfully and consequentially in social relationships, and the categories

1. The first use of the term *relational inequality* was by Charles Tilly (2000) in an essay in *Contemporary Sociology*. This was a summary statement of his monograph *Durable Inequality* (1999). RIT was originally inspired by *Durable Inequality* but has since developed into a more encompassing approach to social inequalities.

of our social world—including the categorization of people and value—are produced in those relationships. The human mind organizes the world into discrete categories, including categories of people, but it is through social relationships that this categorization process plays out. There is no such thing as an individual actor, absent the relationships he or she is embedded within. The idea that you challenge troubling racial and gender inequalities by changing people while leaving the relationships in which they are embedded untouched is a recipe for enduring inequalities. Similarly, a revolution to capture the state that does not constrain the social relations of status and power that people inhabit on a daily basis will simply create new inequalities and categorical distinctions.

The second central premise of RIT is that it is often, if not almost always, within and between organizations that the influential relationships that generate and distribute resources emerge and a local social order develops. In organizations social actors develop and enact hierarchies of power and status, typically around categorical distinctions between roles, jobs, and people. We also negotiate local social orders, importing meaning, status, and power from our environments, and become aware of both local and global cultural and material constraints on meaning and action. The same processes happen between organizations in the negotiation over who has access to organizational roles, exchange opportunities, and opportunities to exploit or cooperate in markets. There is no direct line from culture or social structure or markets to human behavior as all actions are produced in local social contexts. It is organizations that make social life, both its cultural and material production, possible.[2]

In our model, social relations are the corrective to individualistic determinism, and organizations are the antidote to market determinism. The notion that we will reduce inequalities by imposing utopian "free markets" is a policy prescription to empower already powerful market actors. The historical correspondence of the rapid growth in income inequality with the political economic turn to "free-market" ideologies bears this out.

It is from these two premises that the rest of our theoretical argument flows. If organizations are the site of the social relations that generate distributional inequalities, they must create and obtain the resources to be distributed. Thus, organizations must also be understood as resource pooling devices. They accumulate and pool resources, including income and wealth

2. Obviously, there are other organizational forms which are powerful in ways similar to modern workplaces. Historically, we can point to families, tribes, clans, feudal estates, guilds, slave-based plantations, and colonial occupations as alternative organizational forms. All were constituted as sites of production and distribution and organized via power and status distinctions between categories of people and roles.

to be distributed, technology and know-how, and productive skills and capacities. Organizational resources can far exceed what people can acquire as individuals. This happens through a combination of people, technologies, and jobs producing reasonably stable social relationships to accomplish relatively complex tasks.

Through these relationships and tasks, as well as their relative power in market exchange, organizations accumulate the resources that people within them then make claims on. People apply for employment, demand raises, negotiate access to skills and training, and acquire shares of the profits. Within any particular organization some claims come to be recognized as legitimate. When faced with resistance to claims, actors may successfully mobilize discursive or collective power to compel that their claims be honored, validated, or respected. When facing powerful opponents, people often fail in their claims. Many claims are never made, are ignored, or are repressed because the cost and/or probability of failure is too high. When claims are endorsed by powerful others or power dynamics shift, resources are (re)distributed and new inequalities are generated.

These claims on organizational resources operate through the twin social mechanisms of exploitation and social closure (Tilly 1999). *Exploitation* occurs when more powerful actors materially benefit at the expense of less powerful actors, taking increased shares of the resources available in the organization or in exchanges between organizations and their suppliers, customers, or governments. Exploitation is the dynamic face of successful claims-making. *Social closure*, only partly in contrast, is the exclusion of some actors from participation in the organizational production of resources or from valuable organizational positions or opportunities with institutionalized claims on resources. Closure typically has two faces: the reservation of opportunities for the in-group (opportunity hoarding) and the denial of opportunity to the out-group (exclusion). Conversion from closure into exploitation and vice versa can be a short step. For example, the difference between no access to credit and access to credit with high interest rates is the conversion of closure into exploitation.

Central to RIT is that these processes are not a function of disembedded local social relations but that relationships are always embedded in larger fields of action. The field in which an organization exists selectively strengthens some claims over others. Laws, markets, cultures, social movements, and practices copied from other organizations are all field-level resources for claims-making within organizations. Which resources and categorical distinctions generate legitimacy and coercive power are both local relational and external institutional products. Who is in the in-group and who is in the out-group are historical products of particular societies, cultures, and interactional contexts. In Mark Granovetter's (2017) language, actors are simultaneously relationally, structurally, and temporally embedded. As a result, while exploitation, social closure, and claims-making are generic mechanisms generating inequalities, the actual levels and distributions of inequalities are profoundly contingent on actors' response to, locations within, and interpretations of both their organizational and institutional fields.

We summarize our argument as follows. Resources are generated and pool in organizations. Actors with legitimated claims gain access to those resources. Some people and potential trading partners are denied access to organizational resources through processes of social closure. Others appropriate organizational resources based on their ability to exploit weaker actors in production and exchange relationships. Actors are more or less powerful in these claims-making processes to the extent that they have cultural, status, and material advantages in resource distributing relationships. These power generating resources tend to be associated with categorical distinctions such as ownership, occupation, gender, education, citizenship, race, and the like. Which categorical distinctions are the basis for claims-making are institutionally and organizationally variable. Organizational and institutional fields influence, but do not determine, action and opportunities. Rather, actors use cultural and other tools to invent local strategies of action.

We will use the rest of this book to unpack our argument and to provide empirical examples from our own and others' work. But first a few words on where we fit relative to other approaches to the study of inequality.

HOW ELSE DO SOCIAL SCIENTISTS THINK ABOUT INEQUALITY?

There are three general theoretical orientations in the social sciences that dominate the way social scientists practice and engage in the study of stratification and inequality: status attainment, human capital, and heterodox economics/political economy. Our criticism of these three is that none foregrounds the actual social relations and their organizational contexts that are the proximate causes of resource distributions.

Largely missing the inherently relational nature of inequality production, status attainment and human capital theories both focus on individual characteristics related to inequality outcomes. They also both sidestep the organizational space in which these relations play out, with the former fixating on a national occupational structure and the latter on markets. Political economy and heterodox economic approaches take more seriously some notion of social relations, typically organized around power relations, but tend to ignore organizations and treat those social relations within a uniform national political economic context. We will discuss each of these in turn and then return to our central focus on relational processes.

Status Attainment and Human Capital Theories

In sociology there is a robust tradition of *status attainment theory*, which focuses on the biographical resources people develop to be successful in a stratified society. In this approach there is a set of ranked employment positions, most commonly thought of in terms of occupations, constituting a stratification structure. This structure is understood to be produced by the societal division of labor. People have resources for accessing positions, most centrally education, but also ascribed statuses such as sex, race, or the social connections of one's parents and acquaintances. The great strength of status attainment sociology has been to explore the impact of families and schools on the development of individual capacities.

On the other hand, the status attainment approach takes for granted the employment structure of opportunity and asks how people are allocated across that structure. We do not. We see the generation of the opportunity structure as the generation of inequality, and status characteristics such as occupation, education, class, gender, and race as central to both the development of jobs and their associated rewards. In this way we hope to solve some of the issues raised in 1980 when James Baron and William Bielby critiqued status attainment theory and urged sociologists to bring the firm back into our conceptualization of inequalities.

For many years the status attainment perspective was silent on the relational context of inequality, preferring to explore questions about societal meritocracy, especially whether or not particular societies were becoming more meritocratic, rather than ascriptive, over time. This was a classic question of the modern, industrial era, one that the French sociologist Emile Durkheim (1893) predicted must happen to preserve the legitimacy of inequality and prevent class conflict in an increasingly interconnected production system. Durkheim's, and the early status attainment researchers', functionalist assumption that this must happen has since been tempered by a more scientific investigation into where and when it is or is not happening.

In addition, status attainment theory has begun to adopt more relational ideas about cultural and social capital from social theorist Pierre Bourdieu (1986). This turn recognizes that people's resources are not only in themselves but also in their social networks and social capital, as well as in their interactional capacities, or cultural capital. This is an important addition in that it reveals the relational, interactional processes that sort people into positions. We, of course, emphasize this relational approach in our model but embed it in durable social relationships (i.e., organizations) and extend it to not just the sorting of people into positions but the creation and valuation of those positions.

There has also been a clear movement in the status attainment literature toward theoretical accounts that stress the relational resources associated with employment. Le Grand and Tåhlin (2013) have argued that the striking similarity of occupational ranking across countries documented in earlier stratification analyses (e.g., Treiman 1977) reflects real workplace skill distinctions. Employers value skilled workers and pay them more than others. Weeden (2002) pointed out that some occupations (e.g., credentialed professions, skilled trades) extract more pay from their employers because they develop relationships with the state in the form of licensing or other restrictions on labor supply, thus increasing the workplace bargaining power of these workers. The idea that care work is devalued and so occupations with care responsibility are paid less also posits a gendered interactional process that generates inequalities in respect and pay (England and Folbre 1999). In these three accounts, while workplaces are typically not observed empirically, it is the social relations between employers and employees that are the theorized distributional mechanisms.

At its core though, status attainment is an approach to social inequality that highlights the sorting of individuals into national occupational structures. As such, it ignores what we take as the core arena of inequality generation: social relations within organizations.

If status attainment theory is the dominant framework in sociology, human capital theory is the historically dominant approach in economics. In many ways it is also currently the most influential theory of inequality in the social sciences more broadly, and it is used to both explain and legitimate the distribution of employment rewards. In the human capital approach individuals are thought to act like small firms, investing in their productive capacity, getting jobs based on those skill investments, and then getting paid for their contributions to production (Becker 1964). This is a reasonable account, except when people are not paid for their skills or are over- or underpaid relative to their contributions.

Human capital theory incorporates a simultaneously complex and restricted relational lens to explain why productivity is converted into rewards. There is a basic employment relationship between employers and employees, but market competition reduces all action in this relationship to a Pavlovian behavioral response to supply and demand. Employers are reduced to a set of skill preferences, while employees are reduced to their skill profiles.

The theory begins by imagining a world of market competition which ensures that employers fairly reward productivity and efficiency. In this world firms are embedded in competitive product markets. Any firm that does not maximize production efficiency will be outcompeted by other firms and eventually die. Capitalists must care about productivity and do not have the luxury of making status distinctions or pursuing more purely social comparisons and evaluations.

At the same time, competition in labor markets is assumed to discipline employers to pay people what they are worth. Otherwise, workers will quit, taking their skills with them. In this account, employment relations are disciplined by these two competitive markets to focus on efficiency in production and fairness in pay and nothing else. The fact that human beings are social and generate meaning through social relationships in particular contexts has no place in this theory, which reduces the social world to an imaginary, largely asocial, and very powerful set of market contexts. In practice, human capital theorists often recognize that both product and labor market competition routinely fail to produce fair income distributions but treat these as temporary anomalies rather than the norm. RIT does the opposite, treating them as the norm rather than anomalies.

The theoretical linchpin in the human capital approach is the notion of productivity, but the evidence on the link between productivity and the distribution of resources is a weak one. Productivity turns out to be difficult to observe at the individual level (Bishop 1987), and its most common proxy, skill, is clearly a social construct influenced by the power and status of workers (Attewell 1990; Steinberg 1990). Even in organizations that attempt to identify and measure productivity we find both that different status groups can be evaluated differently for similar contributions (Mueller, Mulinge, and Glass 2002) and that they may receive different returns for similar levels of observed productivity (Castilla 2008). Thus, within workplaces productivity is relationally constructed, subject to categorical biases, and routinely contested. One argument we make in this book is that it is more appropriate to think of standard human capital indicators of productivity, such as education and experience, as proxies for claims-making resources or status expectations, rather than mechanical contributors to an organization's productivity or a person's earnings.

Do not mistake us for arguing that markets do not matter. We do think markets are often field-level constraints on organizational behavior, but we see them as one among many. Labor relations organized around efficiency and productivity exist, but firms are also inequality regimes with cultural and institutional practices, status hierarchies, and the routine cognitive limitations of the normal people who work within them. Even in competitive markets, competitors are the same human animals whose cognitive capacities are channeled by past experiences and whose current choices adjust to relationships and opportunity structures. There is no such thing as an asocial, competitive market or organization (Zelizer 2007). In fact, rational productivity-centered efficiency is just as likely to be the product of professional or cultural norms as it is of competitive product market pressures (Nee and Swedberg 2007).

Some labor economists have come to recognize the importance of firm variation in wage-setting. This realization largely follows the availability of administrative data produced by national governments that has allowed them to study how earnings distributions are linked to both individual and organizational traits. Early research in this vein documented the substantial autonomy of organizational wage-setting from individual human capital (Abowd and Kramarz 1999). As this literature has developed some labor economists have come to understand that firms reward human capital in complex ways inconsistent with the model of a single labor market, that wages reflect not only individual but also firm productivity, and that firms producing the same product have wide variations in their productivity (Card et al. 2018). In this book we make a great deal of use of this more recent move to bring the firm back into labor economics.

Both status attainment and human capital theory, in their original forms, are normatively attractive to modern observers in their emphasis on productivity and merit as the primary or eventual mechanisms for distributing resources. Both have the same solution to inequalities–increase investments in education and reduce ascriptive biases around gender, race, and the like. They are optimistic theories. They may even be aspirational theories, telling us stories of which institutions and distinctions we might want to nurture and which we should extinguish. But even here, we should heed Daniel Bell's (1972) warning against embracing "unjust meritocracy" in which the educated or skilled profit at everyone else's expense.

While normatively interesting, these two accounts are not particularly accurate as empirical theories. Nor do either of them routinely theorize the role of institutions or social relations. Rather, like the blind man who mistakes the elephant's tail for a snake, each has discovered one aspect of inequality and mistaken it for the generative whole. At the same time, both status attainment sociologists and human capital labor economists are moving toward a more relational perspective. Sociologists are developing relational models at the individual level, and economists have discovered the importance of the firm. The value added by RIT for both sets of social scientists is the provision of an integrated framework to help bring the larger inequality elephant into focus and develop explanations for both its evolution and its variability.

Economics: Conventional and Heterodox

Conventional macroeconomics is the most influential academic discipline in the policymaking world. Conventional macroeconomic models have developed primarily to explain and even solve the problem of economic growth, either ignoring inequality or assuming that growth will solve inequality problems (e.g., Lucas 2004). The real inequality problem for conventional macroeconomics is the standard of living, and the primary solution is to raise the standard of living of everyone through economic growth and higher productivity. Because these economists begin with the assumption of perfect competition in product and labor markets, the relative power of labor and capital, of various types of labor and of various organizational forms of firms, is assumed away. What remains is technological change and the crucial role of competition in markets to produce societal growth in efficiency, productivity, and total national income.[3]

In addition, much of the theoretical underpinning of conventional economic thinking has assumed the autonomy of the economy from the social. Social ties between trading partners are suspected to be deviations from free competition and rational calculation, allowing collusion and emotion to derail the efficient, power-free action of markets. In contrast, it is clear to us that the economy is always social. Markets are created with moralities (Zelizer 1979), embedded social ties of friendship and trust encourage trade (Granovetter 1985), arms-length relationships permit exploitation (Uzzi 1996), and all trade is strongly conditioned by the normative, power, and legal structures of organizational fields (Fligstein 2002). In Fred Wherry's terms, all markets have cultures (2012). From Harrison White's perspective all markets are networks of positive and negative social relationships (2002).

Heterodox economists, in contrast to their more influential colleagues, tend to begin with the assumption that markets are imperfect and infused with power imbalances. Thus, the relative bargaining power of various actors is an empirical question and is generally assumed to be important, at least to some extent. They have also preserved a focus on institutions and distribution, the latter typically rooted in the relative power of capital and labor.[4] RIT is largely consistent with this approach but goes further, emphasizing

3. By *conventional economics*, we are referring primarily to neoclassical economic theory, the associated deductive theorems and mathematical project (see for examples Becker 1976 and Friedman 2009).

4. In many ways this description masks the valuable heterogeneity among heterodox economists, who include post-Keynesian, institutionalist, feminist, and Marxian economists. What tends to unite these disparate approaches is a rejection of the more extreme assumptions of mainstream economics and a recognition of the role of power in economic life as well as the importance of social and political institutions (Lee 2009). Here we should also note that heterodox economist Nancy Folbre (2016) is exploring the intersection of RIT and labor economics.

the relative power of all actors in production and, of course, focusing on the particularly central role of organizations.

A prominent heterodox example is the recent work of Thomas Piketty. His 2014 book *Capital in the Twenty-First Century* argues that capital tends to get higher rates of return than labor on its investment, so over time the natural outcome of capitalism is increased concentration of wealth in the hands of the wealthy and their descendants. This account has been particularly influential in that it corresponds to the great concentrations of wealth and the high shares of national wealth accumulated by the top rungs of society both during the initial growth of capitalism and again in the contemporary world. This account is simple in its assumptions, is critical of inequality in its argument, and bears a family resemblance to Marxian expectations about the concentration of wealth in the hands of the owners of capital. Although the Piketty account lacks social relations and firms are never mentioned, it does focus on production as the source of earnings and wealth, and sees the relative power of capital and labor to be central drivers of the distribution of new production. The great wealth of the top 0.1% of the world's population is always rooted in the ownership or control of some firm (or in a few instances whole countries).

On the other hand, Piketty's theory is even weaker than status attainment theory in that institutions, culture, and all status distinctions other than capital and labor are largely absent. Instead, an abstract idea—capitalism—is taken to have historically invariant laws. One thing we will see in this book is that there is a great deal of variety in inequality regimes within and between capitalist societies and that variety is precisely about the institutional fields, both societal and in production, that generate categorical distinctions, enable resource accumulation, and legitimate claims on those resources.

Institutional Political Economy

In political science and sociology, as well as elsewhere in the social sciences, there are also political economy traditions which focus on the role of the state and legal institutions in generating national differences in patterns of inequality. We share with these approaches a focus on the importance of institutions for creating the fields of action in which inequalities are generated. National labor market institutions set limits on exploitation and closure mechanisms at the firm level (e.g., Hall and Sokice 2001). National welfare state institutions transfer income and provide services to households, often reducing inequalities produced by the set of jobs produced in the economy and at the same time increasing the bargaining power of employees (e.g., Esping-Andersen 2013). Gender inequalities vary with a country's support of families, women in particular, and gendered cultural expectations (e.g., Budig, Misra, and Boeckmann 2012). These approaches share a common focus on national variation in the political and cultural processes that generate cross-country variation in laws and practices (Brady 2009). Comparative political economy is very clear in pointing out that inequalities vary dramatically across countries as a function of national institutions. Our contribution is to examine how these institutions are filtered through organizational relations and locally negotiated social orders. It is to these relationships that we turn next.

THINKING RELATIONALLY

Our core claim is that inequality must be understood through a relational lens. Relational accounts of social life can be difficult to grasp. Most people understand the world through narratives that give priority to self-conscious choices, decisive leaders, and the tension between individual wisdom and foolishness. Most of the social sciences succumbed at least in part to this individualistic tendency during the mid-twentieth century, with cultural anthropology perhaps being the sole holdout. Status attainment theory and human capital theory are both representative of this individualistic focus.

Late twentieth century economic theory adopted a questionable model of economic behavior that has often been adopted in both economic policy and cultural accounts. *Homo economicus*, the imaginary actor in formal economic theory, is a rational, cognitively powerful, utility maximizer. She is smart, calculative, and out for herself. This imaginary person has been useful for theory building and central to the mathematics of twentieth century economics. When *Homo economicus* is placed in an imaginary world of competitive labor and product markets, in societies that defend property rights, investments in physical and human capital produce gains in production and fair distributions of its fruits. *Homo economicus* was invented and promoted partly to make the deductive scientific system work, but she has no basis in what we know about how real human beings tend to behave.[5]

In contrast, *Homo sociologicus* understands and navigates her world through culture and relationships. She can be self-seeking, but she is also always other-regarding. She can be calculative but also habitual and emotional. She lives in a world not of perfect competition but of status and power imbalances interpreted through cultural and relational lenses. She

5. In general, academic economists are moving away from this stylized view of *Homo economicus*, but we agree with Granovetter (2017) that it remains as the orienting hypothesis in much analysis in economics.

lives in a world of negotiated social orders (Fine 2010). It is the *Homo sociologicus* model of actors and action that we draw on in this book. One downside of building a theory around this model of action embedded in a field of often contradictory and power infused institutions is that there is no simple mathematical solution to the problem of income generation and distribution. Rather, our model predicts considerable complexity in the social configurations that produce inequalities. The crucial advantage of our *Homo sociologicus* understanding of behavior and institutions over the *Homo economicus* model is that it more nearly resembles the real world created by living, breathing, thinking people.

The assumption that social causes inhere in individuals, rather than social relationships, is simply wrong. What makes social life social is not individuals but the relationships among them. Friendships, family ties, workplace divisions of labor, and shared identities—these are the relationships that create social organization. In this book we are particularly concerned with inequalities between people, especially as they are created via some enduring social relations. We focus on workplace inequalities because in contemporary societies most inequalities are generated through the relationships in and around workplaces.

A common mistake in social science, as in life, is to assume that the distribution of resources reflects individual essences or intentions.[6] In somewhat more sophisticated sociological accounts, inequalities are thought to inhere in positions. Both approaches miss the causal logic of relationships. Production is not the sum of individuals or even occupations but of a division of labor that joins people and jobs together relationally in a joint set of tasks. A workplace is not simply a set of individual employees, but rather it is a set of relationships between people, organized in terms of tasks, authority, skills, status characteristics, and jobs. These relationships are then interpreted and negotiated through cultural lenses. The work gets done not because the people have intentions but because they have relationships in terms of the tasks to be accomplished. It is true that their pay to some extent is tied to the position they occupy, but even that pay schedule is derived from current and past relationships.

The basic argument of this book is that if we want to understand the generation of inequalities, we need to focus on the relationships between people, positions, and organizations, rather than individual essences or intentions. Obviously, individuals' bodies, personalities, and intentions

6. Emirbayer (1997), following Bourdieu (1977), makes the distinction between substantialist and relational analyses. In the former, we examine the correlations among things, attributes of objects, or people. In the latter, we begin by asking about the relationships among things or actors and privilege the analysis of transactions between actors.

influence relationships. In fact, they often represent important information incorporated into relationships. Because we think categorically, our brains typically search for distinction in order to produce a relationship. Is this person a friend or a stranger? A man or a woman? Educated or not? A full-time or part-time or temporary worker? A manager or worker? Owner or employee? These categorical distinctions are the bedrock of relationships. They are the moral frontiers we use to allocate respect and reward, to justify exploitation and exclusion. Thus, in some ways, this book should be familiar. We will talk about managers and workers, men and women, ethnic minority and majority, the credentialed and the uncredentialed. But we will insist on talking about them as relationships between people in some organizational context.

We will also talk about intentionality. The fundamental mechanisms for producing inequality are exploitation, social closure, and claims-making. Each of these depends on making categorical distinctions between types of people and then expropriating or reserving resources for the advantaged group. This can be intentional. It can be produced according to a plan devised by the powerful or challenged by insurgents. But intentions are never sufficient. There must also be acquiescence by the exploited and excluded or by third-party bystanders. This acquiescence may be a conscious decision not to fight or resist, but it may also reflect a local or cultural legitimacy to the ranking of categories or people or finally resignation in the face of current pain or promised punishment. Third parties may be unwilling to challenge unjust inequities for fear of reprisal or ridicule. Third parties may not even understand relationships as exclusionary or exploitative because their associated categorical distinctions preclude empathy.

While intentionality may matter, so too do unreflective social psychological processes associated with the legitimation of status hierarchies. Much contemporary inequality is produced via the monopolization of good jobs or the ownership of monopolistic firms. Most of this is legitimated by selection procedures, training decisions, and past pay practices, all of which draw attention to the essences of incumbents, jobs, and firms, not the relational causal processes that originally produced the pay schedules and status-based sorting of people into jobs or the market success of firms.

When Charles Tilly published *Durable Inequality* in 1999 relational theorizing in the social sciences was beginning to be re-established. Status expectations theory in sociological social psychology had firmly located the production of status hierarchies in social interaction, rather than culture or individuals. Class theory had rediscovered the importance of social capital and cultural capital in producing individual advantages. Social network researchers had established that most people found jobs through social ties and asserted that social structure was really just a set of enduring social relationships. Gender theorists had embraced the realization that gender is an interactional accomplishment, rather than a stable biological or even social trait. Some stratification researchers had realized that the value of positions was not simply about structural skill or prestige but also about how jobs assumed gendered or racialized or classed value in local interactional contexts. Since then relational inequality theorizing and research has established itself as a leading alternative to individual-level human capital or status attainment thinking. Importantly, because of its focus on relationships, not essences, RIT is compatible with the relational basis of causality in everyday life and supported by the rich array of qualitative work on how inequalities are produced in practice. We will draw on much of that work across this book.[7]

PLAN OF THE BOOK

We begin with methodological and theoretical overviews of our approach, followed by a chapter illustrating the rich variety of organizational inequality regimes that become visible via the RIT lens. The middle of the book takes the three generic mechanisms in turn, providing conceptual definitions and then empirical examples. We end the book with a look at the scientific and policy implications of the RIT model. We first do this with a chapter on how RIT fits into debates over the role of organizations in the dramatic growth of US income inequality since the 1970s. The final chapter looks into the more general social scientific and political implications of RIT. While we intend the book to be read as a whole, we have also written it to allow each chapter to stand alone. Each chapter tackles a central concept within our theory and so can be read as a deep dive into that particular concept connected to the larger theoretical project of RIT.

Chapter 2 explores the methodological approaches that we think assist social scientists in observing the social relations that undergird the inequalities we seek to explain. We begin with an intellectual history of inequality research in sociology, answering the question of "what went wrong" scientifically in this field. This chapter highlights comparative organizational research as offering particularly fruitful research designs for studying

7. Emily Erikson (2013) has outlined clear distinctions between two types of research in relational sociology—formalism and relationalism. Formalism focuses on the formal structure of relationships and sees these as preceding and determining social life. Relationalism, in contrast, focuses on the content of social ties and how they operate in cultural and institutional contexts. We take the latter approach.

relational inequalities. Such research designs enable focused comparisons of the social relations across organizations, enabling researchers to compare either qualitatively or quantitatively the link between the dynamics of social relations and inequality outcomes within organizations. This chapter highlights two empirical exemplars in the study of inequality. The first is our own quantitative comparison of class inequalities in US and Australian workplaces. The second is Katherine Kellogg's (2011) qualitative comparison of the struggles over professional training and gender among surgeons in three teaching hospitals. We conclude the chapter with an examination of the development of qualitative and quantitative comparative research designs from existing ethnographic work.

In Chapter 3 we outline the basic conceptual components of RIT and their interrelations. We lay out the basic building blocks of our account: categorization and the intersection of categorical distinctions, organizations, exploitation, social closure, claims-making, and organizational fields and institutions. Both Chapters 2 and 3 give the reader the tools necessary to think through the empirical and theoretical content and examples we detail in the subsequent chapters.

Chapters 4–7 detail each of the core conceptual components and the empirical evidence that underlies them. Chapter 4 describes organizations internally as inequality regimes in their own right, highlighting the variability in inequality regimes that exist across organizations. It presents qualitative, quantitative, and historical examples of inequality regime variation in the United States, Japan, Germany, Mexico, and Sweden for gender, education, citizenship, race, and class. This chapter stresses the importance of institutional context, organizational practices, and negotiated orders, as well as intersectional dynamics for the constitution of inequality regimes. Chapters 5–7 take the specific inequality-generating mechanisms—exploitation, social closure, and claims-making—and develop each in greater theoretical and empirical depth. We again take the reader through quantitative and qualitative evidence, providing numerous cases, comparatively when possible, to convince the reader of the plausibility of these mechanisms as generative of inequality within organizations.

Chapters 4–7 have been written so that each potentially stands alone. Exploitation (Chapter 5) and social closure (Chapter 6) will be familiar ideas to many sociologists. The inequality regimes (Chapter 4) and claims-making (Chapter 7) chapters are more innovative contributions within the theory. Neither has been developed in depth in prior relational inequality work. The claims-making chapter also links our work with basic sociological social psychology and cultural theories.

Chapter 8 brings the intraorganizational conceptualization of RIT into dialogue with interorganizational dynamics. In particular, we emphasize the role of market power in inequality dynamics and the recent discovery that the growth of distributional inequality since the late 1970s in the United States and many other countries has largely been about growing inequality between organizations. The trend here is that powerful firms in many countries are reorganizing themselves in order to hoard income for an increasingly smaller and more homogenous set of high-earning employees and owners. While it is still the case that the bulk of distributional inequality is within firms, in many countries if RIT is a useful theory of inequality, it now needs to speak to relationships between organizations.

In Chapter 9 we conclude with a discussion of the theoretical, methodological, and political implications of RIT. For social scientists, we advocate the use of relational thinking, field-level notions of causality, and the power of organizational comparisons for documenting and understanding inequality generation. In particular, we discuss the plausibility of a political movement toward universalism that erodes historically defined categorical distinctions within organizations.

In Chapter 9 we also strongly reject market fundamentalist policy prescriptions with their near religious focus on competitive markets and economic growth. We propose in their stead a simple policy goal of increasing human dignity via reducing the power of categorical distinctions to channel resources. We outline three general mechanisms that will move us in this direction: evolving from tribalism to universalism, from hierarchy to citizenship, and from markets to human dignity.

2

Observing Inequalities[1]

Core to our argument is that by failing to observe inequality through relational and organizational lenses, social scientists have developed an excessively homogenous view of what inequalities actually look like. The failure to observe inequality comparatively makes the actual variation in workplace inequalities invisible. Social scientists worried about societal gender wage gaps or economic returns to education or immigrant group assimilation have failed to realize that there are almost as many gender wage gaps as organizations, that education takes on different meanings and receives different rewards across workplaces, and that immigrants are welcomed in some workplaces but shunned in others. In this chapter, we point researchers toward methodologies for incorporating this variation to explain the convergences and divergences of inequality within and between organizations.

Our theoretical conception of workplace inequalities has led us to embrace the idea that each organization is an inequality regime in its own right.[2] By *inequality regime* we are referring to the knitting of the cultural and material architecture of workplaces with the distribution of respect, resources, and rewards. Each organization exhibits its own intersection between status characteristics such as gender, race, and education among actors, positional hierarchies of power, status, and skill in the local division of labor, and cultural understandings of how to navigate local claims on dignity and rewards. These combine together to produce particular inequality regimes. We do not see this variation in inequality regimes as random but rather as organized by the cultural and material resources available in particular workplaces to define what seems possible, steering actors' behaviors

1. We published an earlier version of this chapter in 2016 as "Observing Organizational Inequality Regimes" *Research in the Sociology of Work* 28: 187–212.

2. The idea of inequality regime was proposed by Joan Acker (2006) and utilized extensively in our earlier work (Stainback and Tomaskovic-Devey 2012). Acker's insight was that the knitting of class, race, gender, divisions of labor, and local culture produced self-legitimizing inequality systems. In our work we stress the potential empirical variation produced by the autonomy of the local. We return to this idea in more depth in Chapter 4.

and choices. In the rest of this chapter we emphasize both the variation in inequality regimes and their nesting in particular institutional fields.[3]

Prior data collection methods used to develop our understandings of resource inequality have mostly focused on statistical analysis of traits associated with individuals embedded in national contexts or on single site ethnographies. When individual-level studies skip over the actual social locations in which inequalities are enacted and distributed, both the interactional dynamics that generate inequality and the degree of variation in real or possible inequality regimes are rendered invisible. Ethnographies that lack comparisons have a difficult time distinguishing generic processes from institutional context. Methodological conventions have led to some fairly odd social science. Labor economists theorize the exchange relationship between employer and employee but do not observe such relationships. Instead, they observe the human capital traits associated with individuals and their correlation with earnings. The social relations and workplaces where employment relationships reside are largely missed. Status attainment sociologists theorize status hierarchies associated with education or gender or race but observe these statuses as individual traits correlated with occupation, earnings, or other valuable resources, typically in a national—not organizational—context. In both cases, relational explanations are present, but the observational methods—random sample surveys of individuals—encourage researchers to ignore the fundamental mismatch between their theory and their data.[4]

Other social scientists utilize ethnographic methods to study workplaces and other organizations. These methods are much more suitable for observing the organizational processes that generate inequalities in respect and occasionally rewards. Most ethnographies, however, focus on a single organization, often for short periods of time. Such single case designs are good at observing the relational production of inequalities but are poorly equipped to embed those relationships in specific institutional environments or capture variation across organizational inequality regimes.

These methodological conventions make it difficult to describe and explain the relational generation of inequality. In this chapter, we offer two observational guidelines: (1) observe social relations in their relational

3. In the next chapter we develop the field idea in more depth and link it to both Pierre Bourdieu's (1977) theory of action and organizational science theories of the firm (e.g., Wooten and Hoffman 2008).

4. We are not arguing that individual survey data are never useful for studying inequalities. They can be very useful at linking categorical distinctions, like educational degree or gender, to inequalities in income, occupations, and social psychological states. We argue instead that organizational data are required to observe the generative processes and real-world variation in inequality outcomes.

contexts and (2) embed relationships in durable contexts, particularly organizations, and further embed those organizations in their institutional fields. We argue that these strictures are best carried out in a comparative organizational research design framework, where we can actually observe variation across organizational context.

FROM THERE TO HERE?

In the mid-twentieth century, two very different methodologies, ethnographies of particular workplaces and surveys of random samples of individuals, came to dominate the study of work and inequality.

In the ethnographic classics, such as Donald Roy's (1959) study of routine work in a garment factory and Tom Juravich's (1985) description of working in a chaotic wire harness factory, sociologists were able to discover how workers coped with each other, with monotonous work, and even with abusive management. Most importantly, these studies, which have a long history leading up to the present, are the best sources of insight into the social relations in organizations that allocate respect, dignity, interesting work, and other interactional rewards. The downside of the ethnographic method is that each case study tends to stand alone, and the cumulative knowledge implied by multiple case studies is typically beyond the reach of any one researcher.

During the same period, technologies for collecting high quality random sample surveys of individuals were developed. These included various strategies for drawing relatively large, national random samples of individuals as well as methodological work on the reliability of standardized survey questions (see Rossi, Wright, and Anderson 1983 for the state of that art by 1980). These data collection methods were strongly enhanced when computer technologies vastly sped up the time and cheapened the cost of statistical analyses and survey administration.

In sociology the big shift in studies of inequality came after the publication of Peter Blau and Otis Dudley Duncan's pathbreaking study *The American Occupational Structure* (1967). In the same year, the IBM360 computer system became available, allowing scientists on major university campuses to perform millions of computations per second for the first time. Routine training in multivariate statistics followed and became the bedrock of both sociology and economics graduate curriculums. The marriage of statistics and survey research encouraged sociologists of stratification and inequality to develop sophisticated statistical models on the educational and occupational careers of individuals. Economists did the same for individual employment and earnings.

Workplace ethnographies and stratification studies drifted—perhaps drove each other—apart on methodological grounds. Ethnographers developed an inductive methodology around grounded theory, prioritizing the discovery of social patterns in specific contexts and the inductive generation of locally valid theories of social processes (Glaser and Straus 1967). Following the statistical path laid out by Blau and Duncan (1967), status attainment researchers pursued a deductive path, estimating statistical models of the partial correlations between individual traits like parent's occupation, respondent's education, attitudes, sex, and race and status outcomes like school grades, graduation, occupational status, and earnings (e.g., Sewell and Hauser 1975). Status attainment theory became hegemonic in US sociology graduate training, probably because of its close ties to the increasingly sophisticated statistical analysis of individual survey data. As this theory strengthened, the organizational production of inequality became increasingly invisible, first methodologically and then theoretically.

But there was resistance. Among the ethnographers a new breed of critical ethnographers followed Harry Braverman's ([1974] 1998) Marxian critique of the deskilling of labor. These labor process researchers saw the face of inequality in the social relations of production but, using the ethnographic methods of their predecessors, had the same problems of generalizability and limited comparisons (e.g., Burawoy 1979; Juravich 1985). Eventually the importance of theorizing, if not always observing, institutional context was offered as a criticism of grounded theory, most prominently by Dorothy Smith (2005) and Michael Burawoy (1998).

A similar criticism of status attainment theory in sociology and human capital theory in economics (both of which shared the individual survey methodology) arose, pointing out that workplaces existed and that labor markets were segmented in terms of organizational resources, the relative power of labor, and both firm and worker exposure to external market competition. This new structuralist framework critiqued status attainment and human capital theories for their disconnect from the workplaces that actually set wages and hire and fire people (e.g., Edwards 1979; Baron and Bielby 1980).[5]

In some sense though, if ethnographers could make up for the lack of comparison by appeals to institutional analysis, new structuralists were never able to similarly overcome data limitations. Despite their attraction

5. This literature followed a somewhat earlier literature which criticized both theories' assumption of a homogenous single national labor market (Reich, Gordon, and Edwards 1973; Hodson 1978). This earlier literature was inspired partly by ethnographies, such as Elliot Liebow's *Talley's Corner* (1967), which showed African American men working in a labor market that did not in any way resemble orthodox accounts.

relative to status attainment and human capital models, the critical new structuralist literature on dual and segmented labor markets foundered on the scarcity of quantitative workplace data. If the social processes that create inequality happen in workplaces and both workers and workplaces vary in their resources and product market constraints, we should be studying workplaces in industrial context, not proving deviations from an unrealistic national labor market or status attainment process (Hodson and Kaufman 1982). But the problem was that nearly the only data anyone had at the time were national, and sometimes local, surveys of individuals.[6]

A key methodological exception to this is the work of Randy Hodson, who made a fundamental methodological intervention to bring the firm back in. Using the 1975 version of the Wisconsin Longitudinal Study of Schooling and Status Attainment, which had collected employer names as well as a self-reported measure of workplace employment size, Hodson coded company data on size, assets, subsidiaries, and profits for the subset of firms large enough to have public records. He also appended data at the industry level to the same survey responses, producing a research design focused on people embedded in workplaces, firms, and industries (Hodson 1984). The collection of survey and administrative data on organizations that followed turned out to be one of many valuable research design strategies to "bring the firm back in."[7]

Today a rich array of comparative organizational designs are emerging to shed light on the processes that generate inequality. Ethnographer Steven Vallas has produced two studies with temporal designs that demonstrate how changes in the relative power of actors as well as the interactional framing of skill and status lead to changes in workplace divisions of labor

6. Erik Olin Wright's class analytic alternative to status attainment occupational analyses provided a similar move to the new structuralism. Building directly from Karl Marx, Wright and Luca Perrone argued that sociologists should be studying the social relations of production using a class analytic lens (Wright and Perrone 1977). Wright went on to build an impressive set of comparative national surveys using his proposed method of asking people in surveys about their authority relationships at work (Wright 1997). Using relational concepts including power and exploitation, the class approach showed that knowing an individual's power in production, rather than his or her occupational title, could be used to predict his or her income as well as explain race and gender inequalities. The comparative project showed that this class process was similar, but not identical, across national contexts. Oddly, this project never theorized or collected data at the workplace level, staying steadfastly within the hegemonic survey of an individual-level research design.

7. There have been several notable attempts to "bring the firm back in" even in the absence of firm data. One has been audit studies of employers' reactions to job applications to get at the level of categorical bias (e.g., Pager 2003). We discuss these studies in depth in Chapter 7. Other studies have used census data to produce occupation-industry-locality cells, to mimic firm-like social structures. Leslie McCall's (2001) book *Complex Inequality* is a prominent example, as are the series of studies by Matt Huffman and Phil Cohen (e.g., 2004).

(Vallas 1993, 2006). Cross-sectional comparative ethnographic designs have demonstrated that similarly situated firms develop quite different gender (Salzinger 2003) and citizenship (Muñoz 2008) inequality regimes. There is even one study by Katherine Kellogg (2011), which we will discuss in detail below (see *Inequality Regimes in Interactional Context: A Qualitative Approach*), that compares the dynamic struggle over the organization of status and power in multiple workplaces. Later in this chapter, in the section *Comparisons of Ethnographic Cases,* we will also discuss emerging meta-analytic strategies as a comparative organizational design to solve the problem of generalizability typically associated with ethnographic case study work.

Among quantitative designs there are now single-firm dynamic studies of class (Fernandez 2001) and gender (Petersen and Saporta 2004) inequality regime shifts. Increasingly common are small- and large-sample comparisons of workplace inequality processes, with longitudinal data collected at the workplace level (e.g., Kalev, Dobbin and Kelly 2006; Gorman and Kmec 2009; Skaggs 2008). Some of the most exciting quantitative designs use multilevel administrative data that link employers to their employees (e.g., Petersen and Morgan 1995; Tomaskovic-Devey, Hällsten, and Avent-Holt 2015).

Finally, there are mixed method designs which incorporate comparative organizational analyses using both quantitative and qualitative data. Mario Small (2009), for example, in his study of social capital inequality among young parents, surveyed childcare centers and conducted in-depth interviews with center directors and young parents in order to learn about both organizational practices and the embedding of organizations in larger institutional fields. Olivier Godechot (2016) conducted in-depth interviews with investment bankers in multiple firms in multiple countries, supplementing these data with quantitative analyses of one bank's bonus distribution system and French linked employer–employee administrative data on investment banks' pay distributions. We highlight Godechot's project in Chapter 8, in which we focus on the core mechanisms of claims-making over organizational resources. Mixed method designs are particularly powerful in that they shed light on the processes generating inequalities while also documenting the inequality outcomes.

What all of these designs share is a comparative organizational framework, typically nested in one or more theoretically relevant institutional contexts. We now have good models to guide the design of studies and collect data to reveal relational inequalities. We take our empirical exemplars from qualitative and quantitative studies that follow our injunction: to understand the relational generation of inequality, we should, whenever possible, compare organizations and embed them in their institutional context.

COMPARATIVE ORGANIZATIONAL RESEARCH EXEMPLARS

In the remainder of this chapter we highlight a few examples of contemporary research using comparative organizational designs and interpret them through the lens of relational inequality theory (RIT). The first example is based on our prior research investigating organizational variation in class inequality in US and Australian workplaces (Tomaskovic-Devey et al. 2009; Avent-Holt and Tomaskovic-Devey 2010). This case highlights the crucial role of workplace-level *intersectionality* in expanding or contracting the social distance between core production workers and their managers. It also highlights the importance of institutional context for these processes. We focus on both national context–the US–Australian comparison–and within-country organizational processes including the role of wage-setting institutions, human resource practice, and product market competition. The nesting of internal organizational fields within national institutional fields is a key contribution of this comparative case.

The second example is based on a comparative ethnography by management scholar Katherine Kellogg (2011). Kellogg did ethnographic work in three teaching hospitals responding to drastic changes in their institutional environment. Regulatory demands to reduce the hours of work required of interns in surgical practices challenged profoundly gendered seniority-based inequality regimes. Because of the ethnographic method, these comparative cases are powerful in revealing the relational nature of inequality practices and claims-making struggles. Because the ethnographies were done during a period of rapid social change, they are perfect for displaying dynamics in these processes. Finally, the three hospitals shared identical *institutional environments*, and all started with identical inequality regimes. The three, however, had markedly different dynamics in adjusting to the regulatory requirement and in the end developed different solutions to external field pressures. Thus, they are good examples of how organizational variation is produced locally in relational spaces.

We then turn to two meta-analyses of existing ethnographies, one using ethnographies of inequality (Schwalbe et al. 2000) and the other using ethnographies of workplaces (Hodson 2001). Both attempt to aggregate up from existing single-case ethnographies to reveal generic social processes. That is, they turn a single-case methodological strategy into a comparative research design. One uses analytic induction to qualitatively extract generic processes, while the other uses statistical techniques to accomplish a similar goal. Our objective with each of these methodological exemplars is to highlight the range of opportunities for developing and implementing comparative organizational research designs to study the generation of inequalities.

Class Inequality Regimes in Institutional Context: A Quantitative Approach

The relational power of actors has typically been observed in quantitative RIT research as the relative status composition of categorically distinct groups within workplaces. In past research the status composition of workgroups has been found to explain organizational variation in class-linked wage gaps, bullying, and sexual harassment among workers; merit evaluation processes; the relative autonomy of workers in the labor process; and sex and race discrimination.[8] In one set of studies, we examined the intersection of gender, race, ethnicity, and employment contract with job authority and skill for random samples of workplaces in both the United States and Australia. This comparison highlights the power of comparative organizational research designs, especially when nested in national and other institutional contexts. Our basic finding is that the power of categorical status distinctions is highly context dependent. It depends on the workplace-level relationships among positions, local intersectionality between jobs and other status characteristics, and the institutional environments that encourage or discourage claims-making in workplaces.

The US National Organizations Study was one of the first large-scale comparative organizational studies. It was designed by a team of organizational and inequality scholars: Arne Kalleberg, Peter Marsden, Joe Spaeth, and David Knoke (1996). The basic design was to interview human resource managers in a random sample of US workplaces about many aspects of their institutional environments and internal practices. It was carried out in 1991 and remains to this day one of the best studies of variation in US organizational practices. In 2002 a similar study was undertaken in Australia by Sandra Harding, Catherine Zimmer, and Tomaskovic-Devey, this one with an explicitly relational conceptualization. Although a decade and a world apart, the two surveys are fairly comparable and do a good job of illuminating both generic processes shared across the two countries and institutional variation both within and between the two countries.

Generic Inequality Processes

Both studies found that the level of class inequality, measured as the wage gap between core production workers and their managers, varied tremendously across workplaces. Core production workers are the people who do

8. Some of these studies are presented in Wilson and Roscigno (2014) and Roscigno and Wilson (2014). We summarize more in Avent-Holt and Tomaskovic-Devey (2014) and Tomaskovic-Devey (2014).

the work most central to the task of a workplace. In a warehouse these are the people who put stock on and take stock off the shelves, in schools they are teachers, and in restaurants they are servers.

Figure 2.1 displays for both countries the workplace variation in inequality between core production workers and their managers that we discovered. While in Australia mangers earn on average 42% more than the core production workers in the same workplace and in the United States in the median workplace managers outearn their core workers by 51%, it would be a mistake to simply summarize the manager-worker wage gap with these numbers. Each workplace has its own wage gap, and there is much more information in this variation than in simple national averages. One of the striking things we can see in the distribution of workplaces illustrated in Figure 2.1 is that in both countries there are long right tails to these distributions. While the median class earnings gap is 42% in Australia, there are some workplaces in which the average wage of managers is 300% higher than that of the core workers they manage. In the United States variation in class inequality is even more extreme, with workplaces in which the average manager is paid 900% more than the average core production worker in the same workplace.

But what is also remarkable is that in both countries there are workplaces in which the average worker's earnings *are larger* than those of the average manager. All of the workplaces graphed to the left of zero are class-inverted workplaces where the average worker is paid more than their managers. Despite its higher level of class inequality, there are actually proportionally more of these class-inverted workplaces in the United States than in Australia.

This basic empirical finding of substantial variation around the median core worker-manager wage gap suggests that a standard status attainment occupational analysis of managers as a distinct occupation makes little sense, unless you embed managers in a workplace relationship with the workers they manage. One of the core insights of relational inequality theory is that we should expect that this class variation is produced by variation in workplace-level inequality regimes. The local social relations in these inequality regimes are not a function simply of manager-worker distinctions but also of local intersectionality between positions and other categorical bases of distinction as well as local practices and organizational cultures.

We found that in both countries when intersectional status distinctions reinforced the manager-worker distinctions, class inequality expanded. When managers were men and workers women, the wage gaps between managers and the core worker in a workplace grew. When managers were educated and workers were not, inequalities expanded. When managers had permanent jobs and workers were on temporary contracts, inequalities

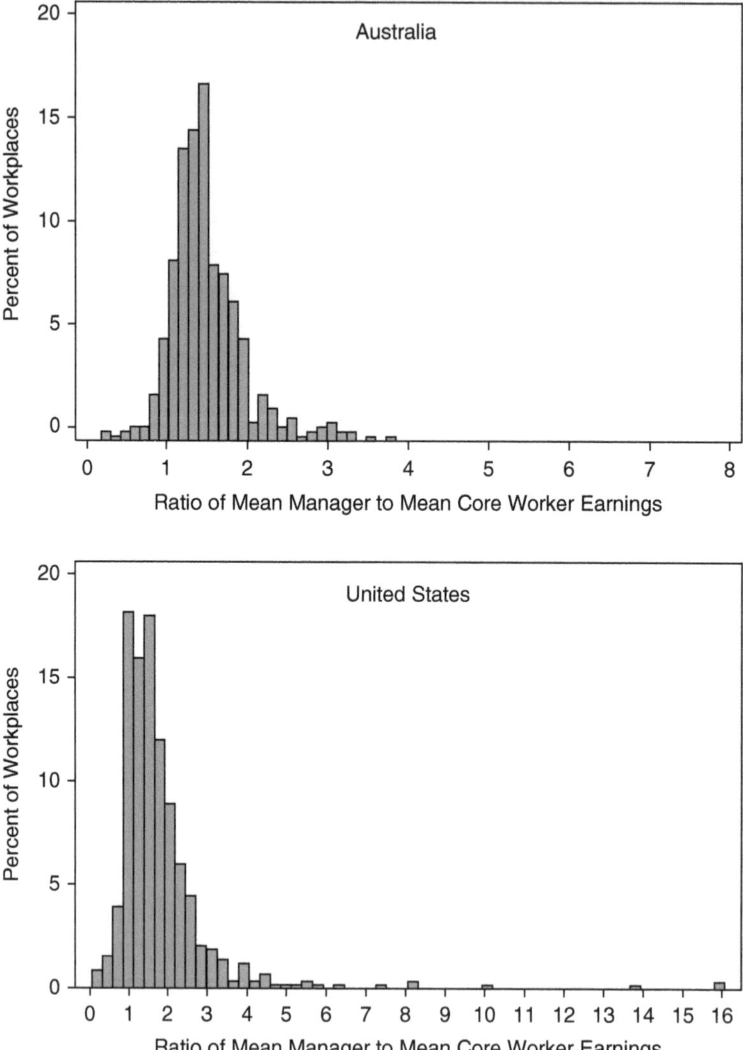

Figure 2.1 The workplace distribution of manager–core production worker earnings inequalities across Australian (2002) and US (1991) workplaces (authors' calculations).

expanded. In the United States, where racial exclusion has a long history, when managers were white and workers were not, inequalities expanded. In Australia, where the distinction between colonists and immigrants is stronger, when managers were native English speakers and workers were not, inequalities expanded. In all of these cases the class distinctions associated with authority in production were exaggerated when they corresponded to other status resources.

Although unobserved, we hypothesized that the dual processes of closure and exploitation were in play. Closure processes segregate men and women, the credentialed and noncredentialed, and permanent and temporary employees into managerial and core production jobs. In turn, status segregation between managerial and production jobs facilitates exploitation—the transfer of organizational resources to managers. In this study we could not directly observe the generic claims-making process that stretched the rubber band of inequality, but the basic pattern was robust across both countries and multiple status hierarchies, suggesting that these locally salient categorical distinctions enabled managers to effectively make claims that augmented their incomes at the expense of the workers they managed.

When we look at inequality regimes as the product of local intersections between production roles and socially recognized status distinctions, the simple notion of binary status hierarchies is overturned. So while we think about, and often react to, other people as inhabiting singular categories, our lived reality always involves much more complex and intersectional categorical distinctions.

What about the case of the class-inverted workplaces? When would the average worker be paid more than their managers? In both Australia and the United States these class-inverted workplaces were populated by very powerful core production workers. Workers were typically professionals who controlled the income flows and their distributions within their workplaces. They tended to be men as well. Their managers tended to be women. One of the hallmarks of professions is their monopoly of specialized knowledge. When a firm is built around professional knowledge and certification—such as in hospitals, accounting firms, engineering firms, law firms—it becomes much less surprising to find that higher earnings go to practitioners of the firm's profession than to the managers who coordinate activity.

From an intersectional point of view, the class advantage lodged in managerial authority is countered, even overcome, by the power in production associated with professional skill monopolies. In terms of social closure mechanisms, the ability of professionals to monopolize professional knowledge gives them power over organizations built around that knowledge. Engineers in manufacturing plants are simply high-skilled workers. Engineers in engineering firms control the surplus and the status order. When these professional-manager distinctions were reinforced by gender distinctions (male professionals, female office managers), the power of professional employees to make claims on firm income grew even stronger.

In other work we have done, some of which we will see later in this book, we find that status-inverted inequality regimes occur all the time. We have found workplaces where women outearn men, migrants outearn citizens, and the less educated outearn college degree holders. As one would expect, these are unusual workplaces. But they do exist if one only looks for them. In general, in status-inverted workplaces the normally subordinate group holds some advantage in terms of occupation, education, gender, or race over the normally dominant group.

The point is that *intersectionality* can both reinforce and disrupt status hierarchies. The idea of intersectionality is one of the most powerful challenges in the social sciences to dualistic categorical thinking. While we are strong advocates of the notion that human beings process information categorically and make categorical status distinctions, the insight that gender and class inequalities always intersect with racial and citizenship distinctions is crucially important to our expectation of variation in organizational and national inequality regimes.[9]

Institutionally Contingent Processes

The US-Australia comparison has so far highlighted a core generic inequality generating process: the matching of status characteristics external to workplaces to hierarchically ranked jobs within the workplace exaggerates the degree of inequality in rewards. When inhabited intersectionality reinforces status hierarchies, inequality increases. But the reverse holds as well. When women become managers, when minorities become educated, or when workers control production and distribution, inequalities are reduced and sometimes even reversed.

But RIT includes the caution that which status relationships are causally powerful at any given moment is steered by the institutional context. We have already seen that both at the median and at the extremes manager-core worker inequalities tend to be higher in the United States than in Australia. The United States is a more highly unequal society with weaker welfare state and labor union protections of its citizens. In general, the United States has more institutional practices than Australia that encourage inequalities and fewer that reduce them.

9. Particularly influential for our thinking is the work of Patricia Hill Collins (2000) at the level of interaction and of Evelyn Glenn (2009) on the institutional production of categorical distinctions.

In 1907 Australia became an independent nation, like the United States 130 years earlier, breaking off from Great Britain. Labor unions were legal and widespread in Australia then, and within a few years of becoming an independent country, Australia legislated a minimum wage sufficient to support a family of four. At that time in the United States labor unions were illegal, and there were essentially no laws protecting labor from predatory employers and no minimum wages, much less a mandatory family wage for all (male) jobs. While Australia, like other former British colonies and England itself, developed a relatively weak welfare state, it started with an institutional commitment to good jobs for white settlers.[10]

Until the 1980s Australia had one of the most strongly regulated labor markets in the world, while the United States had one of the least regulated (Kenworthy 2003). A hallmark of the wage-setting system in Australia up until the mid-1980s was the award system. In the award system the floor on occupational wage rates was based on required educational and skill levels and set by national industrial commissions. This resulted in relatively low wage inequality and removed much of the claims-making struggle over wage distribution from the workplace. Because the award system set a wage floor but no ceiling, internal negotiations could still upwardly influence wages. Since the late 1980s, the influence of industrial commissions on pay levels has declined and the use of award contracts has become voluntary. Awards remain available for most nonprofessional jobs, but local actors (typically unions and management) can elect to use workplace-negotiated union bargains or even individual contracts (Harding and Sappey 2002).

By 2002 (when we collected our data) 62.1% of workplaces had abandoned award-based wage bargains for core production workers in favor of workplace-level wage bargains. This shift away from centralized wage-setting produced a natural experiment that we took advantage of (Avent-Holt and Tomaskovic-Devey 2010). We see local wage bargaining as increasing the space for claims-making processes, especially claims not based on occupational skill levels, to play out. In this study, we again looked at the wage gap between managers and core production workers but added a comparison of the core production workers' wages relative to the lowest-paid job in each workplace. We found, for both comparisons, that when men were in the superordinate job and women in the lower-authority or -skill job, the wage gap became larger. But the striking finding was that for both manager–core production worker and core production worker–low-wage job comparisons, the impact of the relative gender composition was twice as large in workplaces

10. In Australia closure-based exclusion of aboriginal peoples was widespread and supported by the state. In the United States discrimination against African Americans, Mexican-origin peoples, and Native Americans was similarly state-supported and widespread.

that had abandoned the award system. Locally negotiated wages tended to exaggerate the impact of gender-based status distinctions in the inequality generating process. Strikingly, the reverse was true for education. In jobs where the award system controlled local wage bargains, the impact of relative education on the manager–core production and core production–low-wage worker wage gaps was more than twice that in workplaces that did not participate in the award system.

In this case, wage-setting institutions mattered a great deal in selecting which status distinctions were more powerful inequality generators. When the legitimacy of Australian wage claims was governed by national skill-based wage bargains, the impact of educational credentials was magnified and that of gender muted. The reverse happened in workplaces where status hierarchies were negotiated purely locally.

The United States does not have national wage bargains. In fact, when countries are systematically compared in terms of the degree to which their labor markets are regulated, the United States comes out as one of the weakest in the world in terms of institutional protections for workers. The United States has developed social welfare systems tied to employment, rather than more general systems to insure its citizens from the risks associated with capitalist labor markets. Unemployment insurance is paid for by employers. Healthcare benefits are often tied to employment. Even old age pensions via the social security system are tied to employment, and the eventual level of retirement payments is tied to the level of wages when working. In the United States the comparison of centrally versus locally negotiated wages makes no sense. All wages are negotiated locally. Even the relatively weak labor unions in the United States must organize and negotiate at the workplace level.

This does not mean there is no institutional variation in the space for claims-making in US workplaces. In the United States there is substantial variation in the degree to which employers can be described as consciously enacting due process provisions in their local human resource practices. Comparing US workplaces with more formalized human resource practices to those without, we found that formalization tended to increase the power of educational distinctions and weaken the influence of gender-based distinctions in generating the wage inequalities between managers and core production workers. The empirical results paralleled what we found in Australia. The observed types of formalization were quite simple: job descriptions, formal hiring practices, personnel evaluations, and the like. Many US firms lack even such rudimentary organizational barriers to particularism.

In addition to formalization, one of the most powerful predictions about wage-setting, coming largely from human capital models in economics, is that competitive product markets will undermine gender and racial discrimination in employment (Becker 1971). The logic of this prediction is that competition forces employers to produce efficiently and, as a result, reduces the space for exercising "tastes for discrimination." In our analysis of Australian manager–core worker and core worker–low-wage worker earnings gaps we were also able to compare inequality regimes between high and low market competition firms. Contrary to the human capital prediction, we did not find that gender and racial/ethnic inequality generating processes were weaker in more competitive workplaces. We did, however, find that skill-based distinctions between jobs were a stronger basis for allocating wages in competitive markets. Thus, product market competition seemed to do what human capital theory argued it should do: focus managerial attention on socially legitimate productivity-related traits. Competition in the market environment was not so powerful, however, to challenge gender or racial/ethnic hierarchies in rewards. Market competition is a causal force influencing earnings and employment practices. It is, however, not the only or even necessarily a powerful causal force in all relational settings.

The crucial point is that education and gender are not universally important in determining the relative claims-making power of workers and managers. Even in the same country at the same moment in history they can vary substantially in their influence on inequalities, depending on specific organizational practices and external market pressures. Through this quantitative comparative organizational research design we see that variation in national wage-setting institutions, competitive market contexts, organizational practices, and relational intersectionality collectively produce distinctive workplace inequality regimes. Both the variation in manager–core worker inequality and their empirical connection to organizational factors are only observable through a comparative organizational design.

Inequality Regimes in Interactional Context: A Qualitative Approach

We now turn to Katherine Kellogg's (2011) comparative case study of surgery practices in three teaching hospitals to illustrate how comparative organizational ethnographies can illustrate many of the ideas we propose for thinking about organizational inequality. While in much of this book we focus on inequalities in earnings or access to good jobs, we see the underlying claims-making process as strongly tied to interactional power, status attributions, and cultural legitimacy. It is these processes that Kellogg's cases reveal most admirably.

Prior to 2003 surgery practices in teaching hospitals in the United States had strongly institutionalized divisions of labor and associated power and status hierarchies, including norms that first-year residents work well over 100 hours a week, work "days" over 30 hours long were considered normal, and there were strict prohibitions against senior surgical residents and attending surgeons performing "low-status" tasks like prepping a patient for surgery. Like any organization, there was a division of labor, tasks associated with positions, status hierarchies built around categorical distinctions, and both a *habitus* of position-linked appropriate behaviors and deference relationships and legitimating accounts of why current practices were right and proper.[11]

Surgery practices had standardized divisions of labor. Directors, who were also senior surgeons, managed surgery departments and operated on patients. Attending surgeons operated on patients as well. Surgeons were local gods, always right, never in doubt, rarely considerate of subordinates, and to be deferred to without question. The bulk of the actual labor was performed by surgeons-in-training during a five-year surgical residency. Interns, first-year residents, typically worked 100–120 hours a week and did the more routine low-status tasks, such as record-keeping, patient admissions and discharge, test ordering, and getting patients prepped for operations. They also assisted on simple surgical cases. Seniors were second- through fourth-year residents who took responsibility for more complex patient cases and assisted in more complex surgical proceedings. Chiefs were fifth-year residents and were responsible for developing patient care plans and assisting attending surgeons on complex surgeries. Chiefs were also responsible for the supervision and socialization of more junior residents.

The system of very long hours was legitimated through a set of expectations about surgical training. These included the need to complete any in-progress patient work before leaving and not handing off work to the resident on the next shift, the belief that the only way to learn to be a surgeon was through practical on-the-job experience (the more hours, the more experience), and the belief that the life of the surgeon was one of total devotion to work and so new surgeons needed to learn to always be on call. In addition, within each seniority level, the highest status went to "iron men." Among first-year interns, "iron men" were always at work, never handed off patients, never sat down, and did all work at a brisk pace regardless of how tired they were. They were the "workhorses" of the hospital. Iron man chiefs (fifth-year residents) acted like drill sergeants, molding and beating on new interns (and anyone else junior to them in the surgical environment). Senior resident iron men acted as "wingmen" for their chief, supporting his

11. *Habitus* refers to the expected, often taken-for-granted, sometimes embodied set of behaviors and dispositions linked to structured relationships between roles in a field of social relationships (Bourdieu 1977).

authority, attacking enemies, and making sure he had the information necessary to prevent mistakes. Hours of work dropped with seniority.

Regardless of years in the system, all residents were expected to work effectively and briskly despite sleep deprivation and to "live" in the hospital. The prototypical high-status iron man was male, had no family responsibilities or outside distractions, and was ready to party hard. War stories of sleep deprivation, bad surgeries saved, booze blowouts, and sexual exploits were central to the crafting of an iron man image. While junior interns had no power and did the "scut work," they could rise in status in the short run by being junior "iron men" and in the longer run by waiting for their turn to be senior residents, chiefs, and eventually autonomous "gods"—independent surgeons.

In the 1990s, these extreme long hour practices were singled out by reformers external to the surgery profession as dangerous to patients. These reform efforts incited an unsuccessful initial countermovement from the American Academy of Surgeons to preserve the iron man surgical training culture. In 2003, the American Council for Graduate Medical Education in Surgery, in a move to forestall national legislation, promulgated rules limiting residents' weekly hours of work to 80 or less, one free day a week, and a 10-hour break between day- and night-shift work. Kellogg's work documents the implementation of this reform in three hospitals. These comparative cases are quite powerful analytically, revealing the relational nature of power to preserve and change the organizational inequality regime and the crucial role of claims-making in this process.

In all three workplaces, the surgery directors put new "night float" teams in place to implement the mandated reforms. In all three hospitals, a strong majority of residents were in favor of the reforms. Not surprisingly, reform supporters tended to be people socially excluded from becoming iron men. These included most women, residents not destined for the high prestige general surgery practice (e.g., those training for one year in surgery before going into anesthesiology), men who valued time with their families, men who rejected the supermacho iron man ideal, and new interns who had not yet been socialized into the iron man surgical culture. Defenders of the status quo tended to be more senior residents and attending surgeons.

In none of the three hospitals were the original reforms initially implemented successfully. On paper residents' work was reduced to 80 hours a week and seniors, especially on the night shift, had increased responsibility for "scut work" as well as accepting the handoff of patient work that was not completed by first-year interns by shift's end. In practice, the original reforms were merely symbolic compliance with the new regulations, primarily existing on paper produced for consumption by external accreditation bodies. The superexploitation of first-year interns, the status-based allocation of tasks based on seniority, and the expectation of long hours central to the iron man ideology were preserved, despite pressure from the institutional environment, support from hospital surgery directors to adopt the new standards, and a majority of residents favoring reform. Seniors refused to do the new work that would have allowed the reduced hours, and chiefs and attending surgeons supported their resistance.

Iron men residents and attending surgeons were among the most vehement supporters of the status quo, claiming that these changes would endanger patients and weaken surgical training. That they made these claims is not surprising. Reducing the hours of first-year interns challenged the existing division of labor, status hierarchy, legitimating ideology, and the basis of iron men's claims to high status as well as the age-graded hazing system more senior surgeons had survived and embraced.

In two of the hospitals, however, the initial reform failure was eventually challenged. In both of these hospitals Kellogg describes the facilitating role of "relational spaces"—physical and social locations where the supporters of reform could get together without surveillance from supporters of the old order. In these social spaces they developed alternative strategies for patient care, new frames for understanding good surgical practice, and internal solidarity to resist disparaging attacks from defenders of the old order. In the one hospital that lacked these "relational spaces," attempts at reform were necessarily worked out in public spaces and met with derision and harassment by iron men.

In the hospitals with these "relational spaces," reformers organized more successfully and began to insist on using the new rules. Not surprisingly, this produced a counterattack. Senior "defenders" again refused to do the handoff or scut work, disrupting the work flow and angering attending surgeons when patients were not ready for their scheduled morning surgeries. Defenders attacked the reformers, accusing them of endangering patient safety and shirking work, questioning their competency and commitment. Many of the attacks were explicitly gendered. Defenders called reformers weak, softies, wusses, pantywaists, and girls. Male reformers were particularly targeted for these gendered attacks.

These attacks were particularly virulent in "Calhoun," the one hospital with significant representation of women in senior roles. At "Calhoun" the defenders eventually prevailed, convincing surgery directors that the new practices were dangerous, converting the male reformers to the defenders' position, isolating female reformers, and eventually collapsing the reformer coalition. Kellogg concludes that the status threat to iron men posed by women in leadership roles actually intensified their resistance to the reforms.

In "Advent," on the other hand, the reformers eventually prevailed. There, the gendered attack was weaker and failed to disrupt the reformer coalition. The key constituency preserving the reformer coalition was made up of the "other specialty" surgical residents, often on single-year rotations. These were residents who needed surgical skills but did not intend to become full-time surgeons. They were in a fundamental way not committed to the life of a surgeon and all the ideological and status content that this implied. The "other specialty" residents consistently handed off their patients at the end of shifts to the higher-status senior residents and ignored gendered and other types of ridicule and abuse from defender seniors, chiefs, and attending surgeons. In response to these gendered attacks, the reformer coalition invented a new legitimating frame that stressed the efficacy of teamwork, as well as dropped the militaristic and gendered language around surgical training. They eventually proposed a new division of labor in which a first-year intern would be moved to the night shift to do the "scut" work, preserving a key aspect of the age-graded status hierarchy. In the end "Advent" had a modestly changed division of labor, a new legitimating ideology, a preserved status hierarchy, a cooperative rather than individualist notion of what a surgeon was, and workweeks that actually were limited to the mandated 80 hours.

Across the three cases we see a clear example of relational and intersectional processes. Although they started out nearly identical in practices and experienced the same pressures from the external environment, each hospital had a different internal process of reform. And in the end, it was the intersectional complexity that explains why reform failed or succeeded. Strikingly, reform failed in "Calhoun" because of the heightened gendered threat to the iron man ideal posed by women in authority positions. That it succeeded at "Advent" because "other specialty" residents successfully resisted the, for them, temporary status hierarchy and a cross-gender coalition endured despite collective gender combat from defenders is remarkable as well. Relational power as inscribed in positions, status, ideologies, and intersectional coalitions describes the evolution (or not) of these inequality regimes.

Kellogg's comparative ethnography demonstrates the power of going into more than one organization to make sense of the variation across organizations in how social relations develop and produce outcomes. Had she only observed the failure at "Calhoun" or the success at "Advent" she would never have seen the differences in the relational architecture of the organizations that empowered actors at "Advent" while disempowering them at "Calhoun." The comparison across organizations in similar historical moments and institutional fields but with different outcomes is the critical design achievement.

For new research designs we strongly endorse comparative organizational inequality research designs similar to the two we just outlined. But there are ways to also leverage existing isolated case designs by comparing data points across them. We next highlight two complementary research projects that take existing case studies and systematically identify the generic processes that occur across contexts.

Comparisons of Ethnographic Cases: Quantitative and Qualitative Approaches

One of the more innovative comparative organizational designs is to compare across existing ethnographic cases to develop theoretical insights. The two exemplars of this design were organized by Michael Schwalbe and Randy Hodson, respectively. In both designs they began with the body of relevant ethnographies and dove into the cases looking for patterns across them. In the design organized by Michael Schwalbe researchers used an inductive qualitative approach, while in the design organized by Randy Hodson researchers developed a deductive quantitative coding scheme across cases. We will take each in turn, highlighting the benefits of both.

A team of researchers led by sociologist Michael Schwalbe (Schwalbe et al. 2000) revisited a large group of ethnographies to inductively identify generic interactional and identity processes that generate inequality and operate across widely diverse social contexts. They started with a sampling scheme consistent with their symbolic interactionist theoretical framework, including only studies that focused on face-to-face interaction, contained material on symbols and meaning-making among actors, and had implications for inequality. They defined inequality relationally to include the exercise of power, the production of status hierarchies, and the distribution of suffering or reward.

Their basic method was analytic induction. In this method researchers code themes from their observations, group the themes into analytic concepts, and then further collapse the concepts into higher-order, more abstract concepts. Instead of following standard ethnographic practice and using field notes from a single case study, however, they used the published accounts from prior ethnographic studies. One of their main points is that the qualitative literature does permit generalization—to theory—but researchers almost never systematically read across cases to produce general theory. In one study, for example, it could be the case that male workers use a gender frame to exclude women from certain jobs by asserting they are too weak or fragile (Padavic 1991). In another, engineers promote their own technical competencies, excluding skilled workers from the most important production decisions (Vallas 2006). The generic processes common to both accounts are categorization and othering, followed by the discursive creation and policing of job boundaries and ultimately exclusion of some categories of people from a set of jobs and their associated resources. In the language of RIT categorization, social closure and claims-making coalesce to produce resource inequalities.

"Othering" and "boundary maintenance" are two of the generic processes the Schwalbe team identify that people routinely engage in when relationally producing inequalities. Both are directly tied to the categorization processes many social scientists have identified as essential to installing inequalities and which we see as fundamental in RIT. *Othering* is a process through which powerful actors define less powerful groups as distinctive and inferior, while *boundary maintenance* is the interactional process through which actors police group boundaries and hoard resources for themselves. We refer to these, respectively, as *categorization* and *closure*. Schwalbe and colleagues highlight most critically the power of the ethnographic method to observe these interactional processes as central to producing inequality. People make social distinctions in order to promote themselves or exclude others and then police boundaries to maintain control over valued resources. Importantly, excluded actors sometimes resist but often acquiesce. We will come to see much of this as anchored through a claims-making process within organizations that is fundamentally interactional in nature.

Much deductive social science takes categories and their boundaries as given, often referring loosely to culture as the source of distinctions. Thus, we hear about patriarchal or racist or class-inflected cultures promoting those distinctions. The Schwalbe team finds that people do not simply translate or accept cultural distinctions but rather actively construct status distinctions relationally. A central insight from the Schwalbe et al. (2000) project is that these categories do not exist outside of interaction but rather are created and then maintained in interaction. Thus, categories are not sufficient, and othering is only a first step. For inequalities to become durable, boundaries must be maintained and reproduced.

To our knowledge, the Schwalbe symbolic interactionist-inspired project is the only qualitative attempt to *systematically* generate general theory from the large corpus of qualitative studies of inequality processes. The problem of generalizability in ethnographic work is seen by these researchers to be a function not of ethnography per se but rather of the need to develop a research design to produce systematic comparisons across interactional contexts. The power to generalize to theory lies in the ability to recognize inequality processes that generically occur in multiple social settings. This typically requires an additional level of abstraction beyond that contained in the original ethnographic work. Doing gender, racial bias, and class-based exclusion have to be recognized as all being built around categorization, othering, ongoing boundary maintenance, and emotional adaptations.

While the Schwalbe team utilized classic qualitative methods to inductively discover generic inequality processes, Randy Hodson (2001) took a more deductive approach to similar source materials. Hodson first defined his universe as all English-language workplace ethnographies that contained significant material on one or more workgroups. With a team of graduate students he then developed a systematic coding scheme and produced quite nuanced quantitative data on an exhaustive array of workplace social relations, production techniques, market constraints, firm and worker characteristics, and both employee and managerial behaviors. The quantitative codebook is supported with text files of quotes from the original ethnographies to illustrate the concept being tapped by each analysis code. Hodson's *Dignity at Work* (2001) is the signature product of this workplace ethnography project, but these data, at last count, had been used in dozens of publications and involved at least 13 authors.

The topics explored included most centrally the social relations fostering or denying dignity at work. These were found to include employee skill, abuse in situations of low autonomy and direct supervision, bullying and harassment, teamwork and participation, employee claims-making, coworker solidarity, and management citizenship behavior. The last concept, which was developed in the course of his project, was the insight that workers' productivity, dignity, and satisfaction are closely tied to whether or not managers are organizationally effective and recognize employees' dignity. Managerial scholars often worry about the conditions that can foster employees' organizational citizenship behavior, defined as working above and beyond the minimum required effort. Hodson's analysis of the ethnographic literature made clear that the most common and powerful impediments to productivity and worker consent are chaotic mismanagement (Hodson 2002) and abuse (Hodson 2001). Much of the research developed out of this project takes up the theme of employee resistance to abuse and exploitation, highlighting the active relational negotiation of inequality in workplaces (e.g., Roscigno and Hodson 2004).

The Hodson workplace ethnography project has produced the most complete set of analyses of the actual social relations of production that lie behind the relational claims-making processes that generate status and power distinctions in workplaces. For example, one set of analyses of these workplace ethnographies identified direct bullying as a supervisory tactic to control workers (Hodson, Roscigno, and Lopez 2006). Importantly, these tactics vary with the relative power of managers vis-à-vis workers; actors with low relational power (women, minorities, temporary workers, low-skilled job incumbents) are more likely to be bullied (Roscigno, Lopez, and Hodson 2009).

These two meta-analytic approaches to ethnographic cases provide an opportunity for researchers to not only find what is generalizable across ethnographies but also identify processes and mechanisms that neither ethnographers on the ground nor survey designers intuit as critical. For example, managerial citizenship was not a concept recognized by ethnographers or survey designers, but in response to Hodson's identification of its importance across workplace ethnographies, survey analysts are now uncovering its analytic power across multiple workers' experiences of their labor processes (e.g., Rubin and Brody 2011). Importantly, the meta-analytic approach enables researchers to leverage the power of comparative design out of isolated ethnographic cases.

CONCLUDING THOUGHTS

All science is a dynamic dialogue between theory and observational methods. Science progresses when theories incorporate empirical dynamics and when observational strategies have the power to reformulate theoretical assumptions. Science is only as good as that dialogue. For a long time, social science research on inequality suffered from a profound disconnect between the theoretical mechanisms that were thought to generate inequality and the observational strategies used to observe them. Theories that were at heart about power and status relationships in organizational, historical, and institutional contexts withered in the face of data collection techniques that focused on the traits of individuals and lacked contextual variation. Even ethnographies, with their superior ability to observe relationships in context, developed as isolated examples of descriptive and processual prowess with only limited and non-systematic attempts to produce generalizable knowledge.

But now, as studies of inequality have taken a relational and organizational turn, relational analyses focusing on power and status, interactional claims and legitimacy, and cultural and material resources all linked to specific contexts are flourishing. Importantly, we are also learning how to collect and analyze high-quality comparative qualitative and quantitative data on organizational inequality regimes, thus moving these observational strategies closer to our theoretical models of action.

On the qualitative side, where observational strategies always were more in tune with ground realities of action, we see the development of comparative ethnographic methods and meta-analyses of the large body of past ethnographies. On the quantitative side, researchers are also moving toward directly observing organizational variation associated with their external environmental fields. These quantitative, qualitative, and hybrid research designs all share a strategy of collecting comparable, relationally anchored data on inequality processes, mechanisms, and outcomes within interactional and organizational contexts. This observational strategy has revealed substantial heterogeneity in the social world that had hitherto been invisible, while at the same time clarifying what are the generic and what are the contextual processes generating inequality. Comparative organizational research designs have also opened up our observations of the empirical world to a much richer, and empirically realistic, theoretical agenda. These are the designs we seek to highlight throughout this book and hope to inspire researchers to develop in future analyses of organizational inequalities.

3

Relational Inequality Theory

in explanation of the attitude of superiority assumed, it should be shown that intimacy leads to a love of our own customs, and unfamiliarity . . . to dislike and contempt for others' customs.

W. E. B. Du Bois 1911:157

Since at any time the given structure of relations is all that exists . . . in the first instance, social structure is itself the memory of the social process.

Andrew Abbott 2001:259

In answering the central question of this book—where do inequalities come from?—, we build upon the relational inequality model first proposed by Charles Tilly in *Durable Inequality* (1999). This model has been elaborated upon by a network of scholars developing a linked set of ideas around the relational production of workplace inequality (e.g., Avent-Holt and Tomaskovic-Devey 2014; Roscigno and Wilson 2014; Wilson and Roscigno, 2014; Vallas and Cummins 2014; Tomaskovic-Devey 2014). At the heart of our theoretical model is a focus on the role of social relationships between people and positions within and between organizations as the proximate causes of inequalities in access to respect, resources, and rewards. We see these organizational processes as structured by the cognitive and cultural distinctions human beings routinely make between hierarchically ranked categories of people. The status and moral hierarchies produced by categorization strengthen the claims of some and weaken those of others, permit practices of social exclusion and exploitation between categories of people, and steer access to organizationally produced resources. At the same time these "structures of relationships" are dynamically interpreted and reconfigured by the tides of history and the people who inhabit and construct them.

In this chapter we lay out the conceptual building blocks of relational inequality theory (RIT). Later chapters will explore the fundamental concepts in more depth and with extended empirical examples.

BUILDING BLOCKS OF RELATIONAL INEQUALITY

We organize our theoretical architecture around two basic concepts: categorization and organizations. Our premises are 1) that human beings divide a complex world into smaller, more manageable categories to navigate social life and 2) that it is primarily in and around organizations that social categories are created and recreated in ways that generate inequalities in access to resources, rewards, and respect.

Categorization

Among the most fundamental human attributes is our cognitive tendency to understand the world around us by packaging social objects into distinct categories. We distinguish cats from dogs and then group dogs into breeds, culturally inferring temperament from breed. We then encourage our elderly parents to find companionship from a Labrador retriever and tell our children to stay away from pit bulls.

This process of categorizing the world into good and bad, trustworthy and dangerous things has, as psychologists have argued, likely aided in the reproduction of our species. Distinguishing between edible and poisonous plants, predators and prey, people of the tribe and strangers moves us into matters of life and death. Yet when layered with cultural content, categories such as race, gender, ethnicity, and social class routinely produce taunting, harassment, scapegoating, segregation, hate crimes, war, and genocide. Categorization of human beings produces attributions of moral worthiness and facilitates or forbids inequality generating processes of exploitation and closure. Psychologists once assumed that human beings made judgments based on perceptions of absolute values (e.g., musical tone or reservation wage) of continuous stimuli. Most economic models of *Homo economicus* assume that human beings can make fine distinctions in calculating the value of effort and goods. Recent research in psychology and behavioral economics has shown this is not the case. Rather, human beings are quite bad at making absolute distinctions along continua but quite good at making relative and categorical judgments (e.g., Stewart, Brown, and Chater 2005).

We think of categorization as the fundamental human building block of relational inequalities. By embedding this psychological process into sociological terrain we can map onto evolved human traits the socially constructed outcome of social inequality. Claims-making, exploitation, and social closure are inequality generating processes that all rest on the cognitive and moral foundations derived from categorization.

Categorization is an inherently relational process. It is relational in two senses. In the first sense it is relational because we define the social object we are observing in relation to other relevant social objects. We observe a dog relative to other animals, but then we go on to define the meaning of the dog in relation to other dogs. While these meanings appear to us to be embedded in the object itself, they are typically invoked in relation to the cultural meanings of other objects. Thus, pit bulls are stereotyped as aggressive and unpredictable, unlike Labrador retrievers, which are characterized as gentle and loving. Within-breed variation in temperament is culturally erased. In the context of human beings, "we"—our tribe—become defined as moral in relation to the immoral, dangerous "others."

Categorization of humans by humans is ubiquitous in the modern world. Social distinctions form the backbone of all workplace divisions of labor. Job titles—secretary, plant manager, truck driver, accountant—are all categorical distinctions. Attached to these categories are identities, social expectations around tasks, training, skills, authority, pay rates, and relationships with other people and jobs in the workplace. The category of manager is created in relation to support staff in accounting and human resources, workers in production, and executives. While many jobs, like receiver and selector in a warehouse, are not well known outside specific divisions of labor, others have some social meaning across whole societies. In fact, the general esteem associated with familiar occupations, like engineer and cook, tends to be relatively stable, even across countries (Treiman 1977). This stability seems to reflect mostly the typical skill levels associated with these occupations (Le Grand and Tåhlin 2013), and skill expectations are one of the basic ways human beings tend to convert diffuse cultural categories into hierarchies.

Cecilia Ridgeway's work is fundamental in this regard, demonstrating that cultural beliefs about categorically distinct groups shape how others are perceived, evaluated, and esteemed in interaction. Multiple experiments demonstrate that beliefs about which status groups are competent in particular tasks, and therefore deserving of greater material rewards, emerge out of and diffuse through social interactions within task-group settings such as organizations (Ridgeway and Erickson 2000; Ridgeway et al. 1998; Ridgeway and Balkwell 2006; Ridgeway 1997). Cultural beliefs that whites, men, citizens, credentialed, etc. are more competent and deserving facilitate their capacity to claim a greater portion of the jointly produced organizational surplus relative to categorically distinct others, even those who perform as competently.

Often, we do not directly observe the characteristics of a social object in relation to another object but take our memory or cultural expectations of that object into future social interactions. Thus, categorization, when accompanied by past experience or cultural knowledge, tends to generate expectations, stereotypes, and cognitive biases.

Categorization is relational in a second sense as well, related not to the objects of observation but to the social relationships that define a given object in the first place. We come to understand and impose meanings onto social objects with and around others. Coffee shop conversations, family dinners, and television shows create and reinforce such perceptions. Sociologists have demonstrated that from a very young age we learn the basic categories of race and gender (Feagin and Van Ausdale 2001; Thorne 1993). By elementary school, children segregate into gender and often racial groups on the playground and in cafeterias. The fixation of US nightly news on the street crimes of young African American men reinforces perceptions learned at home and in school that young black men are to be feared, injecting a relational meaning connecting "young, black, and male" with "danger." Cognitively, black males come to assume the same cultural position as poisonous plants, dangerous predators, or enemy combatants. In contrast, crew-cut, white-faced, Ivy League college men may be perceived as safe, perhaps even admirable, even in the face of predatory behavior. In a horrific example, a white male athlete at Stanford University was convicted in 2016 of raping an unconscious woman, but the judge handed out an extraordinarily light six-month sentence, reasoning that going to jail would ruin his promising life (Stack 2016).

Professions work to culturally define and legally monopolize a skill set in order to produce both bargaining power and realms of authority in production. In one example, engineers interacted with one another, managers, and production workers in a successful claims-making process to define non-engineer skilled workers as incompetent (Vallas 2001, 2006). As well, male workers often define female workers as insufficiently loyal to the organization, as incompetent, or as sexual objects. These definitions take root within social contexts and come to define the relational architecture of negotiated social orders. At an interactional level we differentiate and then impose meanings laced with social valuations.

Categorization is the foundational component of relational inequality much as cells are the foundational component of living organisms. It is absolutely critical, however, to note that while the process of categorization is most likely hardwired into our brains, the categories we construct are not. These categories are variable across historical and cultural contexts, and part of the job of this book is to understand where, when, and why particular categories become salient and what cultural meanings they incorporate. Referring to citizenship, Evelyn Glenn (2011:2) summarizes our perspective on the origin of categories quite well: "citizenship is constructed through face-to-face interactions and through place-specific practices that occur within larger structural contexts." The interactional and temporal embeddedness of categorization is crucial to understand as well for any political project seeking to ameliorate the inequalities associated with the categories human beings construct.

It is also critical to understand that categorization itself is not inherently problematic. What is problematic is that once we categorize people, we transform those categories into hierarchies, producing inequalities in access to material and social resources. The simplest hierarchies refer to status within groups, such as skilled hunter or brilliant software engineer. These local categories are often used to create local inequalities linked to status hierarchies. But we also use categories to make more global distinctions of in-group and out-group. Categories of in-group when combined with cultural or material power—owner, engineer, man, white, citizen—are the basis of inclusion and exclusion. From the vantage point of in-groups, categorical out-groups are typically seen as less human, less morally deserving, and "not my responsibility." They therefore become targets of exploitation and exclusion.[1]

These hierarchies can quickly become quite complex as categories come to intersect with one another and take on new meanings. In interaction there are typically multiple categorical distinctions in play. In addition, the social meanings attached to categories vary across history and local context. This intersectional complexity creates historically embedded social matrices at the level of biography and interaction and the potential for rich and sometimes surprising local variation in the meaning and impact of categorical distinctions. In US society education, race, class, and gender are among the most prominently institutionalized categorical distinctions, although weight, sexuality, disability, age, language, and religion have in various contexts been and are salient as well. The cultural and political contents of all such distinctions are dynamic, changing with the cultural and political institutions of a given society or locality so that the meanings of categories and their intersections can be, and often are, redefined from one setting to another.

The meanings and cultural power associated with particular categorical intersections incorporate the influence of local interactional and institutional fields, producing complex inequalities (Ken 2008; McCall 2005). In everyday life the various categorical hierarchies intersect, producing, sometimes reinforcing, and sometimes cross-cutting intersections of inequalities. Subordinate races contain superordinate genders. Women become educated and manage men. White men from elite families go to university and

1. There is a rich literature in cultural sociology on the creation of symbolic boundaries and the work they do to legitimate and explain categorical inequalities. Michelle Lamont's (1992, 2009) work on race and class has been particularly important, as have her attempts to summarize this increasingly large literature (Lamont and Molnár 2002).

find themselves instructed by the grandchildren of slaves or hauled into court for raping an unconscious woman. This intersectional complexity only grows as categorical distinctions increasingly cross-cut one another, moving categorically derived hierarchies from bright to blurry.[2] We will return to this distinction in the book's conclusion and touch on it numerous times in this book.

In-group and out-group categorical distinctions are not fixed, even in interaction, but rather are socially produced and negotiated. The meanings of categories and their intersections can be redefined from one setting or time to another. In fact, one can think of some of the most admirable advances in human history as efforts to expand the categorical in-group. The evolution of social organization from tribe to clan to nation to confederations of nations is a sequential broadening of the boundaries of who has rights to be treated as fully human. The outlawing of discrimination based on gender, race, religion, or nationality is an assault on categorical inequalities. The spread of democratic institutions is an extension of governing power to an increasingly wide group of non-elite actors. The notion of human rights, rights that should be given to all human beings on the planet, is perhaps the apogee of a broad institutional movement to limit the power of categorical distinctions to generate inequalities.[3]

Organizations

While categorical distinctions provide the moral and interactional foundation for generating inequalities, these categories must become salient within concrete social contexts to have power. Our premise is that the most central interactional contexts in which contemporary inequalities emerge are organizations. By an *organization* we refer to social inventions which coordinate the efforts of human beings, through interactions with each other, to accomplish some set of tasks. Organizations create and sustain relationships between people, while simultaneously producing the resources we need to survive. In traditional societies the family, tribe, and clan were the most common forms of organization. Modern societies are defined by a plethora

2. These are Richard Alba's (2005) terms for describing strong (bright) categorical distinctions that are sometimes imposed on racial or immigrant groups and the more porous (blurry) boundaries that occur when dominant groups still recognize difference but more nearly equal relationships between groups emerge. Later we make a similar distinction between strongly institutionalized and weakly institutionalized categorical distinctions.

3. We hesitate to push this argument much further but feel compelled to point out that in some fictional worlds (e.g., the *Star Trek* movies and television shows) the aspirational in-group boundary has been expanded to include all sentient beings. Contemporary social movements to extend the notion of human rights to animals exist as well.

of non-familial organizations through which the complex work of society operates and within which individuals interact with one another (Perrow 2009). We are born and die in organizations, and we spend a great deal of our lives working alongside others in organizations. We go to one organization to be educated (schools) and another to get income (workplaces), which we then spend in another (stores) in order to bring food and clothing to a fourth (households). To understand the emergence of economic inequalities that are attached to categorical distinctions, we must focus on the organizational contexts in which these inequalities emerge.

We describe organizations in this book as inequality regimes built around divisions of labor, the matching of categorical distinctions to tasks, and the associated cultural and managerial practices that govern access to rewards, resources, and respect. This description owes a great deal to feminist organizational theorist Joan Acker, who first pointed out that organizations were inflected by status distinctions like gender not only in their divisions of labor but also in their more general cultural understanding of bodies and labor (1990). Acker went on to develop the idea of inequality regimes we have adopted here (2006).

More dynamically we see inequality regimes within organizations as a result of the relative power of organizational stakeholders (March 1962; Pfeffer 1983) and the power struggles over the structure, practices, and resources of the firm (Cyert and March 1963; Pfeffer and Salancik 1974). Although organizations have behavioral expectations and bureaucratic routines, these routines have to be performed, and in those performances actors both affirm and modify the local rules of the game (Feldman and Pentland 2003).

Organizations have been regularly conceptualized by sociologists and organizational theorists as constrained by the broader institutional environments in which they are embedded. In these accounts, organizations within a field become similar to one another through a variety of external pressures to conform to institutionalized expectations of how an organization should operate.[4] Some of these expectations are diffusely cultural, such as our understandings of race and gender.[5] Others are legally proscribed, such as the accounting practices associated with tax law. Still others are technologically produced, such as societal investments in road, electric, and communication networks. If the institutional environment

4. The best-known statement in organizational sociology of this conceptualization of institutions as external expectations comes from Paul DiMaggio and Woody Powell (1983). Good primers on institutional thinking can be found in Mary Brinton and Victor Nee's (1998) and Woody Powell and Paul DiMaggio's (1991) respective edited volumes.

5. John Meyer and Brian Rowan (1977) refer to these institutionalized categories as cognitive "classifications built into a society" (p. 341).

in which organizations are situated were hegemonic, the implication for inequalities would be that categorical distinctions are constituted outside of organizational contexts and the inequalities that develop around those distinctions play out similarly across similar organizations. If this were the case, there would be no need for an organizational conception of inequality and, therefore, no need for us to write this book. Instead, we would move to the organizational field level to explain inequality. However, we argue, and will demonstrate empirically, that organizational fields are not so monolithic and that the organizational context does matter precisely because this is the place in which people interact and negotiate respect and rewards.

Our conceptualization of organizations draws most closely from the inhabited institutionalism (Hallett 2003; Hallett and Ventresca 2006) and the organization-as-field (Emirbayer and Johnson 2008) approaches. In both intellectual traditions organizations are situated within an institutional environment, but organizations are emergent interactional contexts in their own right as well. Organizations develop internally workable practices and cultures, and these may become as important as external institutional environments in shaping the extent and type of inequality that emerges around categorical distinctions. In addition, we foreground the role of power and struggle within organizations (Vallas and Hill 2012). In this way we depart from neo-institutional organizational thinking, which tends to both ignore internal power struggles and emphasize the homogenizing normative power of organizational environments. We see the influence of organizational environments on organizational practices as both contingent upon and refracted through internal power dynamics. Actors pursue pragmatic responses to institutional constraints and in doing so model and shape how institutions matter.

Recognizing this relative autonomy of organizations forces us to reconceptualize the nature of the institutional environment itself. The environment becomes as much a resource for action within organizations as it is a constraint on action. Ideas, categories, and external forces can be used by actors within organizations for a variety of purposes without their external validity mattering. A useful way to think about an organizational environment is as a perception developed by actors within the organization about relevant external pressures, rather than a brute fact imposed on actors (Weick 1995). Perceptions then may or may not align among members within the organization or with actors in other organizations' perceptions of the same environment, but they will shape what goes on inside the organization.

A key implication of this line of reasoning is that categorical distinctions will emerge and operate differently inside of different organizational contexts. Sociologists have long noted fairly extensive gender occupational segregation. However, which occupations are male-dominated and which female-dominated varies across establishments, with the exact same set of tasks switching from male-dominated to female-dominated even within the same organization (see, for example, Bielby and Baron 1986). In a qualitative examination of four maquiladora factories in Mexico, Leslie Salzinger (2003) found that gender, a universally recognized categorical distinction, is actually understood and produced in distinctive ways in each factory. Women are understood as docile, nimble workers in one plant and assertive decision-makers in another nearby factory. Categorical distinctions take on specific meanings inside of particular inequality regimes. Conceptualizing organizations in this way leads us to conclude that a variety of inequality regimes can emerge across different organizational contexts. The extent of inequality that is attached to particular categorical distinctions (and their intersections) will be a product of the local cultures and set of practices that emerge within organizations.

What should be clear in our conceptualization of organizations is that we emphasize local, structured social relations as generative of inequality. Although in our empirical work we focus on workplaces, we rely on a more general conception of social relations as structured in social fields as the theoretical conceptualization that makes organizations what they are. By *fields* we are referring to a set of concrete social relations among actors and positions in which those actors take each other as the reference point for their own actions. Social fields are crucial because they both channel action and provide cultural meaning to those actions. Pierre Bourdieu (1977) describes fields as structured spaces of positions with associated relational expectations for behaviors. Field theories in general stress the concrete social relations that tie actors to each other, providing the frame of reference necessary for action. In this way fields provide the cultural resources necessary to construct and make sense of courses of action, but they also provide the social space in which struggle and contestation over resources and status play out (Fligstein and McAdam 2011).

The notion of field is then, in our view, equally useful for talking about action within organizations as it is between them (e.g., Emirbayer and Johnson 2008). A specifically organizational approach to fields encourages us to think of each workplace as a negotiated interaction order, with a set of expected practices and cultural stories tied to positions within the social relations of that organization (Bechky 2011). These social relations can be the formal divisions of labor, jobs, departments, reports, and audits but also the personal ties between people that may correspond to or cut across the formal structure. Thus, organizations develop local systems of power, status, value, and meaning, which individuals learn and adopt as their taken-for-granted organizational habitus but also sometimes challenge in pursuit of dignity, roles, or income.

Organizations themselves are, however, always located in larger, often multiple, external fields, such as markets, communities, industries, or national legal contexts. Boundary-spanning roles, like CEOs and professional occupations, often import practices from these external fields. These higher-order fields provide meaning systems, legal and material resources and constraints, as well as the people who populate organizations. Field theory encourages us to think about social relationships within organizations as producing a local sensemaking reality tied to position in the field. Claims on respect, resources, and rewards will be governed by both those local social relations and the influence of external institutional fields. Social relations and cultural tools are only partly local. Much is imported, often selectively, from the external fields the organization and its members are embedded within.[6] When thinking about the "causes" of inequality, field theory encourages us to think broadly about cross-cutting and cross-level relationships and to assume that causes are complex, contingent, and pragmatic. This does not preclude examining any particular level—interaction, organization, markets, nations—but encourages us to think of them as interdependent and actions as inherently local.

One of the attractive aspects of field theory is that it dissolves the distinction between structure and agency so common in social theory.[7] Actions take on meanings in fields in relation to a space of possible courses of action. Fields generate goals, power relationships, modes of thought that make some actions possible and intelligible and others not. In a very real sense fields are *simultaneously* relationships, meaning systems, and power dynamics that define the context in which actors act. For example, in economic theory underpaid workers should demand a raise or move. In field theory, on the other hand, workers' pay is tied to their place in a set of relationships, some of which are vertical (co-workers) and some hierarchical (bosses). How would workers know if they were underpaid relative to their bosses? In this case, hierarchical differentiation obscures direct comparison.

6. In our account the key role of external fields is to condition the range of likely social relationships internal to organizations. It is the causal power of the field on action that matters. In this way we do not make strong theoretical distinctions between national and more proximate fields such as locality or market. We see the power of external fields upon action to be an empirical, not a theoretical, question. In this sense field theory is often explanatory rather than predictive.

7. Like William Sewell (1992), we see social structure as a dynamic, evolving outcome of intersectional processes of organized interactions. Unlike Sewell, we see the causally important structure to be the proximate set of more or less stable social relations in a particular field of action. Workplace divisions of labor as structures in our sense are mirrored in the set of recurrent relationships between firms in terms of ownership, sales, and purchases. We are leery of attempts to see structure as an attribute of nations or isms (e.g., capitalism, racism) because they tend toward falsely homogenizing and static accounts of social life.

Economic exploitation is difficult to see within a field. What about the pay of co-workers? Many organizations keep employees' pay secret and discourage employees from sharing wage information. In this case, the agents' habitus, which naturalizes their position, may by way of proscriptions as to allowable conversation hide information even among co-workers. Conversely, a CEO might decide to pursue some set of goals or practices, with little sense of the consequences for actors distant in the field, thus generating opposition or failure through ignorance of more distant positions in the field.

Conceptualizing organizations in this way leads us to our first theoretical proposition. This proposition highlights the substantial variation we expect to see across organizations in the inequality regimes that they produce and reinforce.

> Organizational Variation Proposition: There is substantial variation across workplaces, both over time and across fields, in the relationship between categorical distinctions and inequality.

If inequality regimes vary, one may be tempted to try to a priori systematize the forms these regimes take. Prior use of the regime idea has tended to do just this by truncating variation via a focus on national or historical typologies. Michael Burawoy (1983), for example, suggested that there was a limited number of factory regimes (despotic, hegemonic, and despotic-hegemonic), profoundly linked to their national institutional context. His core model, like ours, sees these regimes as the intersection of power and ideology in production, conditioned by their organizational fields. Unlike our approach, Burawoy's typologizing at the levels of both nation and production leads to a limited set of regime types, obscuring the real-world variation in inequality regimes. The same criticism can be mounted of the varieties of capitalism literature (Hall and Soskice 2001), which identifies a limited set of national "capitalisms" produced by prior political negotiation but assumes an empirically misleading static national homogeneity (Herrigel and Zeitlin 2010). We reject quick movements to typologies of inequality regimes because they will tend to obscure both real-world variation and the relative autonomy of local actors to generate local inequalities. On the other hand, the dynamic configuration of national institutions produces within organizational fields causal pressures that nurture some organizational forms and practices while limiting others (Amable 2003; Davis 2016).

GENERIC INEQUALITY-GENERATING PROCESSES

We have built up the fundamental premise for our relational model of inequality: inequality emerges out of the social construction of categorical distinctions among people and those people's interactions with each other inside organizations as fields of action. Organizational action fields are in turn influenced by both internal dynamics and external environmental fields. But how do these processes produce inequality within and between organizations? What are the processes through which we transform distinctions into inequalities? Tilly (1999) identified two core processes: exploitation and social closure/opportunity hoarding. We identify a third, more foundational, mechanism of relational claims-making that generates the social space for installing and shifting exploitation and closure. We start with the first two more familiar processes and then detail the more novel mechanism of claims-making.

Exploitation and Social Closure

In the original Marxian sense, *exploitation* is simply capitalists' appropriation of the value produced by workers. Capitalists exploit workers, and the concept hinges on the labor theory of value in which all economic value is assumed to be derived from the efforts of workers. Neo-Marxists have since reformulated the concept to avoid the labor theory of value, arguing that capitalists appropriate a portion of the labor efforts of workers even if all value is not derived from workers themselves (Wright 1997, 2000a). Charles Tilly (1999) recast exploitation as simply one group appropriating the labor efforts of another group. This extends Marx's basic insight beyond the capital-labor relationship to also include the possibility that men exploit women, whites exploit blacks, or citizens exploit non-citizens. We will broaden it one step beyond this. For us, exploitation occurs when one group uses its power to appropriate income (or some other scarce resource) from another either within organizations or between them. What is distinctive about our conceptualization is that the process of exploitation happens in and through organizations, either between actors within organizations (e.g., labor power) or between organizations themselves (e.g., market power). Exploitation, however, is not so broad as to become synonymous with inequality. It still entails the appropriation of another's value but simply extends the process to any categorical distinction and to operating both within and between organizations.

The question remains, however—what constitutes the appropriation of the value that belongs to someone else? Marx worked from the ontological and normative assumption that all value is derived from labor, so the mere existence of capitalist profit was evidence of exploitation. Neo-Marxists and some non-Marxists have since abandoned that assumption, instead identifying exploitation as individuals or groups receiving less than their marginal product and other groups receiving more than their marginal product, often called an *economic rent* (Sakamoto and Liu 2006; Sørensen 1996, 2000). *Marginal product* refers to the value of someone's labor (or capital investment) in a perfectly competitive labor (product) market. But this too requires a normative assumption, in this case that individuals *should* receive the earnings that would be produced in a perfectly competitive market environment. Moreover, since productivity is produced in relational divisions of labor both within and between organizations, there is no such thing as the marginal product of an individual, a job, or even a firm. The use of an external "perfect competition" benchmark is fairly unclear in its implications, even while highlighting that power is the underlying mechanism producing exploitation (see Avent-Holt 2015).

We prefer a historical conception of exploitation in which a more powerful group gains income over time at the expense of a less powerful group. In this context, exploitation could happen because the wages attached to a job decline over time as women enter into the occupation (England, Allison, and Wu 2007), because capitalists deskill the labor process to reduce workers' wages (Braverman 1998), or because financial service firms become dominant across an entire economy (Tomaskovic-Devey and Lin 2011). When women's jobs and skills are devalued, capitalists or male workers in other occupations inside a workplace gain income as women lose. When work is deskilled and wages are reduced, capitalists gain income as workers lose. When the financial sector of the economy grows in political and market power, financial institutions become more effective at vacuuming income from their customers' bank accounts. This discussion leads to the following proposition:

> Exploitation Proposition: Inequality emerges when a more powerful group appropriates organizational resources from categorically distinct and less powerful others.

In Chapter 5 we develop our conceptualization of exploitation in considerably more depth and provide a roadmap to the observational strategies social scientists have developed. These include both exploitation in the labor process and exploitation in market relationships.

Our second generic inequality generating process is *social closure*, a process whereby actors limit access to organizational resources to categorically similar others. Closure mechanisms typically use categorical distinctions to prevent or impede categorically distinct others from accessing income, organizations, or positions within organizations and to funnel those resources to categorically similar others. When the categorical distinction is used to monopolize resources for people within an in-group, we can think of it as *opportunity hoarding*. When closure processes are used to exclude categorically defined out-groups, we can think of it as *exclusion*. This distinction reflects what we see as a historical shift away from out-group bias and toward in-group favoritism. With the rise of democracy and a politics of equality in the modern era, the impulse toward closing off access to resources through opportunity hoarding has become dominant. Social psychological research appears to bear this out, finding that in-group favoritism is the more dominant mechanism broadly speaking (DiTomaso, Post, and Parks-Yancy 2007).

The most commonly referenced resource is the job itself, and perhaps the most well-established literature on this is the segregation of men and women across jobs and occupations. Quantitative and case-based qualitative work has repeatedly demonstrated that men and women tend to work in different jobs and to even do different tasks when placed in the same job. Further, the closer one gets to the level of detailed jobs within organizations, the more segregation we see. Trond Petersen and Laurie Morgan (1995), looking at US workplaces around 1980, found almost complete segregation between men and women when looking at jobs within establishments and that gender wage gaps are almost completely explained by this segregation.

While the job is a fundamental resource within organizations, and one which has a clear relationship to income, other resources, such as agreeing to buy or sell from someone, access to training, access to social networks, or even fine-grained organizational status distinctions, can be monopolized as well. Tomaskovic-Devey and Sheryl Skaggs (2002) find that among a sample of establishments in North Carolina access to training time was a central mechanism producing the gender wage gaps associated with sex segregated jobs. Property law is a closure mechanism empowering only owners to direct or consume "private" property. This leads to the following proposition:

> Social Closure Proposition: Inequality emerges when a more powerful group uses categorical distinctions to monopolize positions and other valuable organizational resources.

In Chapter 6 these ideas are developed and brought to empirical life. In that chapter we further develop our conceptualization of social closure, addressing the central role of power within and between organizations. Importantly, we highlight that organizational resources are what are being monopolized and demonstrate this empirically.

One of the central distinctions between our work and much of the existing work on these two concepts is that we see these as operating both within and between organizations. Often, exploitation is conceptualized within organizational division of labor but is empirically assessed with data on individuals devoid of organizational context. The same is true of social closure, though there is more empirical work using organizational data (e.g., Reskin 1988; Reskin and Padavic 1988; Tomaskovic-Devey 1993). There is also a common conceptualization of social closure that definitively locates it as a process within markets (e.g., Sørensen 1996, 2000; Weeden 2002). On this we are decidedly in the organizational camp. The central claims we are making locate exploitation and social closure as fundamentally organizational phenomena.

Claims-Making

We still need to ask how it is that exploitation and closure work at the level of interaction. What is the process through which some groups within organizations are able to exploit other groups or monopolize resources for themselves? Given that we have identified social interactions within organizations as the context in which exploitation and social closure play out, we propose a simple process that is both relational and political, which we refer to as relational *claims-making*. Claims-making involves actors making discursive arguments as to why they are more deserving of some organizational resource than others. This mechanism is political in that it involves negotiation, struggle, and contestation over the legitimacy of a given claim. It is relational in that it involves multiple actors constructing and legitimating claims.

Claims are constructed out of the relational resources actors have at their disposal.[8] These resources include the local meanings of the categorical distinctions of skill, race, citizenship, class, and gender. Categorical distinctions enable groups to organize to both make claims and create the political will to struggle against other groups (Schwalbe et al. 2000). Collective struggles and routine interaction within and between organizations draw on these identities to legitimate claims that certain actors are more deserving of organizational resources than others. Over time, groups that are disadvantaged by the claims of other groups will tend to fight back, either directly challenging the claim or creating new arenas in which to exploit or monopolize resources (Murphy 1988; Sørenson 2000).

Numerous claims can and will be made by various actors within organizations. Despite the potential plethora of claims, not all of them—and perhaps relatively few—will be translated into exploitative resource extractions or the monopolizing of an organizational resource. The translation of a claim into effective exploitation or closure hinges on whether or not other actors,

8. Abstractly we refer to claims by *actors*. However, actors can be either individuals or groups. As individuals, actors can negotiate directly with supervisors over their pay, training time, promotions, and other organizational resources. In such cases, claims are made through individual interaction. As social groups, such as unions, professional associations, departments, and spontaneously organized networks of employees, actors collectively approach employers to negotiate and make claims.

especially powerful actors, find the claim persuasive. This is the critical relational component to the claims-making mechanism. Claims can be made by any actor yet will not generate new inequalities or challenge existing inequalities unless other actors within the organization ratify them. These other actors will often be relationally powerful, such as managers or experts, but can be a substantial contingent of organized co-workers. The question then becomes, who is aligned with whom in the organization around particular claims?

Obviously, those who belong to a categorically distinct group have an interest in promoting claims that enable their in-group to exploit and monopolize. However, unless this particular group has unilateral power—and we would, of course, need to ask how they first obtained unilateral power—they would need some form of consent from other organizational actors. But why would other actors in the organization ratify anyone else's claims? We argue that local organizational cultures produce a sense among actors as to what are appropriate and plausible claims. These cultures are generated by both internal and external understandings. In addition, as social animals human beings tend to take the needs of others into account, controlling impulses to make claims that harm others. The exception to this last tendency is when categorical boundaries are bright enough to render this impulse inoperative. Bright categorical distinctions encourage resource sharing and opportunity hoarding with the in-group and the exploitation and closure of out-groups.

Thus, it is the persuasiveness of a claim, the intensity of the categorical distinction, and the relative power of actors that are central to generating relational inequalities. The persuasiveness of a claim hinges on its resonance with the cultural-historical-institutional context in which the claim is situated, the power of resistance and insistence by actors, and the othering associated with categorical distinctions. Thus, the following proposition:

> Claims-Making Proposition: New inequalities are installed and old inequalities dismantled as a result of actors' categorical mobilization around claims made over organizational practices or resources.

It is in this proposition we come to see the centrality of power as a concept within RIT. Power is in many ways the backdrop behind the entire model, but its role cannot be ignored once claims-making is invoked. Categorical distinctions give some actors power over others, and power becomes a force that is both enacted and legitimated discursively within organizational fields.[9] Claims, as active attempts to redistribute resources,

9. Obviously, power can also be exercised as violence in addition to discursive claims-making. Strong armed robbery and colonial conquest are examples of violent exploitation. Genocide, ethnic cleansing, and the political suppression via arrest of social movements' claims on dignity and access are the violent faces of closure.

are also instances of negotiated power. Organizations are spaces of power struggles, and exploitation and social closure are the fruits of successful power plays.

This discussion suggests a relatively overt political process in which actors are actively constructing claims. Undoubtedly, such overt action routinely occurs, yet much exploitation and closure are institutionalized and taken for granted and often do not involve or invoke active claims-making. Nevertheless, institutionalized exploitation or social closure represents a claim that was made at some earlier historical moment that has since become embedded in the organization's structure and individual's habitus. That is, institutionalized exploitation and social closure reflect taken-for-granted claims that at one point in history involved active claims-making.

A relatively well-institutionalized form of exploitation involves capitalists appropriating value from workers. At the birth of capitalism, newly constituted industrial workers perceived capitalists as exploiting them, interpreting their position in the labor process as "wage slavery." The appropriation of value by capitalists was not yet unambiguously legitimate and was actively struggled against. Today, most employees find it perfectly legitimate for employers to seek profits by increasing their productivity or even reducing their labor costs. Robin Leidner relates a story of such legitimation among the McDonald's workers she worked alongside. At a monthly meeting, workers expressed a desire to pay people for more time to perform non-production related tasks instead of having workers perform those tasks around their main production duties. The manager responded with an explanation of the importance of keeping labor costs down, a counter-claim that workers treated as reasonable (Leidner 1993:79–80). In this case, a claim was made, but it foundered on the taken-for-granted legitimacy of the employer's right to keep labor costs down. One way to think about institutionalized inequalities is that exploitation and social closure between positions or people have become part of the taken-for-granted habitus of everyday life.

> Institutionalized Claims Proposition: The more institutionalized a categorical distinction, the less vulnerable it will be to active claims and the more uniform its impact on inequality distributions.

Here, readers should note that while we have discussed these three as distinct processes, in practice claims-making, closure, and exploitation are tightly linked. Closure processes often exclude people from the ability to make claims. Exploitation is the dynamic face of claims-making, describing the power differences between actors that facilitated the shift of resources from one group to another. In Chapter 7 we develop the notion of claims-making in more depth, building our position on the social psychology of claims and legitimacy in resource distribution and providing examples from the research literature on the multiple ways in which claims-making transpires.

CONTEXTUAL VARIATION IN GENERIC PROCESSES

Exploitation, closure, and claims-making are generic processes that can be expected to generate inequalities within and between organizations. They rest on categorization (a psychological process general to human cognition), emergent category-linked hierarchies of status and power, and the fact that as social animals we create organizations to produce and distribute the resources we depend upon to sustain ourselves. There are not, however, positivist laws ordaining which categories matter or the relative weight and character of the three relational inequality mechanisms. Generic processes create their effects in concrete historical, organizational, and institutional context. We highlight two such crucial contexts that we think are broad enough and general enough across social contexts to merit a theoretical articulation within the context of our generic processes.

Organizational Resources

There is no inequality without a scarce resource to be distributed. Organizations are resource-pooling devices. They generate capital, income streams, and jobs, all of which are then the targets of claims-making, exploitation, and social closure. Sociology has been surprisingly neglectful of the fundamental role of organizational resources in the process of inequality generation. We think this is a mistake. Inequalities both between and within countries are profoundly conditioned by organizational variation in the resources available to be distributed, and the resource bases of both organizations and countries are direct results of organizational efficiencies in production and power in supplier and customer market exchanges. Organizations pool resources through the same process of relational claims-making vis-à-vis other organizations and individuals via mechanisms of social closure and exploitation in market relationships.

Organizations that can attract sufficient revenue from their environment—typically from customers, sometimes from the government in the form of contracts and grants, sometimes from donors in the case of churches and charities, sometimes from family, friends, and venture capitalists in the case of entrepreneurial start-ups—pool the income that stakeholders demand in order to participate in organizational life. Organizations that cannot realize a sufficient income fail, precisely because management, employers, donors, and investors flee or never arrive.[10]

This flow of resources into organizations is a fundamental constraint on both the existence of the organization and its inequality regime. It is these resources on which actors make claims and, therefore, through which exploitation and closure generate inequalities in their distribution. One of the consistent findings in the literature on income distributions is that larger firms and firms in dominant market positions are more likely to pay their workers wages higher than those of workers with similar skills in less resource-rich organizations. Economists refer to this as *rent sharing* (Katz and Summers 1989).[11] Of course, there are actors other than workers and owners who can mobilize claims on this above market surplus. Suppliers can raise their prices if they are powerful and customers may pay less in competitive markets or when they are the only buyer and can insist on lower prices (Burt 1983). Realized organizational surplus is therefore the result of the relative power of customers, suppliers, taxing authorities, and investors to siphon off income, in addition to more routinely recognized internal organizational efficiencies in production.

At the national level, we often think of surplus in terms of the national levels of economic development, typically measured as gross domestic product per capita. How much value is produced in a country for each human being who needs to be supported? Managerial scholars and taxing authorities typically think of organizational surplus as income net of costs, including labor costs. Marxist theory thinks of surplus similarly to management scholars and taxing authorities but sees this surplus income as the illegitimate result of the exploitation of labor.

10. There are many stylized theories of the process of organizational survival. Neo-institutionalists stress the legitimacy of organizational forms and practices (DiMaggio and Powell 1983), population ecologists focus on the match to environmental niche (Hannan and Freeman 1977), and neoclassical economists emphasize price efficiencies in production (Williamson 1981), among others. Our problem is different, although linked, in that we are concerned here with the variation between organizations in the resources available to be distributed to stakeholders.

11. Economists have long documented rent sharing: industries and firms with rising profits tend to subsequently raise wages (e.g., Blanchflower, Oswald, and Sanfey 1996; Mahmood and Heyman 2009). This is in line with the common finding that falling profits do not lead to wage cuts, while increasing profits tend to produce higher employee wages. All workers, however, need not share these rent-driven resource flows equally. Lena Nekby (2003), for example, using matched employer-employee data for Sweden finds that rising profits raise the wages of all workers, but men receive about a 30% larger share of the rent. In addition, rent sharing is more generous with high-wage workers, and it is here that she finds that women are most heavily penalized. Thus, while resource flows influence income, workers with more powerful claims on income—whether derived from skills or positional or cultural resources—tend to benefit the most.

We think it makes more sense to think of organizational surplus as an organizational income net of supplier, distribution, and taxation costs *but including labor costs*. We include labor costs in our conceptualization because these are not external costs constituent to the organization's production of value. The size of labor's share is dynamically produced through numerous rounds of claims-making. In this sense, organizational surplus is the set of resources available for distribution to actors with claims on organizational income—owners, stockholders, managers, workers, taxing authorities. This conceptualization is similar to the calculation by macroeconomists of value added, which includes income distributed to labor and capital as well as earnings retained for future investment. In this sense, it is useful to think of each organization as having a value-added analog, which we refer to as *organizational surplus*.

This idea of surplus was clearly present in Marx's account of the generation of surplus in production as the resource that organizations distributed. Human capital theory in economics also identifies the value accumulated from the sale of goods or services as the material basis for earnings distributed to actors in production (Becker 1964). Following the same insight, Joan Acker (2006) places class relations in production at the center of her notion of inequality regimes. Once resources enter an organization, they are distributed externally to pay for material and service inputs from suppliers. The residual income is a resource to be distributed to actors with claims on the organization's surplus.

In a purely egalitarian country every organizational stakeholder would receive their per capita share of the national organizational surplus. Between workplace inequalities are the deviation from this equal share baseline. In an egalitarian workplace every member of the organization would get their per capita share of organizational income. Workplace earnings inequalities are then the deviation from that pure equality condition. This surplus is partly a function of organizations' divisions of labor and internal efficiencies but also of their power to claim resources from their environment. And, as we will see in Chapter 8, sometimes organizations adjust their boundaries via subcontracting and outsourcing to limit some actors' ability to make claims on the surplus. It is also well recognized in both sociology and economics that organizations vary in both their power to set prices for customers and suppliers and their ability to manipulate the rules that govern their markets. More powerful organizations on both dimensions tend to realize higher levels of surplus as a result of their market and market-making power.

Organizations vary in their productivity as a function of the internal social and technical divisions of labor, the skills embedded in workers, jobs, workgroups, and technologies, and the quality of coordination among roles (Becker 1964; Hodson 2002; Rubin and Brody 2011). But organizations actually accumulate income based on the sale of goods and services. This is not simply about the value produced by people in the organization but also about the value organizations can sell their products for. Resource-pooling reflects both the efficiency of production within organizations and the relative power of organizations in their environment to set prices and avoid taxes.

> Resource Pooling Proposition: Organizations accumulate resources through both structuring internal production and claiming resources in their environment. The volume of resources accumulated shapes resource inequalities between organizations.

By highlighting organizations as resource-pooling devices we not only affirm that the resource base of organizations matters for the emergence of inequality within organizations but can also begin to see that claims-making, exploitation, and closure processes determine the distribution of resources not only within organizations but also between them. Product markets are no more invisible hands than are labor markets. Instead, organizational environments, including product markets, are claims-making arenas. They are relational spaces in which organizational actors establish trust and cooperation or exploitation and social closure. This is true whether we are talking about the product market of private firms or the set of linkages between nonprofits, government agencies, and various public and private funders. The capacity of an organization to claim resources from its environment then becomes a contextual condition shaping the capacity of actors within the organization to claim those resources for themselves.

Institutional Variation

Social scientists have long used the idea of social structure to refer to those relatively durable constraints that steer strategic actions. These "structures" have in our view too often been treated as static attributes of societies or nations. While we agree that both organizational agency and individual agency are typically channeled and constrained by durable forces that appear to be beyond our control, at the same time we do not see these forces as either static or necessarily societal. The "force" in social structure is the pull of relationships in a local field of action.

Actors face limits from both the organizations and organizational fields they inhabit. These limits are structural in the sociological sense that they are both durable and constraining. At the same time, they are neither hegemonic, static, nor typically societal. We agree with Neil Fligstein and Douglas McAdam's (2011) notion that fields limit action but also that there is typically room for strategic action within fields. Actors claim resources in the field, arbitrage structure, negotiate interaction orders, and challenge the habitus they embody. Mostly they fail, and the field, its relations of power and status, and habitus of action dominate. Sometimes they succeed, and access to resources shifts. Sometimes powerful actors actually change their field's rules of the game. Occasionally, the powerful fail and new actors become dominant in fields of power.

Importantly, societies are internally heterogeneous, characterized not by homogeneity of context but by multiple strategic action fields. Actors, who are heterogeneous along race, class, gender, education, and other categorical distinctions, do not face unitary societies or social structures but rather relational fields that empower or limit their opportunities for respect, resources, and rewards. Because they have distinct positions in the fields they inhabit, employers and employees inhabit distinct societies and confront different constraints. The same can be said for races, genders, and any relationally consequential categorical distinction.

Charles Tilly (1999) described organizations as borrowing from the larger society cultural solutions to problems of social organization. The fact that occupations often become associated with particular genders or educational credentials reflects these types of institutional processes. Gender and educational distinctions are widespread and culturally available and so are typically easy distinctions to use when matching people to jobs and recognizing the value of people at work. The matching of cultural status hierarchies to organizational production distinctions both generates and helps legitimate inequalities in respect and rewards at work. Thus, internal organizational fields are profoundly conditioned by the institutions of the external fields they inhabit and react to. This is true not only for market institutions but also for racialized and gendered institutions, which similarly contain both material constraints (e.g., segregation) and cultural understandings (e.g., particular racial ideologies) that inflect and infect claims-making, exploitation, and closure in and around organizations.[12]

The fact that these categorical distinctions are in practice intersectional further fractures society and structure into qualitatively distinct positions within the field of social relationships.

Certainly from the point of view of the actor social constraints often appear to be durable—structural or even stratified in the geological sense. At the same time, actors do not negotiate societies or geological formations but

12. We find helpful the theoretical work of Eduardo Bonilla-Silva (1997) on race and Patricia Martin (2004) on gender for highlighting the interactional impact and historicity of institutions for inequality. Barbara Risman's (1999) work on gender in intimate relationships is valuable in pointing out that gender (and presumably any institutionalized categorical distinction) operates at the individual, interactional, and institutional levels. Her work is simultaneously relational and contextual.

rather must act strategically in local fields. That we often mistake our local action field for societal structures is merely a perceptual error, produced by our limited awareness of field-level properties, much less our inability to perceive whole societies or the historical durability of opportunity structures.

We think of social institutions as powerful influences on local strategic action fields. At the same time actors internal to organizational inequality regimes reinterpret and channel these institutional influences. If we look historically in any one country, we can see social institutions change. Since organizations are lodged in fields, these institutional shifts can be expected to diffuse across organizations. However, how that change happens will be a fundamentally locally negotiated process (Hallett and Ventresca 2006).

> Organizational and Institutional Fields Proposition: Inequality regimes and their internal configurations of categorical distinctions and inequality mechanisms will refract, rather than reflect, the causal pressures from their external organizational and institutional fields.

Cultural and legal institutions within nation states around employment, such as collective bargaining regimes, labor market regulations, and employment laws, are central to the institutional framework shaping what goes on inside organizations. Among industrial societies there are multiple varieties of capitalism and socialism, each of which puts different constraints on organizational processes. In some countries the welfare state insures against risk in the labor market, thus strengthening the bargaining power of labor, especially of low-skilled labor. Countries also vary tremendously in their labor market institutions. Some countries are highly unionized and take for granted that labor has a legitimate claim on organizational resources. In others, including the United States, organized labor is very weak and the law encourages wage bargains at the individual or job level. In some countries the state explicitly supports the bargaining power of capital or of labor, and in some the state acts as a referee. State intervention has been crucial to shifts in the ability of women and ethnic minorities to be treated with respect in workplaces. National variation in cultural and legal institutions will tend to influence most organizations within their borders. Thus, as legal and cultural expectations as to what are legitimate claims on organizational resources shift over time and context, we can expect the observed set of inequality regimes to shift as well. Later in this book we observe such institutional influences on organizational inequality regimes historically, comparatively, and within specific product and labor market institutions. Thus, we expect substantial organizational variation in how inequalities become embedded in local fields and their implications for categories of people based on the cultural and legal institutional frameworks.

We understand the influence of institutions from the point of view of the actor. Actors make decisions in their fields of action. These proximate fields are typically not whole societies but the set of other actors that a person or firm takes into account when deciding on a course of action. Institutions, which we take to be sets of practices and expectations that cross-cut multiple local fields, are at a higher level of abstraction. Like culture more generally, institutions do not so much exist as provide templates for types of action that one might pursue. We can speak of gender, race, and capitalism as institutions, impinging on all fields in a society. But most of the time their impact will need to be transmuted first through a more proximate field of actors and then inhabited in concrete interactional settings within organizations. So even unitary cultural notions of what capitalism should be or of what gender differences or racial stereotypes will be are inhabited and interpreted through the prism of local social relationships.

Similarly, organizations respond to their market or legal or political fields, which in turn are influenced by institutions that cross-cut local fields and provide cultural or material roadmaps for action. Mario Small (2009) has pointed out that because organizations exist simultaneously in multiple fields (e.g., customer, supplier, competitor, regulatory) there is variability in organizational form and action. In this sense the influence of institutions on organizations is indirect, via more proximate fields, and indeterminate in consequences. The imagery here is not so much that of institutions as stacking matryoshka dolls but of a constellation of stars and planets exerting gravitational attraction on each other.

Approaching organizations with this particular institutional lens further forces us to think about organizational inequalities in historical terms. When we think institutionally, we recognize that any cultural, legal, or market practices are temporary, lodged in a specific historical and political moment. That is to say, where you are in history makes a great deal of difference as institutions vary over time as well as place. For example, the spread and legitimacy of educational credentials as criteria for job matching is a relatively new social invention. Educational certification has spread across the globe only in the last 100 years, displacing family and community of origin as the primary job closure criteria in many workplaces and countries. The rise of educational institutions as the primary legitimate source of distinction reflects a host of societal shifts, including initially literacy requirements for workers to match developing technologies, the increased power of educational organizations to define skill and talent, and the political role of some occupations to link their employment monopolies to educational certification. Gender, on the other hand, is a much older basis for distinction, which has only come under widespread attack fairly recently. The thoroughly modern idea that women are fully human is still diffusing across institutional contexts, but in societies where traditional gender distinctions have weakened, gender-based claims over resources are increasingly replaced by or disguised within education or other productivity-linked claims.

RIT stresses the fundamental importance of historical and institutional context for ratifying, exaggerating, or muting status-based claims on organizational resources. Thus, categorical distinctions should not be expected to uniformly generate legitimate claims. If we look across countries and over time, we find examples of multiple institutions, each shaping the inequality regimes that develop within organizations. There are varieties of capitalism, gender regimes, racial formations, and welfare state institutions. And all of these provide the social contexts around which organizations develop inequality regimes.

The salience of particular categorical distinctions—such as gender, education, and occupation—for employment inequalities has been shown to vary as a function of national labor market institutions, the formalization of personnel policy, managerial equal opportunity accountability, local versus centralized wage-setting, product market competition, team versus hierarchical labor process organization, and organizational compensation practices (see our reviews of this literature in Avent-Holt and Tomaskovic-Devey 2014).

> Contextual Variation Proposition: Institutional contexts can legitimate or delegitimate claims and can magnify or mute the exploitation, social closure, and claims-making consequences of any categorical distinction.

CONCLUDING THOUGHTS

This chapter has laid out the formal conceptual building blocks in RIT. Categorization is a ubiquitous process which people use to make distinctions between human beings. These distinctions tend to be converted into moral boundaries between in- and out-groups, low- and high-status traits. Categorization simplifies cognition, encouraging us to rely on cultural stereotypes or past experience in order to evaluate the moral worthiness of people based simply on group membership. Racism, sexism, xenophobia, nationalism, as well as more mundane distinctions such as occupational culture or community pride all put categories into motion, producing inequalities.

But categories are not sufficient. For inequalities to be installed, we need a set of concrete mechanisms in consequential social contexts. Organizations provide that social context as the most profound context in which actors interact with one another to divide up material and social resources. Claims are the active bases upon which organizational resources are distributed, functioning as the interactional mechanism that sets exploitation and social closure into motion to produce inequality. The capacity for claims to be legitimated is conditioned by the institutional arrangements that cross-cut social fields and the resource base of the organization itself. These condition the constitution of claims and their ability to generate inequality but only by intersecting with local organizational cultures to produce distinctive inequality regimes.

It should be clear that our argument is profoundly local. We see local interaction within organizations as the bedrock upon which what come to appear as national and even international systems of inequality emerge. Some readers may wonder what to do with concepts like social structure and how to relate this to our notions of field and institution. We take *social structure* to refer to those relatively durable constraints that steer individual opportunity and action, typically conceptualized at the societal level. Patriarchy, capitalism, and racism are often treated as fairly static societal or national social structures that govern action homogenously across geographic and organizational space. While we agree that individual action is typically channeled and constrained by durable forces beyond any individual's control, at the same time we do not see these forces (e.g., patriarchy, capitalism, racism) as either static or necessarily societal. Instead, we treat these "isms" as institutional forces that must be interpreted and enacted within local social contexts and that are translated through local social relationships (Fine and Hallett 2014). Institutions, conceptualized as both cultural notions constituting what is right and proper and the normative expectations and sometimes formal rules and laws shaping social action, tend to cut across fields, providing cultural material to be adopted and modified within many fields. The fact that the categorical distinctions that make up these "isms" are in practice intersectional further fractures society and structure into qualitatively distinct local social orders. Fields are the local spaces in which cross-cutting institutions get refracted and concretized in particular ways. From the actor's perspective, social structure is not so much a generalized arrangement of constraints and opportunities as it is a discursive framework that is worked out in local social fields. From a more macro perspective, social structure is comprised of the relationships among organizations, fields, and institutions. These relationships produce a structure that appears static but, similar to an atom or a solar system, is in fact held together by a set of relationally attractive and repulsive forces.

One may also wonder how to reconcile our profoundly organizational argument with the recent historical development of the disintegration of organizational forms and the boundaries between organizations. Since the 1980s the boundaries of organizations have been changing rapidly, with many organizations shedding what used to be internal processes of production and contracting these tasks out to other firms. In the contemporary era of organizational devolution organizations control their own boundaries and often do so in strategic ways. In a definitional sense, which tasks happen within the organization versus which are acquired from other organizations define the boundary of organizations. This has produced a growth of inequality between firms as actors in low-wage occupations are excluded from organizations housing core production functions. When high-income organizations externalize production roles, for example, by outsourcing, subcontracting, or hiring needed labor through temporary agencies, they define their boundaries to exclude some stakeholders from claims on organizational resources (Cobb 2016). This means that inequalities between organizations take an increasingly predominant role. We will return to this increasingly important problem of organizational boundaries as it relates to rising income inequality in Chapter 8. Here, it is worth pointing out that organizations are still central, but what matters is how organizations construct their boundaries. The concept of field becomes critical as the organization becomes a set of interlinked organizations that constitutes a field in its own right. In this sense, the field has not shifted as much as has the legal boundaries of organizations.

One of the profound problems with theoretical systems of the sort we have offered here is that theory alone tends to lack sufficient clarity to produce either a real-world image or inspire a research design. In the next chapter we develop these theoretical ideas via a series of examples of distinct organizational inequality regimes. Later chapters develop both conceptually and empirically the inequality generating concepts of exploitation, social closure, and claims-making. The penultimate chapter focuses on the role of market and organizational power in rising earnings inequalities. In the final chapter we return to the theory and point out some practical avenues for further development of the RIT approach to challenge troubling inequalities.

4

Organizational Inequality Regimes

All organizations have inequality regimes, defined as loosely interrelated practices, processes, actions, and meanings that result in and maintain class, gender, and racial inequalities within particular organizations.

Joan Acker (2006:443)

Economic worlds are social worlds; therefore, they operate according to principles like other social worlds. Actors engage in political actions vis-a'-vis one another and construct local cultures to guide that interaction.

Neil Fligstein (1996:657)

In developing relational inequality theory (RIT) we have come to see the intersection of inequality and organizations through the lens of inequality regimes. Drawing primarily on the work of Joan Acker (2006), we define inequality regimes as comprised of 1) the resources available for distribution; 2) the task-, class-, and status-based social relations within organizations; 3) formal and informal practices used to accomplish goals and tasks; and 4) cultural models of people, work, and inequality, often adapted from the society at large to fit local social relationships. Like Vincent Roscigno (2011), we reject the image of organizations as empty positions, rational bureaucracies, or efficiency-obsessed capitalist firms. In contrast, inequality regimes result from the intersection of local narratives, positions, and people infused by historical and institutional context. Like all organizational processes, inequality regimes reflect local technical and social relationships, as well as field-level influences on the emergence of those technical and social systems (Scott and Davis 2015). As a result, the meanings and power resources associated with particular claims-making statuses reflect these local interactional and institutional influences, sometimes producing complex intersectional inequalities (Ken 2008). Thus, inequality regimes reflect both their institutional environments and their internal interactional struggles and negotiated orders over and around production, respect, and rewards.

In developing the concept of inequality regimes, our image of organizations shares more with the inhabited institutionalist approach than with its better-known neo-institutionalist predecessor (Hallett and Ventresca 2006; Hallet 2010). A complementary model can be found in the management literature under the name of *routines theory* (see Feldman and Pentland 2003). DiMaggio and Powell's now famous 1983 paper "The Iron Cage Revisited: Institutional Isomorphism and Collective Rationality in Organizational Fields" outlined generic processes in the institutional environment of organizations that encourage organizations to copy each other's structures, procedures, and practices and that weed out organizations that do not conform. The view of organizations from neo-institutionalism is as generally passive recipients of organizational environments, copying each other's structures, procedures, and practices and leading to fields in which organizations become close copies of one another.

Charles Tilly (1999), in his original relational inequality model, drew strongly on this neo-institutional imagery, pointing toward the matching of cultural status distinctions from the environment such as gender, race, or educational certification to jobs as a low-cost mechanism for installing inequalities between positions and as a tool of organizational legitimation. In this way, Tilly adopted what was then the dominant model of how organizations operate. In contrast, inhabited institutionalism takes organizations as collections of individuals doing things together in ways that reflect organizational models in the environment but that also modify, contradict, and may even explicitly challenge those models (Hallett and Ventresca 2006; Hallet 2010). While we recognize the role of organizational environments in shaping organizations, inhabited institutionalism reminds us that these environments interact with real people inside organizations who adapt, adjust, and translate environmental influences.

THE UBIQUITY OF REGIME VARIATION

A growing body of research demonstrates the utility of thinking of organizations as distinctive inequality regimes rather than mechanical copies of other organizations. Sociologist Kevin Leicht (2008) has pointed out that the focus on mean levels of group-based inequality, such as the national gender pay gap, hides a great deal of substantively important variation. There is increasing evidence that much of this variation is organized at the workplace level. Studies using linked employer-employee data, particularly when they are panel data, are especially useful in allowing researchers to isolate organizational impacts that are independent of or transmute the influence of individual characteristics. Such data are organized through collecting data on both workplaces and the workers who work within them. Organizational data also permit embedding workplaces in their industry and community, thereby revealing field-level influences on organizational resources, processes, and practices. We have conducted a series of studies that use linked employer–employee data in the United States, Japan, Sweden, and Germany, documenting both this variation in inequality regimes and how these regimes are linked to national institutions. We detail some of this work to highlight the importance of recognizing organizational variation and theorizing the variety of inequality regimes that exist or may someday exist.

Gender Wage Gaps in Japan and the United States

In one study we looked at the gender wage gap in the early 1980s in about 100 manufacturing plants in Kanagawa, Japan, and Indianapolis, Indiana (Avent-Holt and Tomaskovic-Devey 2012). Both samples were drawn from similar organizational environments: within each country the national, historical, local labor-market, and production sector fields are nearly identical. This survey, designed by Jim Lincoln and Arne Kalleberg (1992), was one of the first linked employer–employee research designs.[1]

Despite their field similarity, we found that, after controlling for individual differences in education, firm tenure, and labor force experience, there was a wide variety of gender wage gaps across firms in both countries.[2] The average gender wage gap was larger in Japan, reflecting the lack of a women's rights social movement or any legally mandated equal opportunity protections in that country at that historical moment. But as Figure 4.1 makes clear, there was substantial variation in the gender wage gap across plants in both countries. We can also see that, reflecting higher levels of inequality and more locally negotiated wage bargains in the United States, the plants in Indiana had a greater dispersion of gender wage gaps. We were initially surprised to find that in some plants, even in Japan, there was no gender wage gap at all.

1. After randomly sampling manufacturing plants in the two cities, Lincoln and Kalleberg randomly sampled among employees of those plants. An interesting aspect of this study was the data forensics we went through to accomplish it. As we developed the relational inequality model, we realized that linked employer–employee data were ideal for testing our ideas. We remembered the Kanagawa/Indianapolis study done decades earlier. When we went looking for the data, we eventually found the codebook at the University of California, Los Angeles, and the raw data in 1970s-era IBM computer card format at Cornell's social science data center.

2. We stress the important role of cross-cutting intersectionality in producing this variation. It is worth pointing out that especially in small firms some of this variation could simply be the result of random sorting processes, though other studies using data on the complete population of workers in organizations, such as the examples from Sweden and Germany in this chapter, suggest that such variation is not all random sorting.

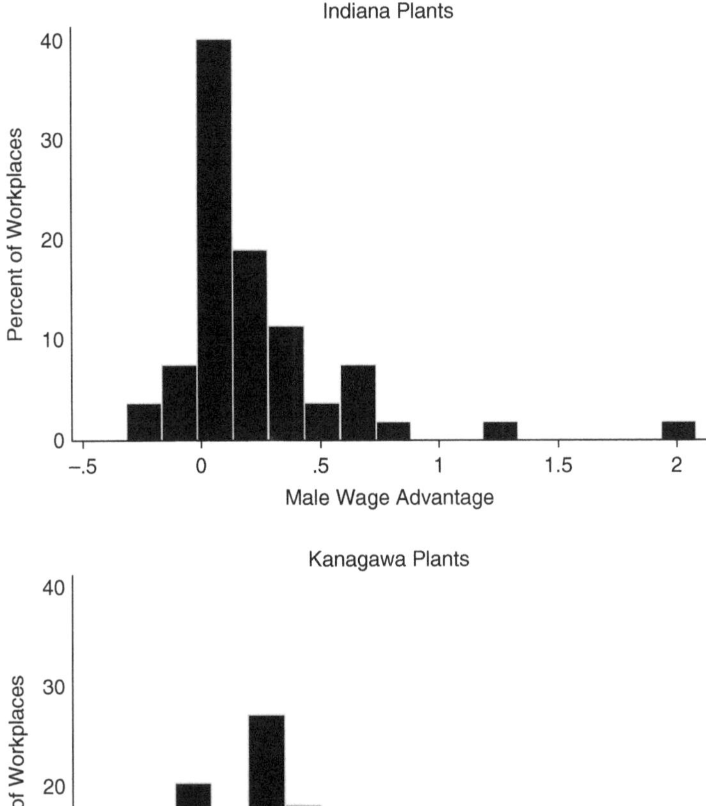

Figure 4.1 Distribution of gender wage gaps across Kanagawa, Japan, and Indianapolis, Indiana, manufacturing plants.

Following our relational inequality model, but perhaps overinfluenced by the US experience, we hypothesized that this variation in the gender wage gap would be a function of the intersection of gender with occupational authority, individual education, and workplace tenure. This is exactly what we found in the United States. But the story was quite a bit different in Japan. There the gender wage gap was created by the sorting of men into higher- and lower-wage firms. Women's wages showed almost no variation across firms. Women's subordination at work was so highly institutionalized in Japan in the early 1980s that there were no intersectional processes in play. In Japan the key inequality-installing categorical distinction appeared to be class distinctions among men and strongly gendered familial norms that consigned women at work to the margins of all firms.

In retrospect this was not surprising as Japan at that point in history had never had a women's movement to struggle to install economic rights for women. The categorical distinction between men and women was a bright line and the exclusion of married women from employment nearly absolute. In contrast, the United States had already experienced at least two women's movements, one in the early twentieth century which gave women the right to vote and a second in the late 1960s and 1970s that legitimated claims to expand both economic and interactional dignity. As we will show in the section on National Institutions later in this chapter, gender segregation in US workplaces had already been falling for a decade when the Indianapolis manufacturing data were collected. Thus, gender in the United States was becoming a blurry categorical distinction, at least relative to the past, and gender inequality was contested in interaction and under the law. As such, variation in the gender wage gap was quite substantial across US workplaces and was being produced in these US manufacturing plants by the intersection of class and gender as categorical distinctions in particular workplaces.

What this means is that gender inequality regimes were more variegated within the US context because the meaning of gender and of women in workplaces, even in the early 1980s, was more locally negotiated. But even Japan's more institutionalized dominance of men intersected with the size and resource base of plants to produce local inequality regimes. In 1980s-era Japan gender and individual women's claims on firm resources were not yet on the table as contestable categories.

Immigrant Status and Skill Distinctions in Sweden

In another project we looked at the wage gaps between native Swedes and non-Western immigrants to Sweden (Tomaskovic-Devey et al. 2015a). We focused on non-Western immigrants, rather than all immigrants, because it is for this group that categorical subordination in Sweden is most clear. This study was for the entire Swedish economy, so there is a great deal more external field variation than in the Japan–US manufacturing

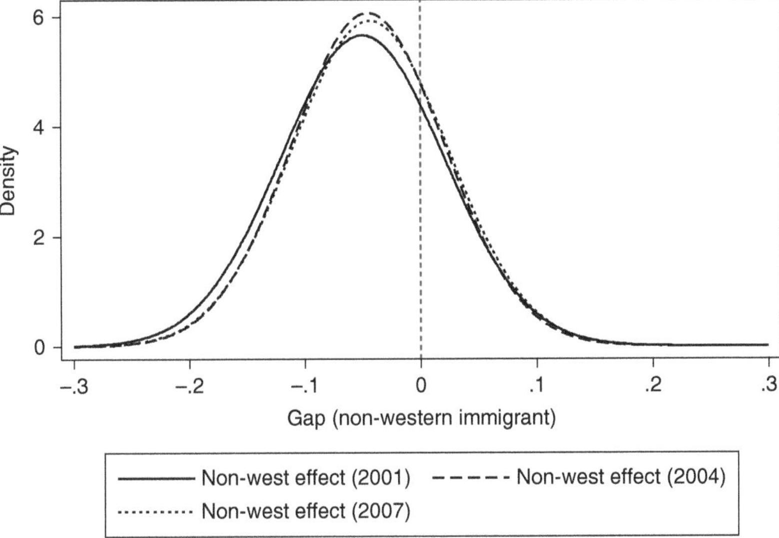

Figure 4.2 Distribution of non-Western immigrant versus native Swede wage gaps across all Swedish workplaces for 2001, 2004, and 2007 (authors' calculations).

comparison.[3] We again discovered a remarkable degree of variability in the native-immigrant wage gap, including in about 20% of workplaces wage advantages for non-Western immigrants over native Swedes. Figure 4.2 displays the distribution of non-Western immigrant-native Swede wage gaps (controlling for education, firm tenure, and employment experience) for all employed workers across all workplaces in Sweden for 2001, 2004, and 2007. The peak of these distributions is at about the average national wage gap between non-Western immigrants and native Swedes (about 7% in 2007), and the leftward movement of the distribution over the periods suggests that, on average, non-Western immigrant pay is becoming more similar to the pay of native Swedes.

But most importantly for our purposes is the striking variation in the size of the wage gap across workplaces. In most workplaces natives outearned similarly qualified immigrants, but in about one-fifth of workplaces immigrants were advantaged over similarly qualified natives. At the extremes there are

3. We controlled for this field variation by estimating organizational fixed effects models, essentially controlling for all stable aspects of the organization and its environment. This allowed us to focus only on the internal social relationships within workplaces and how they were tied to changes in the immigrant-native wage gap. We are indebted to our co-author Martin Hällsten, who constructed and implemented this modeling strategy.

workplaces in which immigrants earn 25% less than similar natives and others in which they earn 15% more. In terms of categorical inequalities, we can conclude that the non-Western immigrant status is less strongly institutionalized in contemporary Sweden than gender distinctions were in 1980s-era United States and Japan, where, despite some workplaces with rough gender equality, there were none with (statistically significant) female advantages.

We found that this organizational variation in Swedish immigrant-native wages was strongly tied to the level of occupational segregation at the workplace level. The matching of external categories to internal production roles was crucial. When segregation was low or favored immigrants, native wage advantages shrank or even reversed. When segregation was high and favored natives, native wage advantages grew. We also found that wage gaps narrowed when non-Western immigrant managerial and overall workplace employment rose and at the individual level as immigrants gained more employment tenure in their firms. All of these results suggested that non-Western immigrant status was a blurry, not bright, categorical distinction and that processes of social closure and exploitation weakened as a result of local workplace intersectional and interactional processes.

Strikingly, the immigrant-native wage gap was much larger in workplaces with high levels of overall inequality. In fact, all categorical distinctions—education, gender, citizenship, parental social class—were exaggerated in their inequality generation consequences in high-inequality workplaces. Figure 4.3 displays this pattern just for skill distinctions, measuring skill in three ways: 1) skill level associated with specific occupations, 2) individual's past earnings history as a signal of personal skill level, and 3) whether or not the individual has a college degree.

Skill distinctions are particularly interesting from the point of view of status attainment and human capital theory. In status attainment theory skill is a stable attribute of occupations. In human capital theory the value of skill is determined externally to the firm, in labor markets. With all three measures we see that the impact of skill—job skill, individual skill, and college degree—on earnings grows dramatically in high-inequality workplaces. The economic value of all three types of skill is between 50% and 100% greater in high-inequality workplaces than in low-inequality workplaces. Thus, the meaning of skill is negotiated locally, and in high-inequality workplaces the claims-making power of the high-skilled is stronger, even in relatively egalitarian Sweden.

Education, Gender, and Immigrant Status and German Wage Gaps

In a third project using linked employer-employee data from Germany, we looked at inequality regimes associated with gender, education, and

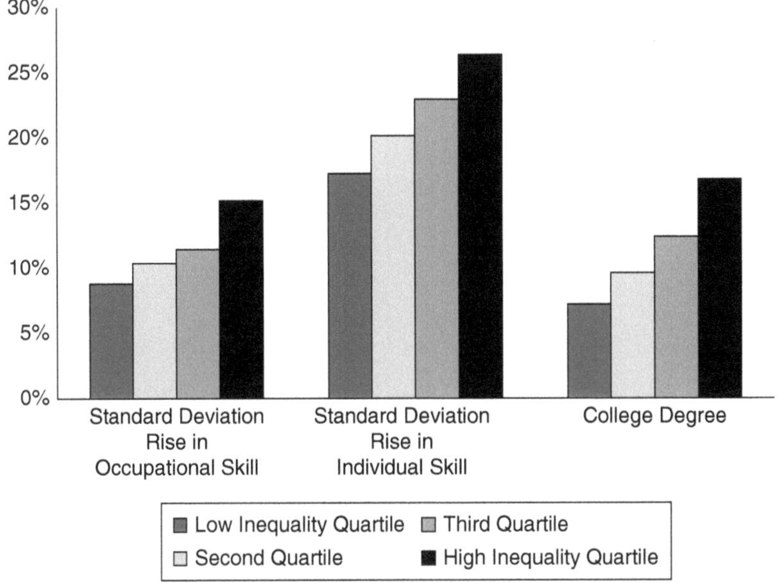

Figure 4.3 Swedish percentage wage gains associated with three measures of individual skill by workplace overall inequality levels (Tomaskovic-Devey, Hällsten, and Avent-Holt, 2015a).

citizenship simultaneously.[4] Again we computed wage gaps—this time between men and women, people with college degrees and those with just a high school-equivalent education, and German citizens and immigrants. By looking at all three simultaneously we can learn something about their relative institutionalization as categorical distinctions in a single country. Figure 4.4 presents another density plot, this time of the wage gap across these three categorical divides for all German workplaces with 20 or more employees in 2010.

For all three categorical comparisons we see the now familiar distributional pattern, with a range of wage gaps that goes from positive where women, high school graduates, and immigrants are favored to a negative range where men, college graduates, and German citizens are favored. Not surprisingly, for all three comparisons most organizations display earnings inequalities favoring the dominant cultural category (men, college graduates, and native Germans), but the mean gap on all three categorical

4. We thank Peter Jacobebbinghaus, then working for the German Institute for Employment Research, for producing these estimates.

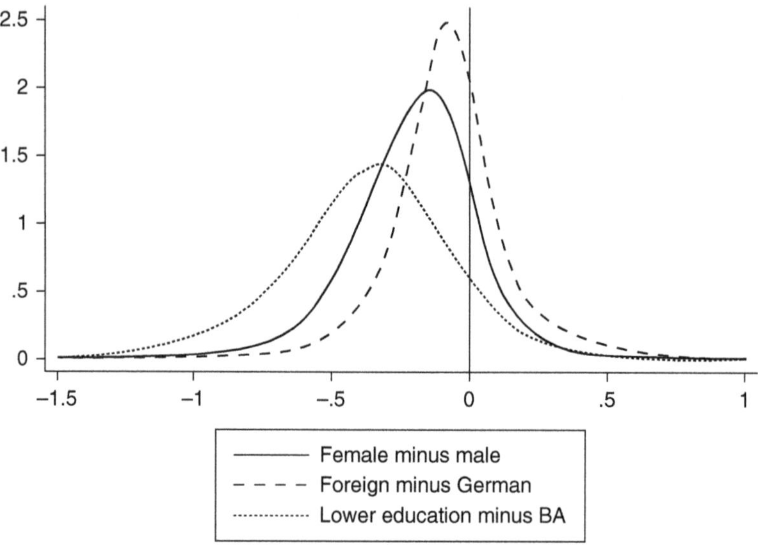

Figure 4.4. The distribution of gender, education, and citizenship wage gaps across all private sector German workplaces with 20 or more employees in 2010 (authors' calculations). BA = bachelor's degree.

dimensions should not distract from the substantial organizational variation in inequality for each categorical pair.

One of the most striking findings for us, however, was the difference between the three comparisons. Educational distinctions are much more highly institutionalized—the mean wage gap is much higher—with college degree holders outearning high school degree holders in the same workplace on average by 45%, often much higher. Only rarely do workplaces show an advantage for high school degree holders. The gender wage gap is on average smaller, and a higher proportion of the curve is to the right of zero, showing women outearning men in some workplaces. The immigrant-citizen wage gap is quite small, on average about 7%; and in many more workplaces immigrants outearn German citizens.

These patterns are not that surprising, once we know a little about German institutions. In Germany there is a very tight coupling between educational certification and occupations, producing a strong pressure to link educational distinctions to job-sorting. Contemporary immigrants to Germany tend to be fairly high-skilled on average, and their primary disadvantage in the labor market is via their lack of German educational certification. The gender wage gap is large by international standards but varies widely across workplaces because German women have access to the same institutionally dominant educational system as German men (Abendroth et al. 2016).

As with the Swedish example, we have further explored the relationship between categorical and overall workplace inequality in the German data. For both gender and college-level degrees in Germany we find the same pattern we found for immigrants and skill levels in Sweden (referred to as "tertiary degrees" in the graph and most of the scientific literature), in which higher overall workplace inequality generates greater categorical wage gaps. In Figure 4.5 you can see that when inequality is very low there is on average no wage benefit associated with a college degree or being a man. But in high-inequality workplaces these benefits are substantial, rising to around 45% higher earnings for college degree holders compared to high school equivalents and 35% for men compared to women in the highest-inequality workplaces. But importantly, we find no such pattern for immigration status in Germany. The flat line for citizenship suggests that high-inequality contexts do not provide additional benefits for citizens over immigrants.

The issue of causal direction is raised by these analyses. Do high-inequality regimes produce more categorical inequalities, or do workplaces with more categorical inequalities produce higher overall inequality? It is not clear, but we have treated the overall level of income inequality as a context in which categorical distinctions are likely intensified, claims by higher-status actors are made more plausible, and thus wage inequality across categorical boundaries is amplified. We suspect that the reverse often holds as well: bright categorical distinctions produce greater overall organizational inequality levels. RIT is agnostic on the outcome of this debate but in both situations recognizes the central role of generic processes playing out in distinctive ways to produce workplace inequality regimes.

Taking stock of all of these studies together, two things become clear. First, there is a substantial amount of heterogeneity across organizations in the form and extent of inequality across categorical distinctions. But, second, while we tend to distribute inequalities in our workplaces along categorical lines, which categories become salient and with what effect are historical and institutional products. One of the basic relational inequality insights is that the meanings and impact of categorical distinctions are institutionally contingent, a proposition confirmed by these comparisons across and within countries. In Germany the strong linkage between the German educational and employment systems strengthens the impact of educational distinctions. At the same time, the strong presence of collective bargaining for low-skilled workers negates the categorical impact of migrant status, even in high-inequality workplaces. Sweden has more autonomous workplace wage-setting institutions, and that autonomy is particularly linked to

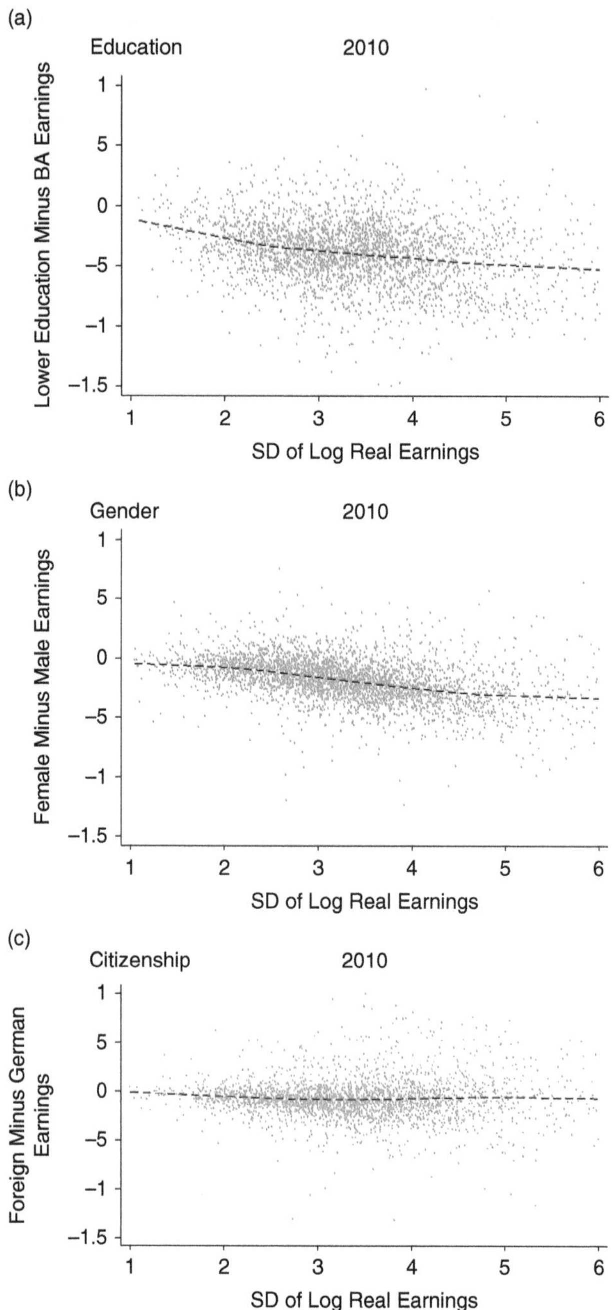

Figure 4.5 Education, gender, and citizenship wage gaps in German workplaces with rising overall workplace inequality (authors' calculations). BA = bachelor's degree; SD = standard deviation.

its high-inequality workplaces. In Japan the relative strength of men as culturally dominant produces a regime centered on variation only in wages for men across organizational contexts, while in the United States a relatively stronger women's movement has weakened institutionalized gender distinctions, producing much more locally negotiated gender inequality regimes within organizations. But, in all cases, substantial variation in categorical inequality across organizations points us toward the fruitfulness of treating organizations as locally negotiated inequality regimes.

We must note that these studies of ours are embedded in a larger literature that finds such variation across organizations in the amount of inequality and even the relationship between categorical distinctions and income inequality. Unexpected workplace variation in wage levels and who gets rewarded has been found in numerous other empirical studies of organizational income inequality using linked employer-employee data (e.g., Cardoso 1999; Abowd, Kramarz, and Margolis 1999; Card et al. 2018; Adams et al. 2017). Similarly, in *Complex Inequality* Leslie McCall (2001) used industry-locality cells to show that the implication for earnings inequalities of the intersection of class, race, and gender varied dramatically across local labor markets, a result consistent with the findings we have produced using organizational data.

Contemporary organizational theory has a bias to expect homogeneity, and most scholars of inequality and wage-setting in sociology and economics are busy looking for national gender or race or citizenship or skill pay gaps. What we should be concerned with is organizational variation in those gaps. This is perhaps even more important from a policy point of view as the ability to see this variation in inequality regimes allows us to target sexist or racist or nativist or classist firms and promote the achievements of egalitarian ones. The ability to recognize more egalitarian organizational contexts, we believe, has the added benefit of making it possible to chart a more egalitarian future, a topic we return to in the final chapter of this book.

ELEMENTS OF INEQUALITY REGIMES

Our argument is that RIT has the capacity to explain this remarkable organizational variation. While organizational fields produce pressures toward homogeneity, actors inside organizations create and reinforce localized meanings, status hierarchies, and practices that tend to be outside of the purview of a neo-institutionalist logic. Here, we identify some elements of organizations and their institutional environments that enable local variation in inequality regimes: resource levels within organizations, variation over time and place in an organization's environment, variations in organizational rules and practices, the local interpretation and incorporation of institutional frameworks, and the intersectionality of status characteristics within workplaces.[5] Each of these contributes to the generation of local inequality regimes by enabling exploitation and social closure claims to be legitimated, negotiated, or rejected, the themes that we will develop in ensuing chapters. In this way these elements should be seen as the contextual factors of organizational life within which inequality processes take particular shape.

Resource Levels

Organizations vary wildly in the resources available to distribute to their members. The consequences of this inequality between organizations are immense. Resource-rich organizations tend to pay higher wages but also to have more generous employee benefits and more stable employment. This is well known among jobseekers and social scientists alike. In an earlier period in the United States it was not unusual for parents to tell their children to get a good "union" or "corporate" or "state" job in order to be set for life as these tended to be the workplaces with substantial resources that could be used to provide better job conditions, security, wages, and benefits. These jobs have become harder to find as unions declined, large firms shed workers, and federal and state employment has been outsourced and downsized. In the previous chapter we stressed that the pooling of resources is a fundamental constraint on claims-making, exploitation, and closure. Inequality regimes vary sharply in the internal social relationships that generate surplus, and these social relationships feed back into processes of exploitation and closure. Organizations with more resources tend to be able to afford to legitimate more claims for higher incomes and job stability, have more opportunities for promotion or wage gains, and can install organizational routines that minimize exploitation and closure strategies. Thus, it is critical to know the resource base of the organization to understand how inequality processes play out.

At perhaps the most basic level, more efficient organizations produce larger volumes of surplus because they produce a greater volume of products and services at lower prices, which can then be sold to generate more revenue. The most misleading explanations of this efficiency variation focus on individual productivity, assuming that the pool of resources accumulated by an organization is the simple sum of the efforts of all of the

5. This list follows from Acker's (2006) inequality regime framework. We do not see it as necessarily exhaustive but only as reflecting some of the dominant elements of organizations that shape inequality regimes at this historical moment in most modern industrialized societies.

individuals in that organization. This version of reality, embodied to some extent in both human capital theory and the everyday interaction orders of many firms, conceptually adds up the productivity of individuals to get to the productivity of organizations, legitimating whatever distribution of income emerges from more relational processes. In this account physical technologies play the primary role, enhancing individual output. But what this general approach ignores is that efficiencies are embodied in social relations as much as, if not more so than, in the individuals attached to machines.

Truly efficient organizations combine physical technologies—machines—with social relations—divisions of labor and managerial practices—to produce goods and services. David Card and colleagues have recently documented that there is a great deal of variation in firm efficiency, even when firms operate in the same market (Card et al. 2018). Physical technologies and effort levels combine with internal divisions of labor, cooperation, and co-ordination among and between co-workers and managers and formal and informal authority relations to produce output. When tasks are shared and coordinated in a division of labor, the importance of the social relational component of production rises. Moreover, technologies and skills are often embedded in jobs and increasingly in work teams within organizations, shaping both organizational and individual productivity levels. Cooperation and coordination in production are social as well as technical accomplishments.

Economists have long recognized that actual national productivity growth is typically much higher than the simple inputs of labor and capital. Robert Solow (1957) won the Nobel Prize for his estimate that *four-fifths* of economic growth was produced by what he referred to as technical progress, pointing to a host of, typically unmeasured, organizational processes that included technological innovation, managerial competence, and various other organizational efficiencies. At about the same time, sociologist Peter Blau (1954) discovered that workgroups organized around competition between employees had lower productivity than those organized cooperatively. As all of these attributes vary across organizations, so do the resulting resource levels available for distribution.

The effects of technological innovations, skills, and the division of labor on organizational efficiencies are fairly well known. Less well understood are the effects of social relations on organizational productivity. Randy Hodson (2001) has done a great deal to move forward our understanding of the relational influences on organizational effectiveness. Most notably he focuses on features of managerial relations with workers, referring to managerial behaviors that encourage production efficiencies as *managerial citizenship behaviors*. Based on a close reading of many case studies of actual production and further statistical analyses of those cases, Hodson identified two dimensions of managerial citizenship behavior: technically workable systems of production and socially effective leadership. Technically workable systems of production involve investment in appropriate technologies, harmonization of input materials and labor, and an efficient coordination across production functions. Socially effective leadership requires respectful interactions between managers and employees and among co-workers, as well as opportunities for employee skill development, security, and freedom from abuse. Organizations are highly variable in the degree to which owners and managers produce workable divisions of labor, supplies of raw materials and technologies, and effective leadership.

Hodson showed across many organizations that managerial behaviors that promoted trust, reciprocity, and legitimacy of organizational practices achieve employee consent and effort in production. Managerial practices that do not provide the technical and social bases for socially efficient production are associated with conflict, co-worker abuse, work avoidance, and resistance to managerial directives. Hodson identified a range of managerial citizenship behaviors across workplaces, from what he identified as exceptional to catastrophic. As can be seen in Figure 4.6, in just around one-third of all ethnographies he identified management behaviors as either

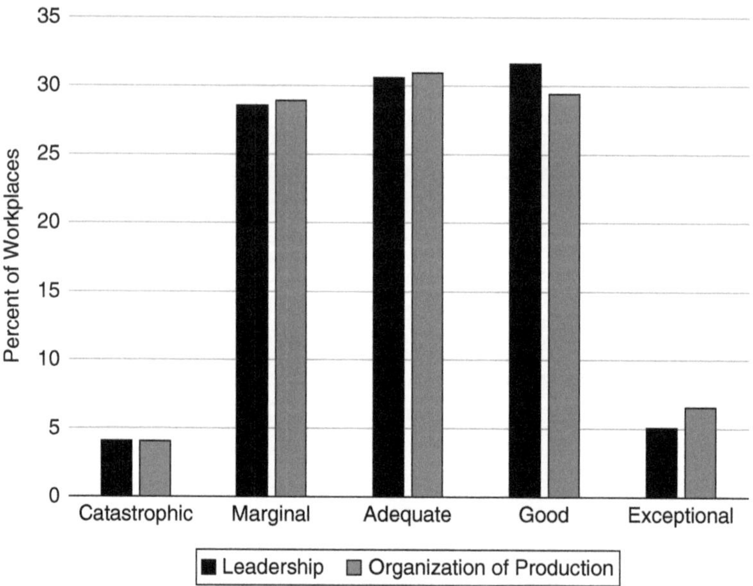

Figure 4.6 Percent distribution of workplace leadership and the quality of production management, 197 workplace ethnographies (Hodson 2004).

catastrophic or marginal on both leadership and the technical organization of production.

Poor managerial citizenship behaviors lead to negative organizational synergies and thus reduce efficiency and surplus. The kind of negative synergies Hodson describes as catastrophic and marginal can lead to poor products or ineffectual services, customer flight, worker sabotage, and potentially organizational failure. Perhaps the best example of catastrophic management in the ethnographies Hodson analyzed is found in Tom Juravich's (1985) *Chaos on the Shop Floor*. Juravich took a job as a machine operator in a wire harness assembly manufacturing plant. What he discovered was that the technical and social organization of the shop floor was both chaotic and abusive. The manager of the plant was incompetent and disrespectful. This manager regularly told workers he could find anyone off the street to do their job as a threat when they complained about technical disorganization. The plant was regularly low on supplies by design as an explicit managerial strategy to keep input costs low. Machines routinely broke down, and when running, they were often dangerous because of disrepair. In response, workers regularly shirked, compounding the organizational inefficiencies derived directly from technological and managerial failure. On both dimensions of technical production and managerial leadership, poor managerial citizenship behavior led to organizational inefficiencies.

Employers, like the one described by Juravich, who maximize the exploitation of labor and minimize investment in production actually drive down efficiency and thus surplus. Solving all production problems with labor and material cost-cutting strategies, driving workers like cattle, and bypassing managerial or technological investments that might raise productivity are recipes for organizational failure. In a recent development of Hodson's concept of managerial citizenship behavior, Martha Crowley (2015) shows that firms that are low in managerial citizenship behavior tend to be particularly harsh places to work. What is particularly striking in Crowley's research is that these same firms have 22% lower productivity and 21% lower profitability than well-managed firms (see Figure 4.7). Not surprisingly, these low-managerial citizenship firms perform poorly on many of the labor process sources of productivity. Employee turnover and absenteeism were higher in these workplaces, as were accidents, defective products, and employee sabotage and theft.

In contrast, positive managerial citizenship behavior produces positive synergies that increase internal production efficiencies. The high-road strategies of some organizations described by Eileen Applebaum, Rosemary Batt, Arne Kalleberg, and others paint a picture of positive managerial citizenship behaviors and the associated positive synergies they generate

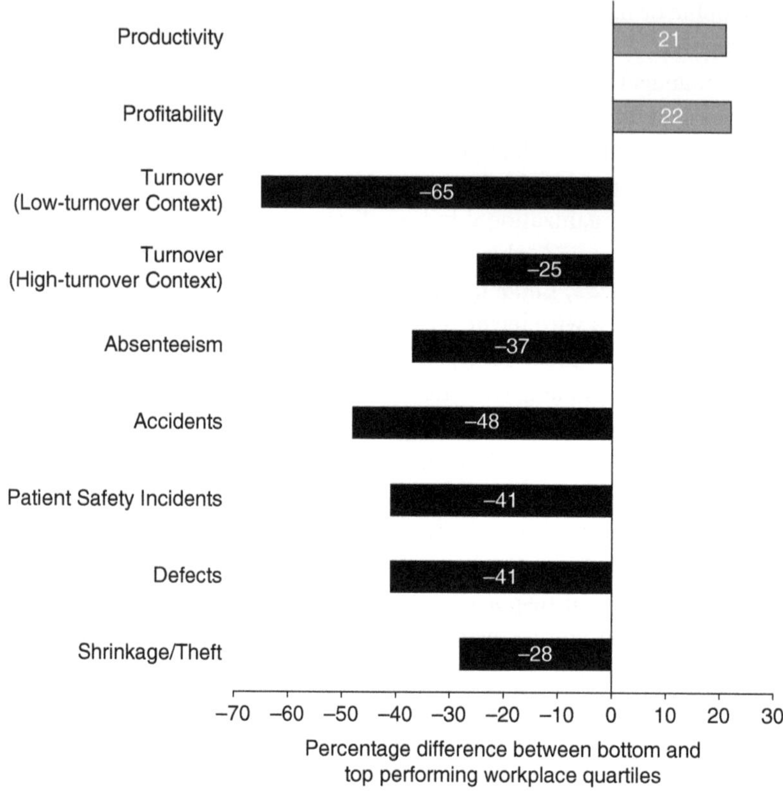

Figure 4.7 Comparisons of the top and bottom quartiles of organizational performance in US firms by managerial citizenship behavior (Crowley 2015).

even as organizations face competition in their product markets. The high-road strategy tends to include some mix of team-based problem-solving, decentralized empowerment in decision-making, and enhancing employees' commitment by linking compensation to organizational performance. Applebaum and Batt (1993) describe this strategic bundle as characteristics of "high performance work organizations."

Applebaum (2000) shows that high-road, high-performance work organizations tend to also achieve higher productivity. Economist Stefan Bender and colleagues have come to the same conclusion, finding that "advanced management practices" when combined with a high-skill labor force are associated with higher productivity (Bender et al. 2018). Consistent with the results reported by Crowley, management scholar Mark Huselid (1995) provides evidence on two mechanisms through which high-performance work practices produce increased productivity: reduced turnover and increased employee productivity. These types of practices correspond well to Hodson's description of workplaces that foster the dignity of employees in production and as a result produce effective organizations.[6]

A key ingredient in these positive synergies is the mutual respect between workers and managers, as well as among co-workers. Respectful social relationships increase reciprocity and joint problem-solving in production, while exploitative and selfish behavior tends to produce production failures. An obvious implication of this account is that exploitation or closure processes within firms, to the extent that they generate perceptions of injustice, run the risk of undermining productivity-enhancing synergies. Internally inefficient organizations emerge from treating individual organizational members as cogs in a machine to be sped up when needed. Real long-term efficiencies emerge from crafting workplace social relations of mutual respect and shared dignity that lead to positive synergies among organizational members. The efficiencies produced from these social relations generate greater organizational surplus, and the possibility for combining high income and egalitarian organizational distributions.

It is possible, however, to run an organization that minimizes labor and other costs and accomplishes production through alienating drive systems. In Chapter 8 we will see that many powerful firms pursue exactly this strategy by outsourcing labor to dependent satellite firms. This has become the recipe for cost savings in multiple industries where dominant brands can permanently exploit subordinate firms. Walmart, Apple, and Amazon all have adopted versions of this low-road strategy.

The level of organizational resources provides a crucial context in which inequality regimes develop. Organizations with more resources have a greater capacity to legitimate claims that minimize exploitation and social closure. Moreover, it is not merely the technical aspects of production that generate the efficiencies that increase surplus, but social relational dynamics within organizations are critical for creating or failing to create greater organizational surplus.

National Institutions

Organizations are situated in distinctive social fields that provide cultural and material resources that can be deployed within organizations to empower particular actors to frame claims and capture resources. Many of these resources are assembled from the national political and economic

6. Of course, if work systems are instituted mechanically (or cynically) by management to produce a higher rate of effort exploitation, then the positive synergies are likely to be lost. The key seems to be whether or not employees have levels of control over the implementation and content of high-performance work systems (Jensen, Patel, and Messersmith 2013).

institutions governing organizations. Here, we focus on spatial and temporal variation in these national institutions as a conduit through which organizational inequality regimes develop.

National institutions influence the types of organizational inequality regimes that can and do develop. There are large national differences in labor market institutions; regulatory environments; the economic rights of women, workers, and citizens; and the levels of workplace and household inequality sanctioned by the state and society. National institutions influence the capacity to exploit the effort of others, with most modern countries developing labor laws that limit exploitation. Most of these institutions operate by limiting the power of employers in the employment relationship or shifting bargaining power toward employees.

We can see the impact of national institutions by examining the impact of welfare state measures and labor market institutions on inequality patterns in the cross section across countries. In strong social welfare states, such as in the Nordic countries, workers have more alternatives to employment through the social provisioning of goods as well as income supports in the absence of employment and, thus, more bargaining power as individuals relative to their employers (Esping-Andersen 2013). In these countries, wage-setting is further constrained by the coordination of bargaining at the industrial and societal levels, which constrains the capacity for exploitation at the organizational level (Hall and Soskice 2001). These coordinated bargaining institutions typically set floors on wages but can also sometimes set ceilings on wages and prices.

The nature of employment contracts is also often determined at the national level, and these contracts can impact the leverage workers have in their workplace negotiations. The classic negative case is the United States, in which most employees can be fired at will, severely constraining what employees can ask for in negotiations for wages and interactional respect. In contrast, while in Sweden new workers can also be fired at will, after two years of employment they become permanent, leaving initially successful employees with substantial protections against firing. These practices reduce the scope for firms to reduce wages and hire and fire workers at will, at least in comparison to the United States. Germany's employment protections are stronger still, with a default presumption of permanent contracts for workers except under specified and limited circumstances. For example, a firm can offer a fixed-term contract of up to two years (four years if it is a new firm) but only for very specific reasons (e.g., replace a worker on maternity or sick leave or training for young workers). Sweden has much stronger institutional employment protections than in the United States, and Germany's are stronger than Sweden's.

It is no coincidence that societal inequality patterns tend to follow these institutional patterns. Our work on rising between-firm earnings inequalities across multiple countries strongly implicates national labor market institutions in producing both the levels and trajectories of national earnings inequalities. Workplaces produce much more inequality in the United States than elsewhere and much less in Sweden and Norway (Tomaskovic-Devey et al. 2017). These national institutions have their impact by influencing the development of inequality regimes within organizations.

Historical change within a country is the temporal analog to cross-country comparisons. Countries have different political, economic, and cultural histories. These histories generate different national institutions. Similarly, within countries historical struggles produce new institutional environments, changing the social space for exploitation, social closure, and claims-making associated with categorical distinctions. In several countries with strong coordinated bargaining institutions we see a historical shift toward decentralized wage-bargaining. In those spaces where wages are decentralizing, organizational inequality regimes are changing and becoming more diverse within countries. For example, we have shown that in Australia organizations that have moved away from the centralized wage award system have higher gender wage gaps between managers and core workers than do organizations that continue to use the system. In general, countries that have weakened their centralized wage-setting institutions, such as Germany, Sweden, and Norway, have seen a concomitant increase in income inequality between organizations (Tomaskovic-Devey et al. 2017).

National institutions observed in the cross section are the dynamic product of past political struggles. These struggles are often over the institutional meanings and laws around categorical distinctions. The rise and decline of union power in the United States is clearly an example, as are particular movements to create and expand LGBTQ, disability, women's, immigrant, and minority rights. More abstractly, variations in national inequality institutions can be understood as a result of dynamic power relations in a society. Political and social movement actors at particular moments in history mobilize to weaken or strengthen citizenship rights, the commodification of labor, or racial distinctions. And these in turn influence the relative power of actors in workplaces (Brady 2009).

Much of the thinking on national institutional contexts tends to emphasize the kinds of labor market and welfare state institutions that largely work through shaping exploitative labor practices within organizations. But here, exploring the case of the civil rights movement and desegregation of jobs in the United States, we want to show that such institutions can also shape how social closure operates within organizations. In doing so, we also demonstrate the power of social movements as transforming the institutions through which inequality regimes develop. In what follows, we draw upon Stainback and Tomaskovic-Devey's *Documenting Desegregation* (2012) to trace the evolution from highly institutionalized racist and sexist *societal* inequality regimes to a highly variable, locally negotiated array of more and less gendered and racialized workplaces.

Prior to the struggles associated first with African Americans' civil rights and later with women's rights social movements, African American's and women's subordination in organizations was deeply institutionalized in the United States. Essentially all workplaces were dominated by white men, and white women and racial minorities were either excluded from employment altogether or employed in a limited set of low-wage jobs. Social closure along racial and gender lines was nearly absolute, the lines were bright between white men and all others, and when women or racial minorities were employed, exploitation and wage discrimination were routine and legal. Slavery and Jim Crow culturally encoded the racial subordination of African Americans across political, economic, and social spaces in the United States. Similarly, the normative presumption of the dependent domestic role of women excluded or subordinated women in schools, public places, and workplaces. Legal codes further reinforced both of these cultural prescriptions.

In this context, most everyone understood that white men would occupy the most desirable jobs and hold authority over other groups. It was also assumed that if they were to be hired at all, women of all races and non-whites of all genders would occupy marginally rewarded jobs with little or no authority over others. However, as a result of pressure from the civil rights movement, in 1964 the US Congress enacted and President Lyndon Johnson signed the Civil Rights Act. Although it was not the first or the last legislative moment of the civil rights movement, it was a pivotal one for workplace inequalities. For the first time in the United States, and perhaps anywhere in the world, the Civil Rights Act outlawed segregation and discrimination by race, ethnicity, and religion in employment. In a desperate attempt to stop the passage of the Civil Rights Act, "sex" was added into the pending legislation as an additional protected status, under the assumption that fewer legislators would view preventing sex discrimination as acceptable. This then created legislation that threatened to curtail the widespread discrimination against women and people of color.

After the Civil Rights Act, both legal and interactional expectations shifted. While racial employment discrimination did not disappear, it became possible for actors, whether federal regulators, personnel managers, unions, or employees, to challenge practices that appeared to be discriminatory. Racial segregation declined, and some African Americans (mostly men) got access to better-paid jobs and jobs with authority. To use Samuel Lucas's language, the era of *condoned racial exploitation* was replaced by one of *contested prejudice* (2009). Similarly, in the 1970s in the face of the women's movement and supported by the 1972 amendment to the Civil Rights Act that made clear that Congress meant it when it added "sex" to the 1964 act, gender employment segregation began to decline.

One way of thinking about this transition is that both racial and gender closure and exploitation went from a near constant across workplaces to locally negotiated both across and within firms. Some workplaces would change their organizational routines around race and gender segregation faster than others. Some might not change at all. Some firms integrated working class jobs but left management the preserve of white men. New workplaces were founded where interactional routines were less strongly tied to pre–civil rights era divisions of labor and status expectations. Some firms, regions, and industries were subject to stronger regulatory, social movement, and employee pressure to shift toward equal employment practices. Workplaces that began to hire women or minorities into lower-level jobs were then faced with internal demands for increased access to higher-level jobs.

In 1966, the first year that the US Equal Employment Opportunity Commission (also created by the 1964 Civil Rights Act) began collecting workplace data, most private sector workplaces remained hypersegregated along the lines of both race and gender. White men monopolized almost all of the most powerful, prestigious, and skilled jobs. The immediate period following the passage of the Civil Rights Act was one in which US corporations became aware that they might soon be held accountable for this highly institutionalized discrimination. Moreover, the new institutions were filtered through the presence of strong and active mobilization of African Americans but relatively weak mobilization for women's rights. As a result, employment gains immediately following the 1964 act were largely confined to black men. Instead of responding directly to the law, employers responded to the more general political pressure in their institutional environment, an institutional pressure which did not yet take claims for women's equal rights seriously. Paradoxically, these initial gains did not come at the expense of advantaged white men, who solidified and even expanded their advantaged access to the best working- and middle-class jobs in the economy. This is because the gains for black men (and for black women and white women to the extent that they made gains) were largely in the lower-skilled jobs, pushing white men up into the higher ranks.

However, in the early 1970s the US government began to exert more direct legal and regulatory pressure on firms. The 1972 Civil Rights Act gave the Equal Employment Opportunity Commission the power to bring lawsuits against discriminating companies, and it began to target large visible firms. And in the case of *Griggs v. Duke Power* (1971) the Supreme Court ruled that employers could be held responsible for unintentional, in addition to intentional, discrimination, broadening the definition of discrimination to include unequal employment outcomes. Given that now ostensibly race-neutral practices could be deemed discriminatory in the eyes of the courts, organizations began empowering corporate personnel managers to develop and implement equal opportunity policies and practices. This led to a period of robust employment gains for black and white women as well as black men and overall decreased segregation in employment.

But the movement toward employment equality quickly stalled for black men and women and eventually for white women. African American mass social movement activity became rare after the early 1970s. This is because of both repression from state and local governments and the incorporation of civil rights leadership into electoral politics. Moreover, national electoral and social movement politics were transformed by the Republican Party nurturing white resentment against the civil rights movement, culminating in the election of Ronald Reagan in 1980. It is at this historical moment that black employment progress in the private sector effectively stopped.

Employment gains for African Americans stalled during this post-1980 period also because organizations transformed their equal opportunity policies in this era. Corporate goals of equal opportunity and proactive methods of affirmative action were largely displaced by goals of interactional tolerance and diversity training. Fuzzy talk about polite accommodation to difference at work replaced clear goals of equality, hiring expansion, and desegregation (Kelly and Dobbin 1998). And while employment advances for white women continued in this period, by the early 2000s white women's gains relative to white men had stalled as well. Figure 4.8 illustrates the initial progress and eventual stall for African American men and women in the 1980s and for white women slowing considerably in the 1990s and stalling after 2000.

It is clear from the US race and sex desegregation case that the national political institutions around race and gender employment opportunities shape organizational inequality regimes and that these national institutions are buttressed by social movement activity. But these national trends can easily hide the more central transformation that the pattern of racial and gender inequality in workplaces shifted from a national apartheid-like inequality regime exhibiting little organizational variation in the 1960s to locally negotiated, highly variable inequality regimes. The civil rights and

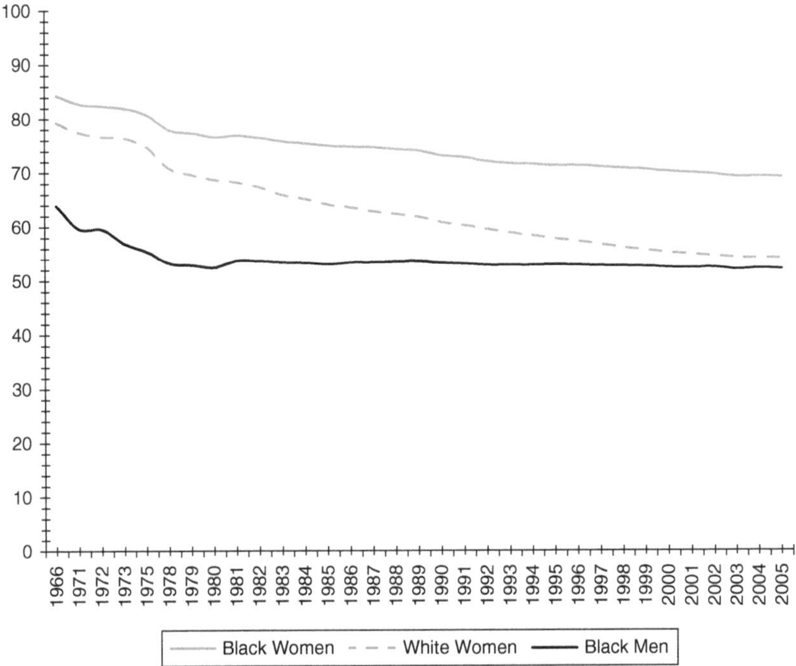

Figure 4.8 Trends in employment segregation of black women, white women, and black men from white men, private sector US workplaces, 1966–2005.

women's movements successfully attacked and defeated the strong institutionalization of racial and gender categories, moving them to locally negotiated status hierarchies.

Figure 4.9 illustrates this historical transition. It reports the distribution of white male managerial representation in every private sector workplace that reported to the Equal Employment Opportunity Commission in 1966, 1980, and 2005. A representation score of zero means that the proportion of managers in a workplace is the same as the proportion in the local labor market in which that workplace is located. A score of 100 indicates that white men are in managerial jobs at 100% more than their representation in the local labor market. In 1966, almost all workplaces were far to the right of zero because white men dominated almost all managerial jobs. There were also a very small number of workplaces at -100% where white men were absent in managerial jobs. This was essentially complete categorical exclusion in which almost all workplaces only had white male managers and the few that had other groups had no white male managers. Over time the distributions flatten out, and we see many more workplaces

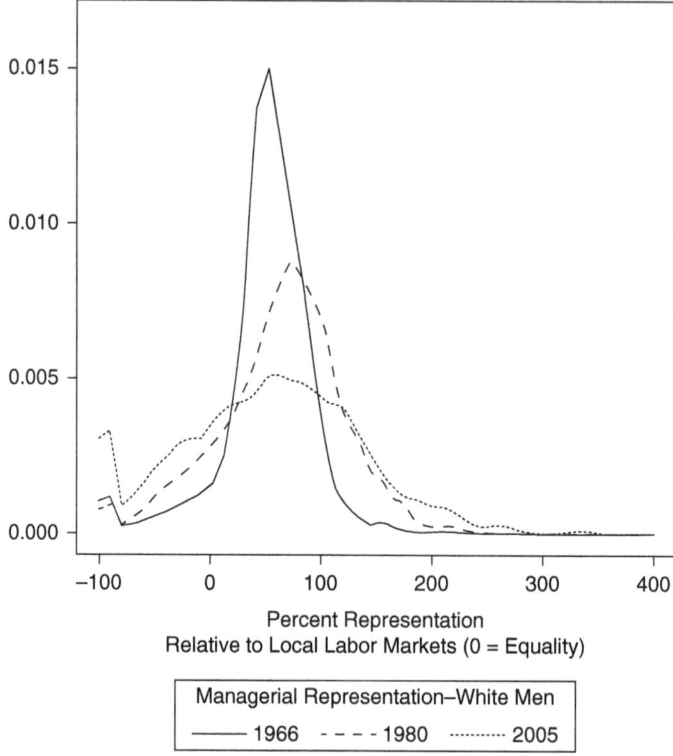

Figure 4.9 Frequencies of workplace white male managerial representation relative to local labor-market white male composition, private sector US workplaces, 1966–2005.

in which white men are represented at or below their labor market representation in local labor markets. Many more organizations become mixed in their managerial composition. At the same time the proportion of workplaces where white men are underrepresented in managerial jobs and those where they are vastly overrepresented both grow to be larger proportions of all workplaces.

National institutions shape the development of organizational inequality regimes by enabling and constraining exploitation, social closure, and claims-making. They are resources within organizational fields that legitimate and delegitimate actors' claims to exploit others or monopolize resources. Critically, while strong institutions can produce homogeneity as in the pre-civil rights era, quite often they are consistent with significant organizational heterogeneity as social orders develop within organizations, producing distinct local inequality regimes. This is increasingly the case as societal institutions break down or are transformed.

Organizational Rules and Practices

We have been stressing the relationships between people and positions as generating within-organizational inequalities. But embedded in those relationships organizations also have normative expectations and routinized practices. Central to modern organizations are human resource practices, which govern the employment contract and workplace behavior. Human resource practices can be inequality-generating or -reducing devices, depending on how they interact with local claims of exploitation and social closure to produce and legitimate inequality regimes.

Perhaps the most central human resource practices shaping inequality regimes are the rules for setting standard wage rates associated with particular jobs in particular workplaces. Most organizations have a standard wage or a wage band associated with particular jobs, especially for starting wages. These standard wages are typically the result of earlier rounds of claims-making over the division of organizational surplus but become embedded in the common-sense notion of what a particular job is worth. Standard wages associated with jobs build the class inequality between positions directly into the division of labor. These specific wage-setting practices are then the skeleton around which job inequalities are hung. As Joan Acker (1990, 2006) pointed out, when organizations have a history of gender or racial or educational segregation in job assignment, the formalization of a job's standard wages will produce gender or racial or educational inequalities that are largely taken for granted because they are built into the compensation structure associated with the organization's division of labor.

Wage-setting rules are fundamental to distributional inequality. Adam Cobb (2016) makes a distinction between firms that use "organizational" and "market" logics in setting wages. Organizational logics stress internal equity among employees as well as internal careers and long-term employment practices. These types of personnel practices reduce internal inequalities among employees. Market logic personnel practices include a more short-term orientation toward labor, less of a focus on internal skill development and more on hiring credentialed workers externally and the use of pay-for-performance systems to determine compensation. All of these market-logic practices tend to lead to higher levels of income inequality within firms through the use of face-to-face wage negotiations, pay-for-performance plans, and bonus systems, as well as between firms through outsourcing and otherwise externalizing production tasks. These practices are fundamental to organizational inequality regimes because they can reinforce or diminish categorical boundaries. Where wage-setting policies allow larger degrees of inequality, categorical boundaries are heightened, which can feed back into legitimating claims that reinforce inequalities or even produce greater inequality.

Linked to general wage-setting practices are policies specifically designed to ameliorate boundaries between categorically distinct status groups in wages as well as hiring, firing, and promotion. Unfortunately, the literature on these policies has shown that it is difficult to suppress categorical inequalities, even when human resource systems endeavor to root out bias. One of the best studies of this process was done by Emilio Castilla (2008). Castilla had access to the personnel records of a company that was heavily invested in performance evaluations and merit-based compensation practices. The company had carefully crafted an evaluation system to prevent gender or racial bias in the evaluation of the work products of its employees. Castilla found that the system worked as designed: there were no average differences in performance evaluations between men and women or between whites and ethnic minorities. However, at the next stage, when managers assigned pay increases to correspond to individuals' merit ratings, they tended to give larger raises for the same merit score to white men than to others. Categorical biases in evaluation, he concluded, are more likely in the absence of accountability and transparency, both of which were present in the initial merit-evaluation stage but not in the second stage, where raises were tied to rankings.[7]

Performance evaluations are one possible practice to reduce status inequality in organizations. But because of the pressures for equal opportunity generated by the civil rights and women's movements, many US firms instituted a whole suite of practices to reduce gender and racial bias in hiring and evaluation. Sandra Kalev, Frank Dobbin, and Erin Kelly have completed the most complete evaluation of the effectiveness of these different human resource practices. For a sample of workplaces they conducted a survey of the adoption of human resource practices and linked them to three decades of employment data (Kalev et al. 2006). They found that many of the most widespread practices had little or no influence on women's and minorities' access to managerial jobs. Looking at three broad types of practices, they found that organizational attempts to directly reduce psychological bias are largely ineffective and sometimes lead to the exaggeration of categorical boundaries, actually increasing female and minority exclusion from managerial jobs. Mentoring-type programs which attempt to create connections for women and minorities with powerful senior managers had small positive effects. The big gains, however, came when managers were held accountable

7. While this is perhaps the most carefully design study of this sort, there is a rich literature showing that performance-evaluation systems tend to exaggerate gender and racial/ethnic inequalities. In a meta-analysis of similar studies, Joshi, Son, and Roh (2015) found no average gender difference in performance evaluations but very large average male advantages in rewards.

for their successes or failures in hiring, promoting, or retaining female and minority employees.

In general, attempts to figure out if the formalization of human resource practices reduces the impact of categorical distinctions, either by increasing employment (reducing closure) or by narrowing wage penalties (decreasing exploitation), have generated quite mixed conclusions. Formalization of hiring seems to reduce gender- or race-based social closure (e.g., Tomaskovic-Devey 1993), but formalization of evaluation is associated with increased wage exploitation (Joshi et al. 2015) and even the harassment of employees who claim to have been discriminated against (Roscigno 2007). In a recent study of large German workplaces, we found that formalization in hiring and in career-planning reduced gender wage inequality but only among employees with college-level credentials (Abendroth et al. 2016). Specific educational credentials in job descriptions reduced managerial discretion in hiring and made women with that credential more competitive, even in what was otherwise a set of firms with high levels of gender bias. Formalization in merit evaluation, however, as in previous studies, was associated with larger gender wage gaps.

A lesson from all of these studies is that because organizations are bundles of social relations, with ongoing local cultures, production practices, and status relationships, the effects of formalized human resource practices are variable (see Feldman and Pentland 2003). As Gouldner (1954) pointed out decades ago, informal norms intersect with and often trump formalized routines within organizations. And as Tim Hallett and Marc Ventresca (2006) remind us in their own rereading of Gouldner, such formal organizational policies are infused with meaning in social interaction, generating divergence across organizations in how they play out. Thus, the same practice can prevent or enable organizational actors from engaging in discriminatory or even retaliatory actions (Dobbin, Schrage, and Kalev 2015; Baron et al. 2007; Roscigno 2007). Creating an organizational practice targeted at reducing categorical inequalities is no guarantee of success but must be understood within the context of the local organizational culture and inequality regime. Organizations are, after all, inhabited by people who are active agents in producing their social worlds.

The local organizational meanings of formal organizational practices are revealed in Joan Meyers and Steve Vallas's (2016) ethnographic account of two worker cooperatives. To the notion of organizational inequality regimes they add the notion of diversity regimes. By *diversity regimes* they refer to "concepts and practices that firms invoke as they define and regulate status group behavior within the firm" (p. 105). With this concept they are identifying a local cultural notion of diversity that is embedded into the local social relations of a given workplace, as a constituent part of the overall inequality regime.

What they find is compelling for RIT as the configurations of practices and inequality outcomes are strikingly different across the two cooperatives. In one firm, a worker-owned bakery, governance was hierarchical, the institutional schema was founded on class identities stressing earnings and job security, and the diversity regime eschewed conversation on race or gender despite being actively worker-managed around class distinctions. This firm also had high levels of gender and racial segregation across departments and jobs and the resulting pay inequalities that typically follow. The second firm, a worker-owned grocery store, in contrast, had a governance system built around elected management roles and multiple empowered work teams, an institutional schema predicated on valuing multicultural difference, and a diversity regime that values and encourages recognizing difference. As a result, it had very low gender and racial wage inequalities, little job segregation, and an atmosphere of mutual respect.

From these two similarly structured cooperatives with distinctive diversity regimes, they suggest that diversity regimes often lie on a continuum, anchored on one end by a utilitarian approach, in which race-, gender-, and skill-diverse employees are hired purely to fulfill functional business needs and on the other by firms that endeavor to produce a communitarian culture that positively values all employees. In the former, integration is common, but the management of diversity is absent. In contrast, communitarian regimes "encourage employees to learn from and positively value the various differences found among their ranks" (p. 106).[8]

We think the Meyers and Vallas approach to organizational rules and practices is a good methodological example of how to think holistically about the social practices that produce and reproduce organizational inequality regimes. Their comparative case study also highlights the variability of real-world inequality regimes, even for two firms with very similar original organizational designs and low inequality worker cooperative goals.

Local Organizational Cultures

The prior element–organizational rules and practices–made central that while formal practices matter, they intersect with the local culture to have their effect. In this section we flesh out more concretely how the organizational culture shapes inequality regimes. The basic fact of all social life is that we as actors draw on our symbolic or cultural understandings in order to negotiate local meaning systems. These local realities should be

8. Their work does not comment on the distribution of diversity regimes along this continuum, but the work of Kalev et al. (2006) suggests to us that most firms in the contemporary United States are clustered near the utilitarian end of the distribution.

understood as negotiated social orders that constitute expected behaviors associated with particular relationships, positions, and peoples (Fine 1984). For our actions to be intelligible to each other we must take into account the implicit interactional rules and procedural expectations of those in our immediate environment (Goffman 1959). We are certainly influenced by status and power hierarchies that we learn from the broader culture, but these hierarchies have to be negotiated locally to become embedded in the routines and practices of the organization.

The implications for inequalities are that local social orders develop and become constituent emergent phenomena within inequality regimes. Actors are disciplined to do gender (West and Zimmerman 1987) and class (Jackall 1988) appropriately in the local organizational context. Actors who do not belong, who are "not appropriate labor" in Melissa Wooten and Enobong Branch's (2012) language, tend to generate a reinforcement of categorical distinctions in interaction, leading to harassment and exclusion (see, for example, Padavic 1991). Violating norms and procedures structured around these relationships risks emotional harm to both violators and their audience. Thus, the audience, including the broader set of relations within the organization beyond particular interactions, holds us accountable for locally expected behavior (Schwalbe 2008).

This notion that organizations have locally negotiated social orders has significant implications for the emergence and evolution of inequality regimes. Turning categorical distinctions into status hierarchies and linking status hierarchies to inequality generating processes are profoundly localized phenomena. While we are influenced by our broader institutions and cultures to understand the existence and content of categories, their meanings must be negotiated within local space where status hierarchies take shape. Thus, the meanings around categorical distinctions emerge as a process within inequalities regimes, and these meanings shape the dynamics of organizational resource distributions. Leslie Salzinger's (2003) work on gender regimes within four factories is fascinating in this regard.

Doing Gender Differently in the Same Organizational Field

Leslie Salzinger (2003) studied four manufacturing plants in a single labor market in Ciudad Juarez, Mexico. All of the maquilas in which she worked are situated within the same intensely competitive global production regime, and because of their shared geography, they rely on the same local labor market. Each operates within the same gendered cultural schema rooted in what Salzinger calls the trope of "female productivity." The imagery floating through this cultural space is that of the hard-working but docile female worker, categorically contrasted to the slothful and disruptive male worker. At least partly as a result of this shared stereotype, in all four plants women are the preferred workers, although not all plants are equally able to attract them. Since the big cultural frames as well as the economic context are identical, one might expect similar gender inequality regimes in the four factories. But this was not the case. Salzinger discovered striking variability in the local enactment of gender, constituting the local inequality regimes in different ways.

Not surprisingly, in all of the plants the managers were predominantly male, but the gender composition of the workforce varied despite managerial preferences for female workers. Only two of the four plants (Panoptimex and Particimex) had predominantly female workforces, yet the ways gender operated were almost mirror images in these two organizations. Panoptimex upholds the "female productivity" trope most clearly, absorbing the cost of busing in female workers from rural areas to maintain an almost exclusively female shop floor. When supervisors request workers for their line to the personnel department, they not only request the number of workers needed but also specify the required gender. The structure of the workforce reinforces the sexualized character of the production line in which "male managers watch male supervisors watch women workers" (p. 60). Salzinger observes that Panoptimex produces an organizational gender regime in which women are passively feminized and highly sexualized.

In contrast, the female workers at Particimex are constituted as active and assertive. The plant is organized through participatory teams, and this enables female production workers to act and be recognized as assertive and agentic. The initial training of workers attempts to socialize them into working in a team context, and this is done through developing their ability to freely share their thoughts. This has real consequences for authority relations on the shop floor. For one, women are more likely to be in positions of authority than they are in other maquilas, where women are virtually absent from supervisory and managerial positions. As well, even production-level women are more assertive in relation to managers. Salzinger relates the story of an all-female work team that successfully corrected their supervisor's behavior when he failed to follow the proper channels of communicating with the members of the group on their work performance (pp. 95–96). Moreover, these powerful gendered scripts, at odds with the gender scripts that operate in the broader community, seem to have sparked new, more assertive female selves both on and beyond the shop floor. Women who work at Particimex contrast the control and responsibility they possess on the shop floor to the more confining institution of marriage and learn to speak up at home as well.

Importantly, at Particimex, outside of the spheres of production traditional femininity resurfaces. In hiring decisions, discourse around women's marital relationships and fertility is routine, with hiring managers openly seeking the permission of parents and husbands for the women to work. One personnel manager even noted, "If her husband isn't in agreement with her working, I won't hire her. She won't last" (p. 94). While women are more likely to be in positions of authority here than they are in other plants, they are still underrepresented in positions of authority and higher skilled jobs such as expert operator and line coordinator.

In contrast to the female-dominated factories, Andromex and Anarchomex each have workforces that are not predominantly female. Andromex is more or less gender-balanced, while 60% of Anarchomex's workforce is male. Both dealt with the shortage of female workers in the local labor market by simply hiring more men. While this gender integration in many ways degendered the shop floor at Andromex, it made gender a contested terrain at Anarchomex.

The gender-mixed workforce at Andromex was in part a response to a series of strikes by those previously imagined "docile" female workers. These strikes resoundingly challenged the controlling image of the compliant, productive female worker. At Andromex the shop floor became a space in which gender was de-emphasized in both discourse and practice. Men and women wore similarly degendered dark blue smocks, with no makeup allowed, diminishing the possibilities of the overt sexualizing of female workers. The division of labor across sections of the plant itself is as close to gender-balanced as possible. This degendering, however, produces a notion of line work that is masculinized as the absence of explicit gender in discourse and practice tends to assume a masculine undertone. Pay is organized through piecework, where each worker is paid per unit produced. This creates an atmosphere of masculinized competitiveness to produce at higher rates. Routine negotiation and conflict on the shop floor between engineers, supervisors, and line workers over production quality, material shortages, and work speed similarly structures the work environment. And both male and female workers deploy "masculine" selves. Moreover, the categorization of workers as "producers" and "breadwinners," while restructuring work to be more autonomous and pay to be higher relative to other maquilas, also defines "workers" as "men." Thus, it is probably incorrect to interpret Andromex as degendered but more accurate to state that both men and women come to behave in ways that are thought of as masculine.

Anarchomex is distinguished by its essentially failed organization of production. Although 60% of its workers are male, managers continue to understand maquila work as "women's work." Managers belittle male workers, leading men on the line to find ways to reassert their masculinity. The hands-off approach of managers, who spend most of their time pouring over production numbers in their offices rather than directly managing on the shop floor, enables men to reassert their masculinity through redefining the work they do as masculine and sexualizing their female co-workers. Though managers regularly define maquila work to Salzinger as "women's work" and explicitly advertise for female workers, male workers act as if they are unaware of this and assert strongly that the difficult work on the line is the natural work of a man. They then treat women on the shop floor less as co-workers and more like sexual targets in a bar. Everyone on the floor seems to understand that men are to engage in catcalls at women, while women are to respond as if they appreciate the gesture. Men and women alike sanction workers for not engaging appropriately in their respective roles as catcaller or responder. Such sexualization of the shop floor constitutes the workplace as a male domain and provides a sense of masculinity to the many male workers engaged in "women's work."

Salzinger wrote this extraordinary study outside of the framework of inhabited institutionalism, local social orders, or RIT, yet the empirics of the case demonstrate a marked similarity to our theoretical orientation. Four organizations operating within the same institutional field and facing the same labor shortage gendered jobs and people in four distinctive ways. This clearly rules out an appeal to broader cultural processes outside of organizations *determining* the gender regime in these workplaces. The controlling image of docile, nimble female labor turns out to be quite flexible in practice. Each plant is populated by managers and workers who embrace the local gender stereotype of superior female productivity, but the emergent gendered meanings in each plant produce distinctive gendered inequality regimes.

Intersectionality

A final important, and typically overlooked, source of organizational variation in inequality regimes is the particular intersection of status characteristics in specific workplaces. While Tilly stresses the complementary matching of high-status people to high-status jobs, one that black feminist theorist Patricia Hill Collins (2002) refers to as a matrix of domination, he does not recognize that multiple categorical statuses also generate contradictions and spaces for social negotiation. Men may have a status advantage over women on average, but particular men and particular women vary in their educational credentials, class resources, age, race, ethnicity, and citizenship status. Collins talks about this matrix of domination as reinforcing the controlling image of black women. We think that sometimes intersectionality does the opposite, producing, as in Salzinger's study, local definitions of categorical distinctions.

Within almost any organization there is some intersectional complexity. Educated women manage less educated men. Black doctors direct the work of white male orderlies. Managers become dependent on skilled workers. In contemporary high-income countries, power and status relationships are never, or rarely, one-dimensional. As a result they must be negotiated and reproduced locally. There may be historical moments when a status characteristic is so thoroughly institutionalized, like race in the United States prior to the civil rights movement or gender in Japan circa 1980, that categorization of this status characteristic dominates all other status distinctions. But because the creation of categorical distinctions is inherently political, what Omi and Winant (2014) refer to for race as "racial projects," they are always contested and often in flux.[9] Thus, there is almost always local variation in status hierarchies that must be enacted and negotiated in specific relational contexts.

As long ago as 1945 sociologist Everett Hughes recognized the interactional space created by cross-cutting status characteristics. He speculated that integration of women or minorities into professional jobs would lead to what he called "status conflict" in the evolution of relationships. He asked us to think about the circumstances in which a woman or an African American could "become simply a lawyer, foreman or whatever." In 1945 it was a radical thought experiment to ask how people—he was mostly thinking about superordinate white, Anglo-Saxon, male people—would react and adapt. His intuition was that formal integration would be joined with informal exclusion, a pattern that was clear early on in the racial and gender integration of workplaces. Rosabeth Kanter (1977) documented the token roles that female managers were confined to in the initial 1970s period of women's integration into managerial jobs. Sharon Collins (1997) showed that the first post-Civil Rights Act generation of black executives got access to power and high earnings but were segregated into "black" tasks like personnel and community relations.

9. In the concluding chapter we return to this flux. There, our argument is that many categorical distinctions, except perhaps education, are declining over time across the globe. As this happens, institutional and interactional protections of previously excluded and exploited groups expand.

Echoing Everett Hughes but preceding contemporary discussions of intersectionality, Rose Loeb Coser (1975) concluded that inhabiting multiple roles might under certain conditions generate individual discretion in the choice of behaviors. In her study of black male professionals, Adia Harvey Wingfield (2013) provides some good examples of the types of intersectional contradictions that arise when categorical distinctions fail to reinforce each other. In this interview-based study of black male professionals in the United States, she finds that the combination of high educational achievement and employment in high-status professional jobs provides for her black male respondents both high income and interactional class advantages. But they remain black, and being black means that their competence is often suspect, especially when encountering new customers or new co-workers. At the same time, being black *men* is often a resource in male-dominated professions, at least relative to women in those jobs, especially in the ability to establish friendships and mentor relationships with senior white men. Being a black man is at the same time a professional threat to white men, leading to emotional and cultural self-policing by black male professionals in order to avoid stereotypes or the reinforcement of racialized categorical distinctions. Wingfield refers to these contradictory tendencies as "partial tokenization" in which being black and male may become a threat or a benefit depending on the interactional context. Our reading of the Wingfield case is that these black professionals are aware of the controlling images associated with black men and self-consciously adjust the dials to negotiate the local context.

Wingfield did not find a consistent sense of racial disadvantage among her respondents but rather found an interactional strategic use and response to the visibility associated with being black and male in white male-dominated workplaces, which included clear understandings of the potential vulnerabilities that this implied. That vulnerability was tied to a sense that class advantages were tenuous, behavioral and professional standards were higher, and that at least in some workplaces superiors would be happy to facilitate, or at least not prevent, black male departures.

Wingfield shows that these black male professionals respond to their complex categorical situation sometimes by embracing solidarity with white or black women and sometimes by expressing a sense of threat from female competition. That is, their experiences or dispositions may lead sometimes to a sense of minority solidarity and other times to a position of male priority. But in all cases they embraced the class advantages associated with their professional standing, often using it as a shield to ward off racialized threats.

Many of Wingfield's accounts of racialized encounters experienced by black male professionals at work were about patients, customers, or support staff who either failed to recognize black males as doctors, lawyers, or college professors or, in the case of medical patients, explicitly rejected working with a black doctor. Our reading of her cases suggested that black men in class-advantaged jobs could count on the class advantage only in so far as the people they interacted with could clearly discern their role as doctor, lawyer, engineer, or college professor. Black doctors used white coats and a formal professional demeanor to accomplish this. Black lawyers, engineers, and college professors could draw on their class advantages when interacting with a familiar set of clients and co-workers but were at risk of being misclassified in new encounters. For example, George, an engineering professor, recounts:

> When I first arrived here . . . I was mistaken for a technician when I was in the copy room. Someone thought I was fixing the copy machine. . . . The same sort of thing happens when I go to a mall and get followed or if a woman rolls up her window when I walk by. It's the same situation. (Wingfield 2013:114)

In this sense the categorical advantages associated with education and position are quite different from the visual categorizations associated with race or gender. If you inhabit a contradictory intersectional set of roles, the most cognitively available signal will guide interaction, at least until class category can be clarified. In this way black MDs have an advantage in that they can wear the white jacket that signals that they are doctors.

CONCLUDING THOUGHTS

RIT has a particular notion of organizations that is sometimes at odds with how some organizational scholars conceive of organizations. Organizations actively constitute a local social order that engages with but does not necessarily mimic the broader social field of which it is a part. Workplaces are dynamic, not passive, social spaces. This leads us to conceptualize organizations as inequality regimes in their own right. Externally constructed categorical distinctions (race, gender, etc.) are certainly imported into organizations and often matched to internal categories like jobs, but the meanings that these categories hold must be constituted within the interactions that take place inside organizational spaces. These interactions take shape through their interface with the resource levels of the organization, the institutional environment with which the organization interacts, the historically situated local social order and organizational routines, and the particular intersections of status characteristics within the organization. These all coalesce in creating a particular organizational inequality regime in which some claims to exploit and monopolize resources become legitimate and others not.

As a result, we can expect that there are generic inequality-producing mechanisms associated with categorical distinctions but that their causal influence will be locally variable. This implies that in practice there are potentially as many organizational inequality regimes as there are organizations, but at the same time there is a limited set of generic processes generating those regimes.

5

Exploitation

Exploitation . . . operates when powerful, connected people command resources from which they draw significantly increased returns by coordinating the efforts of outsiders whom they exclude from the full value added by that effort.

Charles Tilly (1999:10)

The driving motive and determining purpose of capitalist production is the self-valorization of capital to the greatest extent possible, i.e. the greatest possible production of surplus value, hence the greatest possible exploitation of labour-power by the capitalist.

Karl Marx [1867] 1976 Vol 1: 449

In *Capital*, Marx ([1867] 1976) surveys reports from nineteenth-century British factory inspectors describing children as young as seven working from the early hours of the morning until the late hours of night for barely subsistence wages. He then moves on to describe other common methods under the capitalism of his day for extracting surplus value from workers: speeding up work, mechanization, and the detailed division of labor. All four mechanisms–minimizing wages, intensifying labor, adopting labor-saving devices, and deskilling work–remain important methods for extracting value from labor. In each case, from the brutal exploitation of children to reconfiguring the labor process, the goal of the capitalist in Marx's analysis is to wrest as much value as possible from the workers during the time they have paid for workers' labor–that is, to gain as much capital income as possible while remunerating labor as little as possible. This for Marx is exploitation.

Exploitation both predates the early capitalism Marx details and is widespread in contemporary workplaces and market exchanges. In this chapter we outline our conceptualization of exploitation and provide a series of concrete examples. We think that exploitation is most usefully conceptualized as an exercise of power, typically between categorically distinct actors, to transfer income from one actor to another. This conceptualization recognizes that exploitation can happen in markets and be organized around categorical boundaries beyond the labor-capital distinction. It does not require the intentional exploitation of others but can also be routinized, taken for granted, and even morally celebrated, as when a monopolist firm charges high prices and reaps sustained high profits. Sustained exploitation often requires some level of institutional support—either cultural or state-based, and often both. We begin with an example that has echoes of Marx's version of exploitation, in which employers intentionally minimize wages and maximize effort.

In a compelling exposé, journalist Sarah Maslin Nir (2015) documents the process through which young Korean, Chinese, and Hispanic immigrants obtain work in New York City nail salons and the conditions of their employment. New immigrants pay nail salon owners a fee ($100-$200 typically) to begin work in a salon but do not get paid any wages or salary until they prove themselves to be skilled enough. They work for free, until they acquire sufficient skill. Once these workers do make it onto the payroll, they are typically paid far below minimum wage (often around $30-$40 per day or $3 an hour), and it is not uncommon to simply have their employer steal their wages from them by not paying them overtime or the legally required wage supplement when a worker's tips are insufficient to boost his or her pay to reach minimum wage. This is classic Marxian exploitation in which the value produced is appropriated by employers.

Sociologist Millian Kang (2015), responding to Nir's research on nail salons, points out that this exploitation is facilitated by larger institutional forces that permit labor exploitation as well as by consumer demand for low-priced manicures. The rate of exploitation is tied to the relative power of unskilled immigrants, customer demand for low-cost manicures, as well as the absence of government enforcement of wage and hour laws for immigrant workers. It is important to understand that exploitation is not simply the relationship between exploiters and exploited but also the organizational, institutional, and market contexts that permit or forbid such practices. In these nail salons, the level of wage theft is higher for Hispanic immigrants than it is for Chinese immigrants, and Korean manicurists are treated with more respect and higher wages than other groups. Thus, exploitation not only happens across the categorical boundary of employer-employee but is further inflected by the intersection of ethnic boundaries.

CONCEPTUALIZING EXPLOITATION

Exploitation is a relationship in which one party uses power to gain at the expense of another. For relational inequality theory (RIT) this is a core mechanism through which categorical distinctions are turned into inequalities and conflicts around those inequalities develop.

More formally, under exploitative relations some actor(s) *A* activates power he or she has over some other actor(s) *B* to appropriate organizational resources in such a way that *A* gains and *B* loses.[1] Thus, the advantage obtained by *A* comes at the expense of *B*, and the facilitating condition for this is a power imbalance between *A* and *B*. Exploitation follows from a power imbalance when *A* uses his or her relational power to extract resources from *B*. *A*'s willingness to use this power to exploit *B* is markedly higher when *A* sees *B* as in a categorically different social group. This is in no small part because power imbalances are substantially more likely when categorical distinctions dehumanize *B*, culturally and morally permitting and encouraging exploitation. In the traditional Marxian form of exploitation, *A* is a capitalist and *B* a worker. However, any categorical distinction will suffice, such as when *A* is a firm or white or male or native and *B* is a customer or black or female or immigrant. Categorical distinctions tend to both generate and morally legitimate power differentials and these power differentials enable exploitation.

Two elements of this definition are worth further examination. First, exploitation is a relationship in which one actor gains at the expense of another. The phrase *at the expense of* is crucial as it identifies not only that it is an unequal relationship but that the gains of the exploiter are causally dependent upon the losses of the exploited. For the exploiter to gain, the exploited must lose. This connects inequality more deeply to an actual, objective social relationship between two parties, not just one party having more than another. Thus, exploitation is not synonymous with inequality but is a process through which the gains of some are contingent upon the losses of others.

A second element in our definition is that the advantages gained by the exploiters are because of their power over others. The mechanism for extracting economic gains from others is that exploiters exercise relational power over the exploited, enabling them to take more than they otherwise would or could from them. This notion of power is not contentious in and of itself, but it does dramatically expand the process of exploitation beyond the traditional Marxian version. Marx and neo-Marxists have argued that exploitation occurs via a particular form of power: ownership and control of the means of production (Wright 1997, 2005). Capitalists possess and control the productive resources of society, and workers are by definition excluded

1. We remind the reader that actors can be individuals or collectivities such as professions, unions, and firms.

from such ownership and dependent upon the wage relationship for survival. This form of power enables capitalists to exploit workers in all the ways Marx describes in his discussion of exploitation in *Capital.* We fully concur that control over productive resources enables exploitation, but this is not the only form of power that enables it. Nor does capital ownership ensure that employers have the power to exploit employees. Organizational and cultural power can all also lead to or block exploitation.

Managers within organizations seem to be among the biggest winners during the rise of US income inequality since the 1980s, precisely because of their control over administrative hierarchies and resources (Goldstein 2012). In this sense, many top managers may be extracting greater organizational resources for themselves, exploiting both owners and lower-level employees. CEOs can also reconfigure their firms—by externalizing janitors' jobs to local low-wage cleaning vendors or by replacing domestic production with suppliers in low-wage countries—thus reducing costs of production and simultaneously reducing the group of workers with claims on organizational surplus. Exploitation can be accomplished directly in Marx's sense by diverting organizational value to top managers, but it can also be accomplished by reconfiguring firm boundaries so that market rents are available for a smaller, more elite group of workers and the more vulnerable are exiled from the organization and relegated to subordinate and dependent firms.

The power to exploit can also be cultural in nature, such that exploiters are able to gain because an exploitable group is culturally devalued in routine social interactions. This status valuation process helps explain why sociologist Paula England and her colleagues (England et al. 2007; Levanon, England, and Allison 2009) have repeatedly found that when women enter occupations previously held by men, the wages attached to those jobs are likely to decline. We see this devaluation process as exploitative in that it is a shift of organizational resources away from an occupational group because the incumbents of those jobs are less culturally valued. Where the money that women lose goes is an open question that few have attempted to answer and will probably vary from organization to organization based upon its particular inequality regime. But in an analysis of North Carolina firms, Tomaskovic-Devey and Skaggs (1999) found that such devaluations of female-dominated jobs had no impact on employers' profits but led to higher wages for male workers. Male employees, at least on average, appeared to gain from the losses women suffered by working in female-dominated jobs. That study, however, did not rule out the possibility that customers, as in the nail salon example, might have been the beneficiaries of the devalued female labor.

Exploitative processes happen in markets as well as firms. There is good evidence that women and African Americans pay more when they buy a new car (Ayres 1991). Banks charge higher underwriting fees for black college's capital bonds than they do for equivalent bonds offered by white colleges (Dougal et al. 2016). Consumers in the United States pay less for their tomatoes or manicures because undocumented immigrant workers performed the labor, thereby exploiting the labor of those workers. In doing this we move the concept of exploitation beyond a focus on extracting surplus value through labor effort to the extraction of organizational resources flowing into the firm.

Exploitation occurs through the intersection of power relations within and between organizations. Since the rights of capitalists to the fruits of their private property are protected by law, capital ownership is a privileged resource through which exploitation can occur. However, alongside legally protected material power are organizational power in administrative hierarchies and cultural power in social interactions, each facilitating the transfer of income between categorically distinct groups. And, of course, as Peter Blau (1977), Charles Tilly (1999), and Pat Hill Collins (2002) all pointed out, these material, organizational, and cultural resources that generate power over categorically distinct others are likely to overlap such that each reinforces the other. In our own work using organizational data in the United States, Australia, Japan, and Sweden, we have repeatedly found this to be the case (Tomaskovic-Devey et al. 2009, 2015a; Avent-Holt and Tomaskovic-Devey 2010, 2012). When multiple sources of power intersect and reinforce each other, exploitation increases, becoming a durable feature of organizational life.

There are a variety of processes through which exploitation takes place within and through organizations. In the RIT framework the mechanics of exploitation operate through a claims-making process, and material, organizational, and cultural power are each bases for powerful actors to claim organizational resources from categorically distinct, less powerful actors. Thus, it is through making claims on revenue, effort, or dignity that actors are able to take advantage of others and gain at their expense. Sometimes exploitative claims-making is naked and open for all to see. Refusing to pay workers state-mandated overtime and refusing to pay the full minimum wage as in the nail salon case are common ways that employers engage in the naked exploitation of low-wage workers (see Bernhardt et al. 2009 on the distressingly high prevalence of wage theft in the United States). But more often exploitation is hidden and even accepted by those being exploited. The great genius of Marx was to document the appropriation of surplus at the point of production where workers themselves could not see it. Workers sell their time to an employer, who then extracts as much work effort as possible, capturing value beyond the wages paid to the worker by the eventual sale of the goods produced. This wage-effort bargain became a more or less legitimate practice by the turn of the twentieth century. Similarly, because of job segregation, most women are unlikely to even see the devaluation of their own work in female-dominated occupations. Rather, as Cecilia Ridgeway's (2011) work suggests, they come to see their own work as less deserving than similarly situated male peers. The exploitation of female-dominated jobs becomes legitimate over time.

This process of legitimation, in which exploitation moves from open and contested to institutionalized and taken for granted, is common and central to the process of exploitation. Exploitative claims, if they are to persist, are likely to over time become institutionalized in these ways. Conflict around them becomes muted, and most actors simply enter into such relationships without even thinking of them as exploitative. In this way, exploitation is like many other aspects of inequality that become durable. There is initial struggle over the emergence of the exploitative claim. But eventually resistance desists, and new actors enter the exchanges assuming the claim is legitimate.

Our conceptualization of exploitation is broader than most existing approaches. In expanding the bases upon which exploitation rests we have gone beyond the focus on capital-labor relations as the only site of exploitation, expanding exploitation to any categorically distinct group that is arranged hierarchically inside the power relations within or between organizations. Men and whites possess cultural power over women and minorities, and this may give them, at least in some contexts, the capacity to extract value in the form of higher wages. Managers possess organizational power over workers, especially in the deunionized neoliberal environment, and this enables them to reconfigure social relations at work to extract more value. And in some contexts the power imbalance of capital and labor is flipped when skilled workers or managers have power over owners.

Our expansion of the exploitation concept beyond the capital-labor relationship is partially consistent with the move toward a rent-theoretic conceptualization of exploitation. Sociologist Aage Sørensen (2000) proposed a rent-based model of exploitation to supplant the neo-Marxian conceptualization and be more consistent with modern economic theory. Rents are income or profits above what an actor would obtain in a perfectly competitive market, and from this Sørensen argues that exploitation occurs when one set of actors is able to control the supply of or demand for a particular asset in a market to increase the return they obtain for that asset beyond what would be obtained in a perfectly competitive market. In this sense rents are generated from monopolizing particular assets to gain above-market returns. As in our definition (and in the Marxian conceptualization), power is central to Sørenson's rent model, but grounding exploitation in perfectly competitive markets taints the concept with the normative presumption that market distributions are just (see Avent-Holt 2015).

While we suspect our approach is far from the last word on the conceptualization of exploitation, we abandon the normative frameworks of both the labor theory of value and perfect market competition in favor of an action-based process of appropriation from a less powerful by a more powerful actor. Exploitation operates as an exercise of power, so activated power differentials between actors are all that is required to enable exploitation. There is no normative baseline to our definition of exploitation. Readers looking for a normative evaluation of exploitation are free to do so, but our approach here is simply behavioral.

Where our reasoning becomes most challenging is in those cases where a historically less powerful actor succeeds in expanding his or her access to organizational resources. Consider the following example. Unions have historically increased the power of employees relative to their employers. Both economists and sociologists have described them as obtaining rents and the process of declining wages in a period of deunionization as "rent destruction." Moreover, in some cases, such as the deregulated airline industry or the hotel and restaurant industries, profit margins regularly dip into the negative under the backdrop of a unionized workforce. The question then becomes, is it reasonable to conceptualize unionized workers as exploiting their employers? On balance we think that this is generally not reasonable. While these unionized workers have more power relative to their employer than non-unionized workers, declining profits actually are generated by market downturns in the face of relatively fixed labor costs. But the reverse is true also, when demand and profits surge, union contracts keep labor costs fixed. That is, unions provide workers a power that mitigates, but does not override, the power of capital ownership.

One might think of situations in which less powerful actors successfully mobilize and redistribute organizational resources as usurpationary exploitation. That is, they are exercises of power upward to usurp the ability of normally or previously dominant groups to exploit.

Of course, from the point of view of owners and managers, having to pay union wages, even low wages, in the face of declining sales may feel like workers are exploiting their power and extracting income. Owners may *feel* exploited, but under our definition they probably are not. The product market is dynamic, while the labor market has been stabilized by a contract. There is no new taking of resources from capital by unionized labor, merely a decline in the flow of organizational resources associated with recessions or market competition.

On the other hand, the initial unionization of a workplace, to the extent that it transfers income from owners to workers, may be an example of exploitation under our definition. But even this would only be exploitation if unionization was to happen in a zero-sum context. Freeman and Medoff (1984) in a historically important review of the impact of mid-twentieth-century unionization show that in many cases unionization actually led to higher value added and profitability because it increased employee effort and reduced turnover, as well as encouraged better management in terms of investment, accounting, and personnel practices. In Randy Hodson's (2001) sense, unionization encouraged better managerial citizenship behavior and so increased the size of the pie.

OBSERVING EXPLOITATION

Observationally, our conceptualization of exploitation encourages us to look for examples where one actor's income is causally connected to income transferred from others. This may occur in the Marxian sense through a transfer of income in production from workers to owners. It may also occur in production as a transfer of income from less powerful employees to more powerful employees. Finally, it can also happen in markets, where suppliers or customers are exploited by powerful firms. We will explore examples of each.

Comparing Firm Productivity to Wages Paid and Profits Extracted

A rent-theoretic approach to observing exploitation has been to examine the influence of workplace composition on both productivity and wage levels, arguing that if the influence of demographic composition on both productivity and wage levels are the same, then there is no evidence of exploitation. While this approach is inconsistent with our theoretical model in that it takes a normative baseline from human capital theory, studies using rent theory are to date the best available that have indicators of both inequalities in distribution and the pool of organizational resources to be distributed.

Arthur Sakamoto and Changhwan Kim (2010) find that in contemporary US manufacturing industries more status-privileged workers (older, whites, males, credentialed) obtain wages above their contribution to total firm productivity, while less privileged workers (younger, minorities, women, the uncredentialed) receive wages below their estimated productivity contributions. More powerful workers appear to be exploiting less powerful workers. In a similar paper, with Taiwanese workplace-level data, Liu, Sakamoto, and Su (2010) find that in two-thirds of firms at least some workers are underpaid relative to their contribution to productivity and that three-quarters of profits are expropriated from workers. Women and blue-collar workers are the groups likely to be exploited, while managers, professionals, and workers with high seniority are paid commensurately with their contributions to productivity. These findings are consistent with the exploitation of those with less organizational and cultural power relative to those with more such power within organizations.

In a study of Israeli manufacturing plants, economists Hellerstein and Neumark (1998) found that more experienced workers made stronger productivity contributions than less experienced workers but that their wage premium was even higher, suggesting a transfer of income from young to older workers. The same study suggested that women were less productive than men but that the returns to gender composition for both productivity and wages were equivalent, suggesting no gender-based exploitation in wage-setting. Why the gender difference in productivity existed was left unexamined, but it may have arisen from closure-based processes in which women were more likely to be found in low-productivity firms. In a cross-sectional but otherwise similar study of US workplaces, results were reversed, with older workers' wages equivalent to their marginal contribution to productivity and women underpaid (Hellerstein, Neumark, and Troske 1999). This paper also showed that the underpayment of women is larger in larger workplaces and in workplaces where women are a higher proportion of employees. Again, there is some exploitation of lower-status groups by higher-status groups.

We point out these papers because their design and the contextual variation in results are both highly consistent with RIT. Generic processes of exploitation around categorical distinctions generate income inequality, but the specific types of categorical distinctions that matter and the extent of exploitation varies across national/institutional context. We think that firm-level analyses of group contributions to productivity and group shares of rewards are promising avenues for future relational inequality approaches to exploitation.

Rising Income Inequality

Much has been made of the rise of income inequality in the United States and elsewhere in the industrial and developing world. There are good reasons for thinking of rising income inequality in the United States as generated, at least in part, by increased exploitation. One of the key trends suggesting increased exploitation is the simple relationship between the growth in productivity (value added per full-time worker equivalent) and hourly compensation. As shown in Figure 5.1, prior to the mid-1970s these two tended to move together as increased productivity led to increased compensation. The

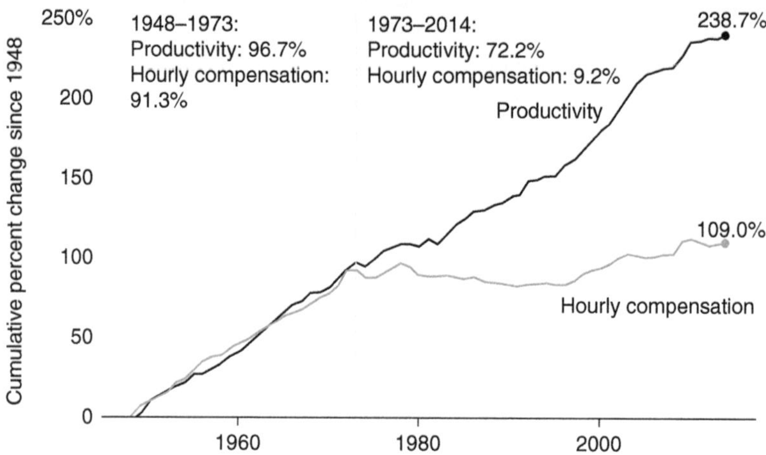

Figure 5.1 Disconnect between rising productivity and private sector, non-supervisor employee hourly compensation, 1948–2014 (Economic Policy Institute 2015).

two time series diverged in the late 1970s, and mean wages have grown very slowly since, even as productivity has surged. At the same time the share of national income going to capital rather than labor surged as well, while wages for the bottom 80% of US workers stagnated or dropped.

This is not, however, clear evidence of exploitation since it does not tell us where the money went or if this income transfer happened within firms or between them. Some of the new wealth generated by productivity growth went to new firms in new industries generating new products, making it a potentially non-exploitative expansion of value added. Of course, this increased variability of firm productivity was an inequality-generating process in its own right, but the mechanism was via differential accumulation of organizational resources, not labor exploitation. We explore the growth in between-firm inequality in organizational resources in more depth in Chapter 8. There is substantial evidence that some of this interindustry shift in resources—particularly into large tech firms, financial services, and pharmaceutical firms—was produced by such firms' ability to use their political and market power to exploit customers and suppliers.

We do know that during the same period only the top 20% of employees realized wage gains and that most of the gains have gone to those at the top 1% of the income distribution. Wages for most have stagnated and, at the very bottom, even declined. Because these are population-level trends, we cannot tell for sure what type of exploitation—within or between firms—created these income shifts, although they do suggest that income gains are accruing to those in powerful positions within organizations such as CEOs and other top managers and elite professionals as well as the owners of capital. The largest gains for the top 1% have been in the states of New York and Connecticut, precisely where many of the largest financial institutions reside (Sommeiller, Price, and Wazeter 2016).

By examining the evidence for when, where, and how incomes have shifted at different parts of the income distribution, and when possible within firm context, we can better see how rising income inequality is driven by processes of exploitation. We start with the surge of incomes at the top and then move to declines at the bottom of the income distribution.

Income Growth at the Very Top

The evidence for exploitation is clearer for the rising incomes of the top 1% or even 0.1%. In the 1980s the idea that firms existed only to provide economic returns to their owners was embraced on Wall Street and by influential economists (Dobbin and Jung 2010). This movement, as well as a late 1980s federal law that tied CEO compensation to firm performance, encouraged firms to reward top managers for stock market performance. The goal of these reforms was to "align" the interests of stockholders and corporate executives. CEO compensation rocketed upward, but profits were largely unaffected, strongly suggesting a transfer of income from other workers to CEOs and other top corporate employees (Fligstein and Shin 2007; Prechel and Morris 2010). This shift to a shareholder value organizational logic led to declining employment and long-term capital investment, both being replaced with increased financial speculation (Lin 2016).

Tom DiPrete, Gregory Eirich, and Matthew Pittinsky (2010) demonstrate just how corporate CEOs used the shareholder value movement to exploit organizational income flows. They examine the rise of CEO pay since the early 1990s, taking a relational view of the process of pay-setting at the top of organizational hierarchies. The general pay of CEOs is critical as there was both a dramatic rise in CEO pay beginning in the 1990s and a new process for setting CEO pay using peer group benchmarks. By the late 1970s large firms were setting CEO pay by having compensation committees create, in consultation with CEOs, a peer group of comparable CEOs to act as a benchmark against which they would evaluate the focal CEO's pay. DiPrete and colleagues track individual CEO pay over time, both within a firm and as they move across firms. They find that the dramatic rise in CEO pay is largely driven by firms' compensation committees using "aspirational peer groups." CEOs would suggest to the compensation committee comparison

CEOs who were already paid more than the focal CEO, enabling them to "leapfrog" over comparable peers, moving to the top of their respective peer group. Essentially, compensation committees are using what looks like a market logic of comparison but only comparing CEOs to the best-paid actors in the market.

But how is leapfrogging exploitation? The money CEOs are capturing must be coming from some other firm stakeholder. As CEO pay goes up, income for other actors in the firm—workers or owners—must be going down. The evidence suggests that the money came from reduced employment as well as stagnating or declining pay of employees and that owners were neither hurt nor helped (Fligstein and Shin 2007; Tomaskovic-Devey, Lin, and Meyers 2015b). CEOs raised their own pay at the expense of their workers, while owners were generally held harmless.

These processes have led to an increasing concentration of income and wealth in the top 1%, 0.1%, and 0.01% of the world's population (Piketty 2014). In Chapter 1, we criticized Piketty for neglecting the role of firms in generating income distributions. This in part reflects data limitations. Piketty and his collaborators have used long time series of national tax and estate data to estimate national wealth and income levels and their distributions. These are necessarily household data. *Forbes* magazine (2017), in contrast, identifies the world's richest people. In 2017 *Forbes* estimates that there were 2,043 billionaires in the world, 95% of whom lived in the United States. The *Forbes* list makes it possible to connect these wealthiest people to the firms that their wealth came from. Table 5.1 lists the 16 richest people on the planet in 2017 and the firms from which they derived their wealth. Not surprisingly, the richest people in the world are associated with the largest

Table 5.1 The 16 Richest People in the World and the Firms That Generated That Wealth

Person	Firm	Person	Firm
1. Bill Gates	Microsoft	9. David Koch	Koch Industries
2. Warren Buffet	Berkshire Hathaway	10. Michael Bloomberg	Bloomberg Industries
3. Jeff Bezos	Amazon	11. *Bernard Arnault*	*Louis Vuitton*
4. *Amancio Ortega*	*Zara*	12. Larry Page	Google
5. Mark Zuckerberg	Facebook	13. Sergey Brin	Google
6. *Carlos Slim Helu*	*América Móvil*	14. *Lillian Bettencourt*	*L'Oreal*
7. Larry Ellison	Oracle	15. S. Robson Walton	Walmart
8. Charles Koch	Koch Industries	16. Jim Walton	Walmart

People listed in italics are not from the United States; all others are from the United States.

Source: Forbes (2017).

and most successful firms in the world. The firms associated with the richest people on the planet tend to be large, dominant in their industries, and powerful relative to their supplier firms.

Importantly, skyrocketing billionaire, CEO, and financier incomes are more accurately described as the property of the top 0.1% or 0.01% of the population. The rising pay of the top 1% represents a much larger group of people, and although we do not have a clear picture yet, firm-level studies suggest to us that skyrocketing CEO pay has pulled the pay of top managers in the same firms up as well (Goldstein 2012). Another likely mechanism raising the wages of top managers is performance pay systems. Many firms in the United States and around the world have instituted pay practices in which pay raises, and bonuses in particular, are linked to performance evaluations. These systems are typically limited to middle managers and higher in firms. Individual-level analyses show that performance-based pay systems raise the wages of initially high-earning employees, presumably at the expense of the rest of the firm's workforce. Olivier Godechot (2016) documents this process extremely well for traders and salespeople in financial service firms. We treat that case in depth in Chapter 7 on claims-making.

In the United States, bonuses and commissions, older forms of performance-based pay systems, are associated with increased earnings inequality (Lemieux, MacLeod, and Parent 2009), and the benefits primarily accrue to highly qualified and white workers (Hanley 2011). In a study of New Zealand firms using linked employer–employee data, Fabling, Grimes, and Maré (2012) find that performance pay systems do not influence the average wage in firms but are associated with increased wage inequality within firms, benefiting mostly male managers. Thus, firm-level productivity does not change, but internal distributions of income do. In a German study of rising earnings inequality from 1995 to 2010, also using linked employer–employee data, Schweiker and Groß (2016) document a clear pattern of declining bonus payments for lower-level workers and rising bonuses for those in the top 1%. This shift in bonus payments, reflecting shifts in pay practices more generally, strongly favors the top 10% of employees in German firms, with the top 1% particularly benefiting. While performance-based systems are often intended to link pay more closely to productivity, they seem to be operating, at least in the United States, New Zealand, and German cases, as reward systems for already advantaged workers at the expense of other employees in the firm.

Wage Theft at the Bottom

In addition to explaining the dramatic income gains at the top, exploitation can help us make sense of declining income for the lowest-wage workers in the United States. As Marx pointed out, employers have a profit incentive to reduce the wage bill. Avoiding high-wage or unionized labor forces was a major motivation for corporate disinvestment in heavily unionized parts of the United States in the 1970s and 1980s and subsequent reinvestment in so-called right-to-work states and in the global south. Declining unionization has been strongly linked to rising inequality in multiple studies (e.g., Western and Rosenfeld 2011; Kristal 2013; Lin and Tomaskovic-Devey 2013). In addition, the basic protections afforded workers by American labor law seem to have weakened, both because the legal provisions that arose in the New Deal and immediate post-World War II eras no longer fit the contemporary economy (Estlund 2002) and because the US federal government embraced market solutions even as employer resistance to workers' claims increased (Rubin 1995).

Since the weakening of general worker protections by the US government during the post-1980 neoliberal period, incidences of wage theft by employers—understood as the failure to pay workers for the work performed—appear to be growing. Studies of wage theft suggest that money may be literally stolen from the least powerful workers. Annette Bernhardt and colleagues (2009) conducted an ambitious study of wage and hour law violations in three cities: Chicago, New York, and Los Angeles. They interviewed low-wage workers about their earnings, hours of work, and workplace experiences, obtaining data on even undocumented immigrant workers and off-the-book workers. They examined a range of violations of labor laws comparing what respondents said happened to them at work in the context of state and federal labor laws. They found that fully one-quarter of low-wage workers did not receive the minimum wage in the previous week of work and that 60% of those who were underpaid received more than $1 an hour less than the minimum wage. Among workers receiving tips, 29% did not receive the mandated base minimum wage for tipped workers, and 15% actually had some portion of their wages garnished by their employer. In all, two-thirds of the low-wage workers surveyed experienced at least one pay-related violation in the prior workweek, which Bernhardt and colleagues estimated to be about a 15% wage loss for the average low-wage worker in their sample. Violations of worker compensation injury laws were also widespread.

Employer exploitation of low-wage workers was widespread across these three cities. Confirming that exploitation is a function of power in interaction, they find that all forms of wage theft are more common for less powerful employees. Since everyone in the sample is a low-wage worker, they are all low-power in a class analytic sense. But exploitation requires the powerful to exercise that power. Among low-wage workers, wage theft is less common among whites, men, citizens, and workers with long tenure.

Race differences were particularly pronounced. Foreign-born Latinos had the highest rate of wage theft, and African Americans' wages were stolen at three times the rate of whites in low-wage jobs. Here, we see that exploitation becomes particularly likely across categorical distinctions of race, ethnicity, gender, and citizenship as these intersect with class distinctions.

Exploitation across Categorical Distinctions in Linked Employer–Employee Data

If we can see patterns that reflect exploitation of low-wage workers and income gains for CEOs and other top managers, this suggests a growth in the extent of exploitation across class boundaries. That is, exploitation is operating to a greater extent across the categorical distinctions around class. But what about exploitation across other categorical distinctions that center on the notion of status such as citizenship, skill, and parental status? Linked employer-employee data have been central in identifying such patterns.

In our analysis of linked employer-employee data, we observed the exploitation of immigrant labor by native Swedes (Tomaskovic-Devey et al. 2015a). In that analysis we looked at within-workplace wage changes associated with immigrant-native segregation and both groups' income returns to skilled jobs. The basic framework of the study is similar to the many studies that have investigated the impact of gender segregation on gender wage gaps (e.g., Levanon et al. 2009) but with the addition of panel data on organizational location and demographics.[2] The devaluation of women's or immigrants' work in production represents an income transfer to someone. The most likely candidates are employers or other more powerful employees.

In the Swedish study we wanted to see if the wage gap between natives and immigrants was high in organizations with high levels of occupational segregation between natives and immigrants from non-Western countries. Tilly (1999) proposed that higher levels of segregation would increase the rate of exploitation. When social distinctions of class and citizenship reinforce each other, they exaggerate categorical distinctions, which in turn legitimates exploitation. We did find that segregation was associated with rising immigrant-native wage gaps. This is not clear evidence of exploitation since this result could be produced simply by closure processes sorting people into high- and low-wage occupations. But after statistically controlling for occupational placement, we found a residual wage gap between

2. Panel data link observations over time. In this example we link all Swedish workplaces over seven years in order to observe the impact of *changes* in demographic composition upon changes in pay. This is a particularly strong research design for disentangling selection of different kinds of employees into firms from changes in firm pay practices.

immigrants and natives but only in very high-inequality workplaces. Thus, exploitation associated with Tilly's segregation mechanism appeared to occur only in high-inequality organizational contexts, where the social space to shift income from one group to another was correspondingly higher. Consistently, that same study found that all categorical distinctions were magnified in high-inequality contexts. The motherhood wage penalty, the daddy bonus, the economic payoffs to skill, as well as preferences for native Swedes were all higher in high-inequality workplaces. There was no motherhood wage penalty, daddy bonus, or citizenship premium in low-inequality workplaces. Exploitation of status groups, observed as wage shifts among employees, was more likely and more extreme in workplaces with high-inequality labor processes.

Thinking about the categorical distinctions around parenthood, sociologists have found interesting patterns of income inequalities. Mothers tend to earn less than non-mothers, while fathers tend to earn more than non-fathers, even beyond what would be expected from differences in the hours each works (e.g., Hodges and Budig 2010; Budig and Hodges 2010). These findings have largely come from survey data on individuals. The general design of these studies looks for the impact of becoming a parent upon earnings, statistically controlling for labor force activity and individual skills and work experience. The residual mommy penalty and daddy bonus after these statistical controls are assumed to reflect, at least in part, cultural preferences among employers for men who are fathers and women who don't have children. There is good evidence that such cultural preferences exist and might in general influence both hiring and wages (Correll, Benard, and Paik 2007). Direct evidence of employers actually paying different wages in response to the birth of children, however, requires organizational data.

One study has examined the potential impact of exploitation based on parental status in both organizational and institutional contexts. Trond Petersen, Andrew Penner, and Gail Høgsnes (2014) used linked employer-employee data for Norway from 1979 to 1996, a period in which Norway rapidly expanded a set of social policies designed to reduce the influence of family status on gendered labor force participation and wage discrimination. They use the language of bias and discrimination rather than exploitation, but the notion is that some unequal treatment in earnings is responding to these familial and gender categorical distinctions.

In 1979 they find that married fathers in the same job in the same workplace outearned married mothers by 3% (one child) to 8% (three children). Their results further showed that men received cultural compensation from their employers primarily for marriage while women were penalized primarily for parenthood. After the significant increase in family-friendly policy interventions—parental leave, childcare subsidies and tax deductions, cash benefits for having children, and increased part-time and flexible-schedule jobs—these within-job gender wage gaps had fallen to between 2% (one child) and 3% (three children) by 1996. Although they cannot directly establish the causal connections between these institutional shifts, they point out that cultural shifts in Norway during this period look a lot like those in the United States and United Kingdom, two countries without comparable institutional shifts that also lack dramatic drops in marriage and parent premiums and penalties.[3]

In an interesting study, Michael Dahl, Christian Dezső, and David Ross (2012) take a firm-level look at a subtler manifestation of this gendered process in Denmark, focusing on the way incomes are redistributed within a firm after the CEO becomes a father. Also using linked employer-employee panel data, they observe changes in the CEO's income after the CEO became a parent. The findings clearly demonstrate that male CEOs shift resources away from both male and female employees and toward themselves after fathering a child. The general finding is that the income of a male CEO who becomes a father increases after he has a child, and the wages of both his male and female employees go down. In an RIT framework, male CEOs are exploiting their employees by reducing the real wages of employees and increasing their own wages after they become fathers and continue to do so with each additional child. Categorically the CEO is favoring his family over his employees in these rounds of exploitation. The shifting of income toward himself after entering fatherhood also demonstrates how persons in positions of power within organizations can claim greater shares of income at the expense of others in that organization. Presumably this power was latent in the CEO role but only activated when the categorical distinction between family and others was heightened. We have not yet seen a panel data-based study of the more general mommy penalty and daddy bonus. If the process includes one of exploitation, we would expect to see shifts in income among co-workers or between employers and employees on the birth of an employee's child. The Petersen et al. (2014) study in Norway, however, reminds us that this—or any—particular manifestation of exploitation is dependent upon the institutional environment. We would expect exploitation around motherhood or fatherhood to be larger in societies with fewer cultural and institutional protections than Norway.

3. This study does not directly examine transitions into marriage or parenthood but is certainly suggestive both of differential payment for the same work and of the importance of institutional context. Petersen et al. (2014) are careful to point out that their models do not control for individual selection, so the declining exploitation interpretation is not definitive.

HOW DOES EXPLOITATION HAPPEN?

The above research gives us a picture of the patterns and trends in exploitation across categorically distinct actors and demonstrates that exploitation is a fundamental feature of the generation of inequality within organizations. But in these quantitative analyses the fundamental mechanism of claims-making to appropriate organizational resources and the variety of ways it operates are difficult to observe. Exploitation can happen through a variety of means, from naked theft to fully legitimated institutional practices. In the previous section (*Wage Theft at the Bottom*), we saw employers skirting the law to rob janitors, domestic workers, restaurant servers, and other low-wage workers of legally mandated wages. Historical examples of slavery and feudal arrangements are other forms of a naked use of power to simply transfer by force income from one party to another. But much exploitation operates through hidden, and often legitimated, exertions of power to transfer income to more powerful actors. Perhaps the most powerful exercise Marx ever engaged in was to demonstrate how value is extracted and then taken from workers without them ever realizing it. However, one can just as easily see the rise of the incomes of CEOs in the same fashion. These actors are able to renegotiate the terms of the employment contract to weaken workers' bargaining power and redirect organizational surplus to themselves. By the twenty-first century it simply became accepted, at least in the United States, that CEOs legitimately earn 250 times the average worker, and few question it.

Qualitative cases enable us to more clearly see how the politics of claims-making enables exploitation. In the following cases we explore detailed accounts of how powerful actors are able to shift income from one set of actors to themselves.

Exploitation on the Shop Floor and in the Office Corridor

Ethnographic studies of the labor process exploded after the publication of Harry Braverman's *Labor and Monopoly Capital* in 1974 (1998), with many of these workplace ethnographies focused on the problem of exploitation. Braverman, echoing Marx, emphasized that the organization of the labor process, both socially and technically, was a central mechanism of exploitation.

Braverman's work led other scholars to ask, how do capitalists extract surplus value from workers? Michael Burawoy's (1979) ethnography of an agricultural equipment manufacturer in Chicago directed this question toward the use of culture as a mechanism to enable capitalists to increase the surplus workers produce and then claim that surplus. Working as a machine operator, Burawoy found other machinists caught up in a game of *making out*, whereby machinists tried to accumulate production beyond the minimum work quota to gain status and impress their co-workers. This game was informally approved by management, even though it contained some formally forbidden practices such as holding back output for future payment from that factory's piece rate system. It was this management-sanctioned game that Burawoy argued enabled the creation and securing of surplus value with workers', often enthusiastic, consent. Burawoy's discovery of complicit self-exploitation was a far cry from Marx's expectation of open class conflict.

Burawoy's vantage point from the shop floor, though, left him unable to really observe management's direct involvement in sanctioning the game. In his account, management was remote, focusing on corporate balance sheets in offices above the shop floor. Gideon Kunda (2009), on the other hand, offers an account of explicit managerial efforts to elicit greater work effort from employees through manipulating the workplace culture. Kunda spent a year at a high-tech firm, which he referred to as "Tech," observing the work lives of engineers. At Tech, worker effort, and indeed a melding together of the self with the organization, was elicited through an organizational and professional culture that promoted and ensured extensive self-exploitation. On the vanguard of the 24/7 model of work in the new economy, engineers had a great deal of autonomy, yet long hours were the norm and bringing work home was common. Engineers came and went into the office as they pleased, though managers and co-workers assumed they were working even if they were not present at any given time.

So, why did the engineers work so hard? Management institutionalized a culture of devotion to the firm that left the engineers either obsessively working on projects or burning out and leaving the firm. The engineers' thoughts, feelings, emotions, and ultimately selves were the focal point of managerial efforts at control, with managers attempting to construct an internalized commitment to the company within employees. This internal commitment then led engineers to work long hours, miss family time to make deadlines, and pull all-nighters. Kunda calls this use of culture to elicit worker effort "normative control."

Normative control was engineered through managers intentionally creating and spreading a cultural framework organized around devotion of one's self to the firm. Much of this operated through a set of managers whose job it was to socialize, and where necessary resocialize, engineers into this cultural framework of self-exploitation. Ellen Cohen and Dave Carpenter were two such managers in Kunda's account. Both describe their job as engineering a culture that accomplishes the company goal of profitability, with Ellen going on to describe her work to accomplish this as "marry[ing] [employees] to the company" (p. 7). To disseminate this ideology of total devotion to the firm, they run "bootcamps" for new employees to get them up to speed with the company culture, provide career seminars for existing employees, write papers on company culture for dissemination through the company, and give speeches at company functions. Through these channels employees learn that this is not a company but a family, one that never lays off its employees, and that that favor should be returned with intensive work effort and total immersion of their selves to the firm. As one mid-level manager describes, "We don't lay off, even though some people deserve to be laid off. So you feel loyalty back. Sam Miller [founder and president] believes in 'taking care of your people' and he gets paid back with loyalty" (pp. 173–174). Autonomy and responsibility are prized, but this is in the context of one having the self-discipline to prioritize one's work above all else. One interviewee describes what it takes to be successful in the firm:

> You have to be a self-starter, an individual who takes chances and risks and moves ahead. The expectation is that everyone is going to work hard, not for hard work's sake, but for the fun of it, and enjoy doing what they are doing, and show commitment no matter what it takes. A core of the environment is individual commitment, a lot of integrity, and a very high level of expectations from yourself. (p. 73).

Thus, the culture creates an ethic of working hard because one is committed and enjoys the intensive work effort. Self-exploitation is the cultural norm, and producing this culture is the key managerial intervention. But this managerial ideology is also part and parcel of a workplace setting that is decentralized and borders on chaotic. Work is organized through projects with teams that have flexible membership. There is no formal organizational chart. Rather, the firm is organized through "matrix management" in which there is a nearly indecipherable network of informal relations among individuals and groups that one must learn over time. Despite this informal labor process, management is under intense pressure to get products to market rapidly and is evaluated formally and informally on its capacity to "ship on time" as time to market is the overarching criterion on which the organization assesses itself (p. 44). The company's founder, Sam Miller, made profit a moral goal for the company, noting in a videotaped interview that gets shown to new employees " 'we've got somebody else's money, and we have to make a return on it'. . . . Everybody in the company understands we've got to make a profit, we want to make it as consistently as possible. We plan to do something in a quarter, we want to get it out, and we're not embarrassed to have people work hard to get it done by the end of the quarter" (pp. 59–60).

Combining the structure and culture of Tech, it is easy to describe this study as an exemplar of exploitative management to extract intensive work effort that generates a surplus to be accumulated by the investors. In this case, exploitation is generated by combining a workplace organized around managerial pressure to make a profit under tight deadlines with a culture of total employee devotion to the firm. What is novel is that this exploitation, this extraction of additional unremunerated work effort, is generated by the conscious engineering of a culture that engenders total devotion of one's self to the company.

Kunda's study is now a classic in the ethnographic literature, but this form of exploitation—the creation of work cultures of maximum commitment and effort—is now widespread among white-collar employees. More generally, in the United States it is now well documented that work hours have grown rapidly among managerial and professional employees, while lower-skilled employees often have difficulty finding sufficient hours and so have to work two or more jobs to make ends meet (Jacobs and Gerson 2004). This pattern—long hours for professionals and managers and part-time work for the low-skilled—was produced institutionally by US wage and hour laws. Under those laws, employers who provide health or pensions to their managers must provide benefits to any worker who works 30 or more hours a week. This has encouraged low-wage employers to create workplaces populated by part-time jobs. Most US retail and service firms are organized in this way. In contrast, full-time workers not only are paid higher wages but get benefits. US wage and hour laws also mandate that workers be paid time and a half if they work more than 40 hours a week or 8 hours in a day. Managers and professionals, however, are exempt from these laws. This has encouraged employers to demand long hours from managers and professionals and to resist efforts to create part-time jobs for them. Managerial and professional labor is thus exploited through more hours of work with no additional compensation, while other workers are exploited through reduced total compensation and by withholding benefits.

Total Exploitation

Among the most striking examples of exploitation are cases where work is simply never paid for. Wage theft in the form of failure to pay departing employees their last paycheck is a common example. Slavery and forced labor, both of which still exist in many parts of the world, including the United States, are other examples (Weitzer 2015). It was once common in the United States for employers to have access to the labor of mentally disabled people and prisoners, and these practices still exist. The Fair Labor Standards Act of 1938 authorized sub-minimum wages for disabled persons.

In 2014 Henry's Turkeys, a firm that provided the labor of mentally disabled men to turkey processing plants, was found guilty of withholding 30 years of wages from these men, who they kept in boarding houses and paid most recently only $65 a month for full-time labor (Barry 2014). Similar practices exist around prison labor in both China and the United States (Cowen 1993).

It is not too difficult to imagine the exploitation of immigrants, mentally disabled people, and prisoners. All three are categorically distinct, are relatively powerless, and tend to lack access to claims-making resources. Immigrants lack the protection of citizenship, disabled people are perceived as incapable of strategic negotiation, and prisoners are stripped of most rights to personhood. But there are also examples of total near-exploitation where subordination is not so obvious. One such example is Ashley Mears' (2011) study of fashion models whose glamorous presence is strategically used to generate nightclub revenue but who are unpaid for their profit-generating work.

Promoters working for high-end New York nightclubs seek out attractive young women, often working or aspiring fashion models, and invite them to attend an exclusive nightclub for free. These women create the club scene, both by lending their beauty and glamor to the place and by "modeling" the consumption of expensive alcohol. Promoters can make up to $1,000 per night plus a cut of the liquor sales by providing these women to the nightclubs. The clubs capture millions of dollars a year. The women get a free dinner and drinks but no pay for their labor. Promoters often use further gifts, masked as favors, like driving the models to castings, lunches, movies, and other amenities. These "gifts" are strategically used by promoters to keep the girls coming out to their clubs, generating profits for the nightclub. Mears describes this gift exchange as exploitation. That it is unpaid reminds us of the case of the mentally disabled turkey slaughterhouse workers: gifts and food, instead of wages, with a labor contractor and a nightclub accumulating the resulting organizational income stream.

In an interesting twist, Mears reports that this gift exchange form of exploitation is so thoroughly accepted by the models that other women who are actually paid by some promoters to attend clubs (generally $40–$80 a night) are derided as akin to prostitutes. In an RIT framework, the clubs then are claiming revenue generated by the relational and emotional work of unpaid women, income on which the women have no claim. Both promoters and models define monetary payment as ruining the experience and thus delegitimate models' claims to the value they are producing for nightclubs.

Interestingly, the rise of tipping as a form of compensation in the United States had a similar origin. After the freeing of black slaves in the nineteenth century, some employers argued that it was immoral to pay former slaves wages and that they should rely instead on tips freely given by customers for good service. The United States is unusual among high-income countries in the degree to which tipping replaces wages in employment, shifting the production relationship from the legally protected employer-employee relationship to the gift exchange embedded in customer-servant liaisons. Tipped workers remain among the most vulnerable of workers, risking exploitation by both their employers and their customers (Jayaraman 2016).

Exploitation in Institutional Context

That exploitation happens across categorical divides should be clear at this point. It is also important to recognize Miliann Kang's (2015) caution that exploitation is facilitated or impeded by institutional context. Wage theft, sexual slavery, prison labor, sub-minimum wages for disabled people, long hours, tipping, expectations of total work effort and commitment all happen in particular legal contexts. They are either legal forms of exploitation or illegal, with laws that are inadequate or are only poorly enforced.

Carolina Bank Muñoz (2008), in *Transnational Tortillas*, provides a fascinating example of the power of institutional context for determining the targets of exploitation in production. She contrasts workplace social relations in two otherwise identical factories on different sides of the US-Mexican border owned by the same global corporation. The pseudonymous Tortimundo is a publicly held corporation, one of the biggest of its kind, with mills all over the world. Hacienda BC is located in Baja California, Mexico, while its twin, Hacienda CA, is located in the United States, in California. Muñoz demonstrates that while workers at the two factories produce the same products, with the same technical division of labor and the same technologies, and both factories have workers of Mexican origin, national context encourages exploitation across distinctly different categorical boundaries.

Managers in both factories create control over their low-wage employees by pitting workers against each other and creating social divisions on the shop floor. However, which workers are pitted against each other and who gets "superexploited" in Muñoz's terms depends on which side of the border one works. On the US side in the Hacienda CA plant, managers pit documented and undocumented workers against each other in order to keep wages low and effort high. Muñoz describes a two-tiered employment structure in the Hacienda CA plant in which documented workers earn higher wages and obtain more favorable working conditions and opportunities for upward mobility. She writes that "documented workers are treated better, paid higher wages, and can look forward to modest upward mobility within the factory, whereas undocumented workers endure poor treatment, poor wages and little internal factory mobility" (p. 3). Two workers, Eugenio (documented) and Jose (undocumented), illustrate this arrangement. Both have worked at the Hacienda CA plant for the same length of time, yet Eugenio has been promoted from a production worker to a line leader, while Jose continues to work the production line during the graveyard shift. Eugenio earns $10.50/hour, while Jose earns $8.50/hour. During the course of her fieldwork she noticed plant managers demoting workers whom they could not match to a Social Security number. Fabian, an undocumented worker, said "the [managers] moved me to packing, and lowered my wage to minimum. They said they were doing me a favor letting me work. I was a liability to the company" (p. 81). Thus, not only are undocumented workers exploited more than documented workers but this exploitation across the documented-undocumented categorical distinction is undergirded by threats of job loss by managers, undoubtedly a feature of the broader legal institutions around employment of immigrants in the United States.

In contrast to the United States, on the Mexican side at the Hacienda BC plant, exploitation revolves around gender, with managers creating distinctions between light-skinned and dark-skinned women. Here, 72% of workers are women, and not only are men in systematically higher-paid jobs than women but women, like undocumented workers in the California plant, are exclusively relegated to production roles. Managers at this plant appear to select particularly vulnerable women to hire, notably single women from the countryside with few local familial networks. One manager explained, "We like hiring women from the interior because they know less, so they complain less" (p. 100). Just as the undocumented status of workers at Hacienda CA makes them vulnerable to managerial exploitation and abuse, their lack of connections and local knowledge appears to make women vulnerable to exploitation and abuse at the Hacienda BC plant.

Much of managerial control of labor at Hacienda BC revolves around sexual harassment. Muñoz notes rampant sexual harassment from managers during her fieldwork. As one worker, Maria, begins her work on the line "she is immediately greeted by a male supervisor who hugs her around the waist and kisses her on the cheek. Maria squirms uncomfortably. The manager laughs and moves to the next woman on the line" (p. 5). This sexual harassment enables further economic exploitation. A production manager asks Maria to dinner, and she is afraid that if she declines, management will "treat her unfairly the next day or dock her pay for being late" (p. 5). Muñoz notes that "When women do not respond positively to manager's advances, they are disciplined. Many women feel that they are at risk of losing their secure employment" (p. 15). Many of the darker-skinned women note that much of the harassment is aimed at lighter-skinned women. Georgina notes that this actually gives lighter-skinned women an advantage because "the *gueritas* (light skin/white) girls don't have to worry about keeping their jobs, because managers are constantly giving them attention" (p. 111). On the other hand, it means they are the recipients of much of the sexual harassment. As a defense mechanism, and reflecting their own participation in the cultural milieu at Hacienda BC, many women dressed up for work and wore makeup in attempts to receive favorable treatment from managers.

The difference in the exploitation dynamics in the two plants reflects differences in national context, particularly the influence of the US and Mexican state on social rights, labor market institutions, and national race and gender dynamics. In the predominantly female labor force in Mexico, the especially harsh treatment of *indios* and the generalized sexism in the plant reflected that women, especially darker women from the interior, were the most vulnerable, most exploitable workers in the local labor market. Sexism unrestrained by legal institutions of equal opportunity or sexual harassment provisions enabled this exploitation. In the United States, exploitation on the basis of gender was more difficult. Managers and workers understood that sexual exploitation was not legal and was socially unacceptable. Perhaps more importantly, they also understood that discrimination against Mexicans and immigrants in general, and the special vulnerability of undocumented male workers, was socially acceptable and legally possible. This made immigrant men the preferred and available exploitable labor force and helps us make sense of the direct evidence of employer wage theft from immigrant labor that Annette Bernhardt and her colleagues (2009) found. Moreover, the militarization of the US border at the end of the twentieth century ensured that undocumented men without wives were always available to work the lines at the US plant. The criminalization of these immigrants further empowered managers, who could threaten to remove their paternalistic protection of the undocumented.

In the end, this case illustrates the role of national context as an environmental force that encourages a particular exploitation target. The force is both legal and cultural, and these legal and cultural institutions generate differences in the relative power of categorically distinct groups.

In the last example we saw how national legal and cultural contexts shifted the target of exploitation for the Tortimundo firm. But often institutions are created for the purpose of enabling exploitation, as well as potentially social closure, rather than simply being contexts in which inequality processes take shape. Thomas Lawrence, Roy Suddaby, and Bernard Leca (2011) refer to this process as institutional work, and Ralph Hamann and Stephanie Bertels (2017) provide an instructive example of this through their historical account of exploitation of black labor by white mining companies in South Africa. Here, we see that firms actively constructed the government and corporate institutions that make exploitation possible, as well as showing that this active cultivation of exploitative institutions is not fixed but interacted with both labor supply and the larger cultural context in South Africa.

In 1867 large deposits of diamonds were discovered in the Kimberly region of South Africa. Similarly, large gold deposits were found in the 1880s. British joint stock companies were founded to mine this wealth, but they faced a profound labor shortage. Instead of passively adapting to labor market conditions, these companies created the institutions needed to generate and control a labor supply. They actively categorized black Africans as "kaffir" labor, particularly suited to the dangerous and extreme conditions associated with mining in the nineteenth century. A standard economic model would predict rapidly rising wages for black labor under conditions of a labor shortage. But this did not occur. Rather, the mine owners combined into a labor cartel, the Chamber of Mines, to avoid competing with each other for labor. In order to motivate pastoral Africans to move to the mines, they encouraged the colonial state to implement a cash tax on black males, forcing them to find paid labor employment. At the same time, they used the traditional authority of tribal chiefs, via payments to chiefs who sent their young men to the mines. In this way the mine owners created the institutional pressures to *conscript* black male labor into their mines. At the mines they created a system of total bodily *control*, in which black laborers were by contract forced to stay at the mine for periods of upward of a year and sleep, eat, and play in massive dormitories staffed by armed guards. This system remained in place from the late nineteenth century through 1987. Wages stayed low. In fact, there was no increase in real wages between 1897 and 1969. Black rural labor was exploited in this way for over a 100 years under the colonial and later apartheid systems.

By the mid-1980s South Africa had shifted to a labor market characterized by high unemployment and labor surpluses. At the same time the anti-apartheid struggle was delegitimating the colonial/apartheid-era system of labor control in the mines. Black workers were demanding that they be allowed to live off the mine property, a right that skilled white miners had long held. Given the now ample supply of surplus labor, mine owners were quick to oblige. Because of the labor surplus there was no pressure to raise wages, and the mine owners outsourced onto their black labor the cost of their own housing and food. Very low wages and repressive, exploitative labor relations in the mines were preserved, while the need to invest capital in (upgraded) housing was abandoned. This *liberalizing* and *outsourcing* employer strategy was offered to black labor as a concession, when in fact it was a deliberate strategy to reproduce their ability to preserve the maximal exploitation of black mine labor. Hamann and Bertels point out that this market externalization of labor costs in the South African diamond, gold, and platinum mines is quite similar to the process of labor cost externalization that is currently widespread among major employers elsewhere. We explore this redefinition of organizational boundaries as an inequality generating strategy in Chapter 8.

CONCLUDING THOUGHTS

Inequality regimes within organizations are generated through and produce exploitation between more and less powerful actors. Exploitation can become inscribed into the social relations between capital and labor, managers and workers, men and women, whites and blacks, citizens and non-citizens, insiders and outsiders—that is, the powerful and less powerful. As well, inequalities in the distribution of organizational resources that organizations are able to accumulate are generated through a process of exploitation within markets. Some organizations have greater market power than others because of limited competition, categorical differences between organizational owners/managers, or network positionality among firms. Importantly, they can translate their market power into gains for themselves at the expense of buyers or sellers in their commodity chain or competitors in their product market.

Thus, our conceptualization of exploitation locates the process within organizations as well as between them and expands the concept beyond the traditional capital-labor relationship. Any categorical difference can be transformed into a power differential that enables exploitative transfers of income. These transfers then translate into within- and between-organization inequalities. At the heart then of distributional inequality is the exploitation of less powerful actors by more powerful ones in institutional contexts that enable or encourage such exploitation.

6

Social Closure

> *The principal motives for closure of a relationship are: (a) the maintenance of quality, which is often combined with the interest in prestige and the consequent opportunities to enjoy honour, and even profit . . . (b) orientation to the scarcity of advantages in their bearing on consumption needs . . . (c) orientation to the scarcity of opportunities for acquisition.*
>
> Max Weber (1947:143)

> *An influx of women into male spheres threatens the differentiation of men and women, and men resist.*
>
> Barbara Reskin (1988:68)

STEM (science, technology, engineering, and mathematics) has become a central acronym in higher education, K-12 education, Silicon Valley, and policymaking circles alike. Much of the policy conversation in the United States has centered on general workforce development issues, but a critical conversation has focused attention on the lack of women and racial minorities in STEM fields, both in college majors and in employment. Women and racial minorities are described as leaking out of the pipeline from college into STEM jobs, and both college classrooms and STEM workplaces are often described as "chilly climates" for women and racial minorities.

The concept of social closure offers us a window into making sense of this phenomenon. This chilly climate in both classrooms and workplaces is part and parcel of the process through which white, and in some STEM contexts Asian, men capture organizational resources for themselves. Chilly climates both emerge from these men's attempts to hoard resources for themselves and produce social spaces that women and racial minorities self-select out of to avoid mistreatment and to find better opportunities elsewhere. That is, the leaky pipeline problem is a problem of categorically dominant groups pushing subordinate groups out of the pipe.

This type of monopolization of organizational resources, or social closure, is commonplace throughout workplaces and the economy broadly. Property laws are examples of closure mechanisms, limiting rights for the use of property and any linked profits to owners. These rights are simultaneously denied to customers and employees, even though their purchases and labor power were necessary to produce the property and any linked profits in the first place. Requiring medical degrees from certified medical schools similarly limits the lucrative and high-prestige practice of medicine to MD degree holders, excluding other skilled medical practitioners from access to the most lucrative markets and positions. Employment discrimination in general on the basis of education, sex, race, sexual orientation, or any other categorical distinction generates closure from jobs, reserving employment or promotion opportunities for the more powerful status group or demanding higher skill levels of the less powerful group in order to get access to jobs. Passing on accumulated wealth to one's descendants or even leftovers from last night's delicious dinner to your immediate family is a form of closure around family ties. And, of course, the creation of an organization in order to accumulate resources is a closure mechanism in its own right, limiting claims-making on organizational resources to those with organizational citizenship rights. Categorically, organized social closure is a fundamental process producing and reproducing inequalities.

The historical and immediate force of social closure is that it produces durable status distinctions and durable inequalities in life chances when they are embedded in and enforced by organizational practices. In this chapter, we describe multiple closure processes around workplaces. These are not, of course, the only organizational fields where closure gives access to or denies resources to groups. Immigration and citizenship requirements hoard national resources for citizens. Racial and class segregation in neighborhoods hoards safety and good schools for those who can afford to get into higher class neighborhoods. Racial, class, and gender segregation in access to exclusive golf and eating clubs hoards elite network access for their members. Families everywhere hoard whatever resources they have for family members and judge socially unacceptable partners for their children harshly.

CONCEPTUALIZING SOCIAL CLOSURE

When we use the term *social closure* we mean a situation in which one group excludes, intentionally or not, another categorically distinct group from accessing some organizational resource. In this sense, social closure refers to the use of categorical distinctions to reserve resource-generating opportunities for one group while excluding others. Central to this conceptualization is the role of power in monopolizing resources as closure requires the capacity to prevent others from accessing a resource and often legitimating a set of principles on which to justify such exclusion. We see this power to close off access to resources operating from two directions. On the one hand, social closure can operate through explicitly excluding a categorically distinct group from a resource. In this case, the monopolizing group is organizing closure on the basis of preventing a morally unworthy out-group from access to the resource. This is social closure based on *exclusion*, and it is often rooted at the social psychological level in out-group bias. In contrast, a monopolizing group may provide preferential treatment for those like them, sharing the resource preferentially with an in-group, rather than focusing on excluding any particular out-group. Here, the monopolizing group is not overtly excluding categorically distinct groups from a resource but instead sharing a resource with those in their own categorical group. Following Tilly (1999), we label this form of social closure *opportunity hoarding*, and this type of social closure is rooted in what social psychologists refer to as "in-group bias."

While clearly exclusion and opportunity hoarding are two sides of the same coin, contemporary social psychology has tended to find that unconscious in-group bias is the more powerful of the two. It is also self-legitimating. While exclusion against outsiders is in some contexts socially reprehensible, even illegal for some status distinctions (e.g., discrimination based on sex or race), affirming the value of yourself and people who share your traits is generally not. In the grand sweep of history, we think it is most likely that closure operated as exclusion up until modernity, when universalizing democratic principles, equality politics, and the cultural valuation of diversity made overt exclusion less culturally acceptable. Today, the power to hoard opportunities for one's in-group remains acceptable, and conscious exclusion has become less culturally legitimate, although still widespread.

Often, scholars think of social closure in binary terms, such as men excluding women, whites excluding blacks, citizens excluding immigrants, and other culturally relevant dyads. While closure is a strategy to position a categorical boundary around who is able to access some organizational resource, organizations are much more complex than binary categories imply. Organizations are fields of social relationships, inhabited by intersectionally complex actors. Therefore, group distinctions are typically based on multiple social categories that can shift and realign over time within organizations and from organization to organization. This means that closure, particularly in-group biases that are unconscious rather than deliberately chosen, is often intersectionally dynamic.

The closure concept has a long history in sociology. Max Weber emphasized the role of closure in producing status groups, identifying closed social relationships as both producing status distinctions and the basis on which groups monopolize resources. Later sociologists, such as

Frank Parkin (1979) and Raymond Murphy (1988), developed the multiple axes along which actors monopolize economic resources, focusing on the monopolization of more rewarding occupations, educational credentials, unionized jobs, and capitalist property rights. They suggest that all of these various closure strategies follow a similar logic of inclusion and exclusion, often with the backing of legal monopolies enforced by the state. Barbara Reskin (1988) used social closure to explain the persistence of sex segregation even in contexts where active social closure is opposed by law and particular regulatory organizations within government (like the Equal Employment Opportunity Commission) and within firms (like human resource managers). She made the fundamental claim that when a particular closure mechanism is challenged, new closure rules will be invented to preserve the original categorical distinction and maintain its associated status hierarchy.

Charles Tilly (1999) substituted the term *opportunity hoarding* for social closure in his germinal relational inequality writings.[1] In some of our previous work, we have employed Tilly's concept of opportunity hoarding, but on reflection we prefer the term social closure to describe this process. We have two reasons for this. First, it connects our work to the dominant sociological conceptualization dating back to Max Weber with its emphasis on status group boundaries and social/moral honor. But our second, and more important, reason is that the term social closure embraces a broader set of social relationships than just market-based opportunities. Weber described closure processes as about both boundary-making and resource distribution between status groups. His examples of closed relationships include familial ties, erotic relationships, religious practices and relations, and political associations. He sees these restrictions on relationships as processually the same as restricting market opportunities through ownership, unions, and professional associations. We do as well. One could update his examples by pointing to current attempts to close off access to political institutions to felons or efforts to deny marital rights to same-sex couples.

Most of our conceptualization is fairly conventional, focusing on the status-based exclusion of categorical outsiders from accessing resources. However, two key elements are worth elaborating. The first has to do with what is being monopolized and the second with why and how actors engage in monopolization.

First, the most distinctive element of our definition, and perhaps the most critical difference from past practices, is that what is being monopolized

1. "Opportunity hoarding . . . operates when members of a categorically bounded network acquire access to a resource that is valuable, renewable, subject to monopoly, supportive of network activities, and enhanced by the network's modus operandi" (Tilly 1999:10).

we define as an organizational resource, as opposed to a market good. An important theme in the relational inequality theory (RIT) approach is to emphasize that markets are not shaped by invisible hands but are made via relationships between actors producing and distributing organizational resources. Most of the contemporary discussion of closure processes has been defined in terms of the monopolization of resources on a market via state-sanctioned mechanisms (Parkin 1979). Property law, licensing, credentialing, unionization, associational representation, and certifications are understood as devices to lock out some groups from being able to access market resources. For example, Kim Weeden (2002) highlights the historical linkage between social closure and higher pay via the mechanism of occupational licensing, which reduces the supply of labor for specific occupations. We have no doubt this is a defining process for some occupations, especially professional occupations such as doctors and lawyers. We agree that governments are often important resources for the creation of formal closure rules by powerful groups. But this market conceptualization hides some, perhaps a majority, of the processes of exclusion that secure greater incomes for some individuals. It is also the case, as Reskin (1988) pointed out, that exclusionary rules are often invented at the interactional and organizational levels.

By identifying organizational resources as what are being monopolized we are being specific about *where* the resources to be monopolized reside. Wages and jobs are organizational phenomena. The specific tasks one fulfills are defined by the organization: one enters an organization to be interviewed, a person or committee selects who is to be hired, and the terms of the employment contract are negotiated between the organization and the potential hire. Similarly, an organization's technology and associated patents and intellectual property rights, as well as its control of all or part of its markets, are resources that organizations struggle to monopolize. Organizations are where the categorical distinctions that generate the power to monopolize reside and where the menu of resources that can be monopolized accumulate. Thus, the exercise of power to exclude categorically distinct others from resources must happen in interaction and typically in some organizational context.

Our second conceptual elaboration concerns the motives of actors involved in monopolizing resources. Most closure accounts emphasize actors—owners, unions, men, whites—working to close off access to resources. Early accounts of social closure around race and gender painted a picture of active monopolization by dominant groups. Reskin (1988) was clear that her argument was linking the economic interests of men to their actions to prevent women from entering male domains. Similarly, Weeden's (2002) account emphasizes how occupational groups actively use the state to reduce supply and thereby increase an occupation's market wage. Our conceptualization breaks from this assumption of intentionality to allow for unintentional, routine, and unconscious processes that lead to the monopolization of organizational resources by categorically distinct groups.[2]

While deliberate social closure is consistent with Max Weber's initial discussion, he does not assume that closure is always generated by intentional action. Weber recognized that while economic and social interests provide a strong rational basis for closing off relationships, tradition and affectual sentiments generate closure as well. Social psychological research on group identity and bias processes suggest that intentional action is not necessary to creating and recreating inequality. Human beings tend to make in-group and out-group distinctions around fundamental identities, like family and tribe. But this process also extends to other identities that are culturally available such as gender, race, religion, region, and occupation, all of which entail an in-group/out-group distinction. Importantly, particularly in the modern era where we are taught to be suspicious of group-based stereotypes and prejudices, these biases around categorical distinctions can be produced without the actors realizing it. Closure processes then can result from implicit cognitive biases channeling cultural messages about group difference.

A great example of the role of unconscious processes in social closure is in Nancy DiTomaso's (2013) important study of contemporary racial inequality in the United States. She finds that almost all of the jobs acquired by her white respondents were achieved by help from a friend or relative. These instances of in-group bias were so routine and ubiquitous that they were largely invisible to her respondents, who tended to claim that their successes were of their own doing. At the same time, many of her respondents believed that their job opportunities were limited by affirmative action for African Americans, and this belief fed into their anti-black racism. While she did not probe the frequency of acts of anti-black bias, her results strongly suggest that hoarding opportunities for friends and family were probably much more frequent and were seen as universally legitimate behaviors. Thus, while the closure process can be an explicit attempt to exclude categorically different groups, it can also be produced by in-group favoritism of which the actor may not even be aware.

Social closure is an organizational process through which some groups, implicitly or explicitly, draw categorical boundaries around themselves and

2. Reskin later (2003) criticized closure theory for an undue focus on intentionality. As a result, she rejected all closure theory in favor of a search for proximate inequality-generating mechanisms. While we are in favor of researching proximate mechanisms, we think that Reskin (1988) and Tilly (1999) were correct in emphasizing the distinction between proximate and ultimate causes. Closure is an ultimate cause, created through proximate practices. Stanley Lieberson's (1985) discussion of ultimate versus proximate causes is very helpful in this regard.

others to monopolize resources. It is about power and the intersections of categorical distinctions steering who gets access to organizational resources.

OBSERVING CLOSURE PROCESSES

Social closure can happen around families, friendships, neighborhoods, churches, firms, and other social networks, as well as around imagined communities such as races, ethnicities, nationalities, religions, genders, or occupations. Mechanisms can include sharing resources, extending help, morally evaluating others, cultural stereotyping, segregating, granting citizenship, enforcing property and labor laws, and developing job descriptions and employee handbooks. Closure processes are ubiquitous and closure mechanisms as varied as human cultural inventions to produce and enforce categorical distinctions. They can emerge from employers in the form of discriminatory hiring, promotion, and wage-setting practices. They can come from employees in the form of refusals to train co-workers, withholding critical tacit skill information, and overt harassment. Most powerfully, they can come from implicit or explicit alliances between categorically similar employers and employees who align their practices to exclude categorically distinct groups from a multitude of organizational resources. And we should remember that firms can also monopolize markets in order to extract resources from other organizations or persons.

The most fundamental resource for most people for securing a particular standard of living is one's job. Income streams are typically tied to jobs, not to the particular people in them. There is an important dynamic between social closure and exploitation associated with jobs. Accumulated value from past exploitation claims becomes institutionalized in job hierarchies, which then becomes the basis for monopolizing certain jobs. Thus, the current wage attached to a job is the result of earlier rounds of exploitation. Becoming an incumbent of a secure high-paying job is the *sine qua non* of upward mobility aspirations. Jobs therefore are, in the first instance, the dominant organizational resource to be monopolized for most people. Because of this, there is no shortage of social scientific research on when, where, and how particular jobs are closed off to categorically distinct groups.

Central to closing off access to jobs is the closing off of access to organizations themselves. Organizations are resource-accumulating machines, so excluding categorically distinct groups from organizations themselves, especially high-resource ones, is a fundamental first step in social closure. Failure to obtain any job is to be excluded from organizations, and in some cases this operates through organizational policy itself. Organizations routinely have closure criteria that identify the categories of people who will be considered. Often, these are educational requirements, sometimes prior experience in a similar job, sometimes specific skills. The matching of people to positions is inherently one of discriminating between acceptable and unacceptable status characteristics. Job descriptions with a list of required skills and experiences are explicit closure mechanisms. Closure rules around jobs are sometimes simply the skills necessary to do the job well, but they also emerge out of a field of struggle and in-group bias that define what skills and experiences are necessary.

Many organizations exclude all applicants who have criminal records. Devah Pager's (2003) landmark study on employers' use of criminal records in hiring decisions documents the extent to which employers use criminal convictions as a status characteristic to exclude some actors from access to organizations themselves.[3] She trained black and white young men to behave identically when applying for entry-level jobs in a single city (Milwaukee, Wisconsin), equipping them with otherwise identical job and educational histories but randomly varying whether or not they had a criminal record in their job history. She uncovered an intersectional story in which having a criminal record led many employers to refuse to hire, but African Americans without a criminal record were no more likely than whites with a criminal record to obtain employment in these organizations. Thus, the closure cost of a criminal conviction for whites was similar to the cost of being African American without a record, and African Americans with criminal records were essentially excluded from most organizations. This provides a view of the organizational decision-making process that explains the widespread finding that those with a criminal record, especially less educated male African Americans, have markedly higher unemployment rates than those without criminal records (Western 2006).

Occupations themselves often take on exclusionary lives of their own, at times beyond the boundaries of particular organizations, when occupational groups control access to education, skills, and employment. Kim Weeden (2002) spelled out five mechanisms through which occupations become closed off to outsiders and thereby increase their average wages: credentialing, licensing, certification, unionization, and professional association. These mechanisms largely operate through state-occupation relationships. That is, representatives of an occupation petition the appropriate government agency to allow them to form a licensing/certification board or a union or professional association and to pass laws to require employers to only hire into those occupations individuals belonging to or

3. Her focus was on access to low-wage employment for which many ex-convicts typically apply, but organizations very often have criteria for employment in virtually any job in the organization that include the absence of a criminal record.

meeting the standards of these entities. Through this process, incumbents of occupations close off access to that occupation to anyone without the required credentials/certifications/license/affiliation, reducing the effective supply of their labor and increasing their organizational power, and thereby increasing their pay.

Occupational closure via the state increases the power of particular actors to get access to jobs in the organizations associated with closure in markets (e.g., medical doctors in hospitals) but also makes those actors more powerful within organizations in making claims on organizational resources. One of the most interesting results from the study of class inequality in Australian and US workplaces that we outlined in Chapter 2 was that in some workplaces the average core production workers actually outearned the average manager. This was the result of exactly the type of occupational closure processes Weeden identified combined with social control of the firm. These class-inverted workplaces tended to be firms dominated by core workers with professional certification–hospitals, engineering firms, accounting practices, law firms, and the like. In these cases, the closure-based power of the occupation was stronger than the more typical authority-based advantages of managers.

Beth Redbird (2017) challenges the notion that occupational licensing necessarily leads to higher earnings. She shows that occupational licensing has expanded in the United States but that the resulting increased supply of labor has also driven down the earnings of newly licensed occupations. In this case, closure around an occupation did not lead to control of labor supply but rather to its expansion, which in turn reduced the bargaining power of people in those occupations. It is also possible that this was a case of closure as a source of worker power being transformed into an opportunity of exploitation of poor people by firms selling the training for licensed occupations. In this case the firms selling training had no interest in controlling supply but rather had an interest in exploiting people desperate to find secure employment.

The closure idea has been most closely associated with occupational and professional closure. But education is probably the more widespread basis. Professions typically have a closure-based educational requirement. Some professions like medicine or the law have also lobbied state governments to award those degree holders' legally enforceable monopolies over tasks and to use their professional power to control the organizations they work in (Abbott 1988). Many occupations, like engineers and computer scientists, have created expectations that jobs will be linked to specific degrees but lack the backing of the state to enforce these closure rules. In these cases the closure rules must be installed in firm-level job descriptions. Even the simple job requirement of holding a high school degree excludes anyone who did not graduate from high school. It is a weak closure mechanism but a closure mechanism nonetheless.

That educational degrees are closure mechanisms, making some people eligible for jobs and excluding others, does not imply that they are not often functional in terms of required skills. They may be or they may simply be imperfect signals that employers can use to eliminate candidates and simplify selection decisions. While closure rules strengthen the claims-making position of the preferred status groups, whether or not they are legitimately tied to productivity requirements is an empirical question. On the other hand, they always limit competition, exclude out-groups, and generate access to organizational resources.

Employment contracts, especially for high-level employees, increasingly include clauses that prohibit employees from leaving a firm and taking a job with a competitor firm. Non-compete clauses are explicit, typically legal, social closure mechanisms. The assumption is that the employee has access to technical or managerial expertise or a set of relationships with clients that the firm has the right to monopolize—and especially to withhold from its direct competitors. It is estimated that 18% of US employees are constrained in their job search by non-compete clauses in their contracts with their current employer (Starr, Prescott, and Bishara 2016). In one interesting case, the global investment banking giant J.P.Morgan lost a top executive and sued the new employer for stealing its "property." Frank Bisignano left J.P.Morgan to become the CEO of a credit card processing company, First Data. Bisignano then hired 10 executives from J.P.Morgan to follow him to First Data. J.P.Morgan sued First Data and eventually was awarded $10,000,000 in compensation. In an exclusionary closure payback move, when First Data, which had been owned by a private equity firm, went public through a massive stock offering, J.P.Morgan was excluded from the ranks of investment firms making the offering (Sidel and Fitzpatrick 2014; de la Merced 2015).

While a criminal record, occupational licensing, and non-compete clauses are legally and organizationally proscribed means of locking actors out of organizations and occupations, the more prominent bases are lodged in cultural status expectations. Moreover, these are often tied to access to specific occupations within workplaces, which produces job-level segregation of categorically distinct groups. Employers often describe making hiring decisions as the result of having a gut feeling about a candidate. When our guts are already inhabited by strong cultural stereotypes about groups and preferences for people like us, then group-based exclusion can arise even without conscious attempts to exclude. Discrimination based on gender, race, religion, and other socially salient distinctions often has at least some basis in these types of cultural biases and provides a basis for employers or hiring managers to exclude categorically distinct groups from organizational resources. Clearly, these biases are weaker closure processes than an occupational license. Therefore, if these are the primary closure processes in play, then they are likely to let some, typically highly qualified, subordinate group members into good jobs. When group stereotypes further invoke beliefs that a group is less qualified, smart, or responsible, pressures for exclusion will increase. In these cases, the gut feeling associated with in-group bias is reinforced by cultural messages about out-group inferiority.

These types of exclusions are exactly the behaviors that equal opportunity laws attempt to prohibit. Explicit racial or gender or religious prohibitions—no blacks, no women, no Muslims need apply—are no longer widespread and in the United States have been illegal since the Civil Rights Act was passed in 1964. However, widespread cultural stereotypes and expectations are difficult to overcome through legal prohibitions and thus tend to mutate and get reinscribed through less overt mechanisms. A consistent problem in social science has been identifying these types of discrimination in practice. Quasi-experimental designs such as audit studies (e.g., Devah Pager's study described earlier in this section) provide the strongest causal evidence of the role of cultural expectations in locking out access to jobs for categorically subordinate groups.

Social closure through employment discrimination around race and gender has been well documented through various versions of these quasi-experimental designs (e.g., Pager 2003; Bertrand and Mullainathan 2004; Correll et al. 2007), but other status characteristics can also be bases of social closure, particularly in specific local contexts. Michael Wallace and his colleagues (Wright et al. 2013; Wallace, Wright, and Hyde 2014) developed an audit study focusing on religion as a status characteristic, identifying religious affiliation as a categorical distinction that in some local contexts generates inequalities. They sent matched resumes that only varied on the religion of the job applicant to employers in both the Southern and New England regions of the United States. They compared a long list of religious affiliations, including no religion, atheist, Catholic, Evangelical, Jewish, Muslim, pagan, and Wallonian. Wallonian is a fictitious religion, included to see if there was an out-group bias associated with pure "difference" not anchored to any cultural stereotypes.

Regionally specific status hierarchies in hiring were evident. As can be seen in Figure 6.1, despite the predominance of religion in the South, resumés not mentioning religion were favored over those that mentioned any religion in this region. There were further status hierarchies among religions. Out-groups such as Muslims, Catholics, and atheists as well as unknown groups such as pagans and Wallonians tended to be excluded more than Jews or Evangelical Christian, with Muslims being the least desired out-group. In New England, there was much less reaction by employers to

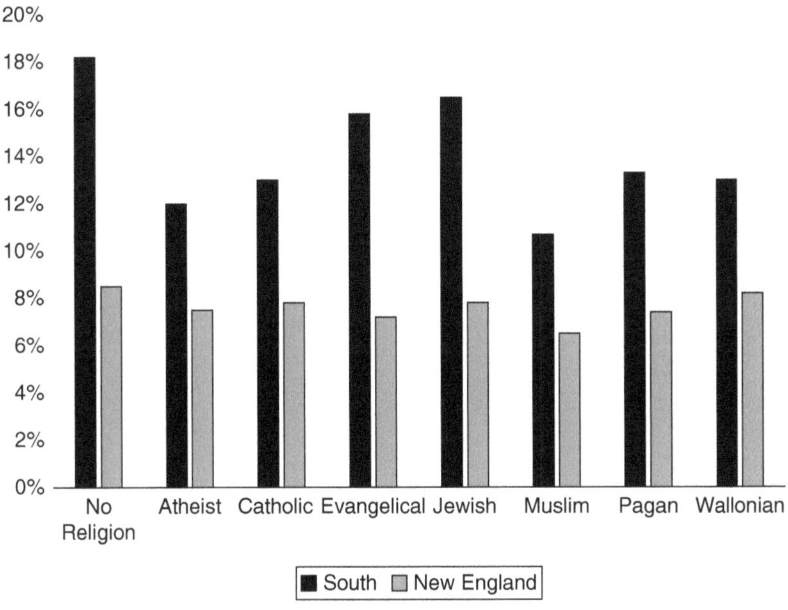

Figure 6.1 Percent of resumés that received employer callbacks by religious categorization in two regions of the United States (Wright et al. 2013; Wallace et al. 2014).

religion, although Muslims again received the fewest callbacks. In the New England study Muslims were the only group with significantly lower chances of getting a positive response. This example illustrates one of the important insights of RIT: status characteristics acquire meanings in specific institutional contexts. Given the cultural inscription of anti-Muslim sentiment in the United States during the period of these studies, it is not surprising that across regions they are the most likely to be excluded, but for other religious distinctions it is within specific regional contexts that religiosity takes on meaning and status hierarchies form into exclusionary criteria.

In a similar design, András Tilcsik (2011) built organizational variation into an audit study of discrimination toward gay men. He matched gay and politically left-leaning resumés of men and sent them to employers. He observed whether the employer was located in a city, county, or state with a law that prohibited sexual orientation discrimination, reasoning that bias would be lower where institutionally prohibited. He also coded the job advertisements, indicating which jobs required masculine stereotypical traits including the words *decisive, aggressive, assertive*, and *ambitious*.

As we can observe in Figure 6.2, across the whole sample gay-signaled resumés received 40% fewer callbacks than the left-signaled resumés,

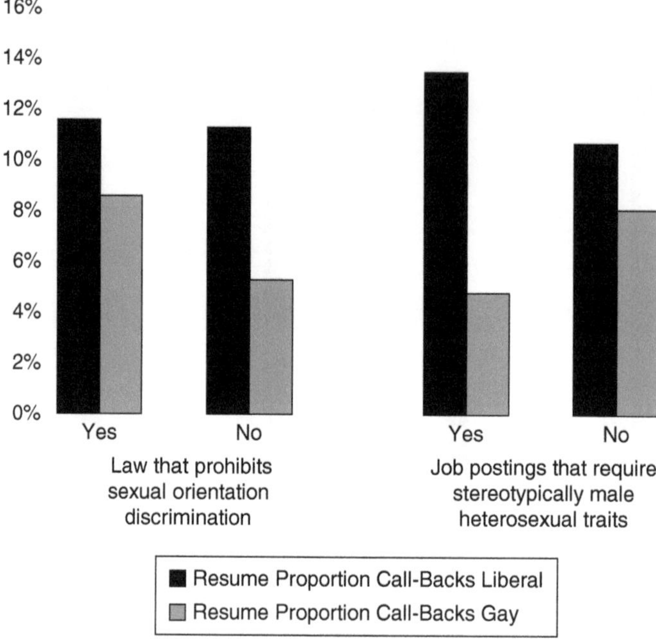

Figure 6.2 Percent of resumés with employer callbacks for gay and liberal job applicants by state anti-gay discrimination laws and employer use of male heterosexual frames in job descriptions (Tilcsik 2011).

suggesting a high level of status bias against gay men. But all employers were not alike. There were regional variations in employer bias against gay resumés associated with legal discrimination prohibitions. In fact, in two states, California and New York, there was no measurable bias against gay resumés at all. At the same time, employers who used stereotypically male adjectives in their job posting were significantly less likely to respond to gay resumés. This study was done just prior to the remarkable social movement success of the LGBT movement in the United States. We imagine that if it was repeated today, the stigma associated with a gay job application would be less than it was in 2005, but also we would expect more regional and employer variation as discrimination against gay job applicants transitioned from highly institutionalized to locally negotiated categorical distinctions.

One of the shortcomings of audit studies is that they do not show exactly how discrimination happens but simply that it does. An interesting research design that gets at how unconscious discrimination transpires was conducted in Sweden by Malmström, Johansson, and Wincent (2017). They sat in on the decision-making discussion of state venture capitalists and then analyzed the conversations in which funding decisions were made.

These are the decision-making processes of the people who allocate venture capital to start up new businesses from the Swedish state.[4] Gender was a powerful force in these intendedly gender-neutral, meritocratic discussions. Women's proposals were rejected 50% more often than men's and, when funded, received half as much start-up capital for their new firms. What the researchers found was that the conversational weighing of the strengths and weaknesses of the proposals was profoundly gendered. When men were young, this was seen as evidence of long-term potential. However, the same information for women was evaluated as inexperience. Men got bonus points for being aggressive and arrogant, while women were dinged for being emotional. Being cautious was prudence when associated with a man and timidity when with a woman. Obviously, all closure is not unconscious, but this study shows how powerful such biases can be even—perhaps especially—when they operate in meritocratic, gender-blind contexts.

These discrimination studies all demonstrate that social closure operates in both generic and local terms. Some status characteristics are widespread, such as race and gender, which operate to some degree in all contexts. Others, such as religion, take on emergent meaning in local contexts. As well, social networks and cultural capital which map onto status groups can become the interactional mechanisms through which organizational resources are closed off to categorically distinct groups and this monopolization is then legitimated. But even the most widespread status distinctions typically take particular shape in organizational contexts as Tilcsik's (2011) study of sexual orientation discrimination demonstrates.

Organizational Data Matched to Employees

While social closure through employer discrimination has been increasingly documented through audit studies, other research has used employer-employee matched data to capture the centrality of organizations in the social closure process. Much social closure around jobs intersects with categorical distinctions around statuses such as race and gender. When jobs or professional degrees become associated with particular genders or races or religions, it produces a feedback loop in which the status distinctions common in the culture become reinforced by status distinctions at work. In the Australian-US comparison we introduced in Chapter 2, we found that income distance between core production and managerial jobs widened whenever the managers faced subordinate status groups in those core

4. In the United States almost all venture capital comes from private sources. In Europe much comes from state entities.

production jobs. Since incomes are tied to jobs, closure in access to organizational resources happened through job assignment. Access to firm resources in that study was governed by a wide array of categorical in-group/out-group distinctions including sex, race, nativity, permanent worker status, and required education.

A well-documented empirical example of these closure processes is the segregation of men into male-dominated jobs and women into female-dominated jobs and its link to the gender wage gap. We used the gender segregation literature in Chapter 5 to demonstrate how men are able to exploit women by devaluing the jobs they are dominant in, but once the jobs are devalued (i.e., exploited) it benefits men to lock women out of access to the higher-paying, male-dominated jobs. This locking-out process can be explicit—women encounter hostility or glass ceilings (or walls) when they try to enter or remain in typically male jobs—or implicit—as when male domains are culturally encoded as male only (Padavic and Reskin 2002). The reverse can hold in typically female jobs, in that cultural expectations discourage men from holding women's jobs, but harassment and hostility have not been documented in this situation. Indeed, the cultural notion that these jobs are inappropriate for men can lead to men being promoted out and up via "glass escalators" (Williams 1992).

This literature has long pointed toward gender-based job segregation as the key source of gender earnings inequalities. A series of studies by Trond Petersen and colleagues used linked employer–employee data to estimate the contribution of occupations, establishments (i.e., workplaces), and jobs (occupation within establishment) to gender earnings inequality and consistently found that the segregation of men and women into different workplaces and jobs within workplaces accounts for most of the gender gap in earnings. At the same time, important institutional variation exists across jobs and organizations in the extent to which segregation shapes the gender wage gap.

Petersen and Morgan (1995) found that 90% of the US gender wage gap in the early 1980s was explained by job-level segregation, leaving only a tiny average wage gap between men and women in the same job. But at that time few men and women worked together in the same job. They repeated this study design in Norway and Sweden, analyzing white- and blue-collar workers separately (Meyersson Milgrom, Petersen, and Snartland 2001). As in the United States, almost the entire gender wage gap was explained by gender-based sorting into jobs, although the within-job gender wage gaps that remain after accounting for segregation were slightly larger in both Norway and Sweden. More recently, they have examined the link between social closure and gender wage gaps in two former socialist countries, the Czech Republic (Křížková, Penner, and Petersen 2010) and Slovenia (Penner et al. 2012). Gender wag gaps tended to be low in both countries under socialism, both because overall inequality was kept low and because the socialist states actively worked to eliminate gender inequalities. After the demise of socialism in the early 1990s, gender wage inequality grew strongly in both the Czech Republic and Slovenia. By the late 1990s and early 2000s both countries had higher within-job gender wage gaps than in the United States (Czech Republic 13%, Slovenia 16%), suggesting either a less tight coupling between the monopolization of jobs and gender wage gaps than in the United States, Norway, and Sweden or finer-grained monopolization of tasks and other resources within jobs in these eastern European countries.

Looking across these national cases, it is clear gender job segregation is prevalent and powerful, producing a substantial portion of the gender wage gaps in all countries. But there is also a story about institutional variation in social closure and its effects on the gender wage gap across organizations and jobs within countries. In all of these countries, managerial and professional workers tend to have greater within-job pay gaps than do blue-collar workers, likely because of differences in the institutional rules for negotiating pay, a point we will return to in the next chapter. As well, some countries experience changes in the institutional rules around pay equity. Men monopolizing higher-paying jobs is widespread and helps to create and perpetuate gender wage inequality, but there is also substantial institutional variation in workplace levels and trends.

Ethnographic Accounts of Closure Processes

When Max Weber originally put forward the notion of closure, it was strongly tied to the process by which elite groups both produced and reproduced their superior social status. Some of the most interesting research in this regard has come from work by Lauren Rivera and Karen Ho.

Rivera (2012) studied the recruitment practices into high-paying entry-level jobs at elite firms—global consultancies, white-shoe law firms, and investment banks. What she found was a two-stage process in which the firms first recruited from a narrow set of elite universities—Harvard, Princeton, Yale, Stanford—largely ignoring grades and coursework and other human capital signals, and then screened on cultural similarity to current employees. These firms first used educational pedigree in the same way a European aristocracy might employ bloodline criteria and then hired people who were culturally similar to the hiring firm. A key hurdle was the "airport test," where interviewers asked themselves, would I want to be stuck for three hours in an airport with this person? Depending on the firm, appropriate credentials might include playing a particular sport, being bookish, or liking math. Screening seemed much more like the process one would use to pick a spouse or a friend than the meritocratic stories favored by many social scientists, indicating substantial in-group bias in elite professional firms.

Karen Ho's (2009) ethnography of financial service dealmakers showed a similar closure process but also provided an ideological link to the merit-based stories so prevalent in social science and everyday life. Confirming Rivera's account, Ho found that global financial service firms recruited almost exclusively from the same set of elite universities identified by Rivera. She observed a consensus narrative on Wall Street during the period of financialization that these were the smartest people of their generation. The firms actively promoted this narrative to legitimate their claims to steer the investment and organizational design decisions of other firms and rich individuals. To be globally influential, the firms presented themselves as populated by the smartest people in the world. Prestigious university degrees became the status signifier of this intelligence. This self-congratulatory cultural story when wed to skyrocketing incomes no doubt produced the status confirmations that justified both high salaries, exclusion of those lacking the university credential and cultural fit, and the financial exploitation of low-status, less smart, less hardworking clients by financial service firms.

Hiring exclusions are but one mechanism of exclusion. Particularly in the wake of equal opportunity legislation and the institutionalization of at least the idea of women's equality, civil rights for African Americans, and broader inclusionary ideologies, subtler closure mechanisms are central to locking out categorically distinct others from access to organizational resources.

Several studies document the variety of ways men prevent women from entering and being successful in male-dominated jobs. The late 1980s and early 1990s witnessed a cottage industry of fieldwork focusing on the experiences of women entering traditionally male jobs, no doubt in part because this was a time in which this was happening more frequently. Harassment, refusal to provide appropriate training, and paternalistic treatment are some mechanisms through which men and other higher-status groups locked women and other categorically distinct groups out of key organizational resources on the job. These mechanisms make it harder for out-groups to perform their job and increase the likelihood they will be fired or quit.

For example, Irene Padavic's fieldwork in a power plant in the late 1980s, combining a survey, in-depth interviews, and participant observation as a coal handler, provides a powerful example of these processes. In the face of a strike, "Urban Utility" temporarily replaced striking male blue-collar workers with female and male workers from other parts of the plant (Reskin and Padavic 1988; Padavic and Reskin 1990). Survey data and interviews showed that a nontrivial proportion of female replacement workers experienced what they described as hostility from male co-workers, including overt forms of sexual harassment such as catcalling and deliberately displaying pornographic images along with nonsexual hostility such as refusing to assist women when they requested it. In a particularly unsettling encounter, they describe how a female worker's coveralls were deliberately torn off her in front of a group of men who laughed at the incident (Padavic and Reskin 1990:620). More common, but equally problematic, was that two-thirds of the women stated they experienced paternalism from co-workers. Women were treated as childlike and therefore in constant need of unasked-for help from male co-workers. This generates the vexing contradiction that when women asked for help, men refused, but when they did not, men often intervened with unneeded aid.

An interesting component of Padavic's analysis of Urban Utility is that supervisors were instrumental in facilitating these closure strategies, reassigning women from plant operator jobs to cleaning jobs and to female-typed tasks within male-defined jobs. Physical demands, like lifting requirements, were the stated reason for gendered job assignments, although the organizationally defined lifting requirements for plant operators and primarily female food-service workers were equivalent.

In a similar study of black workers hired into a manufacturing plant in response to government-mandated affirmative action requirements, Bruce Williams (1987) found a strikingly similar pattern of harassment by white co-workers and supervisors. In addition, he found that management was concerned that the plant itself would get a reputation as a "black plant" and so lose status in the community.

Sharon Collins (1997) explored a quite different closure process, studying black male executives in Chicago firms in the 1970s and 1980s. The firms were major, high-profile employers in the Chicago area and had come under strong pressure from both the community and the federal government to hire African Americans into upper-level jobs. What the firms did was create new job titles, such as community affairs and affirmative action manager, which were in turn filled only by black men. These jobs had power and were highly paid but were not close to the core businesses of manufacturing or sales. When the pressure for affirmative action and equal opportunity evaporated in the 1980s, so too did many of these jobs and the careers of these black men in them. In this case, we see race-based closure, which preserved white executive spaces but did not deny black men good incomes. Since they were segregated from the income-generating functions of the firm, though, in the long run these were dead-end jobs.

The literature is rich in examples where status characteristics intersect with typical occupations generating inequalities in access to rewards. The literature on gender and racial integration of formally segregated jobs is equally rich in documenting the interactional closure mechanisms employed to drive out or contain the threat of women or minorities as they enter desirable jobs. But integration has happened. As we outlined in Chapter 4, the labor force in the United States has transitioned from one of near total race and gender segregation in job assignments and the exclusion of minorities and women from high-skill and high-pay jobs to one of considerable integration.

Integrating Science and Engineering Fields

In the remainder of this chapter, we focus on contemporary closure processes in science-, technology-, and engineering-intensive firms. As we stated at the outset of the chapter, much public policy effort has gone into increasing diversity in these fields, and much has been made in the United States of the science pipeline problem in which women, and sometimes minorities, are described as leaking out of the science pipeline because of the chilly climate first in schools and then in firms. Public policy has as a result focused on increasing diversity in these fields. These integration efforts respond partly to the equal opportunity goals of women and minority scientists and partly to the economic dynamism associated with scientific advances in biotechnology and information technologies.

We have access to firm-level data on the information technology (IT) industry and have explored women's representation at the firm level. Most science was highly dominated by white men prior to 1972. In 1972 the US Congress included an amendment to the 1964 Civil Rights Act that prohibited gender and racial discrimination in colleges and university admissions. Since then, the science pipeline has become substantially more integrated. From a relational inequality perspective, however, we would expect there to be variation from workplace to workplace in the degree of integration, and this is precisely what we find.

Figure 6.3 displays the degree to which women are over- or underrepresented among the 537 US IT firms with 500 or more employees. Most firms show underrepresentation of women, with the average firm having about 15% fewer women than are available to be hired.[5] This is, of course, in line with the notion that these workplaces contain a chilly gender climate, and many are in fact much worse than the average. However, there are also some firms where women are overrepresented, and in these presumably the climate is a bit warmer. This, however, does not exhaust the range of variation in women's representation. Women are more likely to be present in

5. We benchmark availability by the incidence of women in similar jobs in the same or similar industries in the same local labor markets. Details can be found in the industry reports at the Center for Employment Equity, https://www.umass.edu/eeodatanet/industry-ranking.

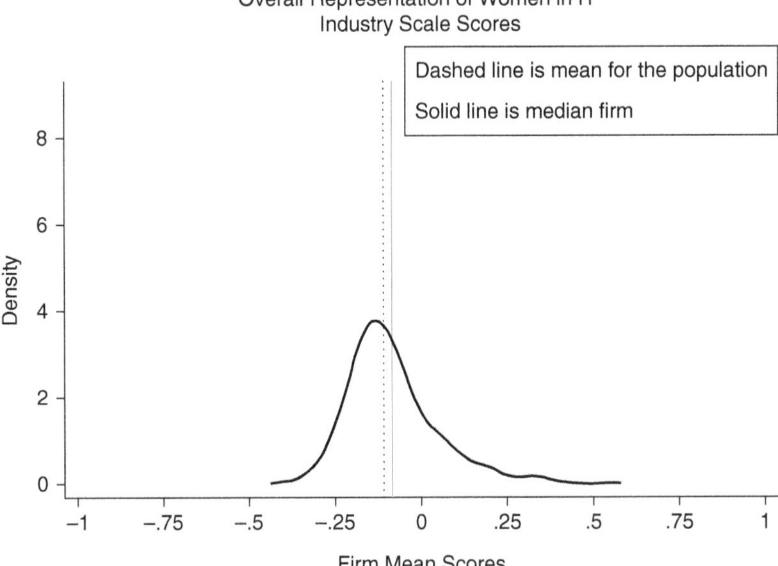

Figure 6.3 The distribution of women's representation in US information technology (IT) firms relative to their labor market availability, all information technology firms with 500 or more employees in 2012 (authors' calculations).

firms where women are in senior leadership or even middle-management positions and are less likely to be present in larger and more complex firms. There are also sectoral differences, with the worst subsectors for women's employment being software publishers, computer system design, and engineering services. So while, in general, women are excluded from IT firms, there is much variation across firms, and that variation intersects with which groups dominate leadership positions, organizational size, and subsector industry fields.

We present two case studies that chart some of the shifts in science field employment since the 1970s. The first focuses on the first female cohorts of engineers, who graduated from college in the late 1970s during a period of strong pressures to desegregate both universities and firms. This case was developed by Judith McIlwee and Gregg Robinson (1992). Despite these pressures, engineering has remained a male-dominated field, though the prevalence of closure practices varies depending upon the organizational context. The second case study is of women's incorporation into biology-linked jobs and is based on the work of Laurel Smith-Doerr (2004). Here, women have made much stronger progress in access to advanced degrees, but their post-education career success depends on sector-specific inequality regimes.

Gender and Engineering in the Age of Affirmative Action

McIlwee and Robinson (1992) studied the experiences of an early cohort of women entering engineering, beginning with their initial interest in engineering, to majoring in engineering in college, to getting a job, to doing the work. These women were the first to be admitted into the two dominant engineering programs in California after Title IX of the 1972 Civil Rights Act required colleges and universities that received federal funds to stop discriminating on the basis of race and sex in admissions. Not surprisingly, these women reported exclusion and harassment in school, but they also had the resolve to work through those gender barriers and get engineering degrees. As this study was done on the first cohort of female engineers in Southern California, the observations are located historically in a period in which equal opportunity expectations and regulation were at their high point in both colleges and workplaces. Since then, federal oversight of federal contractors has weakened considerably (see, for example, the research of Fidan Kurtulus [2012] on this point). In addition, federal oversight of colleges and universities has migrated from admissions to sexual harassment and rape. Pressures in both realms are considerably weaker today than they once were, and engineering today stands out among STEM fields as one in which women have made the weakest inroads.

Engineering was then, as it remains today, a male-dominated field that is largely organized around a culture of masculinity. In general, women are disadvantaged by this culture as the culture tends to privilege interactional resources culturally associated with maleness, including aggressiveness, technical competence, and competitiveness. McIlwee and Robinson found that this culture led to many of the forms of social closure already discussed, including patronizing comments to female engineers and sexual harassment that ranged from calling women "sweetie" to sexual jokes to explicit sexual demands. Equally widespread was the refusal to mentor women, include them in social interactions, or allow them to lead or even participate in the technically challenging job assignments that tended to be higher status and more rewarding.

However, the masculinist culture of engineering intersects with the relations of power within workplaces, giving this toxic masculinity the force of enhancing male power in some places but muting its effects in others. Specifically, in those workplaces where engineers are a powerful occupational group, the interactional power of male engineers relative to female engineers is enhanced. Importantly, in their interviews McIlwee and Robinson obtained information on the kinds of workplaces where the women they interviewed worked. They then investigated in depth two firms in which many of their respondents had found jobs. These firms represented two industries where female engineers had markedly different experiences: Computer Devices Incorporated in the emerging IT industry and United Missiles in the aerospace industry.

Computer Devices Incorporated is a high-tech company, founded by engineers and where engineers have much control over their tasks. The company espouses an official policy of "management by objective" in which managers tell engineers only what needs to be accomplished but not how to do it. Job assignments in the lab are the most prestigious because this is where technical innovation and product design happens, work that is highly valued inside the company. There is also an unofficial open-door policy in which engineers are free to enter managers' offices to discuss work-related matters. In general, engineers are not intimidated by management and feel on an equal footing with them. Engineers even had an annual "Rogue Engineer Award" bestowed on an engineer who "successfully defied management and got the right answer" (p. 114).

Women inside this firm felt especially disadvantaged, interactionally disempowered, and effectively locked out of key organizational resources. For women who worked in the lab, the culture of the organization was especially hostile. And because of its prestige, it was difficult for women to even get assigned there. A key issue for women in the company was that men tended to hoard the most prestigious assignments, with the lab being one of them. All the women who had worked in a lab were excited at the opportunity to do so but eventually left, deeply unsatisfied from their treatment inside of this predominantly male space. Most took lesser assignments just to get out of the lab, often finding themselves in marketing or other relatively lower-status jobs.

When in the lab, women were quickly labeled as incompetent by their male peers, particularly when they had to ask for assistance. And unfortunately this label had sticking power despite the fact that all the women who asked for assistance quickly learned the tasks. One respondent, Ginger, reported being called "lady" by co-workers instead of by her real name, and after two years working together a male engineer concluded "oh you're not just another dumb blonde" (p. 123). In general, she felt uncomfortable with the masculinist self-aggrandizement other engineers displayed about their designs and the seeming necessity of engaging in this behavior in competition with others. This undercut Ginger's self-confidence in her work over time, a feeling commonly expressed by other female engineers. Computer Devices Incorporated had a competitive, male-dominated, engineering culture, which produced a gendered inequality regime that was inhospitable to female engineers, shunting them away from high-status tasks or out of the company altogether.[6]

United Missiles was a vastly different engineering company. It was an aerospace firm dominated by management and highly dependent on federal contracts, contracts which came in that era with strong affirmative action expectations. The work was bureaucratized, and everything operated through a strict hierarchy. This was in part because it operated largely through acquiring government contracts, which involved a great deal of standardization in reporting and billing. Uniform bureaucracy was the thing engineers liked the least about United Missiles. Because of both the hierarchy and rules associated with bureaucratic control of the labor process, managers had a lot more power than engineers. Managers, not engineers, were responsible for approving or denying every engineering decision. Rogue engineers were fired or quit.

However, the bureaucracy was an advantage for women at United Missiles, at least relative to Computer Devices Incorporated. Job promotions and assignments were highly formalized, so it was not as easy for a masculine culture to operate to exclude women from prestigious assignments. Affirmative action reporting to the federal government produced an external pressure to treat women fairly as well. Fair treatment and good assignments fed back to increase women's self-confidence as engineers. Fraternal socialization among engineers was less common at United Missiles, leading to less opportunity for male engineers to exert interactional power. While interactional sexism was widespread at United Missiles, its consequences for locking women out of organizational resources were minimized. For example, one female engineer, Carol, described male co-workers posting images of nude women. This is common in male-dominated professions, but she felt capable of telling them she found it offensive without fearing that this would hurt her job promotion prospects (pp. 133–134).

The masculinist engineering culture was operating in both Computer Devices Incorporated and United Missiles, but the power of this culture to affect women's access to and control over organizational resources varied depending upon the social relations within the firms. Because engineers are so powerful at Computer Devices Incorporated, they are able to use this culture to effectively lock women out of promotions, job assignments, skill development, and a sense of respect within the organization. In contrast, at United Missiles, the masculinist culture is less powerful because the hierarchical bureaucracy, derived in part from the power of affirmative action policy on the firm, diminished the power of

6. A recent study by Erin Cech and colleagues (2011) finds that professional role confidence remains a major impediment to women becoming engineers.

engineers relative to management. Thus, the male-dominated gender regime that developed at United Missiles was weakened, if not eliminated, by the twin contending forces of bureaucratic rules and external pressures for gender equality. The force of social closure is mediated by the social relational power of different actor groups within the firm, which is shaped by the institutional environment that the organization is navigating.

Women in Biotech: Reputation, Bureaucratic, and Network Regimes

In bureaucratic firms the received wisdom is that if management is serious about promoting equal opportunity, it will institute and monitor formal evaluation procedures.[7] That was the lesson McIlwee and Robinson drew from the United Missiles case study. These formal procedures are there to reduce the various closure mechanisms that produce subtle and not-so-subtle discrimination processes such as cognitive bias, in-group preferences, attribution errors, network-based social exclusion, harassment, and targeted discrimination. Laurel Smith-Doerr produced a more recent study on gender integration in the STEM field, where the weakening of gender regimes was dependent not on formal rules but on a cooperative team-based interactional culture. Smith-Doerr explores the careers of PhD-level life scientists, a group that has followed the more common professional gender integration trajectory associated with professional university degrees.

In the 1990s and early 2000s, life science PhDs typically ended up in three destinations: academia, pharmaceutical companies, and biotechnology firms. With a strong mix of historical, qualitative, and quantitative analysis, Smith-Doerr identified very differently gendered inequality regimes in these three organizational contexts. This study reinforces the basic claim of McIlwee and Robinson that organizational forms shape the power of STEM occupations and the gender relations therein. However, which organizational forms reduce social closure practices are reversed in the life sciences: the decentralized, networked organization is best for women, while the bureaucratic form generates worse outcomes. In addition, in academia a reputation-based inequality regime also turns out to be a hostile environment for women. Luckily for this cohort of life scientists, the most exciting science as well as the higher income growth potential was

7. In Chapter 4 we discussed the origins and profound limitations of these practices, pointing toward managerial accountability as more efficacious in reducing categorical bias, whether exclusionary or exploitative, than simple formalization.

happening in the biotech firms, which are notable for their decentralized network structure.

The networked structure of the biotechnology industry required flexibility in firm boundary-spanning, work team organization, and product innovation. These three forms of flexibility nurture, or perhaps even require, diversity in scientists' contributions, leading to a more dynamic organizational culture than the status hierarchies typical in academic and pharmaceutical organizations. As a result, the biotech sector was much more open and welcoming to women (and perhaps non-US nationals) than academia or the pharmaceutical industry. Smith-Doerr finds this in the statistical evidence that female and male PhDs have equal access to biotechnology employment and that women have much higher access to managerial jobs in biotech, perhaps even having an advantage over men, than they do in academia or pharmaceuticals. She further finds this in the qualitative interviews with women, which show a strong contrast between high discrimination, unfriendly environments for women in academia and pharmaceuticals, and more nearly egalitarian welcoming environments in biotech. Though the climate in pharmaceuticals is hostile as it is in academia, the inequality regime in pharmaceutical firms is different, looking more like the bureaucratic promotion ladders McIllwee and Robinson documented in United Missiles but without the affirmative action pressure brought by the federal government in an earlier time.

Our reading of Smith-Doerr's study leads us to suspect that what makes academic workplaces unwelcoming to women is not simply the absence of flexibility but the specific form that flexibility takes. That is, academic inequality regimes are built around individuals' reputations as scientists. Innovation is highly prized in academic labs, but researchers compete against each other to monopolize the reputation-enhancing effect of discovery. In biotech firms, it is cooperation within and across work teams and within and across organizational boundaries that produces innovation. The central logic of academic labs is innovation for career enhancement, while in biotech firms it is innovation for collective (i.e., firm or network) profit. In biotech, the network attempts to monopolize resources while in the academy, it is the principal scientist. It is this contrast that fosters inclusionary versus exclusionary strategies for mobilizing organizational resources. In the academic lab, you get hierarchy and within-team competition as the principal investigator attempts to control and claim discovery and PhD students and postdoctoral scientists attempt to build independent reputations. In the biotech lab, you get networks and cooperation as science for the sake of science is employed to produce collective returns in both reputation and profit. So closure pressures in STEM are not simply the result of categorical distinctions between men and women but the interaction between categorical distinctions and the degree of competition over organizational resources.

CONCLUDING THOUGHTS

While social closure is a central feature of organizations, it is an indeterminate, dynamic process that can be contested by those being excluded. Closure is a strategy to hoard resources, but strategies can fail, especially when opposed. Thus, closure, like exploitation, is an exercise in power. Closure processes can be challenged by usurpationary movements, institutional regulation, and interactional resistance. Raymond Murphy (1988), writing after the civil rights and women's movements had destabilized taken-for-granted racial and gender status hierarchies, observed that usurpationary closure could challenge exclusionary closure rules directly. In the United States, the civil rights and women's movements did this for race and gender in the 1960s and 1970s, directly challenging widespread exclusionary employment practices and strengthening state regulation of equal employment opportunity. More recently, the LGBT rights movement has done this for sexual orientation and gender expression.

Murphy also pointed out that usurpationary movements can also install new forms of closure that benefit the previously excluded. His primary example was labor unions, which while challenging the power of capital to exclude labor from organizational resources created a new category—union member—who obtained access to some of those resources via better earnings or benefits. This new category of union member in turn, however, might include some (e.g., family members or co-ethnics) and exclude others (e.g., women or minorities).

In the United States, almost no managerial positions were held by women or racial minorities before the civil rights movement. In a recent analysis of managerial trajectories in US workplaces, Safi Shams and Tomaskovic-Devey (2017) finds that in a small proportion of US workplaces white women (16.2%), black men (8.9%), and black women (2.5%) are stably overrepresented in managerial roles relative to their participation in their local labor markets. In these workplaces, we might suspect that the closure principle was benefiting white women, black men, and black women. They also found that white men were stably overrepresented in 91% of workplaces, suggesting that closure favoring lower-status groups in managerial jobs, to the extent that it happens, only rarely happens at the expense of white men but rather happens from the exclusion of other, less powerful status groups.

Categorical status advantages do not guarantee that groups can impose social closure mechanisms. Rather, closure mechanisms require field-level, institutional, or cultural support to work. Closure mechanisms need legitimacy, at least among powerful actors, within organizations to operate. They also often require support or at least the absence of attacks from the external fields that organizations inhabit. Equal opportunity laws and enforcement through the courts or government agencies challenge discrimination-based closure around race and sex. Similarly, many governments institute antitrust laws to ensure that product markets do not end up as national or local monopolies. The *trust* in *antitrust* refers to single firms or colluding firms ("trusts") controlling the price and quality of some good in markets. So-called monopoly or oligopolistic markets are closed to competition, and thus, firms therein have control over both the price and quality of products in that market.

When categorical status distinctions are strongly institutionalized, like gender or race in the United States prior to the civil rights and women's social movements, closure mechanisms are likely to be ubiquitous and difficult to challenge. When status hierarchies endure but are no longer hegemonic, closure processes will be challenged politically but also via the intersectional reality of everyday life. Once US colleges integrated on the basis of sex and race, so did most professions. Those studying to become doctors, lawyers, accountants, engineers, and mathematicians in historically white male universities now routinely include women and racial minorities. Workplace social closure around race and gender eroded quickly among professional occupations as a result. On the other hand, bright lines around educational degree closure remained in place. Engineering jobs require engineering degrees, pharmacist jobs pharmacy degrees, and so on. The gender and racial integration of these educational programs led to the weakening of workplace gender- and race-based closure, while leaving unchallenged, perhaps even strengthening, education-based closure as the basis for inclusion and exclusion of many high-status, high-wage professional occupations.

Closure processes are strongest when they are strongly institutionalized at the societal level. When this is not the case and when intersectional complexity flowers, we can expect multiple local inequality regimes. This was the point of the Stainback and Tomaskovic-Devey (2012) case study which we outlined in Chapter 4, documenting the historical transition from institutionalized racial and gender apartheid at work to locally contested inequality regimes around race and gender. Licensing of certain occupations, like accountants, medical doctors, and in some states barbers is a legal closure mechanism. Some professions, like engineers and many academic professions, do not have state licenses but control their workplaces and so are equivalently powerful in controlling both the supply of qualified workers and their screening for employment. But in both types of occupational closure there is an intersectional reality weakening closure on the basis of race and gender, even as closure rules around educational degree remain hegemonic.

Some forms of closure are profoundly local and arise in interaction. When sex and racial employment segregation were made illegal, initial attempts to integrate workplaces were rebuffed by interactional boundary heightening. In her classic work from the late 1970s, Rosabeth Moss Kanter (1977) documented a series of interactional closure processes when women integrated managerial jobs in a large corporate environment: performance pressures, boundary-heightening, and role entrapment. Women's performance was judged more harshly than that of men; men exaggerated the social, cultural, and biological differences between men and women; and female managers were allowed a much more limited range of roles, all of which were circumscribed. Strong female managers were described as bitches, comforting ones as mothers, and the interactionally engaged as temptresses. Thus, managerial gender integration led to a fixation on and exaggeration of gender, rather than the occupational authority normally associated with managerial jobs. Ironically, relaxing an explicit closure rule—the exclusion of all women—led to a new interactional set of rules that served to isolate and undermine the effectiveness of individual women in managerial jobs. Closure became profoundly local.

When we talk about employment discrimination based on race or gender, employers may have an interest as employers in eliminating discrimination, either to drive down labor costs or to keep regulators at bay. At the same time, employers are caught in nets of accountability to their own race or gender identity group and to powerful groups of workers on whom they depend. And while certainly gender stereotypes at the level of individual employers operate during hiring and job placement, these stereotypes are conveniently consistent with attempts to preserve the monopoly advantages of high-status groups (Reskin and Padavic 1988). At a more local level, we should also expect on the shop floor that if occupational groups are powerful enough, supervisors may be inclined or forced to turn a blind eye to overt closure strategies such as refusal to hire women or minorities or the sexual and racial harassment behaviors that encourage them to quit.

7

Relational Claims-Making

> *[D]omains of activity in the workplace are, on a daily basis, allocated, confirmed, guaranteed, extended, stabilized and defended against attacks by rivals. . . . They enable a "this is mine" approach, which asserts its legitimacy both for oneself and for others.*
>
> Godechot (2016:226)

> *These compensation levels are very reasonable in light of the huge amount of value the executives have created for their investors.*
>
> Moorman (1992:107)

Claims are made throughout social life. Politicians make claims about what is needed to enhance the well-being of citizens. Citizens make claims to politicians about what they need to live a decent life. Members of households make claims over who is best suited to which household tasks. Students make claims over what grades they should receive and professors as to what grades students have earned. Employers and employees make claims on organizational resources. We argue that it is through such claims-making that organizational exploitation and closure processes enact inequalities. We take relational claims-making to be the proximate causal mechanism underlying organizational inequalities.

Claims are inherently political and relational acts, made through the power and status dynamics in relationships and the resulting struggles and contests over outcomes (Pfeffer and Salancik 1974; Roscigno 2011). Claims are negotiated in particular fields of action, which as spaces of social relations both define what is culturally recognizable or legitimate to claim and channel the status and power of actors mobilizing claims. We see the causal process around claims-making as strongly tied to the interplay between material, symbolic, and cultural resources in interaction. Relational claims-making is the elementary interactional process distributing organizational resources.

Owners' claims are strongly tied to property rights, giving them legal power over firm surplus, as well as the organization of production and future investment decisions. Status processes associated with class reinforce these legal claims. Employees' claims are commonly based on task competence, personal status, and power invested in positions. Job applications are claims of competence for doing the job, claims that are refined and bolstered in a job interview. Finishing a task and reporting a "good job" to your supervisor is a claim on respect and moral worth and eventually a paycheck. Competing for a promotion or a raise involves numerous claims of superior performance. Unionizing a workforce and professionalizing an occupation are collective claims on tasks. In these cases, workers generate collective power to garner some combination of respect, resources, and rewards, including a larger share of the resource pool, employment security, and perhaps even increased autonomy from supervision. When women or minorities integrate an all-male, all-majority workplace, that is a claim on the resources of those organizations. Groups collectively organize across organizations to make claims on the state in the form of law, regulation, and taxation.

Claims become inequality-generating mechanisms when they are treated as legitimate and so direct or redirect the flow of resources. And it is always the case that any actors' claims can be challenged by other organizational actors and stakeholders, making claims conditional on the legitimacy other actors grant. Claims are relational accomplishments not inherent facts of organizational life.

Situating this process within and between organizations highlights that what we often perceive as abstracted, disembodied market forces involve flesh-and-blood human beings negotiating organizational life. When other social scientists refer to "the market" as allocating income, jobs, and other rewards, they all too often invoke a magical, typically invisible, process. In relational inequality theory (RIT), there is no magic, and the process is often visible, created in the negotiated order human beings construct in exchange (and other) relationships. Markets, whether competitive or monopolistic, only lead to the exchange of value through a process of claims-making in some relational context.

Next, we develop our conceptualization of relational claims-making and then move to examining illustrative cases of relational claims-making within organizations over organizational resources. We examine cases of claims over the labor process, work–family conflicts, dignity at work, wages, union decline, financialization, and the cultural framing of diversity.

CONCEPTUALIZING CLAIMS-MAKING

We refer to *relational claims-making* as the discursive articulation of why one actor is more deserving of organizational resources than others. Within and between organizations, actors routinely maintain that they deserve a particular slice of the pie and, in doing so, regularly respond to other actors' counterclaims over the same resources. Through this claims-making process, some actors are able to acquire new organizational resources (exploitation) and/or prevent others from accessing such resources at all (social closure). Claims-making is a two-step process. First, one or more actors make a claim on organizational resources. Second, a claim is either recognized as legitimate or rejected by influential others. Both the ability to make a claim and its legitimacy reflect the social relations of status and power associated with individual competencies, individual and group power, and structural position within those social relations. Relational claims-making is the interactional process that puts exploitation and social closure into motion. It is also central to the processes that enable resource extraction from an organization's environment. Setting a price for goods or services is a claim on customers' incomes. Negotiating a contract between firms involves claims and counterclaims, often tilted in favor of the more powerful firm in the exchange relationship.

Actors can be either individuals or collections of individuals. Individuals can make claims on jobs, incomes, projects, training, and other organizational resources. But so can unions, occupations, departments, and firms. Representatives of nations, organizations, status groups, and social movements all can make claims on organizational resources.

Actors' claims can be *explicit*, such as applying for a job, demanding to be treated similarly to co-workers, requesting a raise, union bargaining over the terms and conditions of employment, as well as firms marketing a product or filing a patent application on a production process. Past claims often become institutionalized in roles and relationships, becoming implicit claims. *Implicit* claims are embedded in taken-for-granted practices, such as expectations for routine respect from supervisors and co-workers, the standard wage attached to jobs, or routine salary increases after a few months of employment. Claims can also be *silenced*, as when actors fail to apply for a job or demand respect or a raise because they believe that they will not be taken seriously or, worse yet, will be abused.

When influential actors recognize and accept the claim, they direct resources or rewards to the actor making the claim. More powerful and persuasive actors will tend to make more and more ambitious claims and garner both more respect and organizational rewards. In this sense, there is a negotiated inequality order that goes on both within and between organizations over the distribution of rewards, resources, and respect.

Securing and monopolizing organizational resources typically require that one's claim is legitimated by other actors within the organizational field. This process of legitimation is fundamental to relational claims-making.

As scholars since Weber have noted, legitimacy is central to the exercise of power, and power is fundamental to the operation of claims-making (Roscigno 2011). Sometimes the legitimation process is simple with everyone agreeing that one group or job or person is more deserving than others. At other times claims are contested and legitimacy isn't easy to create. Some claims are undermined by competing claims, while at other times a particular claim is simply rejected as implausible. At still other times legitimacy is not achieved, and naked power is the distributional arbiter.

Among scholars of inequality, our position on claims-making is quite close to that articulated by Olivier Godechot (2016). Godechot also sees a two-step process in which actors' claims are "opportunistic calculations" as to potentially legitimate claims and legitimacy hinges on the degree of "belief" other actors have in those claims. People can, and often do, use multiple discursive strategies to make claims. Claims of skill or credentials, claims of friendship or family, claims of fairness or equity or effort or merit or markets or productivity or quality can all be mobilized by actors seeking a share of organizational resources.

In the management negotiations literature, the most efficacious claims are often those based on a generally legitimate characteristic, such as skill or productivity. Claims based simply on authority tend to have less moral force and claims based explicitly on gender or race none at all. Roger Fisher, William L. Ury, and Bruce Patton (2011) refer to this as negotiating based on a "legitimate standard." In our formulation this "legitimate standard" can be thought of as the symbolic capital that has currency in a particular workplace. Skill, professional autonomy, revenue generation, and team-playing could all be local variants of a legitimate basis for claims-making. Categorical distinctions like gender, education, or position may vary greatly in their legitimacy as explicit bases of claims but often operate implicitly in interaction.

The idea of claims-making is also utilized in social movement research as the discursive mobilization of new claims by movement actors (e.g., Gamson 1988; Koopmans and Statham 1999). We share this focus on discursive claims and, like social movement scholars, see the legitimacy of claims as tied to cultural frames and power resources. We focus, however, less on the birth of new discourses around claims and more on the multiple contending claims available in contestations over organizational resources. Our approach draws most explicitly from the negotiated order perspective in sociology, which describes people as acting within the constraints of social structure and available cultural tools but also as active agents in dynamic relational fields (Fine 1984, 2010; Hallett 2007; Fine and Hallett 2014). In addition, claims are often invoked to protect organizational identities. People come to inhabit and believe in the categories they form relationally. When those categories produce valued identities, actors will fight to protect what they see as the rights associated with their identities (Schwalbe, McTague, and Parrotta 2016).

LEGITIMACY AND CLAIMS-MAKING

For claims-making to translate into resources, the claims must be accepted by others, making the issue of legitimacy central to the process of claims-making. Legitimacy is a relational accomplishment, requiring that others in the field find what you are claiming reasonable, which in turn hinges on the personal and collective resources that actors bring to and deploy during organizational negotiations. These resources are used to gain allies in the organization and have them legitimate one's claims (Cyert and March 1963).

We see the local organizational cultural as providing the framework through which claims on organizational resources are legitimated. That is, claims need to be framed within the context of the local cultural milieu to be persuasive to others. Past research on justice perceptions finds that we generally make social comparisons in determining if our own rewards, as well as the rewards of others, are just. People expect higher earnings when they work harder or have more education, experience, or higher-status jobs. Importantly, in work by Carsten Sauer and Meike May (2016) it appears that for most people the referent for these comparisons are other people within our local social worlds, specifically our own workplaces. For claims-making this means that the justness of a distribution, and thereby the legitimacy of a claim, has to be framed within the local meanings of a specific workplace for it to be persuasive. To the extent that claims are framed within the shared cultural understandings within organizations they are more likely to be legitimated by others and thereby shape resource allocations.

The implication of this connection between the local cultural setting and the legitimacy of claims is that the local cultural situation will influence both what kinds of claims are made and which are seen as persuasive. The most basic framing of claims over organizational resources discursively centers on the *competence and skill* of the actor making the claim. Social psychologists regularly find that when people interact around some task they will tend to rank themselves and others in terms of perceived competence on the task (Berger et al. 1977).

It is no wonder then that competence and skill are central discourses around which actors make claims. And the more central productivity is to an organization, the more important skill-based claims are likely to be. For example, in our work on Australian organizations, we found that organizations that operate in more competitive product markets had a tendency to prioritize claims related to skill over those associated with gender (Avent-Holt and Tomaskovic-Devey 2010).

But claims of merit are not the same as actual skill and competence. Rather, the skill and competence discourses pervading contemporary organizations are routinely linked to status hierarchies, such that higher-status actors are more likely to be perceived as competent and skillful. Irrespective of skill and productivity, high-status actors are more likely to both make claims on resources and have those claims legitimated by others. Thus, claims linking actors to productivity are actually linking categorically distinct status groups to claims about their productivity and competence (Ridgeway and Erikson 2000; Ridgeway and Correll 2006). Diffuse status characteristics such as gender or race generate expectations of competence, as do situational characteristics such as current job prestige in addition to or as substitutes for actual skills relevant to the task at hand (Ridgeway and Nakagawa 2014). Conversely, when actors make claims of why they are deserving of a particular organizational resource, they may do so by discursively undermining the competence and thereby deservingness of a categorically distinct outgroup. Social status and rewards, then, exist in a mutual feedback loop in which high-status actors' claims on rewards are more likely to be deferred to and actors with resources are more likely to be perceived as competent. Status orders both reflect and legitimate claims on organizational resources (Della Fave 1980; Ridgeway et al. 1998; Podolny 2010).[1]

When such a link between competence and status is reinforced in the broader culture, this will further legitimate the claims made by higher-status actors. Capital ownership, education, race, gender, and occupational prestige all have strong cultural content, making those statuses powerful bases for claims-making across many organizational contexts. To the extent that localized meanings around categorical distinctions map onto external cultural meanings, claims are likely to be more persuasive and gain more allies within the organization. This is especially true as more elite and powerful actors are likely to worry about the legitimacy of the organization and work to ensure that internal claims mirror external meaning systems. So while the task competence framing of claims likely transcends time and place in its utility, who is seen as more competent, the bases of competence itself, and the relation between competence and deservingness all intersect

1. Campos-Castillo and Ewoodzie (2014) point out the affinities between RIT and status characteristics theory (SCT). Both focus on the relationships between status-ranked actors in producing inequalities. SCT focuses on the translation of status hierarchies into differences in perceptions of competence, trust, and integrity. RIT focuses on the distributional consequences of those status attributions.

with the broader organizational field to make some claims more likely to be made and more likely to be found persuasive.

To give a historical example, in the post-World War II era in the United States, productivity was widely understood to be located within the skills and technologies deployed by unionized workers, whose union status helped legitimate their claim to a rising organizational surplus. However, beginning in the 1970s, their status and union power diminished and was replaced with a notion that capital and elite managers (especially financial managers) were central to production and the economy broadly, recasting both who is competent and who is deserving of organizational resources. By the early twenty-first century, discourses that emphasize the power of markets have become particularly central, limiting unions' and other actors' use of bureaucratic or equality-based claims (Cobb 2016), while enhancing the productivity-based claims of management and capital (Hanley 2011). We will say more about this connection between market fundamentalism and organizational claims-making later in this chapter (see Neoliberalism and the Legitimacy of Claims), but the point here is that organizational claims that link local organizational status hierarchies to broader institutional cultural schemas are likely to be seen as more legitimate within organizational negotiations and struggles over resources.

Translating these status hierarchies and institutional schemas into legitimate claims requires that actors possess the power to persuade others, and this stems at least in part from the symbolic power embedded within local organizational cultures (Hallett 2003). *Symbolic power* refers to the interactional capacity of actors to define the situation. This capacity stems in part from the deference others in the organization extend. At the same time, when actors are able to define what is going on and why it matters, they are defining the situation of the organization. Definitions of the situation are central to claims-making. When actors are able to define themselves (or their group or their skills) as central, productive, and competent while defining others, especially categorically distinct others, as less important, unproductive, and incompetent, their claims become more persuasive. It is this symbolic power that generates the ability—and inability—for actors to harness local status hierarchies and discourses to produce plausible claims on organizational resources.

When symbolic power intersects with the formal authority structure of the workplace, the capacity to legitimate claims is heightened. However, symbolic power need not ride in on the back of formal authority to legitimate claims. For example, Tim Hallett (2007) conducted an ethnography of a school where he found that the claims made by the principal—who was formally in the most powerful position in the school—were seen as almost fully *illegitimate* by the teachers simply because she said them. This was largely because the principal failed to frame claims in a discourse of teacher professionalism, undermining her symbolic power among her formal subordinates. However, when a new vice principal was hired, he gained deference from the teachers because of both his past teaching credentials and his acceptable self-presentation within the discourse of teacher professionalism. As a result, he was able to make the same proposals the principal had and have the teachers accept them willingly. His symbolic power legitimated his arguments, enabling him to accomplish what the principal could not.

In this way, the local organizational culture, including the emergent status hierarchy, is bound up with the power dynamics of the organization and the broader meaning systems of the organizational field. These three things—local organizational cultures, field-level meaning systems, and symbolic power—all intersect to move actors to either legitimate or delegitimate claims made by other actors in the organization.

It must also be recognized that sometimes actors will forgo making a claim at all. Often, actors take for granted the distributional structure of a particular relational context and do not even think of making a claim on a particular organizational resource. Steve Vallas (1993) illustrates this in a comment by a union leader reflecting on an earlier period of union strength:

> Referring to this period of material gains, one former union official recalled, "We almost ran out of things to ask for. I mean, what'd we want, our pants cleaned and pressed for us?" Like many others in his position, this man viewed management prerogatives as unalterable facts of economic life. (Vallas 1993:190)

Even in a historical context where workers were relatively powerful, claims were limited to what could be contemplated—in this case, material resources—but not the usurpation of management's control over the labor process. This case reminds us of economist Amartya Sen's (1992) capabilities and agency approach to action. Sen sees people as needing to cognitively imagine that they have resources on which to base claims and they do so taking into account not only the normative environment around such claims but also the local context. Thus, agency is limited by a locally embedded sense of the possible. Unlike utility-maximizing assumptions in conventional economic models, Sen's approach does not define *a priori* who has the agency to make claims or what claims are likely to be made but rather sees both as emergent and context-specific.

In a similar vein, organizational power is often inscribed, hidden in the technologies and practices that organize work. These are not only the obvious machines and divisions of labor, but also the systems of accounting and record-keeping that train workers to operate from the point of view of managers (DeVault 2013). Thus, the organizational context of inequality, what work counts or is counted, which jobs matter, and whose rules rule are often made invisible within organizational routines and job assignments and, as a result, are not contested. These become the cognitive habitus that guides and limits claims in the field of action. Many claims will never be made, or even contemplated, because the basis of power is not merely legitimated but invisibly encoded in the social and technical architecture of the organization. This does not mean that claims-making is not occurring, but rather that the claim itself is already deeply institutionalized. But institutionalized claims were not always so. At some point in time, within one organization or another, the claim was made, likely contested, and only over time accepted as so legitimate that the claim need not be explicitly made or justified anymore.

It is also the case that actors will avoid making a claim if they have reason to believe that their claim is likely to be unacceptable within the framework of the local culture. Actors, especially low-status actors with less formal and symbolic power, often fear losing face, or even retribution, for making an illegitimate claim. Silenced claims are rooted in the fundamentals of social interaction. In order for our actions to be intelligible to each other, we must take into account actors' power resources as well as the implicit rules and procedural expectations of those around us as our local audiences will hold us accountable for proper behavior (Goffman 1959; West and Zimmerman 1987). Therefore, to make claims above one's station is to invite at least embarrassment and ridicule, perhaps even retribution and violence (Schwalbe and Shay 2014). This means that actors, especially subordinates within an organization, will often avoid making claims that they believe others will see as unreasonably outside of the norm for a person of their status in that interactional context.

When there are large power differentials, such claims may also be punished, thus discouraging further attempts to claim organizational resources. This explains why much of the time subordinate actors within organizations appear to accept their subordinate status and therefore do not make any claims at all. Rather than risk ridicule or retribution, these actors define the best course of action as the path of least resistance. Thus, women propose lower starting wages than do men (Correll 2001), and less than 1% of employees who believe they have been illegally discriminated against at work file discrimination complaints (Neilsen and Nelson 2005). Over time, categorically disadvantaged groups often adapt to their subordinate status as a means of survival, suggesting that accommodation to organizational inequality regimes is often less a matter of belief in subordination than a survival strategy to exist in a categorically exposed position (Schwalbe et al. 2000).

Bringing all of these ideas together, claims are political and relational acts that work to produce inequalities within organizations by enabling exploitation and social closure. For relational claims to do so they must be legitimated within the organization. This legitimacy hinges on the claims most proximately connected to the local cultural milieu (including its status hierarchy) but also to the broader field-level meanings external to the organization and the symbolic power that actors possess within it. Claims can be explicit, implicit, institutionalized, and silenced. Thus, claims-making can be negotiated or not depending on the relative power of actors and the degree to which claims are taken for granted or contested.

OBSERVING CLAIMS-MAKING

Researchers have devised novel ways to observe how actors make claims on wages and other organizational resources. Sometimes this involves just being in the right place at the right time, but often explicit comparative designs can facilitate the observation of claims-making within organizations.

Claims-Making and the Labor Process

Much work on social closure has focused on the monopolization of jobs, in both the organization of the labor process and division of labor as well as who has access to what jobs. This work has largely been ethnographic, which provides us an opportunity to observe exactly how organizational actors lay claim to organizational resources. A team of sociologists organized around Anselm Strauss provided the earliest account of relational claims-making we have discovered. This study was the intellectual origin of the negotiated order perspective that Gary Alan Fine and Tim Hallet (2014) draw on in their analysis of organizational culture and that we draw on in conceptualizing organizational inequality regimes in Chapter 4 and claims-making in this chapter.

Two sociologists on that team, Leonard Schatzman and Rue Bucher, analyzed five hospital wards at a state mental hospital, uncovering variation across those wards in the organization of the division of labor to treat patients (Schatzman and Bucher 1964). Through field observations of work life on each ward and interviews with the mental health professionals on the wards, they uncovered that the variation in the way tasks were organized on each ward emerged through negotiation and claims-making from different work groups.

Prior to the mid-twentieth century, state-run mental hospitals in the United States were places where those who were deemed to be mentally ill were housed but given almost no therapeutic treatment. This custodial model of mental hospitals came under attack in the 1950s from a set of psychiatrists who favored organizing these institutions around promising therapeutic approaches. These psychiatrists began taking jobs in state-run mental hospitals. In the mental hospital Schatzman and Bucher studied, a new superintendent had been hired and was attempting to move the hospital toward psychiatric models of care. He hired young psychiatrists to run individual wards and gave them relative autonomy to organize care. Each ward consisted of a team comprised of a chief psychiatrist, a physician, a psychologist, a social worker, a nurse, a recreational or occupational therapist, and at least one psychiatric aide. The psychiatrist in chief would come into the ward with some *a priori* treatment ideology and then organize the team to implement it. This was not as simple as implementing a single coherent treatment approach. There were multiple new therapeutic approaches, often in conflict with treatment preferences held among other professionals on staff. Moreover, the chief psychiatrists generally had only vague notions of how to implement their therapeutic ideals. The organization of care tasks had to be negotiated among team members, and this involved both explicit and implicit claims-making to obtain control over tasks some members wanted to perform as well as the pushing of undesirable tasks onto others.

Ward B developed a system in which many of the day-to-day tasks were shared more or less equally across team members, much in the style of a worker cooperative. The nurse was initially tasked with overseeing all of the patients, providing surveillance on their daily activities and movements, and came to feel overworked. By rhetorically tapping into the prevailing treatment ideology, which focused on using professional staff to help patients understand their condition and co-develop solutions, she argued that all professionals should be involved in the daily management of patients. This was particularly persuasive to the social worker and psychologist whose professional orientations centered on hands-on patient care. Eventually, in a team meeting the nurse spearheaded a plan to divide the patients across herself, the social worker, the psychologist, and the physician, making individual professionals responsible for the surveillance, management, and treatment of a subset of patients rather than each being responsible for only a specific task across all patients. This required getting those professionals to agree to share tasks they once controlled, such as the physician, reluctantly, giving up his monopoly over drug dosages and psychotherapy techniques. Once in place, this system, which Schatzman and Bucher call the "representative system," meant that initial treatment plans were chosen by the person in charge of specific patients irregardless of professional certification. These decisions were then discussed and either ratified or modified by the others in regular team meetings. This was a radically democratic claims-making project, deconstructing the basic occupational categories.

To legitimate her claims to task-sharing, the nurse appealed to the chief psychiatrist's desire to build consensus within the team and to the social worker's and psychologist's professional orientations toward hands-on patient care. She then developed an alliance with the physician, who came to trust the nurse because she had a medical background he recognized and to which she could appeal in her claims. Once this system was in place, the sharing of tasks involving patient care grew over time.

The other wards were similarly rife with relational claims-making over the division of labor. In Ward E, noted for its lack of a treatment ideology or organizational coherence, the social worker claimed the right to organize small group therapy sessions. But his claim was rejected by the physician (in charge of the ward until a new chief psychiatrist was hired), who delegitimized the social worker as a "young novice." Once a chief psychiatrist was hired, power coalitions shifted, and the social worker was granted the capacity to perform this task. On Ward A, the social worker and psychologist developed an alliance with the chief psychiatrist to organize their work around a new treatment ideology which delegated treatment and management to patient peer groups, succeeding against the counterclaims of the nurse and psychiatrist who favored more expert-based treatment. In doing this, they stripped the psychiatrist of his traditional authority over patient disposition and drug prescriptions.

Importantly, all of these divisions of labor, because they were not yet institutionalized, were routinely up for renegotiations as new claims were made. Mobilized by a social worker, Ward B developed a shared division of labor and adopted a new treatment ideology shortly after Schatzman and Bucher left the field. This transformed what were semi-autonomous modes of treatment developed initially by the professional in charge of his or her patients into a form of treatment shared across all representative units known as patient government, in which patients came to be in charge of their own treatment.

Schatzman and Bucher demonstrate the negotiation of occupational boundaries within organizations, translating into organizational space the jurisdictional disputes that Andrew Abbott (1988) argues define professional occupations. Through analyzing the emergent divisions of labor across these five mental hospital wards, we see remarkable flexibility in the relational claims-making among these professionals over the day-to-day tasks of treating mentally ill patients. This dynamism was a result not only of this variable local claims-making but also of the weak institutionalization of mental health care in that historical moment.

More than 30 years later, Steve Vallas (2001; see also Vallas and Beck 1996) documented a similar form of relational claims-making in the negotiation over the organization of work tasks across four pulp and paper mills. Central to these dynamics were technological changes in the process of papermaking, changes that fundamentally reorganized how work was done.

Paper mills rely on continuous process methods in which chemicals are combined with wood chips to transform the wood chips into a liquid pulp. Traditional methods involved a skilled worker operating one of a series of machines through which this process took place. Workers became immersed in the workings of the machine, accumulating embodied knowledge about production. This knowledge resulted from a sustained physical interaction with the liquid product as it went down the line. Workers would use taste, touch, and smell to assess the quality of the product and what needed to be adjusted to improve it. Having this intimate, sensory connection with production empowered skilled workers to claim and maintain control over critical pieces of production and effectively monopolize key tasks within the paper mill division of labor.

Beginning in the early 1980s, a set of technological changes restructured the production process in these plants, involving the introduction of sensory equipment to test product quality, computer programs to control production, and mill-wide information systems for the collection and processing of data to monitor production. These forms of technology highlighted abstract reasoning skills over sensory skills, disrupting the status hierarchy that favored skilled workers and opening up space for new actors to claim centrality to the production process. The new actors who emerged were engineers who controlled the new computer technologies and the scientific language that interpreted data output. As part of this shift in local power, engineers actively deployed this scientific knowledge frame to redefine the highly accurate sensory data of skilled workers as error-prone and unreliable.

In claiming control over the production process, engineers crafted moral and cultural boundaries between engineers and skilled workers. Engineers defined skilled machine operators as creatures of habit resistant to any change, good or bad, and discursively positioned their own scientific knowledge as superior to the craft knowledge of machine operators. Engineers belittled manual workers' craft knowledge as "voodoo," "black magic," and "witchcraft." Says one process engineer,

> It drives me crazy when operators say you can't control the whole process with the computers. They'll stand there and scrape the stock with their thumbnail, and say they can tell me more about the stock [that way] than with the $40 million Accuray nuclear instruments we just installed. (Vallas 2001:23)

The workers responded to these claims by engineers with counterclaims to both undermine engineers and preserve control over production and their own dignity. Whereas engineers referred to workers' experiential knowledge as "black magic," workers derogatorily referred to engineers' scientific expertise as "book knowledge." Said one skilled worker mockingly, "You ask them what time it is and they tell you how to build a clock!" (Vallas 2001:26). Moreover, skilled workers are able to portray engineers as self-interested, more concerned with their careers than the company, claiming at times that engineers focus on less critical technical innovations over more practical improvements in production in order to climb the corporate ladder.

In the end, though, engineers' claims won the day. A powerful example of this is one of the more open contests between a skilled worker's "black magic" and the engineers' "book knowledge." J. W. was accustomed to the use of sensory knowledge to assess the quality of the pulp. One day he put his hands in the liquefied pulp as he had been accustomed to do even after computer technologies began to monitor the pulp quality, and he decided the end product was not good. He told his superintendent, who got engineers down to conduct lab tests. But the tests came back that the product quality was okay. Ultimately, the engineers won, and the plant continued production, affirming the newfound legitimacy of the scientific claims of engineers. In the long run it turned out that J. W. was right, and there was a chemical impurity. But by then the status order had been inverted, and a machine operator getting it right was not sufficient to undermine the legitimacy of engineers' newly institutionalized claims over control of production.

The legitimacy of engineers' claims transformed the division of labor. New positions such as "shift engineer" were created to move engineers closer to the production process, and the ratio of engineers to machine operators increased. At the same time a newfound emphasis on educational credentials, promoted by engineers, limited the internal mobility of machine operators, locking them out of higher-level managerial positions. The claims to scientific knowledge that engineers espoused combined with the new technological innovations catapulted engineers to a central role in production, relegating machine operators to the sidelines.

Negotiating Work–Family Relationships

Not only is there claims-making around occupational structures and divisions of labor, but who is acceptable in particular jobs and even who a suitable member of the organization is the product of relational claims-making. When Joan Acker introduced the notion of gendered organizations in 1990, she described seemingly neutral organizational roles and practices as actually gendered, and typically gendered male. The assumption of a male worker, one whose family responsibilities are taken care of by an invisible wife, made possible workplace claims on the hours and energies of all workers. The universal worker and the universal job Acker described as requiring 40 or more hours of work and admitted no employer responsibility for the rest of their employees' lives. Over the last quarter-century, this male breadwinner assumption has been challenged across the globe. The mobilization of claims to create family-friendly workplaces has occurred through many channels, including feminist movements, governments concerned with the health and fertility rates of their populations, unions protecting their increasingly gender-integrated membership, and, as the discourse became more legitimated, individual workers making individual claims for family-friendly work.

In the United States, prohibiting discrimination against pregnant women became one of the legal resources in support of these claims. A US-based analysis of pregnancy-related discrimination claims provides one window into this claims-making process. In many organizations, women—especially mothers—are seen as more family-oriented and less dedicated to the organization than either men or fathers (Correll et al. 2007). In fact, this claim is routinely used by managers to delegitimate pregnant women's discrimination claims. Reggie Byron and Vinnie Roscigno (2014) studied pregnancy discrimination claims made by women in Ohio to the Ohio Civil Rights Commission, focusing only on the claims of discrimination that the commission judged had merit. The historical clash between motherhood and employment that permeates the culture of many workplaces was evident in the language that employers developed in countering discrimination claims. One of the most common counterclaims of employers (60% of the time) is that the pregnant employee was fired not for being pregnant but for not being dependable, linking the firing to the culturally accepted trope of mothering getting in the way of loyalty to the organization. Such symbolic vilification of pregnant women led some managers to simply say their organization is too demanding for women with "family problems" (pp. 446–447). The social meaning operating in these discourses is that mothers are less worthy of employment opportunities than non-mothers. In addition, the external act of filing a legal discrimination complaint suggests that these mothers could not directly claim rights as employees within the organization but rather needed to enlist the state to defend against illegal discrimination.

Claims for family-friendly work have diffused across most high-income countries, but permissible discourses vary substantially depending on national cultural frames. In a remarkable piece of comparative organizational research, Alena Křížková and colleagues (2009) examine claims-making around work-family balance in three engineering workplaces in the Czech Republic and simultaneously in their parent firms in Germany, France, and Sweden. Being engineering firms, all six workplaces were predominantly male, and all except one had an explicitly masculinist culture. The researchers identified six unique influences on claims-making. The most local was simply the firm's experience with parents. In two of the Czech firms they studied, the workplaces developed corporate cultures in the context of very young workers. In these workplaces managers had no routines for dealing with requests for work time flexibility from new parents, and co-workers were hostile to new parents' requests for family accommodations. The family claim itself was not recognizable by managers and co-workers as no discourse to support it existed.

The degree to which individual actors were empowered to make claims was important as well. In the Czech Republic, workers were generally passive and made few claims, and managers did not even feel the need to inform them of their legal rights to parental accommodations. In the German and French cases, workers also made few claims as individuals, relying instead on their unions to negotiate collectively for them. In contrast, in Sweden individuals, both men and women, negotiated actively for family accommodations–such as long leaves, short leaves, part-time work, and telecommuting–that fit their family needs. In Sweden, individual agency was supported by a strong culture of non-discrimination, in which discrimination was conceptualized as failure to respond to individual needs around the family. This was in stark contrast to one Czech firm in which discrimination was defined as special favors for parents. The Swedish engineering firm was the only one in which masculinist local cultures were trumped by a commitment to the rights and needs of the individual and their families.

In France, a long-work hour culture prevented women and men from taking shorter hours or extended leaves. In the Czech Republic and Germany, a masculinist culture built with the assumption of mothers' total responsibility for the family predominated. In the Czech Republic, not only was this strong motherhood ideology built into workplace expectations but women were disciplined by co-workers and neighbors if they returned to work before their child was at least three years old.

Finally, the welfare state was a precondition for much of these other constraints on claims-making. The German and Czech welfare states were familial, providing long motherhood leaves and limited or no childcare facilities. The French and especially Swedish welfare states were more universalistic, providing men and women with similar levels of parental accommodation and plentiful high-quality childcare, even for very young children. A historical irony of the Czech case was that prior to the end of socialism in 1989, there was strong organizational and welfare support for women working and for high-quality childcare. With the repudiation of socialism, the Czech Republic embraced an extremely familial form of state-led capitalism that pushed women out of the workforce and into the home.

Křížková and colleagues use these six cases to highlight Joan Acker's (2006) notion that each organization is an inequality regime in its own right, generated by both internal relational dynamics and external environmental influences. This case is also important because it illustrates the nested nature of claims-making. Claims can be made by individual or collective actors, but the ability to conceptualize a claim and its legitimacy are functions of relational power, organizational habitus, and environmental resources, both cultural and structural.

Claims-Making and Wages

Contra the market mechanism so predominant in the social sciences, RIT views wage-setting and the resulting distributional inequality as an outcome of relational claims-making. One way we can see the centrality of claims-making in wage-setting is through examining organizations in different institutional contexts. Local organizational cultures are tied to institutional contexts, so the legitimacy of different claims should be shaped by the fields in which claims are made. We can see this by examining a cross section of organizations with different internal fields as well as observing organizations across national contexts.

Organizations vary a great deal in the degree of transparency, especially financial transparency. How much surplus is available for distribution is often a mystery to workers, but workers know more in some organizations than in others. Jake Rosenfeld and Patrick Denice (2015) compare organizations in terms of resource transparency. They focus on whether or not an organization discloses financial information to employees, arguing that disclosing financial information to employees should constrain managerial claims-making and potentially enhance the bargaining power of workers. If workers know how profitable their employer is, then it becomes harder for managers to claim they cannot afford raises. Using data on British organizations, they demonstrate that this is in fact the case. Organizations that disclose financial information pay higher wages. Their argument hinges on the legitimacy of claims under different organizational practices. In those organizations where firms disclose financial information, the workers' claim that the organization should be sharing profits is understood as more reasonable and the power of managers to undermine workers' claims is diminished.[2]

2. There is a long research record in labor economics showing that workers in more profitable companies get paid more (Card et al. 2018). This research is focused on the organizational resources available to be distributed. The transparency of these resources, that is, the information necessary to make a socially plausible claim, seems important as well.

Michael Schweiker and Martin Groß (2016) take a similar approach, comparing organizations, but link together the organizational and environmental fields. They argue that in firms with greater collective bargaining and seniority rights claims from workers in the bottom part of the income distribution will be legitimated, while high-skill firms with greater skill-enhancing technology and higher human capital will legitimate the claims of workers in the upper part of the income distribution. They focus on bonus payments in German firms and show that each of these organizational contexts shapes which claims are legitimated. High-salary employees gain larger bonus payouts when they are in high-skill firms that value their human capital, while unions and stable firms legitimate the bonus claims of lower-pay workers. Moreover, these claims are mediated by environmental contexts outside the firm. As the German economy became more financialized and globalized, the effects of union coverage and firm stability weakened, and so did bonus claims for workers at the lower end of the income distribution. During the same period, the skill-based claims of those at the top were strengthened. Here, then, we see the interaction between organizational and environmental contexts in legitimating the claims of employees to organizational resources.

We have done similar comparative organizational research focusing on how institutional environments shape claims-making by comparing organizations in different countries with different political economic institutions and by comparing organizations under distinctive institutional bargaining regimes within countries. We have found that where wage-setting institutions are centralized in government wage-setting boards, gender wage gaps are smaller and much of the existing inequality is linked to legitimated skill distinctions. For example, Australia, which has a history of centralized bargaining (the award system), has lower wage gaps between managers and core production workers than does the United States, which has never had centralized wage-bargaining (Tomaskovic-Devey et al. 2009). We find similar results in the immigrant–native wage gaps in Sweden. This inequality tends to be smaller in blue-collar jobs, where wages are negotiated in national industry agreements, but higher in white-collar jobs, where wage claims are made as part of individual negotiations (Tomaskovic-Devey et al. 2015a). Under centralized wage-setting, gender and citizen status are not legitimate status characteristics upon which to build a claim. As a result, other status characteristics such as skill and education become more powerful. And it is precisely around these status distinctions that we see organizational wage inequalities emerging under centralized wage-setting regimes. We also found that organizations facing stronger market pressures in their product markets tend to organize their inequality regimes around skill-linked resources (Avent-Holt and Tomaskovic-Devey 2010). Again, in such environments claims organized around status distinctions that are divorced from productivity concerns are less likely to be legitimated within the organization.

The research we have just reviewed does not directly observe the relational claims-making process. Instead, we observe a link between organizational contexts and practices and organizational wage inequalities and infer that the claims-making process must be going on. Nelson and Bridges' (1999) analysis of sex discrimination lawsuits more directly observes the claims-making processes. They find that at least some of the wage inequality between sex-segregated jobs in their cases is a function of male workers using their organizational power to capture higher wages. Part of this power can be explained in terms of the superior formal organization of men in the observed organizations. Men were more often represented by strong unions, giving them an organizational voice and the capacity to negotiate higher wages. When women were active in unions, they were often in segregated "female" unions that were not as well organized and were not seen as similarly legitimate negotiators, making them less socially persuasive. More generally, men's social status as men enhanced the likelihood that their claims were seen by other actors, management in particular, as legitimate. Gender even influenced the perceptions of labor supply and market value. When male workgroups made claims about the need for higher wages to match the market, those claims were routinely treated as plausible. In at least one case the claims were demonstrably false, but when made by organized male workgroups they were convincing enough to secure higher wages. Thus, men were more successful in claims-making because of both organizational sources of power such as unionization and the interactional power that comes from being male, and they were able to use both to secure greater organizational resources.

Caroline Hanley's (2014) study on the automation of white-collar work at General Electric (GE) makes even more visible the claims-making process as well as the birth of a discursive strategy that managers in many firms have come to rely on for capturing organizational revenue. Using historical documents from GE, including internal memos, strategic reports, and correspondences, Hanley isolates the transformation of claims around productivity and merit that developed as a result of the spread of computers and other information technologies at GE. During the 1960s, computers were introduced at GE, automating many clerical tasks such as record-keeping and, in doing so, reducing total labor costs. In part, this was a labor-saving management strategy, but GE's management also feared that the expansion of clerical work and the increasing number of clerical workers would provide fertile ground for future unionization. This case illustrates the discursive transformation of what counts as productivity in such a way as to enable managers at GE to make plausible claims on greater shares of organizational revenue and to limit the claims of their workforce.

GE engaged in a concerted effort to redefine the meaning of productivity by defining clerical automation as merely information-handling. In a 1959 internal report on the status of clerical automation, GE managers emphasized that "productivity is the effectiveness with which a business utilizes its human, capital, and land resources in creating goods or services to satisfy customer wants" (p. 412). As managers were the ones who organized how the business utilized these things, this redefined productivity as originating in the managers of the firm and away from the productivity of employees, enabling managers to define themselves as central to the productive efficiencies established by clerical automation and thereby claim the increased profits derived from it. This claims-making process defined both the meaning of technological changes and who should reap the benefits of technological innovations. Although Hanley does not discuss it, it seems likely to us that the valorization of managerial productivity was also likely accompanied by the abandonment of earlier forms of job skill ranking in which managerial pay, even top managers' earnings, would have been tethered to the pay and skill levels of lower-ranked workers.

Finally, we explore a case with even more direct observation of the claims-making process over earnings. Olivier Godechot (2016) conducted both participant observation and interviews with employees of financial service firms, revealing the role of claims-making over the skyrocketing revenue of financial firms that emerged in the era of financialization. With the very large volumes of money flowing into financial service firms available to be claimed, he focused in particular on the capacity of employees within these firms to claim this increasing revenue in the form of wages and bonus payments. While any number of actors in the division of labor—owners of capital, salespeople, traders, and back office staff including information technology specialists, those in human resources, accountants, and managers of various sorts—could plausibly capture some portion of these increased revenues, in the end it was the traders who reaped the most fantastic rewards. Why?

Traders positioned themselves, structurally and discursively, as the most central contributors to profit-making within the closely monitored income flows of their financial service firms. The basic accounting system of these firms counts profits after trades, and traders use this to point to themselves as the singular source of profits. While salespeople cultivate personal relationships with rich clients and control the flow of orders and investment activity that generates fees for the bank, their activity is not visible in the accounting system as generating profit; and this diminishes their capacity to make a claim on the new profits. Traders are able to point to tangible proof of their centrality to profit-making and claim to have "created value" for the firm and to thereby own "their profit." Godechot describes this as "opportunistic calculation" because this is the claim that has been legitimated in the past and so becomes a part of their discursive strategy of claims-making.

In addition to the visibility of traders as a source of profit in the accounting system, traders have what Godechot calls "hold-up" power within these organizations. Traders control specialized knowledge including algorithms, specialized trading routines, and specific know-how tied to complex trades. They can threaten to take this person-specific capital and leave for another firm if they do not get what they want. Thus, the organization of the labor process in financial service firms generates power for traders that they use to claim greater income. Salespeople have a similar hold-up power in that they can take clients with them to another firm, and this gives them an edge in claims-making relative to the back office. But their invisibility in the accounting system means they are not able to claim as much income as the traders.

While these cases demonstrate that relational claims-making is a central source of distributional inequality, it has to be borne in mind that jobs vary in the capacity for incumbents to negotiate their wages and thereby to engage in explicit individual-level claims-making of organizational revenue. In the standard economic model, all actors are expected to be income maximizers. Everyone should be negotiating explicitly or via changing exchange partners (e.g., jobs, suppliers, customers) to secure the best deal. But in the real world, some actors are allowed to negotiate, and others are not. This is often a function of the type of jobs we are qualified for and have applied to. Negotiating in product markets varies greatly across transactions as well. Business-to-business transactions often include negotiations over price and sometimes other aspects of the exchange, such as delivery time and product quality. Individuals and households are often more limited in their ability to negotiate.

Systematic research on the ability to negotiate as far as we can ascertain does not yet exist. We designed a few questions for a recent survey of German employees, which produced a window on the frequency of wage negotiations in that labor market. Among the 3,342 respondents to the survey, 56% reported that in their job it was possible to negotiate around salary.[3] Not surprisingly, the ability to negotiate was a function of the relative status of individuals. It was among higher-status workers—those with educational credentials, men, citizens, permanent contract workers—that the ability to negotiate wages was routinely associated with their jobs, and

3. Our calculations from the Expectations towards Economy and Society survey collected at Bielefeld University, Research Center SFB 882, From Heterogeneities to Inequalities. This is a random sample of employed Germans in 2014.

this negotiation was more likely to happen both at hire and during employment. For example, women were two-thirds less likely than men to be hired into jobs where negotiation was possible. When women were hired into such jobs, negotiation tended to happen only at hire but not later. People in precarious work—fixed-term temporary contracts, no contract at all, and part-time work—were typically excluded from any negotiation over wages. Even in jobs where negotiation was possible, women, immigrants, and precarious workers were unlikely to take advantage of the opportunity, perhaps self-censoring, perhaps bullied into concluding that their claims would not be credible in the locally negotiated inequality order.

Claims-Making and Dignity

Up to this point we have discussed mostly claims-making over material resources, but throughout the book we have argued that there are other resources that emerge within organizations that actors can make claims on. Perhaps the most fundamental non-material resource that we have discussed is dignity and respect from others in the organization. The centrality of dignity for organizational inequality is two-sided. It is both an organizational resource that can be claimed and central to the claims-making process itself.

In Chapter 2 we highlighted the important comparative ethnographic work done by Randy Hodson. In his workplace ethnography project, Hodson assembled all English-language ethnographies of workplaces that contained relational data on at least one workgroup. With a team of researchers, he then coded these qualitative accounts into quantitative data comparing workplaces. Hodson's signature work from this project was his 2001 book *Dignity at Work*, in which he found that workers everywhere expect to be treated with dignity. But he also found that access to dignity in interactions varied greatly across workplaces. This is not a surprising finding as inequalities in respect are both the result and cause of other inequalities. The denial of dignity is a denial of the right to make claims.

One of the key findings in *Dignity at Work* was the central role of management in denying dignity to their employees. Hodson points out many ways in which this happens, including outright abuse, attempts to overwork employees in order to exploit more value, failure to recognize excellence or quality work, and even failing to simply provide the tools needed to get work accomplished. Particularistic management, playing favorites, or discriminating against categories of workers demeans those not favored and violates their justice expectations. Sometimes managers are power-hungry and deny workers autonomy or participation in problem-solving. While all of these are relational accomplishments, grounded in managers' structural power, the denial of dignity, because it is not self-legitimating, also produces resistance. Workers react by withholding effort, playing dumb, violating procedures, gossiping and sowing discontent, sabotaging machines, going on strike, organizing unions, and quitting. Not all workers were similar in their ability to resist. Assembly-line workers typically were limited to reducing effort. Professional workers, in contrast, had the capacity to resist but often would not because as salaried workers their futures were too closely tied to the needs and whims of management. It was skilled craftworkers, who had the combination of skill and often union power and career independence, who engaged in the most effective and creative forms of resistance.

The denial of dignity does not always take the form of overt abuse, but sometimes it is lodged in behavior that fails to even recognize the efforts or existence of actors/employees. Kristen Lucas (2016) outlines one such case:

> Vonda accompanied the CEO as he escorted several VIPs around the corporate office to make introductions. "This is where Geoff would sit if he were here today," the CEO said and pointed to an empty chair in an office that belonged to a high level manager who was out for the day. The guests laughed and said "hello" to the empty chair. Then they lingered at the door for a couple more minutes as the CEO outlined Geoff's primary responsibilities and listed several notable accomplishments. Meanwhile Vonda—who did all the behind the scenes work of coordinating the visitors' meetings, meals, and more—was never introduced by name. Vonda was devastated. "I was standing right there with them the whole time and no one said hello. It was like I didn't matter, like I was an invisible nonentity. My boss made it clear that Geoff's empty chair is far more important than me."

It is easy from this example to see the gendered nature of claims and counterclaims to dignity within workplaces. The accomplishment of dignity, and its failure, is often linked to the status characteristics of actors and positions. Perhaps there is no greater example of the gendered nature of dignity at work than in claims around sexual harassment. In the fall of 2017, on the heels of the election of a US president who boasted about his own ability to sexually harass women, the prominent Hollywood producer Harvey Weinstein was forced out of his own company due to a multitude of public sexual harassment allegations (Twohey 2017). This set off a wave of women coming forward to make claims against men in both the media and politics for sexually harassing them. Congresspersons resigned, celebrities were fired, and conservative Alabama even elected a Democrat to the US Senate due to the accounts of sexual harassment (including pedophilia) that surrounded the Republican candidate (Burns and Martin 2017).

At the level of the political field, the discourse around sexual harassment rapidly shifted from routine skepticism silencing women's sexual harassment claims to a new default legitimacy of belief and moral outrage. After the national discourse shifted toward believing women's claims of harassment and abuse, at the Weinstein Company, the National Broadcasting Company, National Public Radio, and the *New York Times*, the organizational response was swift, with suspensions and firings of the accused, suggesting that some organizations were responding to this field-level shift in sexual harassment discourses.

And yet this shift is not universal. Investigative journalist Bernice Yeung has been following the stories of women, often immigrants, in working-class jobs for years, documenting patterns of sexual harassment that are likely to be untouched by these particular field-level, media-driven dynamics (Yeung 2016, 2017). Immigrant women working on farms and cleaning high-rise offices are relatively powerless in the face of much more anonymous bosses than Harvey Weinstein. The dynamics are the same. The managers have power over the paychecks and livelihoods of women and thereby can threaten and make sexual demands upon them. But Yeung notes that these women often are undocumented, almost always are dependent upon their next paycheck for their survival, and are typically physically isolated from others. These conditions increase the likelihood of assault and rape and decrease the likelihood of either the women making a claim against their assailant or anyone else believing the claim.

Sexual abuse at work is an assault on dignity embedded within a world of claims-making. When a manager demands sex from a subordinate, he is making a claim on her body, and her resistance is a claim for her own dignity and control over her body. For centuries the presumption was that men's claim to women's bodies was legitimate, and even in the post–civil rights workplace a woman's counterclaim against sexual abusers was treated as illegitimate. The post-Weinstein field-level transformation has legitimated some women's claims to sexual harassment in the workplace. But this, for the time being, is largely limited to relatively powerful women in white-collar occupations, perhaps inside nationally prominent workplaces. As Yeung points out, in the world of less powerful women in workplaces few others know about or see, women's counterclaims likely remain highly suspect and many, perhaps most, claims are silenced.

NEOLIBERALISM AND THE LEGITIMACY OF CLAIMS

One of the best ways to observe the link between organizational claims-making and resource distributions is to observe how changes in organizational environments are linked to organizational inequality regimes.

Beginning in the 1980s, a seismic shift in political economic institutions transformed the relationship between U.S. unions and management, firms and the state, and the role of free-market discourses in steering distributional claims. This transformation developed out of the crisis in profitability that began in the 1970s, which led to the emergence of the market fundamentalist cultural ideology often referred to as "neoliberalism." We focus here on two of the claims-making consequences of the two most powerful institutional power shifts: deunionization and financialization. Both have had a marked impact on who is able to claim income within organizations, delegitimating claims of workers and legitimating the claims of managers and capital.

Organized Labor

A classic form of claims-making within capitalist organizations operates through labor unions. The logic of unions is to bring together employees within an organization and give them an avenue to make claims on not just wages but also job security, the labor process, and the organization of work. In the United States, unions regularly negotiate with managers over wages and benefits, work hours and time off, work training and assignments, how many workers are needed for tasks, and technology adoption. Grievance procedures can also channel claims of managerial abuse of workers. Given this claims-making role vis-à-vis management, unionized workers regularly receive higher pay than similar non-unionized workers in other organizations. The United States has a low rate of unionization and laws that require unions to organize one workplace at a time. Many European countries have higher rates of unionization, and often negotiations take place at the industry or even national level. At the same time unions and union power have been declining in many countries but most precipitously in the United States (Western 1999).

As unions have declined across Western industrial democracies, their capacity to claim a greater organizational share of income has diminished apace. Tali Kristal (2010) finds this in her work looking at the national division of income between capital and labor. She finds that across most Western industrial democracies labor's share of income has declined and that the decline in the organizational capacities of unionized workers to claim that income is central to explaining this dynamic. As unions have declined in their claims-making capacities, more and more of the total economic surplus has moved into the hands of capital.

One of us (Avent-Holt 2017) brings this type of analysis to an organization level in work on the US airline industry. With archival and accounting data on airline firms going back to 1977, Avent-Holt examined the changes in firm revenue being captured as profits, top managerial salaries, and workers' wages/salaries. As shown in Figure 7.1, between 1977 and 2005 revenue going to worker wages in the average airline declined. Beginning in the 1990s revenue going to top managers in the form of salaries increased. All the while, profit remains a stable share of revenue, dipping toward zero during recessions and shooting up during growth periods in this business cycle-dependent market. The slow but steady decline of worker incomes is partly being redistributed to consumers in the form of lower ticket prices. However, since the 1990s some of this income was siphoned off by managers.

So, what transformed the distribution of income within airlines? As the once oligopolistic airline industry deregulated in the late 1970s and early 1980s, it became a much more competitive industry and firm resources declined. New airlines entered the industry and expanded into old, former monopoly routes, creating a competitive market in the early 1980s. In this context, airline management began searching for ways to reduce costs in order to survive. They cut the cost of airline travel to customers and began demanding wage and other cost savings from airline unions (Cappelli 1985; Northrup 1983).

Deregulation, market competition, and the threat of firm failure put unions in a weaker position relative to management and diminished their

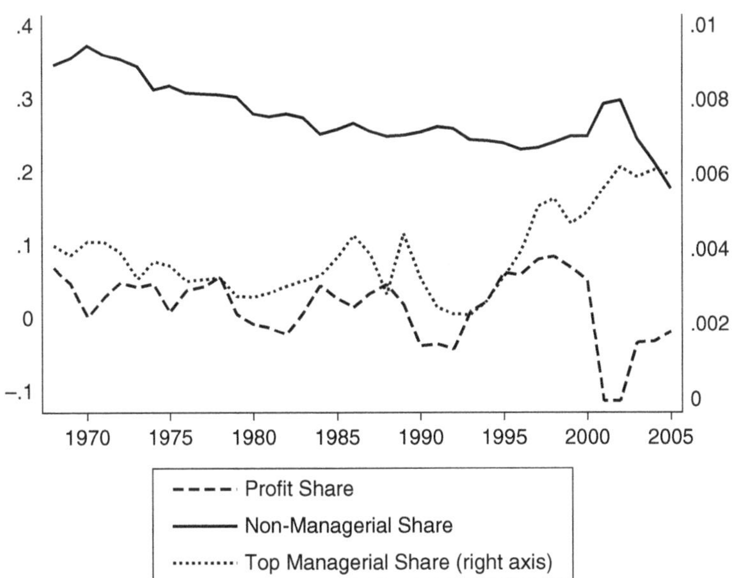

Figure 7.1 Capital, labor, and top managers. share of income in the airline industry, 1965–2005.

capacity to claim income streams. Contract renegotiations involved both direct cuts in wages and benefits and a renegotiation of the organization of work to reduce the income going to workers. American Airlines, for example, adopted a two-tier wage structure in which new workers would be hired at lower wages than current employees. Eastern Airlines, followed by Braniff, Republic, Western, United, and American, pioneered a "variable earnings plan" in which it included workers in profit-sharing in exchange for wage cuts in union contracts. Virtually all airlines began renegotiating union work rules. Management pushed for and eventually won a shift from three-person cockpits to two-person cockpits, despite union claims that these were less safe. Management at most airlines also succeeded in increasing the maximum flying times for pilots and flight crews. At the same time, airlines began to outsource many tasks, not only through partnerships with feeder airlines into their hub-and-spokes market structure but also by outsourcing reservations, check-in, baggage handling, and even, in some cases, airplane maintenance (Rieple and Helm 2008).

The weakening claims-making position of airline unions is most clearly evidenced in the declining power of the strike weapon after deregulation. Historically strikes are among the strongest and most consistent predictors of workers' share of income (Rubin 1986; Wallace, Leicht, and Raffalovich 1999; Kristal 2010), but among airlines strikes are no longer effective relational claims-making tactics. As Figure 7.2 shows, in the year of a strike, non-managerial employees' wages as a share of firm resources go up, but during the post-1980 period strikes actually had a long-term negative effect on workers' share of income. The strike weapon as a means to claim greater income streams for workers appears to have declined, perhaps even turning counterproductive.[4]

Thus, the capacity for workers to claim greater organizational resources has been undermined in the neoliberal era of market deregulation. Unions cannot provide the source of ever higher wages as their power to effectively claim incomes has diminished, just as their prevalence in the economy has shrunk.

Financialization

The increased importance of financial rather than production investments among non-financial firms has transformed the claims-making capacities of various actors as well. Industries where firms began accumulating profits

4. Although lacking firm-level data and the ability to capture the flow of money to other actors (capital, customers, managers), Jake Rosenfeld (2006) shows that in the United States the strike mechanism no longer produces higher earnings across multiple industries.

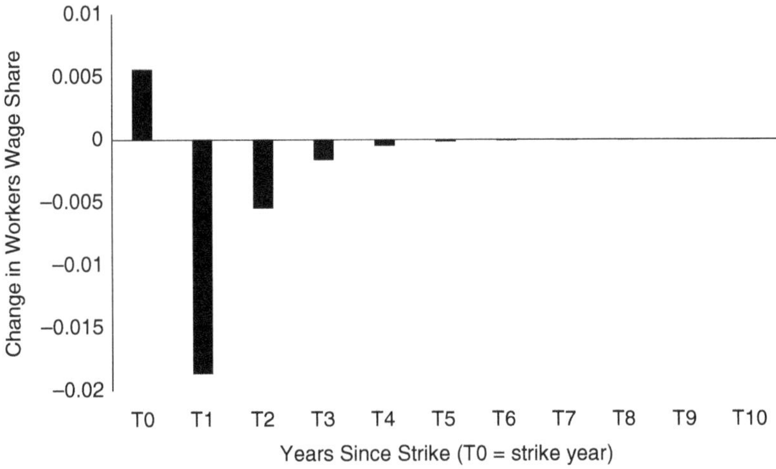

Figure 7.2 The influence of labor strikes in the airline industry on workers' wage share in years since the strike (Avent-Holt 2017).

through financial rather than production channels saw labor's share of income decline, a growth in income inequality among employees, and a greater concentration of income in the hands of top executives (Lin and Tomaskovic-Devey 2013). In such financialized industries executives are able to claim greater portions of organizational revenue for themselves, and workers are less able to do so. In both the airline and financialization cases we see that it is not just workers who make these claims but managers as well, redistributing income into their salaries or stock options. In linked work we find as well that firms that pursued financial, over production, investment strategies had strongly declining employment, had lower total organizational income, and paid less taxes. Profits distributed to the owners of firms' stockholders were not affected one way or the other, although the share of income going to the holders of corporate bonds soared. Financialization reduced economic activity, hurt most employees other than top executives, and benefited financial institutions and rich individuals who held corporate bonds (Tomaskovic-Devey et al. 2015b).

Claims-making took place on multiple levels. First, successful corporate CEOs were redefined from those who achieved a larger market share or more employees to those who delivered a higher return on investment and stock price. This shift legitimated the move away from production and toward financial speculation. Second, this move reduced the importance of production workers' employment and wage claims and encouraged employment downsizing announcements as a strategy to boost stock prices. Finally, the move from production to return on equity metrics for corporate success encouraged firms to shift from stock equity to corporate debt as a source of capital investment. Stockholders' claims on the surplus of firms come into play only after workers and all suppliers of goods and services in production are paid. Debt holders, in contrast, are more akin to suppliers, in this case of capital, and get paid out of revenue, not surplus. Thus, the shift from stock to debt financing reordered capital claims so that capital owners' claims on surplus were temporally equivalent to those of employees.

Both financialization and deunionization are components of the neoliberal remaking of the United States, and more generally of the political economy of many other nations.[5] Understood within RIT, these should be thought of as institutional shifts that reorganize power relations within organizational fields, delegitimating the capacity of workers to claim income and control their work, while enhancing the legitimacy of top managers and capital to claim income and pursue their private agendas. Market fundamentalist ideas and policies have increased income inequality through transforming the claims-making capacities of actors.

MOBILIZING CLAIMS IN CULTURAL CONTEXT

We end this chapter with a short discussion of the role of culture in the generation of inequality. Our model of claims-making sees cultural discourses as central to the mobilization of claims. However, we also see cultural claims as filtered through local relationships and mutable in local organizational context.

In a recent high-profile article, Michelle Lamont, Stefan Beljean, and Matthew Clair (2014) argued that social scientists should see culture as the essential interactional basis of inequalities. Given the role we place on an organization's culture in legitimating claims, we obviously see merit in this argument. At the same time, we think that cultural analyses of inequality must be located concretely in specific relational contexts to be plausible, linking culture to the local negotiated order of organizations. Cultural ideas do not simply flow from societies through people's heads and then into their behaviors. Culture is not intracranial but interactional and organizational.[6]

In RIT, key analytic roles are given to power and to claims-making. Power is located in the relationships among actors, positions, and organizations.

5. In many other countries, neoliberalism is referred to as the "Washington consensus," to underline that this model has been both exported from and to some extent enforced via institutions influenced, if not controlled, by the United States (Babb 2013; Stiglitz 2005).

6. We provide a more formal development of this position in Tomaskovic-Devey and Avent-Holt (2014).

Claims are attempts by actors to access organizational resources like money or power or respect. The legitimacy of claims is tied to the relational power and status of actors and cognitively lodged in routine practice and organizational habitus. Power and claims, in our view, are located not in societies or cultures or individuals but in relationships and organizations in particular historical moments and institutional contexts. Cultures must flow through these relational processes of power and claims to have their influence on inequality.

This does not mean societal cultural discourses are unimportant. Just as categorical distinctions become linked to cultural stereotypes cementing inequality, actors mobilize cultural frames to enable some actions and block others. Culture in action legitimates power and claims, but culture is plastic to context, enacted in relationships, organizations, and the historical/institutional context. We end this chapter by looking comparatively at how a single cultural frame, the value of diversity, evolved within the institutional logics and emergent discourses in three quite different organizational fields. The lesson we highlight is that local relational context steers cultural frames—sometimes in quite unexpected directions—and provides a local cultural context in which claims on organizational resources are constructed and legitimated.

The civil rights movement utilized and expanded the democratic cultural frame of rights and reparations to African Americans and eventually to other subordinate status groups. African Americans were framed as having rights to equal opportunity in access to employment, school admission, housing, and public accommodations. Organizations, particularly schools and workplaces, responded by practicing, and in some cases were mandated to practice, affirmative action as a form of local reparation for historical exclusion. By the late 1970s, affirmative action and quotas began to be challenged in the courts. In case after case, the US Supreme Court limited affirmative action and banned numerical quotas, but affirmed the idea that diversity, because it enhanced learning, was an acceptable criterion to take into account in college admissions. Corporations adopted the same rationale, building a business case for diversity that emphasized the economic value of diverse viewpoints for problem-solving and diverse workers for reaching diverse customer bases.

The language of diversity has transformed rights claims into a liberally endorsed, white-friendly cultural frame that obscures categorical subordination in favor of a narrative of cultural equivalence. Ellen Berrey in *The Enigma of Diversity* (2015) presents three cases studies on the use of cultural discourses around diversity in three quite distinct organizational fields. These cases highlight how societal cultural frames evolve to fit local relational claims-making. The three cases studies—student admissions at the University of Michigan; neighborhood development in Rogers Heights,

Chicago; and diversity management at the "Star" Corporation—all share a focus on the process and context of diversity discourses. In all three cases diversity talk eventually steers actors away from recognizing racial rights claims. While there is a similarity in outcomes, there is not in process. By looking across cases and within cases over time, Berrey shows that diversity discourses are used by actors in different contexts to do different work. The cultural diversity frame is transmitted and transmuted through local social relationships.

Following the Supreme Court's 1978 *Bakke* decision banning quotas but endorsing diversity in college admissions, diversity discourses were defended as producing a better elite education by many selective admission universities, including the University of Michigan. In the late 1990s the University of Michigan was sued for reverse discrimination in two cases—one focused on undergraduate admission and the other on admission to the law school. To fight the lawsuit, the university made claims both internally to the organization and externally in its field. Internally Michigan crafted a well-scripted celebration of the role of diversity in producing excellence in education, which was repeated verbatim by university spokespeople to internal and external audiences and subsequently adopted by most student groups. A more radical student group that tried to make claims based on rights was marginalized in the debate, and a right-wing student group adopted the diversity discourse to participate in the debate—although it emphasized the need for political, rather than racial, diversity.

Externally, Michigan and its allies mobilized dozens of friend-of-the-court amicus briefs from diverse external constituencies to defend the concept of diversity. This cultural discourse was produced organizationally and included an internal framing by elites to produce local legitimacy and an external mobilization of allies to produce legal legitimacy. Eventually, the Supreme Court ruled in favor of Michigan's law school admission process, which looked qualitatively at the whole application package, including the value of bringing diversity to campus, but against the undergraduate college's practice of awarding admission points based on race.

In the second case, the Chicago neighborhood of Rogers Heights, the diversity cultural frame was used to make claims on the use of housing stock. The replacement of poor minority residents and low-income rental housing with condominiums for better-off Chicagoans was justified by the need to diversify the neighborhood. Diversity was presented as a morally good principle. In this case the diversity frame was used to legitimate gentrification. The neighborhood needed income diversity—more high-income people—and poor black neighborhoods were examples of segregation. Diversity frames justified the claims of urban developers on profitable real estate. Rights-based claims by and for long-term poor neighbors were marginalized.

This claims-making process again happened through a set of organizationally embedded actors. Although the neighborhood was predominantly made up of renters, the alderman who controlled real estate variances was strongly connected to one group representing real estate developers, another group representing predominantly white local businesses, and a third group representing predominantly white homeowners. A fourth group of social service agencies became captured by the language of diversity in much the same way that the University of Michigan captured most of its internal constituencies by staying on message, and again the actors mobilizing rights claims failed, mobilizing a weaker cultural frame that few could recognize through the diversity haze.

In the corporate case, the affirmative action expectations that arose for federal contractors out of the civil rights movement and subsequent federal enforcement efforts were displaced in human resources (HR) practice by the business case for diversity. Diversity it turns out is morally good in the shareholder value society but only because it is good for sales and profits. But the discourse in practice is quite a bit more narrowly deployed than the "good for business frame." It is "tethered" to two corporate goals. The first is to produce sufficient demographic diversity among top executives to prevent corporate embarrassment, in an era when all-white-male optics lack legitimacy. The second is to prevent too much turnover among targeted "diversity" groups that would make the crafting of minimally diverse leadership teams impossible.

At the Star Corporation, the entire language of diversity was decoupled from any discourse on discrimination or rights. It was even decoupled from federal affirmative action compliance and from most of the workforce. The 70% of the workforce who were not in managerial or professional jobs were also not in the organizational regions in which the diversity cultural tool was deployed. The key actors here are internal to the organization—diversity HR managers, line managers, and top executives. The language of diversity as productivity-enhancing was present. However, the goal was much more narrowly framed, and no one, except perhaps a few naive HR managers, actually believed the cultural frame that diversity was good for business. Executive diversity, however, was necessary for the corporation's external legitimacy.

What do we learn from these three cases? Cultural objects are deployed discursively to both enable and disable courses of action. The production of claims happens by mobilizing cultural objects—like diversity—in specific organizational fields of power. These fields are both the internal social relationships among actors in organizations and the larger fields of power in which organizations are embedded. These fields, both internal to the organization and external, shift over time, changing the meaning of cultural objects and the social practices to which they are tethered. These are the generic processes. On the other hand, the specifics, how diversity discourse is framed, mobilized, and contested, like action more generally, are profoundly local.

CONCLUDING THOUGHTS

Claims-making is the proximate process through which exploitation and closure mechanisms are enacted and inequalities in access to organizational resources are formed. Claims are discursive moments in which divisions of labor, criteria for organizational membership and job assignment, and reward systems and their beneficiaries are developed. Older claims-making processes become cemented into the habitus of organizational divisions of labor, status hierarchies, taken-for-granted practices, and the local rules of the game. They become "right and proper," as institutional theorists like to say, and so are taken as legitimate. Plausible cultural framing and status-based power within an organizational inequality regime drive discursive legitimacy. When the legitimacy of claims fails, conflict-based power—whether executive authority or employee resistance—emerges as a claims-making strategy. These processes, like categorization, exploitation, and closure, are always embedded in both organizational and institutional contexts. The processes are generic and widespread; the social content is historical and local.

8

Organizational Surplus and Rising Inequality

People of the same trade seldom meet together, even for merriment and diversion, but the conversation ends in a conspiracy against the public, or in some contrivance to raise prices.

Adam Smith ([1776] 1994, book I, chap. X)

These companies–Apple, Amazon, Facebook, Microsoft and Alphabet, Google's parent–have created a set of inescapable tech platforms that govern much of the business world. The five have grown expansive in their business aims and invincible to just about any competition. Their collective powers are a source of pride and fear for Americans. These companies thoroughly dominate the news and entertainment industries, they rule advertising and retail sales, and they are pushing into health care, energy and automobiles.

Farhad Manjoo (2016b)

Recently, five information technology (IT) firms have been dubbed the "Frightful Five" because of their global market domination (Manjoo 2016a, 2016b). They include Amazon, Apple, Facebook, Google, and Microsoft. Amazon controls 78% of all e-commerce.[1] Apple dominates the mobile phone and music streaming markets, as well as the market for smart phone and tablet applications. Facebook dominates Internet advertising and, in some dimensions, human social relationships. Ninety-three percent of all social media users in the United States are on Facebook, 73% of them return at least once a day, and they average 31 hours a month on the application. Google dominates Web search and online advertising. Google's search engine is so ubiquitous that it has become a verb: "google it." Google and its parent company, Alphabet, also own the Android operating system, which powers almost half of all smart phone and tablet devices. The other half is controlled by Apple. And finally Microsoft's operating system runs more than 90% of desktop and laptop PCs around the world. Most of the

1. Market share and usage estimates in this paragraph were produced by Verto Analytics and downloaded from their website on August 8, 2017 (http://www.vertoanalytics.com).

remainder are Apple machines with Apple operating systems. Amazon, Microsoft, and Alphabet are also emerging as dominant in data storage and cloud computing.

Each of these five companies has its hands in lots of other aspects of the IT market, but their dominance of these specific platforms gives them what scholars have begun to refer to as "network" power, referring to the feedback loop—as more people use an information platform, it draws others in, cementing the power of that platform in the market (Choudary, Van Alstyne, and Parker 2016). Tech writer Farhad Manjoo dubbed these firms the "Frightful Five" because this network-based power has the potential to give fairly unlimited market power to these companies. They may compete against each other for pride of place in the IT market, but all other IT and non-IT companies need to adopt their software or hardware or advertising or social network strategies to the software platforms owned by these five. By virtue of their user base, these companies also have more data on the population of users than any new entrants to the market. Whether or not that remains the case probably depends on governments' reactions to platform closure and their exploitation of market power.

In their relatively short lives, these companies have generated some of the richest people on the planet. The richest person in the world in 2017 was Bill Gates, the founder of Microsoft, and he was worth an estimated $86 billion. Number three was Jeff Bezos (Amazon, $73 billion). Mark Zuckerberg (Facebook, $56 billion) was number five, while Sergey Brin and Larry Page split the Google wealth at $40 billion each. Steve Jobs (Apple) died in 2011 with an estate worth only $10 billion. His heirs now have a fortune worth $20 billion (*Forbes* 2017).

That a few companies dominate a market is nothing new. General Motors, Ford, and Chrysler dominated the US auto market for decades. Before there were the Frightful Five, there was Microsoft alone dominating the personal computer (PC) operating system market, and before that there was "Big Blue." IBM, nicknamed "Big Blue" because of the color of its dominant product, the IBM 360, controlled the market for mainframe computers between the mid-1960s and the late 1980s (at which point mainframes were replaced by desktops and distributed computing). Eventually, General Motors, Ford, and Chrysler were forced to compete with car companies from around the world, as well as other modes of transportation. What is different about the Frightful Five is that they control not merely markets but platforms. Even in monopoly markets, if prices get too high, consumers can switch products, what economists talk about as *substitution effects*. Since the platforms have already rolled up the customer base and new IT companies must use the platforms or operating systems owned by the Frightful Five, it is difficult to see a market solution to their considerable closure-based market power. This does not preclude other limits on this power. Political regulation of how they do business, limiting these firms' control over other firms' use of their platforms, could mitigate their market power. Governments could also choose to treat them as "natural monopolies," as the US government once treated the airline industry, and regulate pricing to limit the exercise of monopoly power.

The Frightful Five make clear that the processes we have been developing in the preceding chapters, relational claims-making, social closure, and exploitation, impact the flow of resources not merely within organizations but also between them. When a firm or group of firms has closure-based market power, it can set prices, exploiting both customers and suppliers. It can also use its market dominance to make claims on the resources of other organizations.

One of the consistent findings in the literature on income distributions is that larger firms and firms in dominant market positions are more likely to pay their workers' wages higher than workers with similar skills in less resource-rich organizations. Economists refer to this as *rent-sharing* (Katz and Summers 1989). Economists have long documented rent-sharing: industries and firms with rising profits tend to subsequently raise wages (e.g., Blanchflower et al. 1996; Mahmood and Heyman 2009). All workers, however, do not share these rent-driven resource flows equally. Lena Nekby (2003), for example, using matched employer–employee data for Sweden, finds that rising profits raise the wages of both men and women but that men receive about a 30% larger share of the rent. In addition, rent-sharing is more generous with high-wage workers, and it is here that she finds that women are most heavily penalized. Thus, while resource flows influence income, workers with more powerful skill, positional, and cultural claims on income benefit the most.

Of course, there are actors other than workers and owners who can mobilize claims on this above-market surplus. Suppliers can raise their prices if they are powerful, and customers may pay less in competitive markets or when they are the only buyer and can insist on lower prices (Burt 1983). Realized organizational resources are therefore the result of the relative power of customers, suppliers, taxing authorities, and investors to siphon off income, in addition to internal organizational efficiencies and claims-making in production.

Differences in the volume of resources available at the firm level to be claimed by stakeholders generate a substantial portion of total inequality in any population. In fact, much current research suggests that increased variability across firms in their average wage rates and profitability is a key driver of rising national inequality in multiple countries. In the US case the best estimates are that virtually all of rising earnings inequalities since 1980 are produced by shifts in the organization-level size of the pie (Song et al. 2016). Our research suggests that wage polarization between firms can be found in many high-income countries (Tomaskovic-Devey et al. 2017).

Organizations are social inventions designed to absorb resources from their environment, employing those resources to motivate members to do the work necessary to accomplish organizational goals. In this chapter, we refer to this process of resource absorption as *resource-pooling*, although it sometimes goes by other names such as *value added, surplus generation*, and *cash flow*. In Chapter 3 we focused on this process of generating and capturing organizational resources as a key constraint on the operation of claims-making, exploitation, and closure. There, the focus was on the combination of internal social relations in the production process and external market power to condition the volume of organizational resources that stakeholders could make claims on, close off access to, and exploit from one another. Most of the examples in the intervening chapters focused on these processes. Our argument in this chapter is that much of the rise in income and wealth inequality in the United States—and in many other countries—since the late 1970s can be traced back to the rise in firms' market power. We understand this rise of market power as a process in which dominant firms capture national and global income through the key processes of social closure and exploitation in product and service markets, as well as relational claims-making vis-à-vis the state, other organizations, and households. As in other claims-making processes, the relative power and status of firms are crucial to the claims-making process.

MARKET POWER

In Chapter 4 we outlined the role of internal production regimes in the generation of organizational surplus. Of course, internal productivity alone does not govern the flow of resources into organizations. Organizational income streams are also a function of the power of firms in their organizational environments and the social relations between suppliers, customers, and the state. Organizations accumulate income based on the sale or provision of goods and services, so the organizational surplus is as much about the value organizations can sell their products for as it is about the efficiencies produced by people within the organization. While in the neoclassical economic model the price of goods is assumed to be fully disciplined by market competition, and therefore to only reflect the value added in production, this competition is rarely, if ever, fierce enough to generate such an outcome.

Institutional economists have long recognized that market competition should be treated not as an assumption but rather as a variable (e.g., Scherer 1970), and economic sociologists have pointed out that market competition (or lack thereof) is an institutional accomplishment that can take multiple forms with multiple consequences (Fligstein 2002). Real markets are organized through social relations of power, networks of exchange in which some actors exert greater control over prices and therefore shape the capacity of organizations to accumulate (or lose) resources in their environment. In addition, powerful firms attempt to adjust, and often succeed at adjusting, the basic legal and regulatory environment to favor themselves or their market (Mizruchi 2013).

In the early 1980s organizational sociologist Ronald Burt (1983) suggested that market power should be thought of as network power in a field of actors. Using industry data, he showed that industries that trade with industries (as suppliers and/or customers) that have few competitors have lower profits. The less market competition in an industry, the greater the power to extract resources from both suppliers and customers. Even more interestingly, he showed that this was a network phenomenon that rippled across the economy, treating market power as an income-extraction mechanism from the entire exchange network. At about the same time, Marxist sociologist Luca Perrone (1983) demonstrated that these same network dependencies generate higher wage gains for striking unions. Thus, power in a network of market relations can be used by actors within the firm to claim greater gains for themselves, shifting some of the surplus captured in market relations onto powerful actors within powerful firms. Burt focused on capital and Perrone on labor, but in our model both are stakeholders with potential claims on the resulting market power–supplied flow of organizational resources.

Thinking of market power as a network of relations has crystallized into a new hybrid science called *econophysics*, which marries the network models from sociology to the mathematics of physicists. A series of papers (Vitali, Glattfelder, and Battiston 2011; Battiston et al. 2012a, 2012b) used data on co-ownership of all global corporations in 2007 to establish that the entire contemporary global economy can be described as one big co-ownership network (network below on left). They go on to identify 22 financial firms that have the most ties to each other and to the other global firms, making them the most central players in the global economy (see Figure 8.1). These 22 firms are the powerful actors in the earlier network models of Burt and Perrone and are so central to the trade network that almost all firms that wish to participate in global trade have to go through one or more of these financial institutions to do so. In simulations in which a single firm's revenue flow was reduced, even relatively small shocks to any of the 22 systemically

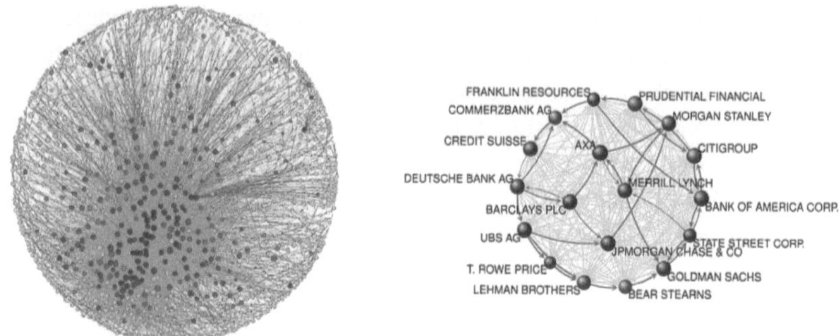

Figure 8.1 The 2007 network structure of global firms defined in terms of ownership/debt stakes in each other. Left picture is the global network. Right picture is structurally central core firms (Vitali et al. 2011).

important financial firms had the potential to destabilize the entire world economy—which is, of course, exactly what happened a year later, producing the deepest global recession since the 1930s.

Market power, like power within production, is a relational phenomenon, operating through networks of opportunities and constraints on a firm's capacity to extract resources from its environment. Resource extraction requires forming social relations with the state, suppliers, customers, and/or other producers to limit competitors' access to markets. Just as we can describe various actors as relatively powerful within firms, firms and their customers should be thought of as relatively powerful in their markets.

Importantly, this should be understood not as an aberration from normal market activity but as something that firms routinely seek out in the course of their normal business. Firms desire to avoid, not engage in, competition with other firms and develop business strategies from seeking market niches to patent protection to collusion as a means to protect themselves from market competition (Baker and Faulkner 1993; White 1981, 2002). To the extent that market power is a product of property rights and barriers to entry, it should be thought of as the product of closure processes. When that power is used to extract higher prices from customers or lower prices from suppliers, exploitation is in play. When powerful firms lobby Congress to adjust regulations in their favor, they are undertaking a claims-making process. Economic sociologists have stressed status (Podolny 2010) and normative organizational structures (e.g., Cohen and Haveman 2016) as influencing price, access to capital, and economic survival. These mechanisms behave in the same way that status does in claims-making—they support or erode the legitimacy of claims on resources from the environment.

There are a variety of mechanisms through which firms can structure networks of social relations that enable them to extract greater revenue from their environment. We present a series of organizational studies to highlight how organizations manage relationships in their field, including relationships with competitors, suppliers, buyers, and the state, to limit competition and funnel income to themselves. We then detail how these resource-pooling processes shape organizational inequality dynamics.

CLOSURE, EXPLOITATION, AND POWER IN MARKETS

Market closure is one of the basic sources of economic rent in conventional economic accounts. In these accounts, efficient markets should in theory be characterized by open competition, with many sellers competing for sales to many discerning, price- and quality-sensitive customers. Many markets are not open in this idealized sense, and it may be that smart capitalists are always in some sense trying to get out of competitive markets. The trend in the United States has been toward less competition in markets. This is true in many industries, including agriculture, financial services, and hospitals. As a result, profits in the economy have become concentrated in fewer, more powerful firms.[2] When firms get big and rich enough, there is a political feedback loop in which market power generates wealth and prestige, which can be brokered into political power. That power can then be used to influence the institutional rules for the firm's market and tax rates on its expanding profits.

Relationality and Market Closure in Biotech Innovation

In the late 1990s there was an explosion of science-based innovation fueled by new biologically based technologies. The field, which came to be called *biotech*, generated new agricultural, industrial, and especially pharmaceutical products. The organizational problem was how to both encourage and capture innovation. Patents on inventions and production processes were the main closure mechanisms for securing property rights to these innovations.

2. A good summary of this trend can be found in the 2016 report of the president's Council of Economic Advisers, *Benefits of Competition and Indicators of Market Power*, which can be found here: https://obamawhitehouse.archives.gov/sites/default/files/page/files/20160414_cea_competition_issue_brief.pdf. The report is useful for both documenting the increased concentration of economic power in most industries in the United States and the implications for rising inequality between capital and both labor and consumers. It also illustrates the continued naive embrace of market competition as an antidote to market power among economists.

Studying the rise of biotech, a team led by Woody Powell, which included Laurel Smith-Doerr, discussed in the Chapter 6 case on PhD scientists' careers, adopted an explicitly relational view of innovation and organizational strategy (Powell, Koput, and Smith-Doerr 1996; Powell et al. 2002, 2005). The biotech field included university laboratories, biotech research-intensive start-up firms, and traditional large pharmaceutical and chemical firms that could move the new products to market. They found that innovation in this field required a network structure that crossed firms, mostly among the biotech research-intensive start-ups. Scientists moved frequently across firms, sometimes between biotech firms and university labs and sometimes between biotech firms and the large pharmaceutical or chemical companies (but rarely between universities and the large firms). The invention of new products and production processes required fluid network cooperation within and between organizations. There was remarkably little organizational closure in employment.

At the same time, the ability to capture the vast new streams of income associated with these innovations required considerable closure around ownership of the biotech start-ups and biotech patents. Initially, biotech patents came out of university laboratories. Universities changed their employment relationships with professors, insisting that the university, like private sector firms, would own the patents associated with discoveries or manufacturing processes emanating from university labs. This encouraged scientists to leave their labs and found new firms to develop and capture the swelling income streams flowing toward biotech innovations. That is, as universities made claims on the income streams derived from scientific innovations within their walls, scientists moved themselves outside those walls in order to secure their claims on the fruits of their innovations.

Venture capital firms played a central role in providing the initial capital behind these externalizing biotech start-ups, making many bets on future innovation success and then having a claim on the tidal wave of money associated with new products. In addition, pharmaceutical firms, especially those facing revenue declines associated with impending loss of patent protection over older products, would pay top dollar to acquire the biotech firm and its patents from the venture capital firms and initial scientist owners. The top 10 most profitable pharmaceutical companies in the world earn over 70% of their profits from acquisitions of other firms that actually developed the new drug (Behnke et al. 2014).

Universities trying to capture the value being produced by their scientists faced limited success but propelled new alliances between scientists and venture capital. Venture capital's strategy was to create ownership-based rights to products even before they had been invented. Large pharmaceutical companies came later, achieving patent and product-based monopolies after the inventions were protected by patents for drugs with no or limited competition in fighting specific diseases.

Victor Roy and Lawrence King (2016) provide a case study of one drug and show how this process works. Sofosbuvir produces a 90% cure rate for people suffering from hepatitis C. Hepatitis C is a common disease among chronically ill people, including those with HIV/AIDS and injection drug users. From 2% to 3% of the world's population, about 3 million of whom live in the United States, are infected with hepatitis C (Averhoff, Glass, and Holtzman 2012). A biotech firm, Pharmasset, was founded by scientists originally based at Emory University in Atlanta, Georgia. The initial science that made sofosbuvir possible was funded by the US and German governments. The lab that was spun off as the new biotech firm Pharmasset had received its funding from the US National Institutes of Health and the Veterans Administration. Using venture capital and at later stages a stock offering, Pharmasset invested $271 million in drug development, $62 million of which went into the development of sofosbuvir and taking it through two of four stages of clinical trials. At this point, Gilead Sciences, one of the most successful biotech companies in the world, acquired Pharmasset and sofosbuvir for $11 billion and spent an additional $880 million to get sofosbuvir and at least one other failed product through the next two stages of clinical trials. Thus, while the cost of producing sofosbuvir was less than $1 billion, Gilead Sciences was willing to pay 10 times that to acquire the patents on a drug that would have a virtual monopoly for treating 185 million people worldwide. In the first 30 months on the market selling sofosbuvir for $1,000 a pill Gilead Sciences realized $40 billion in revenue from sofosbuvir and a spin-off drug called Harvoni.

A set of relationships made this drug discovery possible. The most important among these were initial investments by government agencies in the United States and Germany, lab science at a major American university, and the final science at a biotech start-up. The start-up scientists and their venture capital backers made a tremendous profit from ownership of the patent. Gilead, which grew quickly into one of the most profitable pharmaceutical companies in the world, however, realized the biggest enduring gains as it bought monopoly rights to cure hepatitis C. Thus, closing off access to the new drug through a patent-driven monopoly secured market power to price its drugs.

There are two further national institutional dimensions to this story. Because countries vary greatly in their intellectual property laws and in the freedom they grant drug companies to set prices, Gilead licensed sofosbuvir to other companies to sell at less than $1,000 dollars a pill in other countries. In this way, Gilead could capture lower profits in those markets, rather than losing its patent rights in local courts (Harris 2014). Finally, Gilead relocated its corporate headquarters from the United States to Ireland in order to avoid higher US taxes on its enormous profits.

The relational architecture of the biotech industry elucidated by Powell and his colleagues then helps us make sense of the monopolization of drug patents. The patent is the most valuable closure mechanism around the revenue stream, providing a virtual monopoly on treating particular medical conditions. A set of personnel relationships between universities, scientists, and biotech start-ups generates the potential for monopolization through patenting. This relationality in the biotech field is underscored by market institutions that structure drug development through a patenting system that enables and encourages market closure and legitimates monopolistic claims on income streams from pharmaceutical innovations.

Institutionalizing Airline Monopolies

Sociologist Neil Fligstein has been central to developing a theoretical understanding of how firms shape their institutional fields in concert with the state and other market actors. Fligstein (2002) points out that the market itself is not simply the place where buyers and sellers meet but rather a field where institutional rules are produced to define the market. Intellectual property, labor, and contract law; health, licensing, and product quality regulations; and socially legitimate business models all define who can operate in any given market, how goods or services are produced, and if that market can even exist at all. In this way markets are fields, in the same way we used *field* earlier in the book as the set of relevant actors and institutions, in which a set of political and cultural rules define who can operate and in what capacities. It is through a process of constituting the rules that define markets where actors most effectively lock out potential competitors.

The market for air travel in the United States provides a case in point.[3] The US airline industry barely existed before World War I, but the war-making needs of the US government led it to invest in the nascent aircraft technology. As the war came to a close, it became clear that these machines had civilian uses. The industry was initially organized around transporting mail for the federal government, although by the 1930s a very small luxury travel market had emerged.

In 1925 the US Congress passed the Kelly Airmail Act to enable the post office to contract its airmail service through a competitive bidding process to private airlines. This established a competitive, unregulated market

3. This case study is based on the history of airline regulation and deregulation found in Avent-Holt (2012).

for contracts to transport mail. During the mid-1930s the industry began experiencing declining profits and high rates of firm failure. It was then that the organization of the airline industry as an unregulated, competitive market was questioned by multiple actors in the field.

The competitive bidding process came to be blamed for the industry's decline. Politicians, bureaucrats, economists, industry analysts, and the airlines themselves all argued that unregulated competitive bidding was creating "destructive competition." Bidding wars between airlines were argued to produce a downward spiraling of prices, and there was concern that this would leave only one or a few firms to survive and monopolize the market in the long run. The alternative of state management of competition in the industry emerged as a solution. Under such a regime, competition would be allowed, but it would be managed by the state to ensure that it did not become destructive or monopolistic.

State management of competition gained full force in the 1938 Civil Aeronautics Act. The act institutionalized a five-member independent regulatory commission, initially called the Civil Aeronautics Authority but later renamed the Civil Aeronautics Board (CAB), to promote the "sound development" of an economically viable industry in the public interest. Competition was to be allowed "to the extent necessary" to achieve this goal, creating a system of "regulated competition." The CAB regulated who could fly commercially, where they could fly, and what they could charge for this service, all to ensure the presumed benefits of competition while avoiding its destructive tendencies. Very quickly the board declared that the industry needed no new airlines, effectively locking in 18 airlines in the 1940s. This oligopoly would be reduced to 11 airlines through orchestrated mergers of financially unsound airlines into more stable ones, again with the CAB as the central architect. Moreover, as the airlines were spread out over a large route structure, they rarely directly competed with one another, and they actively sought to preserve this system. These incumbent airlines maintained their monopolistic advantages for 30 years, regularly petitioning the CAB to block airlines that tried to enter the industry and to block existing airlines seeking authority to fly on other airlines' already established routes. And when the CAB did expand the industry, allowing new entrants, it did so by only allowing them in as a new subordinate class of carriers (called "local airlines") to serve the routes that the incumbent airlines did not find profitable.

In the airline case we see the constitution of a market as a set of rules organized first to create and then to preserve the monopolistic advantages of incumbent airlines. The rules were structured to make it likely that incumbent airlines could, and would, easily use the petitioning process to lock out potential competitors from the industry and their respective markets.

The result was a series of local near-monopolies for a handful of airlines. Through the regulated period, city-pair markets were largely oligopolies, with most city-pair routes having no more than three airlines on them and many having only one or two (Caves 1962:20, table 3). By using the state to construct rules that locked out competition, these oligopolistic airlines made a lot of money whenever the economy was growing, which was most years from 1940 to 1970. Their unionized workforces were also well paid as the strong flow of income into these managed monopolies supported union wage claims without threatening the profits of owners.

This all changed in the 1970s when consumer advocate organizations led by Ralph Nader aligned with progressive congressional leaders such as Senator Ted Kennedy challenged the monopoly power of incumbent airlines. These consumer advocates relied on the free-market ideas of a new breed of anti-regulation economists who saw markets as the solution to all economic problems, pushing forward the 1978 Airline Deregulation Act, which eliminated the institutional structure of regulated competition.

Upon passage of the act, US airlines entered a world governed by market competition around prices, in which competitors could relatively quickly jump into previously protected market niches to undercut dominant airlines. And this is precisely what happened. New start-up airlines, such as People Express and New York Air, emerged. And firms that were once relegated to marginal niches in the industry, such as Southwest Airlines, were able to expand onto more lucrative routes. Dominant incumbent airlines such as Eastern, United, and American began expanding their scheduled flight network into routes previously monopolized by other airlines. Throughout the early 1980s, price wars were common and favored customers. Airlines began seriously worrying about how to capture and maintain declining revenue streams that were increasingly dispersed across more and more airlines. This was particularly alarming to the previously powerful incumbent airlines that were accustomed to stable streams of revenue from the earlier era of regulated competition.

In response, the largest airlines began reconfiguring their field with a new set of rules to protect themselves from competition, ultimately reproducing the dominance of a few large firms at the top of the market status hierarchy. Incumbent airlines restructured their markets around a hub-and-spoke network fed by smaller subcontractor airlines, which acted to consolidate incumbent airline power around particular hub airports. Rather than flying directly to every city in their network as they had done under regulated competition, incumbents developed major hubs to fly passengers between. Passengers were fed into the hubs on many more indirect flights by smaller, dependent subcontracted airlines (Donoghue 1988). These produced a more efficient route system but also generated monopolistic barriers to entry into particular cities as incumbents at a hub typically control much of the terminal and gate space through long-term lease agreements with the local municipalities that control airports (Borenstein 1989; Donoghue 1988). These "fortress hubs" enabled incumbent airlines to retain market share and protect themselves from the hypercompetition envisioned by airline deregulation. Market structure effectively moved from federal regulation to airline-city contractual closure around terminal gates.

Incumbent airlines also organized alliances with smaller, low-cost regional and commuter airlines to maximize passenger feed from smaller cities and markets into their hubs. These relations were solidified through incumbent airlines' monopolization of computer reservation systems that travel agents used to book passengers. By owning and operating these systems, incumbent airlines programmed them to display their flights first and to display flights operated by their known regional partners as if they were their own flights. This technological protection from competition, a form of implicit claims-making, was challenged as monopolistic by challenger airlines, consumer groups, and the increasingly marginal commuter airlines that failed to contract as suppliers with major carriers. But in the current neoliberal environment, the Department of Justice saw its mission as protecting private businesses from the state and ruled that hub-and-spoke monopolies were "fair competition."

We see multiple attempts by the largest airlines to protect themselves from the vagaries of competition. This took the form of regulated competition in the postwar era of state economic management and a hub-and-spoke niching strategy in the free-market, anti-regulation environment. Both sets of market practices produced a relatively stable status hierarchy of firms and depended on relationships with governments, generating larger external resource flows to the same basic set of firms under both market environments. Even after deregulation, incumbent airlines continued to dominate the market, with seven former trunk airlines capturing over 75% of the revenue in the market into the early 1980s (Avent-Holt 2012). This meant they tended to control large shares of the market on most of the major routes across the United States. To be sure, a few challenger firms, such as JetBlue and Southwest Airlines, rose to strong positions within the industry, and some incumbent firms, such as Eastern, TWA, and Pan Am, did not survive. However, the basic status hierarchy remained.

As demonstrated in Table 8.1, American and United had the largest market shares in 1978 prior to deregulation, and this remained true well into the 2000s. Delta moved from number six in 1978 to number three in 1988 as TWA, Eastern, and Pan Am approached their own bankruptcies. Since 2005, United acquired number five Continental, Delta merged with number four Northwest, and American acquired US Airways. Thus, post-deregulation,

Table 8.1 The Six US Airlines with the Highest Market Share, 1978–2016

1978	1988	2005	2016
United	United	American	American
15.5	15.3	17.1	19.5
American	American	United	Southwest
12.0	14.9	14.3	18.2
TWA	Delta	Delta	Delta
10.9	12.9	13.3	16.9
Eastern	Northwest	Northwest	United
10.5	9.7	10.2	14.4
Pan Am	Continental	Continental	JetBlue
10.0	7.9	9.2	5.5
Delta	TWA	Southwest	Alaska
9.9	7.6	6.3	4.6

Note: Entries are the percent of industry revenue captured by the airline.

Source: Avent-Holt (2012) and US Department of Transportation, Bureau of Transportation Statistics (http://www.transtats.bts.gov/, retrieved 12/12/2016).

the dominant firms re-established their market power through new tactics sanctioned through the state. In 1975, the top four airlines controlled just less than half the market. By 2016, the top four airlines controlled 69% of the market. The era of free-market deregulation produced a more oligopolistic market and, for small cities, virtual monopolies.

This case demonstrates that market monopolies can be constructed through constituting the basic rules of the field. Airlines were not passive in producing regulated competition but in fact were central to legitimating the idea to state actors. Moreover, the deregulated period suggests that even as fields shift under institutional transformations, dominant actors devise strategies of monopolization to constitute new institutionalized practices that close off access to market opportunities. This is precisely what the hub-and-spokes and the computer reservations systems accomplished. The case also holds lessons for the more general process of adjusting organizational boundaries to shift risk and hoard income.

Embedded Exchange and the Limits of Exploitation

Organizations can acquire revenue from their environment in less nefarious ways than using the state to protect them from competition or creating patent or network monopolies. A relational alternative to market power is the embedding of market exchange in social relationships, which for quite distinctive reasons tends to increase the revenue flowing into organizations. Scholars have come to refer to these embedded exchanges in and around organizations as "relational wealth." *Relational wealth* refers to the value, both real and reputational, produced by trustworthy, collaborative relationships within workplaces, as well as in the external relationships with suppliers and customers (Leana and Rousseau 2000). We see this type of economic embeddedness as the high-productivity, low-inequality alternative to exploitation and closure mechanisms.

Economic sociologists who have studied supplier–customer relationships in firm-to-firm exchange have often noted a tension between "embedded" and "arms-length" exchange relationships. Embedded exchange relationships tend to have high levels of trust and mutual reciprocity and are often stable and long-term. Arms-length relationships, by contrast, are more self-interested and transitory, and the social room to exploit market power is correspondingly higher.

The primary information organizing arms-length transactions is price (Uzzi 1996, 1997). Price-driven relationships are typically described as instrumental exchange built around a short-term profit calculus. The central behavioral motivator is price and profit, in which a buyer (seller) uses price and quality information to find the least costly (most profitable) exchange option for a product of a given quality. These arms-length exchange relationships are typically characterized as transitory because a buyer (seller) chooses among many potential trading partners on the basis of a purely price/profit calculus. The essence of this relationship is its asocial character, in which non-price content in the relationship is at best unnecessary but also potentially detrimental to efficient exploitation of power imbalances (Dyer and Singh 1998).

It also seems reasonable to think of the rise of subcontracting relationships in which the main brand—American Airlines, Nike, Apple, or Amazon—collects the market rents but subcontracts production to low-wage, nonunion firms as this type of arms-length relationship. In these examples, however, it is not competitive markets that create these arms-length relationships but rather sole-source, monopoly buying power by the main brand firm. The dependent exchange relationship enables the monopolist to exploit the value produced by the subcontracting firm in much the same way that a capitalist exploits the value produced by low-power workers in the classic capitalist-worker relationship.

In contrast, embedded relationships are characterized by trust and reciprocity. Such relationships are typically long-term and provide tacit market and production information unlikely to be transmitted solely through the price signal (Uzzi 1997). Embeddedness analyses suggest that social relationships are often a necessary precondition for long-term successful economic transactions and will be mutually beneficial to both exchange partners. As Uzzi (1996) concludes, social relationships "prime the pump" for successful economic exchange (p. 680). Just as positive management citizenship behaviors are associated with higher productivity within firms, embedded ties between firms encourage mutual respect, cooperation, and joint problem-solving.

Economists have long observed that prices are "sticky," noting they do not quickly respond to changes in supply and demand. One explanation, proposed by economist Arthur Okun, sounds a lot like the economic sociologist's notion of embedded social ties. Okun (1981) suggested that when buyers and sellers are in long-term relationships "implicit contracts" arise in which sellers are expected to refrain from taking advantage of the kind of market power associated with rising demand, and buyers similarly refrain from demanding price cuts when demand falls. Motives behind these implicit contracts include notions of fairness as well as simply valuing the relationship itself for both economic and social reasons. The similarity to the embeddedness logic should be apparent. In both cases, actors refrain from exploiting their power in the market in favor of nurturing the ongoing relationship.

Economist Alan Blinder and colleagues (1998) conducted a very interesting study to examine the many theories economists had about price stickiness, including Okun's notion of implicit contracts. Their basic method was to draw a random sample of firms and ask the managers responsible for pricing about the plausibility of 10 or so theories that economists had come up with to explain the often observed failure of prices to adjust to market signals. Implicit contracts turned out to be widespread: two-thirds of firms report having implicit contracts of the sort Okun described. This makes good sense in that 85% of sales were reported to be made to repeat customers. Blinder and colleagues estimate that in the late 1980s 60% of US gross domestic product was sold under implicit contracts. Importantly, they also found that implicit contracts were less frequent in industries with high levels of market concentration, suggesting that monopolistic and oligopolistic firms are more likely to disregard social relationships and exercise their power to manipulate prices.

The empirical record on embeddedness is impressive. Familiarity and friendship reduce monitoring costs and the risk of exploitation (Rooks et al. 2000). The trust that is generated in socially embedded ties can provide cushions from price or supply shocks because it encourages mutually regarding behavior (Uzzi 1997; Ingram and Rogers 2000). Financing is acquired on more favorable terms through embedded ties (Uzzi 1999), and general firm performance can be enhanced by being embedded in cooperative, rather than competitive, networks (Uzzi 1996; Ingram and Roberts 2000; Zuckerman and Sgourev 2006). Even the foundation of economic theory, the price mechanism, has been found to be contingent on the social ties between actors (Uzzi and Lancaster 2004; Fernandez-Mateo 2007). In short, social embeddedness is an economic resource that both reduces the transaction costs of exchange and facilitates the value creation of firms (Dyer and Singh 1998; Kostova and Roth 2003; Adler and Kwon 2002). Importantly, embedded relationships are built around ties of trust and reciprocity, the opposite of relationships that are built across categorical distinctions, which permit exploitation and closure.

Using the same Australian establishment data we used in Chapter 2 to examine organizational inequality regimes, we have explored the relationship between the quality of market exchanges and socially embedded exchange relationships (Tomaskovic-Devey, Avent-Holt, Zimmer, and Harding 2016a). These data focus on the relationship between an organization and its largest supplier. We operationalize social embeddedness as the degree to which the organization describes the relationship with the supplier as mutually beneficial and trusting, with a high level of familiarity with people and routines. We measure the success of market exchange as the stated importance of product price, quality, reliability, and delivery timeliness in that relationship.[4] As one would expect, embedded relationships and successful market exchange are strongly positively correlated with each other ($r = 0.54$), even in the presence of multiple statistical controls for the degree of market competition. In more sophisticated statistical models we find that the two generate positive synergies. Successful exchange builds trust, and trust in turn leads to successful market exchanges.

In Figure 8.2 we plot out that relationship between social embeddedness and market synergies by the length of the exchange relationship. In our Australian data, the average exchange relationship with the largest supplier was 11 years, and the longest exchange relationship was a remarkable 144 years. In the neoclassical market model, exchange relationships are typically thought of as transitory, with many arms-length buyers and sellers in the same market, each potentially disposable for a more economically attractive buyer or seller. Real firm-to-firm markets tend to be more stable, as Alan Blinder and colleagues documented, with recurrent exchange between trading partners. We investigated if the relationship between social embeddedness and successful market exchanges was dependent on

4. Reliability of the social embeddedness measure is 0.71. The market exchange scale has a reliability of 0.74.

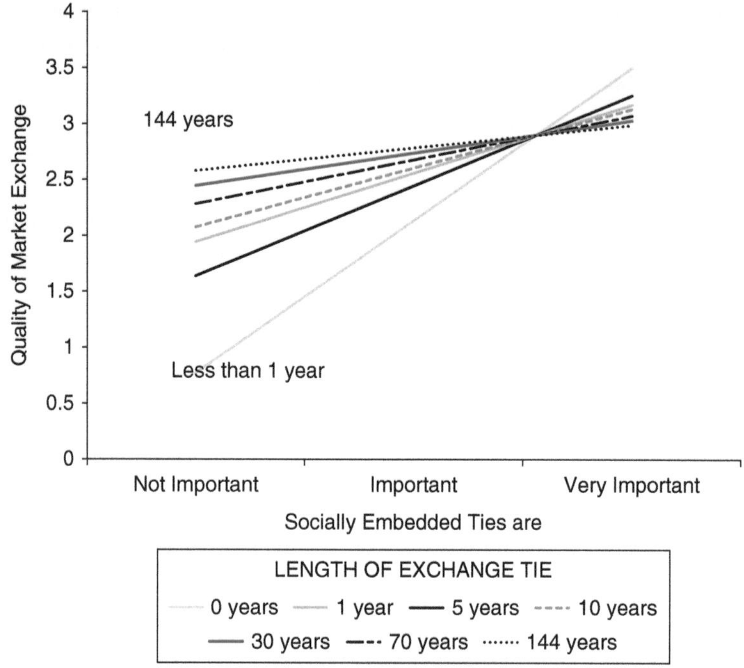

Figure 8.2 Market synergies and levels of social embeddedness for longer exchange relationships (authors' calculations, Australian National Organizations Survey).

the length of the exchange relationship, since the length of the relationship is theorized to produce greater embeddedness. While market synergies and embeddedness are always positively correlated, this positive feedback loop between the two was much stronger in new trading relationships. In new trading relationships, we see the strongest trade-off between trust and quality in the market exchange.

Embedded market relationships and implicit contracts produce the same types of positive synergies in trade relationships as managerial citizenship behaviors (Chapter 4) do in production. An important insight from these analyses of the processes that produce organizational value is that socially embedded, cooperative relationships tend to be more productive than exploitative ones. Exploitation, whether through markets or in production, may produce short-term economic gains but is unlikely to lead to the synergies that produce long-term efficiency gains within production. An important lesson from this discussion is that exploitation produces negative synergies at the actor and system levels. If the system is an organization, exploitation of the workforce will stymie innovation and cooperation in production. When the system is the whole economy, it will lower total productivity and its growth.

There is an apparent paradox in our analyses of positive synergies in trade and in production. In both cases, the evidence suggests that cooperative, socially embedded, respectful relationships are more likely to produce creative, innovative, income-enhancing outcomes. But why then is exploitation in markets and production so widespread? Part of the answer lies in short- versus long-term time horizons. Socially embedded relationships pay off in the long term, but exploitation of power advantages generates an immediate return. A firm facing bankruptcy as a result of mismanagement or market competition can drive down labor costs or sell shoddy goods as a short-term strategy. This is the classic recipe of competitive, exploitative capitalism. In the longer run, powerful companies can place the synergistic function of new product and market development in the parent company and subcontract out production to lower-cost firms, whether locally or globally. This externalization strategy is consistent with both innovation and exploitation, or as Josh Whitford concludes, it is a "double edged sword" (2005:20). Finally, there are also widespread ideologies that promote exploitation of markets as reasonable solutions to organizational dilemmas in production.

LINKING ORGANIZATIONAL INEQUALITY AND RESOURCE-POOLING

The cases detailed in this chapter demonstrate how firms manipulate relationships in their field to monopolize markets and funnel money into their organization. This process becomes particularly relevant to relational inequality theory (RIT) when it can be linked to distributional inequalities within organizations. We argue that this happens largely through two distinct processes. First, extracting revenue from the environment increases the size of resources that can be claimed by stakeholders within organizations. Second, firms can reconfigure their boundaries in such a way that stakeholders can no longer legitimately claim the increased revenue flowing into these monopolistic firms.

Financialization and Shifting Claims

We illustrate the interrelation between organizational inequality and the organizational environment with a case study of the financialization of the US economy. One of the most powerful economic trends, beginning in the 1980s, has been the financialization of both the US and global economies more generally. *Financialization* refers to both the rising political and economic power of financial service firms and the growing importance of financial, rather than production, strategies in all sectors of the economy. In the US case at least, financialization also accompanied a shift from values associated with employment and production to a normative elevation of financial investment as preferable to physical capital investment. This movement has led to a tremendous concentration of income in the finance sector as well as a retreat from production-led income generation in many sectors of the economy, redirecting streams of income into both financial organizations and non-financial firms that reorganized themselves into vehicles of financial investments.

US bank regulations were instituted in the Glass-Steagall Act of 1933 in response to the US bank–led financial speculation that led to the worldwide depression of that decade. Glass-Steagall limited the economic power of financial service firms, prevented banks from growing too large or operating across state lines, required different firms for different financial service activities (e.g., insurance, savings and loans, commercial banks, investment banks), and imposed tight regulation on all financial service firms. As a result, the US financial service sector was small, stable, and boring from 1935 until around 1980.

Beginning in the late 1970s but accelerating through the 1990s, the United States dismantled this regulatory structure, and prohibitions on risky financial activities evaporated. A few integrated financial service firms came to dominate the US and increasingly other economies. This economic power was the result not of invisible hand market processes but of specific political pressures from financial services in the context of the growing power of market fundamentalist ideology. Regulators came to be captured by financial economists' efficient market theory, which stated that financial markets were inherently self-regulating and efficient, allowing new, sometimes risky and often predatory, organizational arrangements and financial instruments to flourish (Fligstein and Goldstein 2010; Hacker and Pierson 2010; Krippner 2011; Tomaskovic-Devey and Lin 2011).

Together, these institutional shifts reduced state regulatory oversight over current and emerging investment devices, encouraged financial investment over physical capital investment, and unleashed speculation in financial assets. Because these policies led to increased volatility in interest rates and stock-market performance, they also encouraged the creation of new unregulated financial instruments to profit from the increased volatility, including variable rate mortgages, credit default swaps, and mortgage-backed and other derivative securities (Harvey 2010; Krippner 2011).

These shifts fundamentally redistributed income from other organizations and households into the coffers of financial service firms. From the end of World War II until the early 1980s financial services realized between

10% and 15% of corporate profits in the US economy. After 1980, the share of profits in this sector soared, rising to over 40% of all corporate profits in the US economy in the mid-2000s (Tomaskovic-Devey and Lin 2011). The collapse of the US financial service industry in 2008 and subsequent rescue by the federal government led to further concentrations of power and wealth in fewer firms. By 2012, the three largest US banks controlled 35% of all banking assets and the top 10, over 50% (Tomaskovic-Devey and Lin 2013). Pointing to the post-1980 history of bank bailouts, Harvey (2007) suggests that one of the defining actions of neoliberal public policy was to protect financial institutions at all costs, despite the recurrent contradiction of bank bailouts with free-market ideology.

Much of the soaring financial service firm income appears to have been shared with the top employees of those firms. Financial service sector employee income as a share of national income was remarkably stable prior to 1980 but grew rapidly afterward. The growth in employee income in the securities, commodities, and investment industry was particularly steep. In 2007, workers employed in this industry earned $6,891 per week nationally, $16,918 per week if employed in New York City, compared to the national weekly earnings average of $884. Between 2006 and 2007, just prior to the collapse of the US and much of the global financial systems, first-quarter wages in the securities and commodities industry grew a remarkable 16.4% nationwide and 21.5% in New York City (Sum et al. 2008). Not surprisingly, employees on Wall Street, including CEOs and investment managers in commercial and investment banks, bank holding companies, and hedge funds made up an increasing share of the very highest earners in the US economy (Kaplan and Rauh 2010).[5] Ken-Hou Lin (2015) found that in the 1970s financial service firms tended to pay their lowest-skilled employees wages slightly better than comparably skilled employees in other industries. Across the period of financialization, low-skill employees' earnings dropped, and it was the top 10% of employees in this sector who captured all of the emerging surging employee income generated by the rising economic power of financial service firms.

The normative shift toward finance has also had consequences for resource-pooling in non-financial firms. At this point there is a scholarly consensus that the management of non-financial firms has, since the early 1980s, been increasingly responsive to and disciplined by financial rather than product markets (Fligstein 1993; Fligstein and Shin 2007). The rise of a shareholder value movement emanating from Wall Street encouraged

5. Olivier Godechot (2012) discovered a similar pattern for France. We focused on his work on claims-making in Chapter 7 (Godechot 2016).

non-financial firms to prioritize wealth creation for shareholders over corporate growth, market share, or employment size (Dobbin and Jung 2010). As the growth and market share metric of CEO success was displaced by goals of short-term profitability and stock price gains, shareholder value goals came to dominate corporate strategy (Dobbin and Zorn 2005). The latter was accomplished at least in part by improving corporate returns on equity (stock) by simply reducing the number of stock shares. Profits were used to buy back stock, and new investments increasingly became dependent on corporate debt rather than retained earnings.

This has had negative employment consequences in non-financial firms in the United States, as also documented by Ken-Hou Lin (2016). He looks at three financialization behaviors that grew rapidly after 1980: the replacement of investments in production with investments in financial assets, the replacement of equity and retained earnings to finance firm operations with corporate debt, and increased payouts to stock holders, primarily in the form of stock buy-backs. All three, he argues reduce the importance of production and the bargaining power of production workers. He finds that all three financially oriented investment strategies led to reduced employment of production workers and that this job destruction accelerated over time. Conversely, the same investment behavior marginally increased the employment of managerial and professional workers. Rising debt-based financing and stock buy-backs led to lower employment for all classes of workers but most steeply for production workers. These effects also accelerated over time, although these patterns were weaker when unions were present to challenge managerial downsizing strategies (Jung 2016).

Financialization is a product of regulatory decisions, both decisions to deregulate and encourage the concentration of financial power in a few large institutions and decisions that fail to regulate new financial instruments or strategies. It is at its root a system of income redistribution which favors the finance sector over the non-finance sector, financial investments over investments in production, and shareholders and top executives over workers and other citizens.

As an ideology, financialization was promised to increase competition, reduce costs, and increase innovation, thereby increasing standards of living and economic growth in the standard economic policy model. This, however, has not been the case. In the United States, during the post-1980 financialization period there has been a large transfer of income into the financial services industry (Krippner 2011; Phillipon and Reshef 2013) but no increase in financial service productivity (Phillipon 2015), declining investment in production (Orhangazi 2008; Davis 2013), and declining total value added in the economy (Tomaskovic-Devey et al. 2015b). And during this period household debt—credit cards, college, mortgage—has skyrocketed as financial service firms have created new technologies of income extraction from families, creating instability and insecurity within households (Hyman 2012). What financialization has given us then is a new source of resource-pooling across and within organizations that has led to less competition, greater concentration of income at the top, and the exacerbation of systemic risk. Financialization has been a recipe for the most powerful firms and corporate CEOs to accumulate a larger share of the pie.

Reconfiguring Organizational Boundaries to Monopolize Surplus

RIT tends to emphasize how stakeholders can make claims on the resources that organizations accumulate. But when thinking about organizations pooling resources from their environment, the manipulation of firm boundaries can have a decisive effect on who can claim those resources. In the remainder of this chapter, we explore contemporary trends that shift the structure and location of production, concentrating surplus accumulation into certain core firms and limiting the actors who can make claims on that surplus. Our goal here is to document that much of rising inequality in contemporary high-income economies is tied to changes in the size of the pie across organizations, rather than to increased inequality within organizations in how the pie is distributed.

By the 1970s, the landscape of the US and global economies was changing. Large manufacturing firms suddenly found themselves competing with higher-productivity, more efficient producers from both Asia and Europe. US banks, which had been tied to domestic economic growth, had to seek out new markets. The social contract between labor and capital that developed after World War II suddenly seemed expensive. Firms looked for ways to cut their costs in order to survive in a newly competitive global economy.

Much of this cost-cutting was accomplished through externalizing either the employment relationship or the production process or both. At the level of the employment relationship, this externalization adjusts the size of an organization's workforce away from regular full-time employees through the use of part-time, temporary, and independent contractors. This allows the powerful brand firms to limit the duration of employment to particular projects or periods of high demand and avoid creating relationships in which some reciprocity between capital and labor is present. Arne Kalleberg (2003) refers to this as "externalized flexibility." Doing this creates a new categorical distinction around organizational citizenship, permanent versus temporary employee, limiting the capacity for temporary, part-time, and independent contractor employees to make claims on the surplus of the organization. An emblematic case is the reorganization of long-distance truck driving, from a heavily unionized firm employment regime to being almost completely dominated by independent contractor truck drivers, who not only drive but become responsible for the capital investment in their trucks. Income plummeted as truck drivers became self-employed, but for the transportation firms that distribute goods, flexibility and profitability soared (Viscelli 2016).

At the level of the production process, externalization shifts parts of production to other organizations. This can be done by moving parts of production to lower-wage labor markets or by using subcontracting, outsourcing, franchising, and other legal maneuvers to shift production to other organizations while keeping profits in the dominant firm. This externalization of the production process has been fundamental to reshaping how organizations claim resources in their environment and ultimately to the dynamics of increasing inequality since the 1980s. The hub-and-spokes reorganization of the airline market did precisely this, by externalizing all the less profitable routes to branded subcontract airlines, while still monopolizing the customers delivered to the hubs by the dependent feeder firms.

David Weil (2014) has shown that one way that externalization is accomplished is by shifting the boundaries of the organization so that the lead or core firm controls both the production process and brand linked surplus but externalizes most of production labor and the risk of failure to dependent subcontractors and suppliers. Two examples will make this clear:

> A maid works at the San Francisco Marriot on Fisherman's Wharf. The hotel property is owned by Host Hotels and Resorts Inc., a lodging real estate company. The maid, however, is evaluated and supervised daily and her hours and payroll managed by Crestline Hotels and Resorts Inc., a national third-party hotel management company. Yet she follows daily procedures (and risks losing her job for failure to accomplish them) regarding cleaning, room set-up, overall pace, and quality standards established by Marriot, whose name the property bears.
>
> A cable installer in Dayton, Ohio works as an independent contractor (in essence a self-employed business provider), paid on a job-by-job basis by Cascom Inc., a cable installation company. Cascom's primary client is the international media giant Time Warner, which owns cable systems across the United States. The cable installer is paid solely on the basis of the job completed and is entitled to no protections normally afforded employees. Yet all installation contracts are supplied solely by Cascom, which also sets the price for jobs and collects payment for them. The installer must wear a shirt with the Cascom logo and can be removed as a contractor at will. (Weil 2014:1)

Weil's analysis is that under external stock market pressure to focus on their core competencies and generate high returns to shareholders, many firms found ways to shift their organizational boundaries, externalizing the actual production while retaining control over revenue streams. When this happened, the externalized labor and their third-party employers became costs to Marriot or Time Warner with limited or no claims on the surplus associated with the brand's market power.

The externalization of both employment and the production process led to decentralized networks of organizations with different capacities to claim resources in the environment. Work that was once done in vertically integrated firms is now done via contractual relationships with supplier firms, transforming who has legitimate claim to the surplus. Ultimately, the externalized employees or firms do not have the same social claims on the surplus produced by the core firm (Weil 2014). They do the work to produce that surplus, but because they do so through an arms-length, subordinate market relationship, rather than from an internal organizational citizenship position, they have no or only weak claims. Since these external relationships are typically organized as dependent on the core firm, bargaining power is typically weak as well. One exception seems to be some highly skilled technical contract labor (e.g., computer engineers) who tend to realize high wages associated with movement between technically dynamic firms (Kalleberg, Reskin, and Hudson 2000). It is important to recognize that the same firm can potentially take a high-road strategy with its core of internal employees and a low-road strategy with its externalized employment practices. Thus, the same firm can create socially embedded, respectful employment relationships with its permanent workforce and exploitative relationships via short-term and contractual market relationships with less powerful others.[6] Kalleberg (2003) estimated that about 18% of establishments that pursued a low-road, externalization labor strategy for some of their workforce also pursued high-performance work practices for others.

Arin Dube and Ethan Kaplan (2010) provide an in-depth look at the outsourcing of janitors and guards in the United States. They find that between 1983 and 2000 employment in both occupations shifted into business service industries, by 5% and 10%, respectively. This outsourcing was most likely to happen in high-wage industries, so externalization reduced the ability of these relatively low-skill jobs to make claims on the surplus of high-wage firms. Outsourcing reduced wages an estimated 4%–7% for janitors and 8%–24% for guards. In addition, outsourced workers lost access to employment benefits such as pensions and health insurance and were

6. This reminds us of the rise of adjunct faculty in the United States and their differential treatment relative to tenured and tenure-track faculty, at least at many US universities.

more likely to be nonunion, women, and racial minorities. Outsourcing was most likely to happen to employees with low claims-making power to begin with.

The externalization strategy has been central to the growth of income inequality since the 1980s, producing a set of high-skill, high-wage firms closing off resources and exploiting lower-skill, lower-wage workplaces. Tracking organizational surplus, or the size of the pie, is crucial for linking external organizational environments to internal inequality regimes. Thus, even if there were no internal inequalities within firms, there still might be considerable inequality between firms as a function of firm resource inequalities.

One way to measure the size of the pie is to conceptualize each organization as having a mean wage—the per capita wage that would be paid to everyone if there were no internal inequalities. Recent research in Sweden, Germany, and the United States suggests that companies are becoming more internally homogenous in this regard, with some firms specializing in high-skill, high-paid work and others in lower-skill, lower-paid, typically nonunion, noncredentialed work (Skans, Edin, and Holmlund 2009; Tomaskovic-Devey et al. 2016b; Song et al. 2016). This research also shows that most of the rising earnings inequalities in these three countries are the result of new levels of skill segregation between firms produced by polarization of employment into low- and high-wage firms.

Some of this polarization is the result of the outsourcing, franchising, temporary, and independent contracting externalization process. Some is produced by the rise of sectors with closure-based market power as in the finance, tech, and pharmaceutical examples outlined at the beginning of the chapter. No one has yet done the research to say exactly how much of rising inequality in the United States or elsewhere is a function of the two processes, and, of course, they are complementary to some extent as well.

Using US Internal Revenue Service data that match workers to firms, Song et al. (2016) estimate that two-thirds of the steep rise in US earnings inequality between 1978 and 2012 was produced by this increased income polarization between firms. In a similar analysis of the rise in German between-workplace inequalities, we found that 63% of the steeply rising earnings inequalities in Germany between 1993 and 2012 was the result of the increasing between-workplace segregation in the size of the pie available for distribution to employees accompanied by increasingly skill-homogenous firm divisions of labor. In that research the contribution of between-industry earnings polarization, a rough indicator of outsourcing, to rising between-firm inequality was very high (Tomaskovic-Devey et al. 2016b). This is exactly the pattern of employment shifts documented by

Weil (2014) with his focus on the externalization of production. Lin (2016) similarly shows that the largest US firms became increasingly dominant in the flow of income, while simultaneously accounting for a shrinking share of employment. This shifting of firm boundaries changed who had claims on surplus but left intact the lead firms' control over production and profits.

This kind of interorganizational power relationship externalizes the claims of less powerful workers and production units, excludes organizational citizenship-based claims, and increases the rate of exploitation of core firms over their dependent exchange partners. Examples include winner-take-all markets such as the global dominance of a few technology firms like Google and Amazon (Freeman 2016), the power of financial service firms in some countries to accumulate national and even global income (e.g., the United States [Tomaskovic-Devey and Lin 2011] and France [Godechot 2012]), automakers spinning off supplier functions (Whitford 2005), branded companies subcontracting out most low-skill labor while absorbing the profits associated with the brand (Weil 2014), and global commodity chains in which routine production are sourced from low-wage locales by retailers in high-income countries (Gereffi 1996).

Recent research by Nathan Wilmers (2017) looks directly at the influence of consolidated buyer power on the wages of workers in dependent supplier firms. Focusing on firms' exchange relationships with buyers that account for 10% or more of a firm's sales, Wilmer finds that workers' wages decline the larger the share of sales goes to a dominant customer. These results are stronger when there is a single dominant buyer, when the firm had high profits to be plundered, and the longer the exploitative exchange relationship lasts. Importantly, these results do not hold before 1980 and the rise of the shareholder value movement with its emphasis on profit exploitation over embedded exchange relationships. It also does not hold for financial service firms, whose dominant buyers are each other and where predatory market behavior is reserved for households.

That the rise in earnings inequalities is so strongly tied to emerging organizational earnings segregation is striking. Much has been written on the demise of vertically integrated firms, the rise of subcontracting, and the new networked firm (e.g., Powell 1990; Whitford 2005). If contemporary theories of management and monitoring technologies are encouraging the formation of skill-homogenous firms organized around "core competencies" and encouraging exploitation of other firms rather than embedded exchange, and it seems that they are, then we are moving toward an economic system in which only the high-skilled in powerful firms have the capacity to make claims on the income that pools in these powerful firms. Those income pools, however, are the social production not only of the lead firm but also of the subcontractor, supplier, and franchisee firms that the lead firm controls. Exploitation is moving into markets and outside of firm labor processes.

This rising firm-level inequality is also reflected in the emergence of a new stratum of very rich people, whose wealth does not arise from inheritance but rather is tied by ownership or managerial roles or both to the superstar firms that have come to dominate national and global markets. We discussed this in Chapter 5, where all of the top billionaires in the world derive their wealth from their connection to particularly successful firms. We criticized Thomas Piketty, the author of the monumentally successful *Capital in the Twenty-First Century* (2014), in Chapter 1 for his neglect of the organizational context of rising inequality. To be fair, he had tax data, so it was not possible for him to identify where the rising wealth of the super-rich was coming from. As a result, he could not distinguish between wealth based on inheritance and investments and that based on contemporary winner-take-all firms. A recent analysis of the shifting composition of the world's billionaires between 1996 and 2014 helps to sort this out (Freund and Oliver 2016).

In 1996, there were 423 billionaires in the world. By 2017, this elite group had almost quintupled to 2,043 people. Across this period of rapid growth in extreme wealth, the source of the large wealth shifted from inheritance- to firm-based riches. In 1996, more than half (55.3%) of those 423 billionaires entered this elite club based on inherited wealth. By 2014, inheritance had been cut in half, and 70% of the world's richest people had acquired their wealth during their own lifetime through their ties to particular firms. Piketty (2014) did comment on the United States as the one place in the world where the "working rich" seemed to be more prominent. The trend, however, appears to be more general, with all regions of the world increasingly producing billionaires tied to corporate fortunes.

CONCLUDING THOUGHTS

Inequality generation is an organizational phenomenon, and it must be understood as both an interorganizational process and an intraorganizational process. However, the processes governing inequality between organizations is fundamentally the same as that governing inequality within organizations: relational claims-making, exploitation, and social closure. Organizations monopolize resources (patents, land rights, customer revenue, tax dollars, donations, etc.), closing off access to those resources from other organizations in their field. Organizations exploit weaker trading partners, siphoning off value produced by them. Closure and exploitation intersect when organizations monopolize markets as a means to exploit customers and other organizations and to accumulate value. Monopolizing markets happens through a claims-making process where claims are constructed by organizations to establish product or market monopolies and legitimate exploitative practices over other organizations within a field. Thus, incumbent airlines constructed hub-and-spoke networks and computerized reservation systems as a means to monopolize routes. When challenged by smaller firms that this was a remonopolization of the industry, they claimed it was just competitive business practices and ultimately convinced the Department of Justice of the legitimacy of their claims. This process can be seen in many other industries with large, powerful actors, including those discussed in this chapter: finance, tech, and pharmaceuticals.

Ultimately, this all matters because resource-pooling shapes the volume of resources struggled over within organizations. If RIT is correct and inequality is generated through the interactional mechanisms of relational claims-making, exploitation, and social closure as outlined, those same processes are shaping how much is organizationally available to struggle over in the first place.

The size of the pie matters and perhaps increasingly matters in a world where organizations are segregated by income flows and organizational power. This chapter has demonstrated that thinking of organizations as resource-pooling devices is central to understanding inequality, even more so in a world of externalized production through organizational networks. The concept of organizational surplus transforms our thinking from the neoclassical imagery of market competition to a network of social relations within and between firms, relations that are often imbued with power and steered by status and ideological claims, shaping the capacity for organizations to create and capture organizational surplus.

Carrie Leana and Denise Rousseau (2000), creators of the notion of relational wealth, question whether externalization strategies, with their reliance on dependent suppliers, temporary and contract workers, and other forms of organizational labor flexibility, will create value in the long run. These are essentially systems of exploitation which sacrifice the joint problem-solving and creative synergies of workgroups for short-term profitability. Of course, firms with monopoly or platform-based market power may still be able to exploit actors elsewhere in the economy. In these cases, we would expect foregone growth in the national economy, even as powerful firms continue to absorb income from suppliers, customers, and superexploited workforces.

In the next chapter, we recap RIT, briefly outline some implications for how we should pursue a social science of inequality generation, and then turn to the implications of a relational inequality lens for pursuing more embedded, synergistic, and egalitarian futures.

9

Expanding the Moral Circle

A theory is only as good as it is useful. In this chapter we draw out the implications of relational inequality theory (RIT) for how we should do social science and, perhaps more importantly, for the types of organizational and institutional designs it implies for developing more just, dignity-enhancing organizations and institutions.

We stress the importance for all social science to focus on the interactional level of durable social networks in order to advance theoretical and empirical models of inequality-generating processes. Current practice, at least when there is a primary focus on individuals, markets, or societies, is ill-equipped to discover causal processes or explain societal dynamics.

In terms of the real-world application of an RIT model to advance equality and justice agendas, we propose a series of global goals for challenging inequalities. These include moving from tribalism to universalism, from hierarchy to citizenship rights, and from markets to human dignity. We reject robotic recipes, all too common in contemporary policy discourses, particularly the religious reliance on market solutions, economic growth, and expanding education. These will not mechanically reduce inequality or enhance human dignity in a world of dynamic social relations.

We begin by recapping RIT:

> Resources are generated and pool in organizations. Actors with legitimated claims gain access to those resources. Some people and potential trading partners are denied access to organizational resources through processes of social closure. Others appropriate organizational resources based on their ability to exploit weaker actors in interactional and exchange relationships. To the extent that they have cultural, status, and material advantages in resource-distributing relationships, actors are more or less powerful in these claims-making processes. These power-generating resources tend to be associated with categorical distinctions such as class, occupation, gender, education, citizenship, race, and the like. Which categorical distinctions are the basis for claims-making are institutionally and organizationally variable. Institutions, markets, and organizational fields influence, but do not determine, action and opportunities. Rather, actors use cultural and other tools to invent local strategies of action within field level constraints.

Most broadly, RIT implies that changing distributional inequality patterns in a society or even in a single firm requires shifting the basic organizational architecture of social relations in ways that alter what claims are articulated and legitimated and thereby the flow of resources.

This chapter provides an explicit—but we think realistic—alternative to market fundamentalism in organizational and public policy design. We leave it to others to provide the specific policies and political roadmaps to foster the transition from fixations on growth and market mechanisms to ones of human dignity and embedded exchange.

IMPLICATIONS FOR SOCIAL SCIENCE

RIT encourages social scientists to embrace a relational explanatory framework. We think that much, perhaps most, social theory is already relational in its causal assumptions but that relational dynamics are hidden by explanations of action that exaggerate the autonomy of individuals or the homogeneity of societal structures. Actions are always chosen in a relational context, and the menu of available choices is influenced, but not determined, by the institutional frameworks and organizational fields in which actions are pursued, as well as the relative power of actors in those fields.

One of the most common mistakes social scientists make, even when they explicitly theorize the power of social relationships to channel action, is to ignore the organizational context of action. People do not live their everyday lives in nations or societies or within their own heads but rather navigate life in relationships with family, neighbors, suppliers, customers, employers, and co-workers. These relationships take on inequality consequences when there are resources to be acquired and distributed. That is, they become inequality-generating relationships when there is some organizational process that accumulates resources to be claimed, exploited, or monopolized. To acknowledge that African Americans are culturally denigrated in the United States does not tell us how racial inequalities are generated. To do that requires the social scientist to show the organizational resources that African Americans are excluded from making claims on or the exploitation of resources produced by African Americans and transferred to whites.

The failure to recognize this organizational level of action produces analyses that are simultaneously too individual and too societal. The actual processes and mechanisms that constitute social life, including the generation of inequalities, become as a result invisible. Vague theoretical attributions to individual rational choice or prejudice or to societal, cultural, or institutional norms end up substituting for careful scientific analyses of generative forces.

Skipping over the generative social processes not only makes for bad science but also obscures much of the real-world variation in inequalities, making it impossible to observe consequential dynamics at the levels of interactional processes and distributive mechanisms. Slavery in the Americas was a system of exploitation in which slave owners exploited the effort and bodies of human beings of African origin in order to enrich themselves. Contemporary racism in the United States is built much more clearly around closure processes in which many people with dark skin are not granted access to resource-rich organizations and neighborhoods, an exclusion that is manifest in high rates of unemployment and imprisonment.

At the same time, some African Americans, particularly those with some social class advantages, get access to higher education and as a result can take advantage of education-based closure to secure access to richer organizations and jobs. They may then be subject to more opportunities to be treated disrespectfully in these integrated settings. Focusing on the structural continuity of black disadvantage hides the changing relational mechanisms, categorical boundaries, and intersectional complexity, rendering discussions about equality, progress, and regress incoherent. In essence, a focus purely on historical continuities misses the variation in the relational spaces, the continuity and discontinuity in inequality regimes.

We are not arguing that only organizations matter for inequality. Individual expectations, interpretations, and motives operate as well. National institutions that transcend individuals and organizations are clearly influential. It is here that we think field theory is an important corrective to overly individualistic or static institutional accounts of social action. Individuals act in a field of social relationships, taking into account other actors in the field as well as "nets of accountability" beyond their immediate relationships. Similarly, organizations operate in fields populated by other actors, both other organizations and individuals, that must be taken into account, as well as their extended nets of accountability institutionalized into laws, regulations, and field-level norms. Actors, whether individuals or agents representing collectivities, utilize cultural knowledge about what is right, proper, and possible when choosing courses of action and developing organizational routines and practices.

Crucially, causality does not flow from individual choice, nor from societal constraint. Rather, causality happens in fields of social relationships, where more powerful actors in the field, like suns in a solar system, exert particular influence on the structure of the field and courses of action. But at the same time, even the smallest person has some gravitational pull that can influence the chain of action. When weak actors combine via social organization, they can magnify their influence. Thus, closure and exploitation tend to favor the powerful, but usurpationary claims to organizational resources are latent in the system of social relationships, waiting for weak individual actors to combine their gravitational power and shift the interactional rules and resource distributions.

The more nuts-and-bolts implications of RIT for data collection and analysis are littered throughout this book. Whenever possible, social scientists should design research to compare organizations (and similarly consequential meso-level relational networks, such as police–citizen or teacher–student relationships) within their institutional contexts. That is, social relations must be situated in their organizational and institutional contexts, and comparing these contexts links the variability in outcomes to field-level relationships. Methodological choices to focus on individuals or societies, rather than the meso level of relationships and their durable manifestation in organizations, create steep barriers to observing the social processes in play. We need a social science that is focused on relationships in their field-level contexts. A social science of inequality needs to focus in particular on the durable resource-distributing relationships within and between organizations.

We have highlighted and drawn on both surveys that sample individuals in their organizational context and ethnographies that compare organizations and the relations within them. These are the chief methodological devices implicated by RIT. But there are others as well, each of which can be used within a comparative organizational design. In-depth interview techniques can focus on social relationships as well as individual experiences within organizations/networks. Survey sampling of individuals can be dislodged from a fixation on the independence assumption in sampling theory to recruiting individuals who share a relationship, such as husbands and wives, co-workers in the same unit, supervisors and subordinates, customers and merchants. Relational sampling, whether in qualitative or quantitative approaches to data collection, can produce useful relational accounts of inequality processes and meaning-making within them. Experimental research can also be conducted within organizational walls, and experimental designs can construct organizational situations in vignettes or more creative ways that vary relationships and contexts. Even individual-level surveys can be conducted with the goal of collecting relational information on respondents, a position advocated by James Coleman (1958) decades ago. Finally, we foresee widespread application of the RIT model within a relational social network analytic framework, albeit one that recognizes institutional context and cultural power as conditioning network processes. RIT lends itself to primarily being examined through comparative organizational research designs, but the meat of such designs is only limited by the methodological creativity of researchers.[1]

1. We recognize that the methodological and theoretical pluralism of RIT weakens the probability of creating a strong scientific paradigm. Strong scientific paradigms typically have narrow theory scope conjoined with methodological consensus. Like religions, however, such strong science versions when applied to social science produce misleadingly simple models of the world. The cost of parsimony is often the inability to recognize an elephant when holding its tail.

RIT AND THE POLITICS OF EGALITARIANISM

Many contemporary social scientists studying inequality share a normative impulse that judges at least some inequalities as, not only inefficient, but unjust. What exactly makes inequality unjust remains, however, a matter of considerable debate. In this sense, the enduring justice questions, we think, are not scientific but normative. How should resources be produced and distributed? For many social scientists inequalities based on status attributes unrelated to individual merit are seen as unjust. But clearly which categorical distinctions are unjust and which are legitimate bases for moral distinction varies across historical, institutional, and organizational contexts. The great rise in inequalities in the contemporary period associated with firm market power, capital ownership, managerial power, and educational closure suggests that even categorical distinctions often treated as legitimate are increasingly suspect. We may have moved into the world of unjust meritocracy Daniel Bell warned against in 1972. Social scientists have largely skirted the issue of what makes some resource distributions just and others unjust. However, we think this need not–and in fact cannot–remain the case.[2]

Social science always has normative implications. The decision to study the bases of social order versus social change implies a preference for the reproduction of current inequality-generating processes or their destruction. Causal accounts that highlight the power and efficiency of markets imply a certain morality and justness to market-linked distributional outcomes. Asking how meritocratic a society or firm is implies that inequalities are desirable, so long as they are not associated with illegitimate categorical distinctions such as class, national origin, race, gender, or sexual orientation. We might think of all social science as implying a moral package that incorporates, and in many cases fosters, normative preferences.[3] Our

2. Given the political and social complexity of these normative inequality issues, social scientists' wariness is understandable. That said, it is unavoidable, and social scientists would do well to engage the large literature in philosophy on these problems. Good starting points include the works of John Rawls (1971), Ronald Dworkin (1981), Amartya Sen (1992), G. A. Cohen (1995, 2008), Elizabeth Anderson (1999), and Scheffler (2003). Among sociologists, Erik Olin Wright (2000b, 2013) also provides key insights into the importance of specifying the moral principles of an egalitarian social science.

3. We take this idea of a "moral package" from Vivianna Zelizer (2012). Zelizer argues that all economic activity is built around a moral package of ideas, technologies, and relationships that legitimate, and even sanctify, economic practices. To the extent that social science influences exchange practices, the morality of the market, of shareholder claims, of efficiency and merit, of diversity, or of any economic practices is fostered. Even when the influence of social science on the moral package of firms is limited, social scientists may inadvertently mistake the moral packages of the market or prominent firms for invariant or inevitable causal forces.

position is that pretending that there are no normative implications to any particular social science is misleading and even potentially dangerous.

RIT points to an important dimension to thinking about the normative implications of inequality: the relational nature of production. Material redistribution is not simply a matter of charity but can also be justified by the joint production embedded in the practical relationships both within and between firms and increasingly in global production chains and exchange relationships. The production and distribution of value occur not at the level of individuals but in the relationships between them. There is no scientific boundary at which we can confidently say that the organizational resources within were produced by, and so should belong to, an identifiable set of actors, such as individuals, firms, or nations. There are only normative boundaries as to whom we admit within the moral circle of stakeholders and whom we can exploit, exclude, or ignore.

While we cannot resolve the normative issues in this chapter, we do think that RIT offers a scientific basis for establishing inequality-reducing goals and mechanisms. At its heart, RIT understands inequality as the predictable result of status distinctions lodged within organizations and that status distinctions will tend to arise out of differences in perceptions of competence. In addition to actual differences in task competence, status hierarchies are created by cultural frames, the post hoc attribution of competency to those who control resources, and segregation processes that exaggerate in-group and out-group distinctions. It is these status-exaggerating social practices that need to be targeted by any politics of egalitarianism.

So, what does RIT suggest might be appropriate social goals to increase equality? We think it suggests a focus on transforming organizational inequality regimes and that there are multiple avenues for doing so, including both organizational design and institutional pressures. Egalitarian movements can and should engage in claims-making within organizations as well as at the institutional policy level to reshape inequality regimes.

We see the RIT model as generating three universal goals for reducing unjust inequalities: move from tribalism to universalism, from hierarchy to citizenship, and from market ideologies to meaning systems that valorize the primacy of human dignity. At the center of all three goals is the leveling of categorical distinctions and their associated status and power differentials, thereby making human dignity the central cultural framework through which organizational decisions should be made and policy goals identified.

From Tribalism to Universalism

We are a tribal species. Human beings evolved in small groups with strong bonds to the tribe and suspicions of outsiders. For most of human history we lived in small bands of 50–100 people, and strong tribal boundaries were functional. Over time our tribal boundaries have expanded, including for many a tribal identification with whole nations and for some all of humanity. While once our laws and norms of extending routine dignity in interaction applied only to members of the tribe, we now have declarations and expectations fostering widespread human rights.

The march of history has slowly, unevenly, and with painful reversals been moving toward a more inclusive universalism. This does not mean that categorical boundaries disappear, but it does mean that our "tribes" have gotten larger and more diverse. Nationalism is a useful indicator of this process. Identifying with a nation of a million or even a billion people, recognizing the shared humanity of the citizens we share a nation with, is a wide extension of tribal boundaries, at least compared to our evolutionary heritage. Contemporary identity movements, such as movements for equal treatment associated with race, ethnicity, gender, sexual preference, and gender identity, are precisely about extending the moral claims to citizenship within nations. At the same time, nationalism remains a tribal boundary, one that continues to encourage and legitimate the citizenship distinctions that permit exclusion, exploitation, and even state-sponsored murder.

Much of this movement toward universal human dignity has occurred via institutional politics aimed at law and the state. The goals of democratic and identity-oriented social movements have been to extend human rights both within and across national borders. The extension of democracy redefines citizens from property holders and those who control the state to a widening circle of full citizens, eventually moving in many countries to most or all adults. The extension of social and economic citizenship, including expectations of respect, free movement, and equal opportunities in the market, is a parallel development. Older status distinctions, ones that once seemed universal and legitimate, around property, gender, race, and citizenship, are challenged by multiple social and political movements, eroding categorical exclusions.

The movement from tribalism to universalism is clearly reversible as the frequent outbreaks of nativist resentment toward immigrants and ethnic minorities in even the most egalitarian of countries make clear. In the United States, the country we know the best, immigrant, racial, and gender resentments have been routinely harnessed to advance the political power of major political parties and, as we write this in the spring of 2018, have come to dominate political discourse once again. Illegal discrimination in markets remains widespread, and legal exclusion from citizenship rights of felons and immigrants is actively promoted by some and supported by more.

At the same time, the long march of history shows a broadening of the definition of who is to be treated as truly human: from the tribe to the nation to the species and within nations from property-holder to citizen and from ethnic or religious majorities, men, the able-bodied, and heterosexuals to all human beings. The increased complexity of production and trade, moving from tribal to global production and exchange vastly expands the functional definition of the tribe, even as identity and cultural definitions lag. We are now a globally interdependent species, and our tribal hardwiring must catch up with this basic fact. Luckily, we are also a profoundly cultural species. Our actions are much more heavily influenced by cultural inventions than tendencies toward tribalism. The proof is clearly there in the explosive expansion of our tribal boundaries, productive capacity, and organizational practices.

One lesson that we draw from the extension of rights and respect is that it is easier to enact equality-promoting laws than to nurture equality in interaction. Status hierarchies are remarkably easy to create among human beings. This is probably also a result of our species' evolution in which the key distinctions within the tribe were in terms of survival skills. Evolutionarily, we tended to admire the most skilled and knowledgeable among us, granting them status and deference. We continue to defer to those with cultural or local status, even as the evolutionary survival function has withered.

As a result, equality in interaction is much more difficult to achieve than changes in law or organizational policy, particularly when there are cultural messages that reinforce categorical status distinctions. Interactional racism and sexism are probably the most widely recognized forms of this interactional disrespect. Anytime a status category gets married to a skill or authority-invested position, cultural status expectations will be invoked and new ones evolve. Segregation exaggerates status distinctions and reinforces stereotype bias. Even among otherwise equal actors, cultural status expectations can produce implicit status hierarchies and the interactional disrespect that can follow.

Class-based status hierarchies around earnings, education, skill, and authority are also widespread but perhaps less commonly recognized as having their origin in the same interactional processes. Intersectional approaches to inequality focus our attention on the joint production of status hierarchies, which will always include class resources in interaction with other status distinctions. At the same time, even in gender or race or educationally homogenous settings, we can expect class inequalities to generate relational inequalities. Thus, to reduce tribalism at the level of interaction requires reducing both hierarchy and segregation. Equal status interaction is a prerequisite for interactional status equality.

From Hierarchy to Organizational Citizenship

While our evolutionary heritage makes us susceptible to form and act on categorical distinctions, expanding levels of hierarchy and task segregation are much more modern innovations. Complex divisions of labor engender much finer skill- and authority-based distinctions than our hunter-gatherer tribal evolution ever produced. Firms further exaggerate those distinctions when they adopt authority-based managerial strategies and high levels of inequality in pay. Segregation of tasks along educational, gender, ethnic, race, and age lines further cements and exaggerates these status distinctions by tying them to skill- or authority-ranked roles in the division of labor.

What expanded hierarchy and task segregation mean in practices within organizations is that all individuals do not share equal citizenship. Actors in more marginalized positions are treated as less important, and their needs and contributions are less respected and recognized. This hinders their capacity to legitimately claim organizational resources, including perhaps most perniciously their claim to dignified treatment. In more extreme forms, the most marginalized actors are explicitly excluded from organizational citizenship through subcontracting, temporary labor contracts, and the outsourcing of organizational tasks. In such situations, actors may temporarily enter the organizational space but have no claim to any of the organization's material or symbolic resources.

Whether or not workplaces exaggerate or mute hierarchical distinctions are choices in organizational design. Whether compensation procedures increase status hierarchies or flatten them are as well. Since both choices, increasing hierarchical distinctions and the rewards associated with superior positions, favor more powerful actors, it is not surprising when organizational designs turn out to be inequality-enhancing. High-inequality organizations further cement the claims-making power and interactional status advantage of actors in superior roles.

Often, those in power justify inequality-enhancing practices as necessary to ensure productivity, but the evidence for these claims is weak at best. High-inequality organizations are not more productive (Kim and Sakamoto 2008). As we demonstrated in Chapter 8, innovative high-performance work organizations tend to adopt labor processes that generate respect and cooperation among employees and employers. Flatter hierarchies are also associated with more equal-status gender and racial integration (Smith-Doerr 2004; Kalev 2009). Real employee involvement in decision-making does not harm productivity and probably increases it in many circumstances, and such involvement increases employee and managerial well-being in many organizations as well (Doucouliagos 1995; Freeman and Kleiner 2000). In addition, employee ownership increases productivity, reduces layoffs during economic downturns, and increases firm survival (Kurtulus and Kruse 2017). Command and control organizational designs slow innovation and are built on the false premise that denying human dignity is somehow functional for the firm. Even the more benign form of command and control designs—legal rational democratic control—founder under the bureaucratic focus on procedures and rules and audits of behavior rather than goal orientations toward inclusion and dignity (Rothschild 2016).

Command and control management is functional only in the short term and then primarily for the benefit of the powerful who can immediately exploit the effort of subordinates or exclude other stakeholders from organizational resources. While these models of management are as old as hierarchy, shareholder value ideologies have more recently shifted the moral evaluation of the firm toward only a vehicle for producing profits for stockholders (Ho 2009). This financial conceptualization of production and organizational resources has led to declining value of production at both the firm and societal levels (Tomaskovic-Devey et al. 2015b) and given executives increased permission to exploit other firms and their own employees (Lazonick and O'Sullivan 2000).

While organizing production and market exchanges around embedded, equal-status relationships is more economically efficient in the long run, exploitation, threats, and predatory economic practices are often used to reach short-term goals. Since inequality-exaggerating practices will tend to mechanically increase the status and the power of those already in authority- or skill-invested roles, it is not hard to understand why denial of dignity and exploitative organizational strategies are often pursued. At the same time, it is difficult to ruthlessly exploit others you interact with on a daily basis. We suspect that this is one reason why the current increase in inequality in the United States and other nations is so strongly associated with increased exploitation via markets and the polarization of the economy into high- and low-wage firms. It is easier to exploit strangers than family, neighbors, or even co-workers.

To reduce status-based claims-making and categorical exclusion within workplaces requires targeting goals of flatter organizational hierarchies, lower earnings inequalities within them, and reduced task segregation between categorically distinct groups. We believe that such goals, when achieved, would also go a long way toward reducing the routine disrespect in interaction associated with class, gender, race, and other categorical distinctions in workplaces. Simply telling people to respect diversity can never work as long as there are status-generating class inequalities and segregation-reinscribing status hierarchies in interaction. On the contrary, telling employees to respect diversity without flattening organizational hierarchies is just as likely to exaggerate categorical biases (Dobbin, Kalev, and Kelly 2009). Creating dignity at work requires dignity-respecting divisions of labor, reward systems built around the assumption that all people are morally worthy, and challenging claims that categorical distinctions justify closure and exploitation.

From Markets to Dignity

Market fundamentalism, the notion that markets are the morally as well as economically superior solution to all production and coordination problems, has not only justified exploitation of labor, customers, and suppliers in the name of shareholder value but also largely reframed what matters in how we organize economies and organizations. Market competition has become a moral package, self-legitimating despite a built-in bias to reward the already powerful. The mantra of governments has become to secure economic growth through competitive market forces with, at most, a latent presumption that this will benefit human welfare. Currently, most governments take economic growth as their primary social goal.[4] In a world of scarce resources, this is certainly important, and the expansion of productivity has done much to improve the quality of human life. But it has also produced unanticipated consequences of ecological destruction and inequality generation. This logic has infected firms as well. The shareholder value ideology has turned organizations into piles of assets to be shuffled and reshuffled to maximize economic returns to owners, with limited regard for employees and their families and communities. Organizational goals have been reframed to align with owner wealth creation goals, suppressing any understanding of a more general welfare goal that would justify their existence.

Importantly, the view that productivity growth requires high levels of inequality is simply unsupported by empirical evidence (see, for example, Kenworthy 2004). Yes, differences in task competence lead to probably unavoidable status hierarchies in interaction. But this interactional observation has limited, perhaps no, implications for collective efficiencies. Productivity growth requires innovation. Innovation, whether technical or social, requires cooperative behavior. Contemporary innovation requires cooperation both within and between organizations. It is simply not an individual-level phenomenon.

4. There is a movement to push development metrics away from gross domestic product and toward goals of human well-being. In 2016, the Organisation for Economic Co-operation and Development affirmed a commitment to promoting human well-being over production volume. Countries are now being ranked on their overall happiness levels as well (Helliwell, Layard, and Sachs 2017). Countries tend to do well on this index if they have reasonably high standards of living but also low inequality and high access to human dignity.

Rather than maximizing economic growth or economic returns, our goal should be to create normative expectations and institutional pressures to encourage transactions built on the dignity of every human being. That is, the role of the state, firms, and other organizations should be to promote human well-being and dignity, not economic expansion for the sake of economic expansion. In its most dangerous form, market ideology assumes that economic expansion necessarily results in increases in human dignity when, in practice, in many forms it may undermine it. Central to a politics of egalitarianism is reframing the role of states and organizations as dignity-enhancing, rather than market, machines. In treating the market as if it will mechanically produce human flourishing, we have blinded ourselves to the ways in which markets fail precisely because they reinforce the power of the already powerful.

To understand the centrality of placing our social goals ahead of market technologies, let's engage in a thought experiment. Imagine for a moment that we decide we need to build a bridge across a river. Economic theory would suggest that we create a bidding system to get firms to compete on price and quality for building that bridge. But before we ask for bids to build the bridge, we would need to specify where it was to start and end and what it was to carry across the river. Once the social goals of the bridge were specified, market mechanisms might produce some cost efficiencies, although there is no guarantee that this will be the case. It is imperative that we specify our social goals before we invoke market or any other organizational mechanism for generating and allocating production and value in order to ensure that the techniques we employ in fact accomplish the goals we set out. The expansion of market-like institutions for their own sake is an inappropriate design goal and, in the presence of (typically ubiquitous) power inequalities and categorical status hierarchies, will always lead to further inequalities through claims-making, exploitation, and social closure channels.

We should build our bridges with design specifications that begin with goals of promoting human dignity. As a result, it is necessary to reframe the role of government from promoting markets and economic growth to promoting human well-being. Tribalism reserves dignity for the tribal in-group and heaps an extra measure of respect on the skilled or otherwise admirable. Exploitation and closure are built around these basic categorical distinctions. Reducing tribalism requires us to expand the boundaries of who deserves to be treated with respect and dignity. As we recognize a larger circle of people eligible for embedded, trustworthy, respectful interaction, we narrow the pool of people eligible for exclusion and exploitation.

In the context of this book, one might be tempted to consider inequality reduction as the primary social goal. We are reluctant to endorse this as the central alternative to market fundamentalism. Doing so would run the danger of fetishizing equality in the way that policy discussions fetishize economic growth. What we are really after is a world in which we build social relations inscribed with human dignity at the center. Reducing inequality is merely one possible means to that end. Clearly, reducing inequalities reduces both power- and status-based claims-making advantages. Reducing inequalities will also reduce status distinctions and blur status boundaries. But these must be framed as dignity-enhancing political strategies. Worker, gender, sexuality, immigrant, and civil rights movements become morally compelling when they are based around claims of universal human rights to dignity and respect, not when they are simply usurpationary exploitation and closure claims on more income.

There may also be a growth argument for embracing dignity as a primary social goal given the evidence that participatory, respectful managerial practices are productivity-enhancing and that the denial of dignity leads to chaotic production processes and market exploitation. But we think that in the end the question is normative, not scientific. We note that many religious theologies incorporate the injunction to treat all human beings with dignity and respect. In this sense, we are more comfortable with a theology of dignity and respect than with a magical belief in the powerless efficacy of markets or the automatic benefits of economic growth or educational credentialism.

Universalism, organizational citizenship, and dignity are then three normative goals we think can be built out of the RIT framework. However, RIT also has explicit connections to the political strategies for pursuing these goals as it focuses our attention on particular social spaces (i.e., organizations and fields) in which to pursue universalism, citizenship, and dignity. Therefore, in the next section we become somewhat more pragmatic, outlining some implications of the three goals outlined in this section for conventional institutional politics and for the organizational design of workplaces. We focus on institutional politics and organizational design as these are the basic field-level processes implicated in RIT. At the most basic level, accomplishing these three goals—universalism, citizenship, dignity—requires finding ways to legitimate claims of inclusion, level categorical distinctions, and recognize claims of the intrinsic worth of all organizational members. In the end, we must infuse a routinized preference for dignity and respect into both organizations and market exchanges.

INSTITUTIONAL AND ORGANIZATIONAL POLITICS

RIT implies two basic avenues for accomplishing the goals of universalism, citizenship, and dignity. One avenue is to focus on shaping the institutional landscape in which organizations operate, replacing tribalism with universalism and market logics with dignity logics. Much of the politics around egalitarianism already focuses on this level, highlighting opportunities to transform state institutions that directly influence inequality practices (e.g., Brady 2009; Esping-Andersen 2013). These remain appropriate targets of inequality-reducing and dignity-enhancing political interventions. At the same time, the RIT approach adds a caution that societal interventions must be targeted at specific organizations or organizational practices to have their desired effects. The dominant policy recipe of nudging or coercing individuals to make different choices is profoundly mistaken. People make choices in relational contexts. Organizations pool resources and define the choice set. Policies must target the organizations that both generate the opportunities and distribute them.

The second, and in the long run more efficacious, avenue is to directly intervene into organizations, redesigning them in such a way as to replace tribalism with universalism and hierarchy with citizenship. Such an explicit focus on organizational design is implicated in much of the literature seeking to reduce status discrimination as well as the literature on workplace democracy and participation (e.g., Smith-Doerr 2004; Kalev 2009; Kurtulus and Kruse 2017). Such organizational designs are becoming more prominent in many spheres and perhaps are the vanguard of a low-inequality, high-productivity, morally expansive economic future (Rothschild 2016).

Social movements, both inside and outside organizations, are often central to both strategies. But mobilization strategies do not provide a generic roadmap for reducing the space for organizations to generate inequality, other than the observation that state- and firm-oriented politics matters. Here, we provide three simple guideposts for reducing inequalities and enhancing dignity via three mechanisms of institutional transformation: destabilize inequality-distributing categorical distinctions, increase the bargaining power of the least powerful, and reduce organizational resource inequalities. These three goals can be attached to institutional politics at the state or organizational levels.

Destabilize Status Hierarchies

At the heart of RIT's understanding of inequality generation is the translation of categorical distinctions into status hierarchies. Status hierarchies are pernicious and particularly difficult to dislodge once they emerge in conjunction with categorical social distinctions. Organizational routines and local cultures develop around status hierarchies, and interests develop among advantaged actors to preserve them. As Joan Acker (2006) notes, race, class, gender, and other distinctions get written into the relational architecture of firms. We advocate two broad strategies to transform these tribally based hierarchies into universally based organizational citizenship regimes.

One strategy is to delegitimate the differential moral valuation of categorical distinctions. The most effective inequality-reducing social movements across history have struggled for universal human dignity and the recognition of full citizenship rights by fighting for expanded civil, economic, and social rights. They challenge the notion that categorical distinctions of class, of race, of religion, of gender, of sexual orientation, of ability, and of citizenship—to name only the most prominent—must matter for the distribution of resources and respect. The expansion of democratic participation in politics and production as well as the delegitimation of explicit status-based closure and exploitation have been their accomplishments. Many hierarchical status distinctions, such as those around property ownership, race and ethnicity, religion, gender, sexual orientation, and even national citizenship, which were once seen as broadly legitimate have been challenged legally and eroded interactionally.

The most effective of these social movements have also targeted organizations, such as firms, schools, and churches, in their quest for equality. States, particularly democratic states with broad-based political inclusion, are particularly vulnerable to such movements. In response to these movements, many firms in the United States and elsewhere have committed themselves to providing equal employment opportunities irrespective of race, gender, sexual orientation, ability, and other status distinctions. These commitments have often followed legislative and legal interventions promoted by social movements but have also resonated with meritocracy ideologies common in many contemporary societies.

Achieving equal opportunity in practice has been more difficult, but there are some lessons on what works for challenging categorical distinctions. Broadening transparency in hiring and promotion decisions and in pay practices provides resources to counter invidious distinctions. In contrast, evaluation exercises that incorporate information on status hierarchies or simply reassure decision-makers that bias is absent do the opposite. Reducing task segregation both through the formation of cooperative workgroups and integrating jobs, organizations, and teams in terms of their demographic and skill composition challenge status hierarchies and reduce the social space for exploitation. Making workers owners and owners workers erases the boundary across which exploitation so commonly occurs.

Something similar can be said about education. While more education is associated at the individual level with a reduction in tribalism and an increased capacity to solve problems and innovate, it has also been fetishized as a productivity signal and in this way legitimates systems of unjust meritocracy. Organizational activists looking to produce more equal opportunity often stop when the impact of race or gender approaches zero, but the correlation between education and rewards remains unexamined. But this human capital- or status attainment-inspired version of meritocracy is silent on the level or degree of inequality associated with education. If the point of organizational interventions is to enhance dignity, educational disparities need to be contained. Flattening hierarchies as a goal of organization design should not be limited to CEO pay or gender and racial disparities, but we should also interrogate the legitimated inequalities associated with educational credentialism.

It is important to remember, however, that to achieve more than simply symbolic success requires changing interactions and relationships at the meso level of relational life. That is, status beliefs can re-emerge at the interactional level if organizations do not actively work to explicitly undermine the translation of categorical distinctions into status hierarchies.

A second strategy to undermine status hierarchies within firms is to promote status heterogeneity across positions within organizations. This may require making fewer job and occupational distinctions as well as integrating now segregated positions. RIT highlights that one fundamental process of translating categorical distinctions into status hierarchies involves segregating categorically distinct people into distinctive and hierarchical roles within organizations. Such segregation patterns install and reinforce status distinctions, devalue some actors and jobs, and legitimate higher-status actors' claims on organizational resources. The relational composition of a workplace is a signal of inclusion in the organization, and status heterogeneity provides an equal footing for categorically distinct others to make claims. Equal-status contact also makes the translation of categorical distinctions into status hierarchies harder to institutionalize and therefore less likely to justify exclusion and exploitation.

Thus, integrating social relations within organizations can enable a shift toward a more egalitarian local culture. Reorganizing the relational structure and composition of organizations as a means to reconfigure local status hierarchies is crucial for generating local cultures that broadly value the dignity of all organizational roles and actors. The ease of deriving this implication from the elements of RIT, however, masks the complexity and difficulty of turning that goal into a reality. Cultures are notably resistant to change and thereby reinforce segregation patterns and social relations. The most likely scenario for actually rewiring the cultural landscape of an organization is for actors to seize upon exogenous shocks in the organizational field, which tend to disrupt dominant frameworks for sense-making (Avent-Holt 2012). This suggests the potential efficacy of transforming the institutions around the organization as a means to transform the plausibility of categorical claims. Cultural schemata that foster a broad moral circle, the inclusion of all stakeholders, and the inherent dignity of actors can rewrite the local culture in such a way that legitimates the claims of previously marginalized actors and limits the capacity for high-status actors to exploit and hoard resources.

Increase the Bargaining Power of the Least Powerful

RIT identifies relational claims-making as the proximate mechanism underlying resource inequalities, making the relative bargaining power of actors crucial to inequality regimes. Thus, reconfiguring power relations to narrow the gap in actors' individual and collective resources to make legitimate claims is a powerful policy lever in the move toward universal citizenship and human dignity. Accomplishing this goal can target both institutional and organizational practices.

Organizational policies and practices themselves can generate more or less power for some actors to claim organizational resources. A central strategy is to expand the actors within organizations who are considered stakeholders with legitimate claims on resources. Two of the most inequality-enhancing of contemporary organizational practices are pay-for-performance and executive pay via stock options schemes. The stated goal of these is to improve individual productivity, but in effect they both install market logics into the way firms distribute their resources, thereby institutionalizing power asymmetries and submerging citizenship and dignity goals. In practice, both end up redirecting organizational resources away from lower-level employees or dependent suppliers and toward top managers and executives. In contrast, systems that bureaucratize the wage-setting process by linking pay to formal job hierarchies and tenure, which characterized the structure of the postwar capital-labor accords of the mid-twentieth-century US manufacturing economy, generate lower levels of inequality, greater economic security, and a more solidaristic organizational culture. Such systems treat all actors as legitimate stakeholders, improving the bargaining position of the least powerful.

Of course, much of what laid beneath this political economic arrangement was unionization. Unions are the classic organizational actors increasing the bargaining power of the least powerful workers. And in the US context especially, union organizing at the local organizational level was critical to the high-wage, low-inequality mid-twentieth-century manufacturing regime. Despite their historic success, unions in the United States do not now provide the relational claims-making leverage they once did (Rosenfeld 2014). Regardless, expanding the categories of recognized stakeholders to include lower-level workers is a central strategy to increasing the bargaining power of the least powerful within organizations. Including upstream (customers) and downstream (suppliers) actors, as well as community stakeholders, as key constituents with legitimate claims would further broaden organizational citizenship and level inequality-generating hierarchies.

Worker cooperatives are perhaps the organizational structure that most clearly institutionalizes a stakeholder position for all organizational actors while blurring categorical distinctions. In their idealized form, all workers share in both decision-making and the profits generated in the process of production. This organizational form then legitimates the lowest-status members' claim to organizational resources by virtue of simple membership. Relative to conventional capitalist firms, power is much more evenly distributed, and the claims of all actors have a higher baseline legitimacy.

Regardless of the relative power of actors within firms, if the organizational field prohibits certain practices or enforces others, a floor can be set on the level of exploitation. Prohibitions against slavery are perhaps the most obvious. Minimum wages are another. Wage and hour laws and their enforcement to prevent wage theft are a third. Enforceable laws that support the citizenship rights of workers in the employment relationship, either through collective bargaining, health and safety, job security, or equal pay provisions, limit the allowable level of exploitation in the employment relationship. These are all exploitation-reducing policies. They vary in their strength and enforceability across countries and time. The United States has the weakest labor protections among high- and medium-wage countries in the world and, not surprisingly, the highest levels of class inequality. On the other hand, the United States has some of the strongest anti-discrimination laws and some of the lowest levels of gender inequality.

Laws to prohibit exploitation between organizations are less widespread and perhaps more in need of development. One lesson from global financialization is that the globally dominant financial service firms have been willing to use their power to exploit customers through markets. Much of this exploitation, such as creating an unsustainable market for mortgages and repackaging them as worthless mortgage-backed securities or processing debits on checking accounts in order to maximize overdraft penalties, were clearly legal, if immoral. Other practices, like banks trading ahead of their own customers based on customer buy-and-sell information and the LIBOR scandal, in which the largest banks colluded to manipulate the interest rates paid on variable credit instruments like car loans and credit cards, while illegal, were carried out nonetheless. One of the casualties of the rise of market fundamentalism is to obscure that profiteering from market power is a widespread form of exploitation.

The dominant approach in western European countries has been to collectively organize the working class at the societal level, instituting national wage-bargaining over the distribution of the national economic surplus. Other countries have had various forms of corporatist bargaining over the distribution of income associated with capitalist production. One of the most interesting was the "Rehn-Meidner" plan. This plan was introduced in 1951 by two Swedish economists, Gösta Rehn and Rudolf Meidner, and was the dominant income-distribution mechanisms in the Swedish economy until 1983. The Rehn-Meidner wage model emphasized solidaristic wage-bargaining, where all wages were centrally negotiated with wage gains limited by national productivity growth and wage rates directly tied to occupational skill levels, but income for low-skill occupations rose slightly faster than that for high-skill occupations, thus narrowing inequalities over time. Individual or workplace productivity and bargaining power were not rewarded. As a result, everyone's wage rose with increases in national wealth. However, wages for those at the bottom rose faster, and wage distributions were, as a consequence, compressed. Because labor costs tended to rise the fastest in low-skill jobs and because wages were tied to worker skill rather than organizational productivity, this model encouraged technological innovations that increased the skill requirements of low-skill jobs and punished low-productivity firms that had to pay the same wage as their high-productivity competitors (Alexopoulos and Cohen 2003). This market model tied earnings to national productivity and task skill requirements but resisted unjust meritocracy while encouraging productivity improvement and eliminating low-productivity firms.

Decommodification provides another set of public policies that provide alternatives to market distribution of various social and individual necessities (Vail 2010; Esping-Andersen 2013). Such policies include housing subsidies, healthcare benefits, food subsidies, and child support payments as well as other income transfers to households. Universal basic income provides the most widespread attempt to decommodify income and labor itself. In the United States, many of these policies do not exist or are tied to prior labor-market activity. In other countries, some mix of these policies often exists, and they are simply tied to being a resident in the country. The more expansive the welfare state benefits, the less dependent individuals and households are on employment. Universal basic income and more modest income replacement policies are particularly effective in raising the negotiating power of the least powerful because they provide an alternative to exploitative relationships in the workplace and a partial antidote to social closure from employment or from household supporting jobs.

These types of income transfer policies require taxation systems in which governments tax high earners in order to support more vulnerable citizens. In many of the more generous welfare state countries, the goal is precisely to prevent social exclusion by raising incomes high enough to ensure full participation in society. Citizenship rights are assumed to take precedence over property rights.

Reduce Organizational Resource Inequalities

One of the most remarkable of recent findings on the rise of inequality is that a great deal of it is produced through the increase in inequality between the resource bases of different firms. Globally dominant financial service firms, such as Goldman Sachs, and similarly powerful information technology (IT) firms, such as Apple and Microsoft, are the most familiar faces of this transformation. The disintegration of the vertically integrated firm, designed to pool market power in the dominant firm while shifting risk and labor costs onto subcontractor, franchise, and global supply chain firms, is less visible but probably no less important in driving these changes.

Inequalities across organizations in their resource bases are crucial in relational claims-making as the volume of organizational resources provides the fundamental limiting condition on claims-making. Typically, actors make claims on resources that flow into organizations, so if resource streams dry up, so do claims on incomes and other organizational resources. Because high-resource firms tend also to hire white, male, and highly educated workers, there is also a substantial feedback loop exaggerating more familiar categorical bases of inequality. The evolving world of inequality between organizations then produces a world of unequal organizational citizens not within organizations but between them. For universal human dignity to flourish, everyone must have access to the same resource base.

One plausible solution is to weaken the legal and normative boundaries between organizations, enabling actors involved in the process of producing goods and services in one organization to claim the resources that flow out of that firm. Even as we have pointed out the equality-reducing effect of expanding the moral boundaries of the tribe, we could contemplate expanding the legal boundary of the firm. Current law in all countries, as far as we are aware, defines the boundaries of the firm in terms of its legal structure. As a result, firms have figured out how to shift boundaries in order to create new avenues of exploitation and exclusion, monopolizing resources in core firms, exploiting satellite suppliers, franchisees, and independent contractors. If the law was to shift the definition of the firm to the boundaries of control over production, many more actors—subcontractors, temporary labor suppliers, franchisees, upstream commodity suppliers—would begin to have legitimate claims on the surplus generated by joint production. Economist Edith Penrose (2009) has offered a theory of the firm consistent with this insight. Penrose sees the firm not as a production function like other economists or as a legal entity like most governments, but as the entity that coordinates production. The boundaries of the firm in this conceptualization are the boundaries of coordinating authority over production. In the Penrosian version of the firm, a McDonald's franchise would be part of McDonald's, a sole supplier to Walmart located in Thailand would be part of Walmart, and the entire IT industry would be subsidiaries of the "Frightful Five."

If one pushed this idea even further, all actors in an economy are linked via exchange relationships, and firm boundaries and legal conventions tell us little about the actual social organization of production. Network notions of whole economies imply this kind of joint dependency (e.g., Burt 1983; Battison et al. 2012a, 2012b). This was also Emile Durkheim's ([1893] 2014) early insight that people in industrial societies must someday recognize their shared fate through the interdependencies created by complex divisions of labor or suffer from increasingly illegitimate inequalities.

An older, and perhaps less plausible, strategy in the current political moment is the nationalization of industries. Such a policy would concentrate resources into a single revenue stream flowing into entire industries, coordinated through state action in the distribution of resources. In today's neoliberal, market fundamentalist ideological environment, nationalization seems unrealistic. However, there are numerous historical precedents in industries once considered natural monopolies (e.g., utilities) or collective patrimony (e.g., natural resources), and these may be the most plausible industries and sectors in which to pursue such a strategy. But for other industries, this may be plausible as well, particularly if a public good can be articulated from nationalization. Global financial service firms may be a case in point. Global trade depends on their existence, but at the same time they are systemically risky and so essentially already favored by state subsidies. Too-big-to-fail banks may be necessary, but their risks are already nationalized even as their profits remain private.

Another approach would be to define socially acceptable levels of profit for firms. In the United States, financial service firms have controlled up to 40% of all profits in the national economy (see Tomaskovic-Devey and Lin 2011). Since the function of finance is to facilitate productive investment, limiting global financial service firm profits to the global or national rate of economic growth and then redistributing income above that level to support the development of relatively poorer local economies and organizations might both produce investment capital for poor places and reduce the incentives for financial service giants to exploit their global market power. This may be a historical moment in which the logic for treating finance as a public good would find a ready audience.

Any policy goal of organizational income redistribution can be expected to generate resistance from powerful firms and their owners. Countries that contain globally powerful firms, like the United States, whose IT and finance firms are globally dominant, will be reluctant to reduce the global monopoly power of those firms. As the pharmaceutical example in Chapter 8 pointed out, the United States has been reluctant to reduce the power of any firm to extract surplus from the rest of the society, even when those same firms' price-setting powers are limited in other countries.

One of the paradoxes produced by the shareholder value movement has been the declining importance of powerful firms as employers. In the odd set of social welfare configurations that evolved in the United States in the twentieth century, large oligopolistic firms were the source of employment, surplus distribution, health insurance, and retirement savings (Davis 2013). They effectively reduced inequality by pooling economic surplus and sharing it with all employees in the firm. Their decline as employers and expansion as resource-poolers has been a fundamental driver of rising inequality in the United States.

Gerald Davis (2013) has suggested some rules for organizational forms that would counter both the increased pooling of surplus in fewer, low-employment firms in the United States, which may also have more general implications for other countries. First, for production functions that require the wide pooling of resources to be practical–social insurance, transportation and communication systems, mining, transport–large-scale organizational forms are preferable. If market systems are pooling resources elsewhere, these require income transfers into those sectors to support collective activity. In many countries, most of these functions are provided by national governments or are highly regulated to ensure widespread, even universal, access. In terms of direct production and distributions of consumable goods, Davis argues that technological (e.g., cheap computerized machine tools, 3D printers), communication (Web-based applications), and free intellectual property (e.g., Linux operating systems) trends imply that many types of production no longer need large firms and can be produced locally. Local production is much more easily organized as worker or community cooperatives, democratizing production, reducing the cost of consumption, and more equally distributing surplus.

These are, of course, not exhaustive of the possible approaches to reducing the inequalities produced by organizational resource variation. We think the most important political implication of our analysis is to recognize that firm income polarization is an important and rising source of inequalities. Simply recognizing this source of inequality focuses attention on organizations as a source of inequality, and the tactic then is to find creative policy solutions that produce more egalitarian fields of organizations and organizational forms.

IN CLOSING

Human beings evolved in tribal groups. We are social animals, attuned to the wisdom, myth, and prejudices of our tribe. From the collective wisdom of our tribe, we learn the solutions that were invented to solve past problems of social organization and survival. From these myths, we derive explanations as to why those solutions work, as well as parables about how the world should work. From our prejudices, we define the boundaries of our tribe and the limits of our moral responsibility. Crucially, human beings have the capacity for remarkable innovation in their social and material tools, in their myths, and in their tribal boundaries. And it is this innovative capacity that makes a shift from tribalism to universalism a real possibility and gives us hope for generating more egalitarian societies.

While we often imagine our modern selves as qualitatively different from our forebears, and in some ways we are, belief in our own wisdom, exulted through myth and prejudice, is as true of modern humans as it was of our ancestors. Contemporary global societies rely on technocratic experts in the way that tribal societies relied on shamans and medieval societies on monks and priests. Experts provide guidance based on their theories of how the world works. The mythic nature of much of our modern world is often obscured in scientific theories, which purport to be purely mechanical stories about how some aspect of the world works. The big innovation in science has been to elevate and systematize the experimental tendencies that were always there in human populations above static faith in origin stories and their explanatory myths.

But scientists remain human and so often convert their theories into myths, with the same moral (and tribal) tendencies. Macroeconomic theories valorize economic growth, while microeconomic theories valorize market competition. The stronger the belief in theories, the more fervent the belief in the moral superiority of the tribe and of its solutions to problems of social organization. It is easy then to see why strong economic theory cannot be the solution to contemporary social problems and why in the case of the neoliberal policy consensus in Washington, DC, these theories have helped to generate and legitimate some of the most fundamental inequality problems we confront today.

To say that science and technocratic expertise share the tendencies of the species is at some level a mundane insight. We use such experts for the same reason other humans used shamans: they provide us with useful stories about how the world works. But one of the great dangers has been to raise economic theory from the realm of context-specific expertise, for example, a prediction of the effect of drought on the price of wheat, to a global myth used to evaluate the morality of behavior and predict the efficacy of policy. Growing profitability and the extension of markets as moral imperatives are a long way from the narrow scientific question of where wheat prices might go next winter given a drought this spring. What many governments have done with economic theory is equivalent to permitting the expertise of a particular operating system–inspired set of software engineers or national tax accountants or NASA scientists to define the goals and morality of corporate or national economic decisions. But, of course, contemporary economic theory had an advantage that engineers, accountants, and physicists do not: it provides a scientific cover for the exercise of power via mechanisms of exploitation and exclusion while simultaneously denying their existence. Clearly, this has been a science the powerful and acquisitive could get behind.

The ideology of market fundamentalism works against all three of the goals we set out. In setting the market above all else, it permits, and to some extent encourages, an ethos of self-regarding gain over a universalistic moral compass. The assumption underlying market fundamentalism that individuals will maximize their payoff in exchange relationships actually endorses, rather than merely describes, behavior that RIT notes leads to strategies of exploitation and closure as mechanisms to hoard opportunities or take advantage of others' vulnerabilities. Competition is the explicit goal of the game, crowding out the expansion of citizenship and dignity. Market fundamentalism as a moral package, one that has been very beneficial to the wealth and psychological well-being of the rich and their powerful organizations, has been masquerading as science. Academic economists have long understood the difference between a model of how the economy might work and a description of reality, and it is increasingly the case that some mainstream economists have begun to call into question the basic assumptions of the utility of the free market, limited regulation policy recipe they once endorsed for aspirational theoretical reasons.[5]

RIT does not provide a simple recipe for growth or equality or for countering market fundamentalism. And even though we have placed our

5. We look forward to a history of this process which is only now beginning and is far from complete. Nobel Prize recipient Joseph Stiglitz has been the foremost proponent of this movement relative to the problem of inequality (2015). Marion Fourcade's (2009) work does a great job of explaining how the neoclassical theory developed in the economics profession. Sarah Babb, with Fourcade (Fourcade-Gourinchas and Babb 2002; Babb 2001), has also tracked the translation of this abstract theory into neoliberal policy practice.

normative eggs in an egalitarian basket, RIT in and of itself is agnostic on such goals. From the point of myth-making, this is a clear weakness. From a scientific point of view, we see it as a strength.

We have, however, been able to derive a number of implications for the design of organizational and public policy. At the core of these though is that the tribal boundaries that characterized the world of our ancestors are artificial and mutable. Value is not produced by managers or capital or labor or engineers but via coordinated divisions of labor, investment, training, and effort both between and within organizations. Economic actors, whether individuals or firms, are embedded in complex divisions of labor that include the organizations that produce people and customers such as households and schools, firms that supply and consume the output of firms, and the organizations that set the legal and moral boundaries on acceptable exchange behavior such as churches, social movements, political parties, courts, and governments. There is no economy without this complex web of organizations, each of which is influenced by where the money pools and how it is distributed. In such an interdependent world, our ancient tribalism will get us nowhere. To define productivity as something done by executives and managers and then pay them for that is simply extraction of organizational surplus disguised as meritocracy. To outsource low-skilled labor because it is a cheaper way to generate profits is simply closure around the boundary of the tribe designed to hoard income for shareholders and the residual employees. Pretending that individual actors, whether firms or people, are somehow independent of this web of relationships is merely mythology.

We are a relational species. We learn, act, innovate, and create in cooperation with others. Tribal societies could draw tribal boundaries because most learning, innovation, and cooperation happened within the tribe. Modern societies are not tribal in this way. The boundaries of production, innovation, and cooperation are constantly expanding. The globalization of culture and production pushes the functional boundary of the real tribe to include all human beings. We lag behind this organic interdependence in our reliance on categorical distinctions between human beings, artificially narrowing the limits of our moral responsibility to various local tribes—family, community, firm, religion, race, nationality. Narrowing our categorical inclusions broadens the population of people we can morally justify exploiting and excluding. Expanding our categorical boundaries to extend human rights and dignity to all people is the most basic recipe for reducing inequalities, expanding dignity, and promoting human well-being.

References

Abbott, Andrew. 1988. *The System of Professions: An Essay on the Division of Labor*. Chicago: University of Chicago Press.

Abbott, Andrew. 2001. *Chaos of Disciplines*. Chicago: University of Chicago Press.

Abendroth, Anja-Kristin, Silvia Melzer, Alexandra Kalev, and Donald Tomaskovic-Devey. 2016. "Women at Work: Women's Access to Power and the Gender Earnings Gap." *Industrial and Labor Relations Review* 70: 190-222.

Abowd, John M., and Francis Kramarz. 1999. "The Analysis of Labor Markets Using Matched Employer-Employee Data." *Handbook of Labor Economics* 3: 2629-2710.

Abowd, John M., Francis Kramarz, and David N. Margolis. 1999. "High Wage Workers and High Wage Firms." *Econometrica* 67: 251-333.

Acker, Joan. 1990. "Hierarchies, Jobs, Dodies: A Theory of Gendered Organizations." *Gender & Society* 4: 139-158.

Acker, Joan. 2006. "Inequality Regimes: Gender, Class, and Race in Organizations." *Gender & Society* 20: 441-464.

Adams, Britni L., Joe King, Andrew M. Penner, Nina Bandelj, and Aleksandra Kanjuo-Mrčela. 2017. "The Returns to Education and Labor Market Sorting in Slovenia, 1993-2007." *Research in Social Stratification and Mobility* 47: 55-65.

Adler, Paul S., and Seok-Woo Kwon. 2002. "Social Capital: Prospects for a New Concept." *Academy of Management Review* 27: 17-40.

Alba, Richard. 2005. "Bright vs. Blurred Boundaries: Second Generation Assimilation and Exclusion in France, Germany, and the United States." *Ethnic and Racial Studies* 28: 20-49.

Alexopoulos, Michelle, and Jon Cohen. 2003. "Centralised Wage Bargaining and Structural Change in Sweden." *European Review of Economic History* 7: 331-363.

Amable, Bruno. 2003. *The Diversity of Modern Capitalism*. New York: Oxford University Press.

Anderson, Elizabth S. 1999. "What Is the Point of Equality?" *Ethics* 109: 287-337.

Applebaum, Eileen. 2000. *Manufacturing Advantage: Why High-Performance Work Systems Pay Off*. Ithaca, NY: Cornell University Press.

Appelbaum, Eileen, and Rosemary Batt. 1993. *The New American Workplace: Transforming Work Systems in the United States*. Ithaca, NY: Cornell University Press.

Attewell, Paul. 1990. "What Is Skill?" *Work and Occupations* 17: 422-448.

Avent-Holt, Dustin. 2012. "Organizing Markets: The Structuring of Neoliberalism in the US Airline Industry." PhD diss., University of Massachusetts Amherst.

Avent-Holt, Dustin. 2015. "Reconceptualizing Exploitation: New Directions for an Old Concept in Social Stratification." *Social Currents* 2: 213-221.

Avent-Holt, Dustin. 2017. "The Class Dynamics of Income Shares: Effects of the Declining Power of Unions in the US Airline Industry, 1977–2005." *Socio-Economic Review*. https://doi.org/10.1093/ser/mwx048.

Avent-Holt, Dustin, and Donald Tomaskovic-Devey. 2010. "The Relational Basis of Inequality: Generic and Contingent Wage Distribution Processes." *Work and Occupations* 37: 162–193.

Avent-Holt, Dustin, and Donald Tomaskovic-Devey. 2012. "Relational Inequality: Gender Earnings Inequality in US and Japanese Manufacturing Plants in the Early 1980s." *Social Forces* 91: 157–180.

Avent-Holt, Dustin, and Donald Tomaskovic-Devey. 2014. "A Relational Theory of Earnings Inequality." *American Behavioral Scientist* 58: 379–399.

Averhoff, Francisco M., Nancy Glass, and Deborah Holtzman. 2012. "Global Burden of Hepatitis C: Considerations for Healthcare Providers in the United States." *Clinical Infectious Diseases* 55: S10–S15.

Ayres, Ian. 1991. "Fair Driving: Gender and Race Discrimination in Retail Car Negotiations." *Harvard Law Review* 104: 817–872.

Babb, Sarah L. 2001. *Managing Mexico: Economists from Nationalism to Neoliberalism*. Princeton, NJ: Princeton University Press.

Babb, Sarah. 2013. "The Washington Consensus as Transnational Policy Paradigm: Its Origins, Trajectory and Likely Successor." *Review of International Political Economy* 20: 268–297.

Baker, Wayne E., and Robert R. Faulkner. 1993. "The Social Organization of Conspiracy: Illegal Networks in the Heavy Electrical Equipment Industry." *American Sociological Review* 58: 837–860.

Baron, James N., and William T. Bielby. 1980. "Bringing the Firms Back In: Stratification, Segmentation, and the Organization of Work." *American Sociological Review* 45: 737–765.

Baron, James N., Michael T. Hannan, Greta Hsu, and Özgecan Koçak. 2007. "In the Company of Women: Gender Inequality and the Logic of Bureaucracy in Start-up Firms." *Work and Occupations* 34: 35–66.

Barry, Dan. 2014. "The Boys in the Bunkhouse: Toil, Abuse and Endurance in the Heartland." *New York Times*, March 9.

Battiston, Stefano, Domenico Delli Gatti, Mauro Gallegati, Bruce Greenwald, and Joseph E. Stiglitz. 2012a. "Liaisons Dangereuse: Increasing Connectivity, Risk Sharing, and Systemic Risk." *Journal of Economic Dynamics and Control* 36: 1121–1141.

Battiston, Stefano, Michelangelo Puliga, Rahul Kaushik, Paolo Tasca, and Guido Caldarelli. 2012b. "Debtrank: Too Central to Fail? Financial Networks, the Fed and Systemic Risk." *Scientific Reports* 2: 1–6.

Bechky, Beth A. 2011. "Making Organizational Theory Work: Institutions, Occupations, and Negotiated Orders." *Organization Science* 22: 1157–1167.

Becker, Gary. 1964. *Human Capital: A Theoretical and Empirical Analysis, with Special Reference to Education*. Chicago: University of Chicago Press.

Becker, Gary. 1971. *The Economics of Discrimination*. Chicago: University of Chicago Press.

Becker, Gary. 1976. *The Economic Approach to Human Behavior*. Chicago: University of Chicago Press.

Behnke, Nils, Michael Retterath, Todd Sangster, and Ashish Singh. 2014. *New Paths to Value Creation for Pharma*. http://www.bain.com/Images/BAIN_BRIEF_New_paths_to_value_creation_in_pharma.pdf

Bell, Daniel. 1972. "Meritocracy and Equality." *Public Interest* 29: 2968.

Bender, Stefan, Nicholas Bloom, David Card, John Van Reenen, and Stefanie Wolter. 2018. "Management Practices, Workforce Selection, and Productivity." *Journal of Labor Economics* 36, S1: S371-S409.

Berger, Joseph, M. Hamit Fisek, Robert Z. Norman, and Morris Zelditch Jr. 1977. *Status Characteristics and Interaction: An Expectation States Approach*. New York: Elsevier.

Bernhardt, Annette, Ruth Milkman, Nik Theodore, Douglas Heckathorn, Mirabai Auer, James DeFilippis, Ana Luz Gonzalez, Victor Narro, Jason Perelshteyn, Diana Polson, and Michael Spiller. 2009. *Broken Laws, Unprotected Workers*. National Employment Law Project.

Berrey, Ellen. 2015. *The Enigma of Diversity: The Language of Race and the Limits of Racial Justice*. Chicago: University of Chicago Press.

Bertrand, Marianne, and Sendhil Mullainathan. 2004. "Are Emily and Greg More Employable than Lakisha and Jamal? A Field Experiment on Labor Market Discrimination." *American Economic Review* 94: 991-1013.

Bielby, William T., and James N. Baron. 1986. "Men and Women at Work: Sex Segregation and Statistical Discrimination." *American Journal of Sociology* 91: 759-799.

Bishop, John. 1987. "The Recognition and Reward of Employee Performance." *Journal of Labor Economics* 5: S36-S56.

Blanchflower, David G., Andre J. Oswald, and Peter Sanfey. 1996. "Wages, Profits, and Rent-Sharing." *Quarterly Journal of Economics* 111: 227-251.

Blau, Peter M. 1954. "Co-operation and Competition in a Bureaucracy." *American Journal of Sociology* 59: 530-535.

Blau, Peter M. 1977. *Inequality and Heterogeneity: A Primitive Theory of Social Structure*. New York: Free Press.

Blau, Peter M., and Otis Dudley Duncan. 1967. *The American Occupational Structure*. New York: John Wiley & Sons.

Blinder, Alan S., Elie R. Canetti, David E. Lebow, and Jeremy B. Rudd. 1998. *Asking About Prices: A New Approach to Understanding Price Stickiness*. New York: Russell Sage Press.

Bonilla-Silva, Eduardo. 1997. "Rethinking Racism: Toward a Structural Interpretation." *American Sociological Review* 62: 465-480.

Borenstein, Severin. 1989. "Hubs and High Fares: Dominance and Market Power in the U.S. Airline Industry." *Rand Journal of Economics* 20: 344-365.

Bourdieu, Pierre. 1977. *Outline of a Theory of Practice*. Cambridge: Cambridge University Press.

Bourdieu, Pierre. 1986. "The Forms of Capital," trans. Richard Nice. In *Handbook of Theory and Research for the Sociology of Education*, edited by John G. Richardson, 241-258. Westport, CT: Greenwood Press.

Brady, David. 2009. *Rich Democracies, Poor People: How Politics Explain Poverty*. New York: Oxford University Press.

Braverman, Harry. [1974] 1998. *Labor and Monopoly Capital: The Degradation of Work in the Twentieth Century*. New York: NYU Press.

Brinton, Mary C., and Victor Nee, eds. 1998. *The New Institutionalism in Sociology*. New York: Russell Sage Press.

Budig, Michelle J., and Melissa J. Hodges. 2010. "Differences in Disadvantage Variation in the Motherhood Penalty Across White Women's Earnings Distribution." *American Sociological Review* 75: 705-728.

Budig, Michelle J., Joya Misra, and Irene Boeckmann. 2012. "The Motherhood Penalty in Cross-National Perspective: The Importance of Work-Family Policies and Cultural Attitudes." *Social Politics* 19: 163-193.

Burawoy, Michael. 1979. *Manufacturing Consent: Changes in the Labor Process Under Monopoly Capitalism.* Chicago: University of Chicago Press.

Burawoy, Michael. 1983. "Between the Labor Process and the State: The Changing Face of Factory Regimes Under Advanced Capitalism." *American Sociological Review* 48: 587-605.

Burawoy, Michael. 1998. "The Extended Case Method." *Sociological Theory* 16: 4-33.

Burns, Alexander, and Jonathan Martin. 2017. "Once a Long Shot, Democrat Doug Jones Wins Alabama Senate Seat." *New York Times*, December 12.

Burt, Ronald S. 1983. *Corporate Profits and Cooptation: Networks of Market Constraints and Directorate Ties in the American Economy.* New York: Academic Press.

Byron, Reginald A., and Vincent J. Roscigno. 2014. "Relational Power, Legitimation, and Pregnancy Discrimination." *Gender & Society* 28: 435-462.

Campos-Castillo, Celeste, and Kwesi Ewoodzie. 2014. "Relational Trustworthiness: How Status Affects Intra-Organizational Inequality in Jobs Autonomy." *Social Science Research* 44:60-74.

Cappelli, Peter. 1985. "Competitive Pressures and Labor Relations in the Airline Industry." *Industrial Relations* 24: 316-338.

Card, David, Ana Rute Cardoso, Jörg Heining, and Patrick Kline. 2018. "Firms and Labor Market Inequality: Evidence and Some Theory." *Journal of Labor Economics* 36: S13-S70.

Cardoso, Ana Rute. 1999. "Firms' Wage Policies and the Rise in Labor Market Inequality: The Case of Portugal." *Industrial & Labor Relations Review* 53: 87-102.

Castilla, Emilio J. 2008. "Gender, Race, and Meritocracy in Organizational Careers." *American Journal of Sociology* 113: 1479-1526.

Caves, Richard E. 1962. *Air Transport and Its Regulators: An Industry Study.* Economic Studies, Vol. 120. Cambridge, MA: Harvard University Press.

Cech, Erin, Brian Rubineau, Susan Silbey, and Caroll Seron. 2011. "Professional Role Confidence and Gendered Persistence in Engineering." *American Sociological Review* 76: 641-666.

Choudary, Sangeet Paul, Marshall W. Van Alstyne, and Geoffrey G. Parker. 2016. *Platform Revolution: How Networked Markets Are Transforming the Economy.* New York: W.W. Norton & Company.

Cobb, J. Adam. 2016. "How Firms Shape Income Inequality: Stakeholder Power, Executive Decision Making, and the Structuring of Employment Relationships." *Academy of Management Review* 41: 324-348.

Cohen, G. A. 1995. *Self-Ownership, Freedom, and Equality.* Cambridge: Cambridge University Press.

Cohen, G. A. 2008. *Rescuing Justice and Equality.* Cambridge, MA: Harvard University Press.

Cohen, Lisa, and Heather Haveman. 2016. "Starting off on the Wrong Foot? Newly Founded Firms, TMT Structures, and the Unusualness Penalty." SocArXiv https://osf.io/preprints/socarxiv/ua2t5/

Cohen, Philip N., and Matt L. Huffman. 2003. "Individuals, Jobs, and Labor Markets: The Devaluation of Women's Work." *American Sociological Review* 68: 443-463.

Coleman, James. 1958. "Relational Analysis: The Study of Social Organizations with Survey Methods." *Human Organization* 17: 28–36.

Collins, Patricia Hill. 2000. "Gender, Black Feminism, and Black Political Economy." *Annals of the American Academy of Political and Social Science* 568: 41–53.

Collins, Patricia Hill. 2002. *Black Feminist Thought: Knowledge, Consciousness, and the Politics of Empowerment*. New York: Routledge.

Collins, Sharon M. 1997. *Black Corporate Executives: The Making and Breaking of a Black Middle Class*. Philadelphia: Temple University Press.

Correll, Shelley J. 2001. "Gender and the Career Choice Process: The Role of Biased Self-Assessments." *American Journal of Sociology* 106: 1691–1730.

Correll, Shelley J., Stephen Benard, and In Paik. 2007. "Getting a Jobs: Is There a Motherhood Penalty?" *American Journal of Sociology* 112: 1297–1339.

Coser, Rose Laub. 1975. "The Complexity of Roles as a Seedbed of Individual Autonomy." In *The Idea of Social Structure: Papers in Honor of Robert K. Merton*, edited by Lewis A. Coser, 237–263. New York: Harcourt Brace Jovanovich.

Cowen, Jonathan M. 1993. "One Nation's Gulag Is Another Nation's Factory Within a Fence: Prison-Labor in the People's Republic of China and the United States of America." *Pacific Basin Law Journal* 12: 191–236.

Crowley, Martha. 2015. "Neoliberalism, Managerial Citizenship Behaviors, and Firm Fiscal Performance." *Research in the Sociology of Work* 28: 213–232.

Cyert, Richard M., and James G. March. 1963. *A Behavioral Theory of the Firm*. Upper Saddle River, NJ: Prentice Hall.

Dahl, Michael S., Cristian L. Dezső, and David Gaddis Ross. 2012. "Fatherhood and Managerial Style: How a Male CEO's Children Affect the Wages of His Employees." *Administrative Science Quarterly* 57: 669–693.

Davis, Gerald F. 2013. "After the Corporation." *Politics & Society* 41:283–308.

Davis, Gerald F. 2016. "Organizations, Institutions, and Inequality." In *Handbook of Organizational Institutionalism*, edited by Royston Greenwood. Prepared for forthcoming.

de la Merced, Michael. 2015. "First Data Names 15 Banks Chosen to Lead Public Offering." *New York Times*, August 25. https://www.nytimes.com/2015/08/26/business/dealbook/first-data-names-15-banks-chosen-to-lead-public-offering.html?rref=collection%2Ftimestopic%2FFirst%20Data%20Corporation&action=click&contentCollection=business®ion=stream&module=stream_unit&version=latest&contentPlacement=3&pgtype=collection. Retrieved 7/9/2018.

Della Fave, L. Richard. 1980. "The Meek Shall Not Inherit the Earth: Self-Evaluation and the Legitimacy of Stratification." *American Sociological Review* 45: 955–971.

DeVault, Marjore. 2013. "Institutional Ethnography: A Feminist Sociology of Institutional Power." *Contemporary Sociology* 42: 332–340.

DiMaggio, Paul, and Walter W. Powell. 1983. "The Iron Cage Revisited: Institutional Isomorphism and Collective Rationality in Organizational Fields." *American Sociological Review* 48: 147–160.

DiMaggio, Paul, and Walter W. Powell. 1991. *The New Institutionalism in Organizational Analysis*. Chicago: University of Chicago Press.

DiPrete, Thomas A., Gregory M. Eirich, and Matthew Pittinsky. 2010. "Compensation Benchmarking, Leapfrogs, and the Surge in Executive Pay." *American Journal of Sociology* 115: 1671–1712.

DiTomaso, Nancy. 2013. *The American Non-Dilemma: Racial Inequality Without Racism*. New York: Russell Sage Press.

DiTomaso, Nancy, Corinne Post, and Rochelle Parks-Yancy. 2007. "Workforce Diversity and Inequality: Power, Status, and Numbers." *Annual Review of Sociology* 33: 473–501.

Dobbin, Frank, and Jiwook Jung. 2010. "The Misapplication of Mr. Michael Jensen: How Agency Theory Brought Down the Economy and Why It Might Again." *Research in the Sociology of Organizations* 30: 29–64.

Dobbin, Frank, Alexandra Kalev, and Erin Kelly. 2009. "Diversity Management in Corporate America." *Contexts* 6: 21–27.

Dobbin, Frank, Daniel Schrage, and Alexandra Kalev. 2015. "Rage Against the Iron Cage: The Varied Effects of Bureaucratic Personnel Reforms on Diversity." *American Sociological Review* 80: 1014–1044.

Dobbin, Frank, and Dirk Zorn. 2005. "Corporate Malfeasance and the Myth of Shareholder Lalue." *Political Power and Social Theory* 17: 179–198.

Donoghue, J. A. 1988. "The Big Squeeze: Fortress Hubs and Other Barriers." *Air Transport World* 12: 58–65.

Doucouliagos, Chris. 1995. "Worker Participation and Productivity in Labor-Managed and Participatory Capitalist Firms: A Meta-Analysis." *Industrial and Labor Relations Review* 49: 58–77.

Dougal, Casey, Pengjie Gao, William J. Mayew, and Christopher A. Parsons. 2016. "What's in a (School) Name? Racial Discrimination in Higher Education Bond Markets." *Social Science Research Network*. http://ssrn.com/abstract=2727763.

Dube, Arindrajit, and Ethan Kaplan. 2010. "Does Outsourcing Reduce Wages in the Low-Wage Service Occupations? Evidence from Janitors and Guards." *Industrial and Labor Relations Review* 63: 287–306.

Du Bois, W. E. B. 1911. "Races." *The Crisis* 2: 157–158.

Durkheim, Emile. 2014 (1893). *The Division of Labor in Society*. New York: Simon & Schuster.

Dworkin, Ronald. 1981. "What Is Equality? Equality of Resources." *Philosophy and Public Affairs* 10: 283–345.

Dyer, Jeffrey H., and Harbir Singh. 1998. "The Relational View: Cooperative Strategy and Sources of Interorganizational Competitive Advantage." *Academy of Management Review* 23: 660–679.

Economic Policy Institute. 2015. "Understanding the Historic Divergence Between Productivity and a Typical Worker's Pay." Briefing Paper #406.

Edwards, Richard C. 1979. *Contested Terrain: The Transformation of the Workplace in the Twentieth Century*. New York: Basic Books.

Emirbayer, Mustafa. 1997. "Manifesto for a Relational Sociology." *American Journal of Sociology* 103: 281–317.

Emirbayer, Mustafa, and Victoria Johnson. 2008. "Bourdieu and Organizational Analysis." *Theory and Society* 37: 1–44.

England, Paula, Paul Allison, and Yuxiao Wu. 2007. "Does Bad Pay Cause Occupations to Feminize, Does Feminization Reduce Pay, and How Can We Tell with Longitudinal Data?" *Social Science Research* 36: 1237–1256.

England, Paula, and Nancy Folbre. 1999. "The Cost of Caring." *Annals of the American Academy of Political and Social Science* 561: 39–51.

Erikson, Emily. 2013. "Formalist and Relationalist Theory in Social Network Analysis." *Sociological Theory* 31:219–242.

Esping-Andersen, Gosta. 2013. *The Three Worlds of Welfare Capitalism*. Chichester: John Wiley & Sons.

Estlund, Cynthia L. 2002. "The Ossification of American Labor Law." *Columbia Law Review* 102: 1527–1612.

Fabling, Richard, Arthur Grimes, and David C. Maré. 2012. "Performance Pay Systems and the Gender Wage Gap." Motu Working Paper 12-13. Motu Economic and Public Policy Research. http://motu-www.motu.org.nz/wpapers/12_13.pdf. Retrieved 10/3/2014.

Feagin, Joe R., and Debra Van Ausdale. 2001. *The First R: How Children Learn Race and Racism*. Lanham, MD: Rowman & Littlefield.

Feldman, Martha S., and Brian T. Pentland. 2003. "Reconceptualizing Organizational Routines as a Source of Flexibility and Change." *Administrative Science Quarterly* 48: 94–118.

Fernandez, Roberto M. 2001. "Skill-Biased Technological Change and Wage Inequality: Evidence from a Plant Retooling." *American Journal of Sociology* 107: 273–320.

Fernandez-Mateo, Isabel. 2007. "Who Pays the Price of Brokerage? Transferring Constraint Through Price Setting in the Staffing Sector." *American Sociological Review* 72: 291–317.

Fine, Gary Alan. 1984. "Negotiated Orders and Organizational Cultures." *Annual Review of Sociology* 10: 239–262.

Fine, Gary Alan. 2010. "The Sociology of the Local: Action and Its Publics." *Sociological Theory* 28: 355–376.

Fine, Gary Alan, and Tim Hallett. 2014. "Group Cultures and the Everyday Life of Organizations: Interaction Orders and Meso-Analysis." *Organization Studies* 35: 1773–1792.

Fisher, Roger, William L. Ury, and Bruce Patton. 2011. *Getting to Yes: Negotiating Agreement Without Giving In*. New York: Penguin.

Fligstein, Neil. 1993. *The Transformation of Corporate Control*. Cambridge, MA: Harvard University Press.

Fligstein, Neil. 1996. "Markets as Politics: A Political-Cultural Approach to Market Institutions." *American Sociological Review* 61: 656–673.

Fligstein, Neil. 2002. *The Architecture of Markets: An Economic Sociology of Twenty-First Century Capitalist Societies*. Princeton, NJ: Princeton University Press.

Fligstein, Neil, and Adam Goldstein. 2010. "The Anatomy of the Mortgage Securitization Crisis." *Research in the Sociology of Organizations* 30: 29–70.

Fligstein, Neil, and Doug McAdam. 2011. "Toward a General Theory of Strategic Action Fields." *Sociological Theory* 29: 1–26.

Fligstein, Neil, and Taekjin Shin. 2007. "Shareholder Value and the Transformation of the US Economy, 1984–2001." *Sociological Forum* 22: 399–424.

Fobre, Nancy. 2016. "Just Deserts? Earnings Inequality and Bargaining Power in the U.S. Economy." Washington Center for Equitable Growth. Working Paper. https://equitablegrowth.org/working-papers/earnings-inequality-and-bargaining-power/.

Forbes. 2017. "The World's Billionaires." https://www.forbes.com/billionaires/#615a165d251c. Retrieved 8/5/2017.

Fourcade, Marion. 2009. *Economists and Societies: Discipline and Profession in the United States, Britain, and France, 1890s to 1990s*. Princeton, NJ: Princeton University Press.

Fourcade-Gourinchas, Marion, and Sarah L. Babb. 2002. "The Rebirth of the Liberal Creed: Paths to Neoliberalism in Four Countries." *American Journal of Sociology* 108: 533–579.

Freeman, Richard. 2016. "A Tale of Two Clones: A New Perspective on Inequality." Third Way. http://www.thirdway.org/report/a-tale-of-two-clones.

Freeman, Richard B., and Morris M. Kleiner. 2000. "Who Benefits Most from Employee Involvement: Firms or Workers?" *American Economic Review* 90: 219–223.

Freeman, Richard B., and James L. Medoff. 1984. *What Do Unions Do?* New York: Basic Books.

Freund, Caroline, and Sarah Oliver. 2016. "The Origins of the Superrich: The Billionaire Characteristics Database." Working Paper 16-1. Peterson Institute for International Economics.

Friedman, Milton. 2009. *Capitalism and Freedom*. Chicago: University of Chicago Press.

Gamson, William. 1988. "Political Discourse and Collective Action." In *International Social Movement Research: From Structure to Action*, edited by Bert Klandermans, Kriesi Hanspeter, and Sidney Tarrow, 219–244. Stamford, CT: JAI Press.

Gereffi, Gary. 1996. "Global Commodity Chains: New Forms of Coordination and Control Among Nations and Firms in International Industries." *Competition & Change* 1: 427–439.

Glaser, Barry, and Anslem Strauss. 1967. *The Discovery of Grounded Theory: Strategies for Qualitative Research*. London: Aldine.

Glenn, Evelyn Nakano. 2009. *Unequal Freedom: How Race and Gender Shaped American Citizenship and Labor*. Cambridge, MA: Harvard University Press.

Glenn, Evelyn Nakano. 2011. "Constructing Citizenship Exclusion, Subordination, and Resistance." *American Sociological Review* 76: 1–24.

Godechot, Olivier. 2012. "Is Finance Responsible for the Rise in Wage Inequality in France?" *Socio-Economic Review* 10: 447–470.

Godechot, Olivier. 2016. *Wages, Bonuses and Appropriation of Profit in the Financial Industry: The Working Rich*. London and New York: Routledge.

Goffman, Erving. 1959. *The Presentation of Self in Everyday Life*. New York: Doubleday.

Goldstein, Adam. 2012. "Revenge of the Managers: Labor Cost-Cutting and the Paradoxical Resurgence of Managerialism in the Shareholder Value Era, 1984 to 2001." *American Sociological Review* 77: 268–294.

Gorman, Elizabeth H., and Julie A. Kmec. 2009. "Hierarchical Rank and Women's Organizational Mobility: Glass Ceilings in Corporate Law Firms." *American Journal of Sociology* 114: 1428–1474.

Gouldner, Alvin W. 1954. *Patterns of Industrial Bureaucracy*. New York: Free Press.

Granovetter, Mark. 1985. "Economic Action and Social Structure: The Problem of Embeddedness." *American Journal of Sociology* 91: 481–510.

Granovetter, Mark. 2017. *Society and Economy: Framework and Principles*. Cambridge, MA: Harvard University Press.

Hacker, Jacob S., and Paul Pierson. 2010. "Winner-Take-All Politics: Public Policy, Political Organization, and the Precipitous Rise of Top Incomes in the United States." *Politics & Society* 38: 152–204.

Hall, Peter A., and David Soskice, eds. 2001. *Varieties of Capitalism: The Institutional Foundations of Comparative Advantage*. Oxford: Oxford University Press.

Hallett, Tim. 2003. "Symbolic Power and Organizational Culture." *Sociological Theory* 21: 128–149.

Hallett, Tim. 2007. "Between Deference and Distinction: Interaction Ritual Through Symbolic Power in an Educational Institution." *Social Psychology Quarterly* 70: 148–171.

Hallett, Tim. 2010. "The Myth Incarnate: Recoupling Processes, Turmoil, and Inhabited Institutions in an Urban Elementary School." *American Sociological Review* 75: 52–74.

Hallett, Tim, and Marc J. Ventresca. 2006. "Inhabited Institutions: Social Interactions and Organizational Forms in Gouldner's Patterns of Industrial Bureaucracy." *Theory and Society* 35: 213–236.

Hamann, Ralph, and Stephanie Bertels. 2017. "The Institutional Work of Exploitation: Employers' Work to Create and Perpetuate Inequality." *Journal of Management Studies* 55: 394–423.

Hanley, Caroline. 2011. "Investigating the Organizational Sources of High-Wage Earnings Growth and Rising Inequality." *Social Science Research* 40: 902–916.

Hanley, Caroline. 2014. "Putting the Bias in Skill-Biased Technological Change? A Relational Perspective on White-Collar Automation at General Electric." *American Behavioral Scientist* 58: 400–415.

Hannan, Michael T., and John Freeman. 1977. "The Population Ecology of Organizations." *American Journal of Sociology* 82: 929–964.

Harding, Sandra L., and Robert Sappey. 2002. "Australia." In *Worlds of Work: Building an International Sociology of Work*, edited by Daniel B. Cornfield and Randy Hodson, 113–130. New York: Kluwer Academic.

Harris, Gardiner. 2014. "Maker of Costly Hepatitis C Drug Solvadi Strikes Deal on Generics for Poor Countries." *New York Times*, September 15.

Harvey, David. 2007. *A Brief History of Neoliberalism*. Oxford: Oxford University Press.

Harvey, David. 2010. *The Enigma of Capital and the Crisis of Capitalism*. New York: Oxford University Press.

Hellerstein, Judith K., and David Neumark. 1998. "Wage Discrimination, Segregation, and Sex Differences in Wages and Productivity Within and Between Plants." *Industrial Relations* 37: 232–260.

Hellerstein, Judith K., David Neumark, and Kenneth R. Troske. 2002. "Market Forces and Sex Discrimination." *Journal of Human Resources* 37: 353–380.

Helliwell, John, Richard Layard, and Jeffrey Sachs, eds. 2017. *World Happiness Report*. http://worldhappiness.report/wp-content/uploads/sites/2/2017/03/HR17.pdf

Herrigal, Gary, and Jonathan Zietlin. 2010. "Alternatives to Varieties of Capitalism." *Business History Review* 84: 667–674.

Ho, Karen. 2009. *Liquidated: An Ethnography of Wall Street*. Durham, NC: Duke University Press.

Hodges, Melissa J., and Michelle J. Budig. 2010. "Who Gets the Daddy Bonus? Organizational Hegemonic Masculinity and the Impact of Fatherhood on Earnings." *Gender & Society* 24: 717–745.

Hodson, Randy. 1978. "Labor in the Monopoly, Competitive, and State Sectors of Production." *Politics & Society* 8: 429–480.

Hodson, Randy. 1984. *Workers' Earnings and Corporate Economic Structure*. New York: Academic Press.

Hodson, Randy. 2001. *Dignity at Work*. New York: Cambridge University Press.

Hodson, Randy. 2002. "Management Citizenship Behavior and Its Consequences." *Work and Occupations* 29: 64–96.

Hodson, Randy. 2004. Workplace Ethnography (WE) Project, 1944–2002. 2004. ICPSR version. Ann Arbor, MI: Inter-University Consortium for Political and Social Research [distributor].

Hodson, Randy, and Robert L. Kaufman. 1982. "Economic Dualism: A Critical Review." *American Sociological Review* 47: 727–739.

Hodson, Randy, Vincent J. Roscigno, and Steven H. Lopez. 2006. "Chaos and the Abuse of Power Workplace Bullying in Organizational and Interactional Context." *Work and Occupations* 33: 382–416.

Huffman, Matt L., and Philip N. Cohen. 2004. "Racial Wage Inequality: Jobs Segregation and Devaluation Across US Labor Markets." *American Journal of Sociology* 109: 902-936.

Hughes, Everett C. 1945. "Dilemmas and Contradictions of Status." *American Journal of Sociology* 50: 353–359.

Huselid, Mark A. 1995. "The Impact of Human Resource Management Practices on Turnover, Productivity, and Corporate Financial Performance." *Academy of Management Journal* 38: 635–672.

Hyman, Louis. 2012. "The Politics of Consumer Debt US State Policy and the Rise of Investment in Consumer Credit, 1920–2008." *Annals of the American Academy of Political and Social Science* 644: 40–49.

Ingram, Paul, and Peter W. Roberts. 2000. "Friendships Among Competitors in the Sydney Hotel Industry." *American Journal of Sociology* 106: 387–423.

Jackall, Robert. 1988. *Moral Mazes: The World of Corporate Managers*. New York: Oxford University Press.

Jacobs, Jerry A., and Kathleen Gerson. 2004. *The Time Divide: Work, Family, and Gender Inequality*. Cambridge, MA: Harvard University Press.

Jayaraman, Saru. 2016. *Forked: A New Standard for American Dining*. New York: Oxford University Press.

Jensen, Jaclyn M., Pankaj C. Patel, and Jake G. Messersmith. 2013. "High-Performance Work Systems and Jobs Control: Consequences for Anxiety, Role Overload, and Turnover Intentions." *Journal of Management* 39: 1699-1724.

Joshi, Aparna, Jooyeon Son, and Hyuntak Roh. 2015. "When Can Women Close the Gap? A Meta-Analytic Test of Sex Differences in Performance and Rewards." *Academy of Management Journal* 58: 1516-1545.

Jung, Jiwook. 2016. "Through the Contested Terrain: Implementation of Downsizing Announcements by Large US Firms, 1984 to 2005." *American Sociological Review* 81: 347-373.

Juravich, Tom. 1985. *Chaos on the Shop Floor: A Worker's View of Quality, Productivity, and Management*. Philadelphia: Temple University Press.

Kalev, Alexandra. 2009. "Cracking the Glass Cages? Restructuring and Ascriptive Inequality at Work." *American Journal of Sociology* 114: 1591-1643.

Kalev, Alexandra, Frank Dobbin, and Erin Kelly. 2006. "Best Practices or Best Quesses? Assessing the Efficacy of Corporate Affirmative Action and Diversity Policies." *American Sociological Review* 71: 589–617.

Kalleberg, Arne L., David Knoke, Peter V. Marsden, and Joe L. Spaeth, eds. 1996. *Organizations in America: Analysing Their Structures and Human Resource Practices*. Thousand Oaks, CA: Sage.

Kalleberg, Arne. 2003. "Flexible Firms and Labor Market Segmentation: Effects of Workplace Restructuring on Jobs and Workplaces." *Work and Occupations* 30: 154-175.

Kalleberg, Arne L., Barbara F. Reskin, and Ken Hudson. 2000. "Bad Jobs in America: Standard and Nonstandard Employment Relations and Jobs Quality in the United States." *American Sociological Review* 65: 256–278.

Kalleberg, Arne L., Michael Wallace, and Robert P. Althauser. 1981. "Economic Segmentation, Worker Power, and Income Inequality." *American Journal of Sociology* 87: 651-683.

Kang, Miliann. 2015. "Trouble in the Nail Industry." *Contexts Blog*, May 11. https://contexts.org/blog/trouble-in-the-nail-Industry/

Kanter, Rosabeth Moss. 1977. *Men and Women of the Corporation*. New York: Basic Books.

Kaplan, Steven N., and Joshua Rauh. 2010. "Wall Street and Main Street: What Contributes to the Rise in the Highest Incomes?" *Review of Financial Studies* 23: 1004-1050.

Katz, Lawrence F., and Lawrence H. Summers. 1989. "Industry Rents: Evidence and Implications." *Brookings Papers on Economic Activity: Microeconomics* 1989: 209-290.

Kellogg, Katherine C. 2011. *Challenging Operations: Medical Reform and Resistance in Surgery*. Chicago: University of Chicago Press.

Kelly, Erin, and Frank Dobbin. 1998. "How Affirmative Action Became Diversity Management Employer Response to Antidiscrimination Law, 1961 to 1996." *American Behavioral Scientist* 41: 960-984.

Ken, Ivy. 2008. "Beyond the Intersection: A New Culinary Metaphor for Race-Class-Gender Studies." *Sociological Theory* 26: 152-172.

Kenworthy, Lane. 2003. "Quantitative Indicators of Corporatism." *International Journal of Sociology* 33: 10-44.

Kenworthy, Lane. 2004. *Egalitarian Capitalism: Jobs, Incomes, and Growth in Affluent Countries*. New York: Russell Sage Press.

Kim, ChangHwan, and Arthur Sakamoto. 2008. "Does Inequality Increase Productivity? Evidence from US Manufacturing Industries, 1979 to 1996." *Work and Occupations* 35: 85-114.

Koopmans, Ruud, and Paul Statham. 1999. "Political Claims Analysis: Integrating Protest Event and Political Discourse Approaches." *Mobilization: An International Quarterly* 4: 203-221.

Kostova, Tatiana, and Kendall Roth. 2003. "Social Capital in Multinational Corporations and a Micro-Macro Model of Its Formation." *Academy of Management Review* 28: 297-317.

Krippner, Greta R. 2011. *Capitalizing on Crisis*. Cambridge, MA: Harvard University Press.

Kristal, Tali. 2010. "Good Times, Bad Times Postwar Labor's Share of National Income in Capitalist Democracies." *American Sociological Review* 75: 729-763.

Kristal, Tali. 2013. "The Capitalist Machine: Computerization, Workers' Power, and the Decline in Labor's Share Within US Industries." *American Sociological Review* 78: 361-389.

Křížková, Alena, Andrew Penner, and Trond Petersen. 2010. "The Legacy of Equality and the Weakness of Law: Within-Jobs Gender Wage Inequality in the Czech Republic." *European Sociological Review* 26: 83-95.

Křížková, Alena, Hana Maříková, Radka Dudová, and Zdeněk Sloboda. 2009. "The Conditions of Parenthood in Organisations: An International Comparison." *Czech Sociological Review* 45: 519-547.

Kunda, Gideon. 2009. *Engineering Culture: Control and Commitment in a High-Tech Corporation*. Philadelphia: Temple University Press.

Kurtulus, Fidan Ana. 2012. "Affirmative Action and the Occupational Advancement of Minorities and Women During 1973-2003." *Industrial Relations* 51: 213-246.

Kurtulus, Fidan Ana, and Douglas L. Kruse. 2017. *How Did Employee Ownership Firms Weather the Last Two Recessions? Employee Ownership, Employment Stability, and Firm Survival: 1999-2011*. Kalamazoo, MI: WE Upjohn Institute for Employment Research.

Lamont, Michèle. 1992. *Money, Morals, and Manners: The Culture of the French and the American Upper-Middle Class*. Chicago: University of Chicago Press.

Lamont, Michèle. 2009. *The Dignity of Working Men: Morality and the Boundaries of Race, Class, and Immigration*. Cambridge, MA: Harvard University Press.

Lamont, Michèle, Stefan Beljean, and Matthew Clair. 2014. "What Is Missing? Cultural Processes and Causal Pathways to Inequality." *Socio-Economic Review* 12: 573-608.

Lamont, Michèle, and Virág Molnár. 2002. "The Study of Boundaries in the Social Sciences." *Annual Review of Sociology* 28: 167-195.

Lawrence, Thomas, Roy Suddaby, and Bernard Leca. 2011. "Institutional Work: Refocusing Institutional Studies of Organization." *Journal of Management Inquiry* 20: 52-58.

Lazonick, William, and Mary O'Sullivan. 2000. "Maximizing Shareholder Value: A New Ideology for Corporate Governance." *Economy and Society* 29: 13-35.

Leana, Carrie R., and Denise M. Rousseau. 2000. *Relational Wealth: The Advantages of Stability in a Changing Economy*. New York: Oxford University Press.

Lee, Frederic. 2009. *A History of Heterodox Economics: Challenging the Mainstream in the Twentieth Century*. London and New York: Routledge.

Le Grand, Carl, and Michael Tåhlin. 2013. "Class, Occupation, Wages, and Skills: The Iron Law of Labor Market Inequality." *Comparative Social Research* 30: 3-46.

Leicht, Kevin T. 2008. "Broken Down by Race and Gender? Sociological Explanations of New Sources of Earnings Inequality." *Annual Review of Sociology* 34: 237-255.

Leidner, Robin. 1993. *Fast Food, Fast Talk: Service Work and the Routinization of Everyday Life*. Berkeley: University of California Press.

Lemieux, Thomas, W. Bentley MacLeod, and Daniel Parent. 2009. "Performance Pay and Wage Inequality." *Quarterly Journal of Economics* 124: 1-49.

Levanon, Asaf, Paula England, and Paul Allison. 2009. "Occupational Feminization and Pay: Assessing Causal Dynamics Using 1950-2000 US Census Data." *Social Forces* 88: 865-891.

Lieberson, Stanley. 1985. *Making It Count: The Improvement of Social Research and Theory*. Berkeley: University of California Press.

Liebow, Elliot. 1967. *Tally's Corner: A Study of Negro Streetcorner Men*. Boston: Little Brown.

Lin, Ken-Hou. 2015. "The Financial Premium in the US Labor Market: A Distributional Analysis." *Social Forces* 94: 1-30.

Lin, Ken-Hou. 2016. "The Rise of Finance and Firm Employment Dynamics." *Organizational Science* 27: 972-988.

Lin, Ken-Hou, and Donald Tomaskovic-Devey. 2013. "Financialization and US Income Inequality, 1970-20081." *American Journal of Sociology* 118: 1284-1329.

Lincoln, James R., and Arne L. Kalleberg. 1992. *Culture, Control and Commitment: A Study of Work Organization and Work Attitudes in the United States and Japan*. Cambridge: Cambridge University Press.

Liu, Jeng, Arthur Sakamoto, and Kuo-Hsien Su. 2010. "Exploitation in Contemporary Capitalism: An Empirical Analysis of the Case of Taiwan." *Sociological Focus* 43: 259–281.

Lucas, Kristen. 2016. "If Dignity Is so Simple, Then Why Is It so difficult?" *Work in Progress Blog*, June 9. https://Workinprogress.oowsection.org/2016/06/09/if-dignity-is-so-simple-then-why-is-it-so-difficult/. Retrieved 7/20/2018.

Lucas, Robert C. 2004. "The Industrial Revolution: Past and Future." *Banking and Policy Issues Magazine* (Federal Reserve Bank of Minneapolis) https://minneapolisfed.org/publications/the-region/the-industrial-revolution-past-and-future. Retrieved 4/18/2014.

Lucas, Samuel. 2009. *Theorizing Discrimination in an Era of Contested Prejudice: Discrimination in the United States*. Philadelphia: Temple University Press.

Mahmood, Arai, and Fredrik Heyman. 2009. "Microdata Evidence on Rent-Sharing." *Applied Economics* 41: 2965–2976.

Malmström, Malin, Jeaneth Johansson, and Joakim Wincent. 2017. "Gender Stereotypes and Venture Support Decisions: How Governmental Venture Capitalists Socially Construct Entrepreneurs' Potential." *Entrepreneurship Theory and Practice* 41: 833–860.

Manjoo, Farhad. 2016a. "Tech's 'Frightful 5' Will Dominate Digital Life for Foreseeable Future." *New York Times*, January 20.

Manjoo, Farhad. 2016b. "Why the World Is Drawing Battle Lines Against American Tech Giants." *New York Times*, June 1.

March, James G. 1962. "The Business Firm as a Political Coalition." *Journal of Politics* 24: 662–678.

Martin, Patricia Yancey. 2004. "Gender as Social Institution." *Social Forces* 82: 1249–1273.

Marx, Karl. 1976 (1867). *Capital: A Critique of Political Economy*, Vol. 1. London: Penguin.

McCall, Leslie. 2001. *Complex Inequality: Gender, Class and Race in the New Economy*. London and New York: Routledge.

McCall, Leslie. 2005. "The Complexity of Intersectionality." *Signs* 30: 1771–1800.

McIlwee, Judith S., and J. Gregg Robinson. 1992. *Women in Engineering: Gender, Power, and Workplace Culture*. Albany: State University of New York Press.

Mears, Ashley. 2011. *Pricing Beauty: The Making of a Fashion Model*. Berkeley: University of California Press.

Meyers, Joan S. M., and Steven Peter Vallas. 2016. "Diversity Regimes in Worker Cooperatives: Workplace Inequality Under Conditions of Worker Control." *Sociological Quarterly* 57: 98–128.

Meyer, John W., and Brian Rowan. 1977. "Institutionalized Organizations: Formal Structure as Myth and Ceremony." *American Journal of Sociology* 83: 340–363.

Meyersson Milgrom, Eva M., Trond Petersen, and Vemund Snartland. 2001. "Equal Pay for Equal Work? Evidence from Sweden and a Comparison with Norway and the US." *Scandinavian Journal of Economics* 103: 559–583.

Mizruchi, Mark S. 2013. *The Fracturing of the American Corporate Elite*. Cambridge, MA: Harvard University Press.

Moorman, R. W. 1992. "Raking in the Big Bucks. Regional Airline Executives' Compensation Parallels Carrier Profits." *Air Transport World* 29: 107.

Mueller, Charles W., Munyae Mulinge, and Jennifer Glass. 2002. "Interactional Processes and Gender Workplace Inequalities." *Social Psychology Quarterly* 65: 163-185.

Muñoz, Carolina Bank. 2008. *Transnational Tortillas: Race, Gender, and Shop-Floor Politics in Mexico and the United States*. Ithaca, NY: Cornell University Press.

Murphy, Raymond. 1988. *Social Closure: The Theory of Monopolization and Exclusion*. Oxford: Oxford University Press.

Nee, Victor, and Richard Swedberg. 2007. *On Capitalism*. Stanford, CA: Stanford University Press.

Nekby, Lena. 2003. "Gender Differences in Rent Sharing and Its Implications for the Gender Wage Gap, Evidence from Sweden." *Economics Letters* 81: 403-410.

Nelson, Robert L., and William P. Bridges. 1999. *Legalizing Gender Inequality: Courts, Markets, and Unequal Pay for Women in America*. Cambridge: Cambridge University Press.

Nielson, Laura Beth, and Robert L. Nelson. 2005. "Rights Realized—An Empirical Analysis of Employment Discrimination Litigation as a Claiming System." *Wisconsin Law Review* 2005: 663-711.

Nir, Sara Maslin. 2015. "The Price of Nice Nails." *New York Times*, May 7.

Northrup, Herbert R. 1983. "The New Employee-Relations Climate in Airlines." *Industrial & Labor Relations Review* 36: 167-181.

Okun, Arthur. 1981. *Prices and Quantities: A Macroeconomic Analysis*. Washington, DC: Brookings Institution Press.

Omi, Michael, and Howard Winant. 2014. *Racial Formation in the United States*. New York and London: Routledge.

Orhangazi, È. 2008. *Financialization and the US Economy*. Cheltenham, UK: Edward Elgar Publishing.

Padavic, Irene. 1991. "The Re-Creation of Gender in a Male Workplace." *Symbolic Interaction* 14: 279-294.

Padavic, Irene, and Barbara F. Reskin. 1990. "Men's Behavior and Women's Interest in Blue-Collar Jobs." *Social Problems* 37: 613-628.

Padavic, Irene, and Barbara F. Reskin. 2002. *Women and Men at Work*. Thousand Oaks, CA: Pine Forge Press.

Pager, Devah. 2003. "The Mark of a Criminal Record." *American Journal of Sociology* 108: 937-975.

Parkin, Frank. 1979. *The Marxist Theory of Class: A Bourgeois Critique*. London: Tavistock.

Penner, Andrew M., Aleksandra Kanjuo-Mrčela, Nina Bandelj, and Trond Petersen. 2012. "Neenakost po spolu v Sloveniji od 1993 do 2007: razlike v plačah na ravni delovnega mesta v perspektivi ekonomske sociologije." ["Gender Inequality in Slovenia, 1993-2007: An Economic Sociology Perspective on Jobs-Level Pay Differences." In Slovenian.] *Teorija in Praksa* 49: 854-877.

Penrose, Edith. 2009. *The Theory of the Growth of the Firm*. Oxford: Oxford University Press.

Perrone, Luca. 1983. "Positional Power and Propensity to Strike." *Politics & Society* 12: 231-261.

Perrow, Charles. 2009. *Organizing America: Wealth, Power, and the Origins of Corporate Capitalism*. Princeton, NJ: Princeton University Press.

Petersen, Trond, and Laurie A. Morgan. 1995. "Separate and Unequal: Occupation-Establishment Sex Segregation and the Gender Wage Gap." *American Journal of Sociology* 101: 329-365.

Petersen, Trond, Andrew M. Penner, and Geir Høgsnes. 2014. "From Motherhood Penalties to Husband Premia: The New Challenge for Gender Equality and Family Policy: Lessons from Norway." *American Journal of Sociology* 119: 1434-1472.

Petersen, Trond, and Ishak Saporta. 2004. "The Opportunity Structure for Discrimination." *American Journal of Sociology* 109: 852-901.

Pfeffer, Jeffrey. 1983. "A Political Perspective on Careers: Interests, Networks, and Environments." In *Handbook of Career Theory*, edited by M. B. Arthur, D. T. Hall, and B. S. Lawrence, 380-396. Cambridge: Cambridge University Press.

Pfeffer, Jeffrey, and Gerald R. Salancik. 1974. "Organizational Decision Making as a Political Process: The Case of a University Budget." *Administrative Science Quarterly* 19: 135-151.

Philippon, Thomas. 2015. "Has the US Finance Industry Become Less Efficient? On the Theory and Measurement of Financial Intermediation." *American Economic Review* 105: 1408-1438.

Philippon, Thomas, and Ariell Reshef. 2013. "An International Look at the Growth of Modern Finance." *Journal of Economic Perspectives* 27: 73-96.

Piketty, Thomas. 2014. *Capital in the Twenty-First Century*. Cambridge, MA: Harvard University Press.

Podolny, Joel M. 1993. "A Status-Based Model of Market Competition." *American Journal of Sociology* 98: 829-872.

Podolny, Joel M. 2010. *Status Signals: A Sociological Study of Market Competition*. Princeton, NJ: Princeton University Press.

Powell, Walter. 1990. "Neither Market nor Hierarchy." *Research in Organizational Behavior* 12: 295-336.

Powell, Walter W., Kenneth W. Koput, James I. Bowie, and Laurel Smith-Doerr. 2002. "The Spatial Clustering of Science and Capital: Accounting for Biotech Firm-Venture Capital Relationships." *Regional Studies* 36: 291-305.

Powell, Walter W., Kenneth W. Koput, and Laurel Smith-Doerr. 1996. "Interorganizational Collaboration and the Locus of Innovation: Networks of Learning in Biotechnology." *Administrative Science Quarterly* 41: 116-145.

Powell, Walter W., Douglas R. White, Kenneth W. Koput, and Jason Owen-Smith. 2005. "Network Dynamics and Field Evolution: The Growth of Interorganizational Collaboration in the Life Sciences." *American Journal of Sociology* 110: 1132-1205.

Prechel, Harland, and Theresa Morris. 2010. "The Effects of Organizational and Political Embeddedness on Financial Malfeasance in the Largest US Corporations: Dependence, Incentives, and Opportunities." *American Sociological Review* 75: 331-354.

Rawls, John. 1971. *A Theory of Justice*. Cambridge, MA: Harvard University Press.

Redbird, Beth. 2017. "The New Closed Shop? The Economic and Structural Effects of Occupational Licensure." *American Sociological Review* 82: 600-624.

Reich, Michael, David M. Gordon, and Richard C. Edwards. 1973. "A Theory of Labor Market Segmentation." *American Economic Review* 63: 359-365.

Reskin, Barbara F. 1988. "Bringing the Men Back In: Sex Differentiation and the Devaluation of Women's Work." *Gender & Society* 2: 58-81.

Reskin, Barbara F. 2003. "Modeling Ascriptive Inequality: From Motives to Mechanisms." *American Sociological Review* 68: 1-21.

Reskin, Barbara F., and Irene Padavic. 1988. "Supervisors as Gatekeepers: Male Supervisors' Response to Women's Integration in Plant Jobs." *Social Problems* 35: 536-550.

Ridgeway, Cecilia L. 1997. "Interaction and the Conservation of Gender Inequality: Considering Employment." *American Sociological Review* 62: 218-235.

Ridgeway, Cecilia L. 2011. *Framed by Gender: How Gender Inequality Persists in the Modern World.* New York: Oxford University Press.

Ridgeway, Cecilia L., and James W. Balkwell. 2006. "Group Processes and the Diffusion of Status Beliefs." *Social Psychology Quarterly* 60: 14-31.

Ridgeway, Cecilia L., and Shelley J. Correll. 2006. "Consensus and the Creation of Status Beliefs." *Social Forces* 85: 431-453.

Ridgeway, Cecilia L., and Kristan Glasgow Erickson. 2000. "Creating and Spreading Status Beliefs." *American Journal of Sociology* 106: 579-615.

Ridgeway, Cecilia L., Elizabeth Heger Boyle, Kathy J. Kuipers, and Dawn T. Robinson. 1998. "How Do Status Beliefs Develop? The Role of Resources and Interactional Experience." *American Sociological Review* 63: 331-350.

Ridgeway, Cecilia L., and Sandra Nakagawa. 2014. "Status." In *Handbook of the Social Psychology of Inequality*, edited by Jane McLeod, Edward Lawler, and Michael Schwalbe, 3-25. Dordrecht, The Netherlands: Springer.

Rieple, Alison, and Clive Helm. 2008. "Outsourcing for Competitive Advantage: An Examination of Seven Legacy Airlines." *Journal of Air Transport Management* 14: 280-285.

Risman, Barbara J. 1999. *Gender Vertigo: American Families in Transition.* New Haven, CT: Yale University Press.

Rivera, Lauren A. 2012. "Hiring as Cultural Matching the Case of Elite Professional Service Firms." *American Sociological Review* 77: 999-1022.

Rooks, Gerrit, Werner Raub, Robert Selten, and Frits Tazelaar. 2000. "How Inter-Firm Co-operation Depends on Social Embeddedness: A Vignette Study." *Acta Sociologica* 43: 123-137.

Roscigno, Vincent J. 2007. *The Face of Discrimination: How Race and Gender Impact Work and Home Lives.* Lanham, MD: Rowman & Littlefield Publishers.

Roscigno, Vincent J. 2011. "Power, Revisited." *Social Forces* 90: 349-374.

Roscigno, Vincent J., and Randy Hodson. 2004. "The Organizational and Social Foundations of Worker Resistance." *American Sociological Review* 69: 14-39.

Roscigno, Vincent J., Steven H. Lopez, and Randy Hodson. 2009. "Supervisory Bullying, Status Inequalities and Organizational Context." *Social Forces* 87: 1561-1589.

Roscigno, Vincent J., and George Wilson. 2014. "The Relational Foundations of Inequality at Work I: Status, Interaction, and Culture." *American Behavioral Scientist* 58: 219-227.

Rosenfeld, Jake. 2006. "Desperate Measures: Strikes and Wages in Post-Accord America." *Social Forces* 85: 235-265.

Rosenfeld, Jake. 2014. *What Unions No Longer Do.* Cambridge, MA: Harvard University Press.

Rosenfeld, Jake, and Patrick Denice. 2015. "The Power of Transparency: Evidence from a British Workplace Survey." *American Sociological Review* 80: 1045-1068.

Rossi, Peter H., James D. Wright, and Andy B. Anderson, eds. 1983. *Handbook of Survey Research.* New York: Academic Press.

Rothschild, Joyce. 2016. "The Logic of a Co-operative Economy and Democracy 2.0: Recovering the Possibilities for Autonomy, Creativity, Solidarity, and Common Purpose." *Sociological Quarterly* 57: 7-35.

Roy, Donald. 1959. "Banana Time: Jobs Satisfaction and Informal Interaction." *Human Organization* 18: 158-168.

Roy, Victor, and Lawrence King. 2016. "Betting on Hepatitis C: How Financial Speculation in Drug Development Influences Access to Medicines." *BMJ* 354: i3718.

Rubin, Beth A. 1986. "Class Struggle American Style: Unions, Strikes and Wages." *American Sociological Review* 51: 618-633.

Rubin, Beth. 1995. *Shifts in the Social Contract: Understanding Change in American Society*. Thousand Oaks, CA: Sage.

Rubin, Beth A., and Charles J. Brody. 2011. "Operationalizing Management Citizenship Behavior and Testing Its Impact on Employee Commitment, Satisfaction, and Mental Health." *Work and Occupations* 38: 465-499.

Sakamoto, Arthur, and ChangHwan Kim. 2010. "Is Rising Earnings Inequality Associated with Increased Exploitation? Evidence for US Manufacturing Industries, 1971-1996." *Sociological Perspectives* 53: 19-43.

Sakamoto, Arthur, and Jeng Liu. 2006. "A Critique of Wright's Analysis of Exploitation." *Research in Social Stratification and Mobility* 24: 209-221.

Salzinger, Leslie. 2003. *Genders in Production: Making Workers in Mexico's Global Factories*. Berkeley and London: University of California Press.

Sauer, Carsten, and Meike J. May. 2016. "Determinants of Just Earnings: The Importance of Comparisons with Similar Others and Social Relations with Supervisors and Coworkers in Organizations." *Research in Social Stratification and Mobility* 47: 45-54.

Schatzman, Leonard, and Rue Bucher. 1964. "Negotiating a Division of Labor Among Professionals in the State Mental Hospital." *Psychiatry* 27: 266-277.

Scheffler, Samuel. 2003. "What Is Egalitarianism?" *Philosophy & Public Affairs* 31: 5-39.

Scherer, Frederic M. 1970. *Industrial Pricing: Theory and Evidence*. Chicago: Rand McNally.

Schwalbe, Michael. 2008. *Rigging the Game: How Inequality Is Reproduced in Everyday Life*. New York: Oxford University Press.

Schwalbe, Michael, Daphne Holden, Douglas Schrock, Sandra Godwin, Shealy Thompson, and Michele Wolkomir. 2000. "Generic Processes in the Reproduction of Inequality: An Interactionist Analysis." *Social Forces* 79: 419-452.

Schwalbe, Michael, Tricia McTague, and Kylie Parrotta. 2016. "Identity Contests and the Negotiation of Organizational Change" *Advances in Group Processes* 13: 57-92.

Schwalbe, Michael, and Heather Shay. 2014. "Dramaturgy and Dominance." In *Handbook of the Social Psychology of Inequality*, edited by Jane McLeod, Edward Lawler, and Michael Schwalbe, 155-180. Dordrecht, The Netherlands: Springer.

Schweiker, Michael, and Martin Groß. 2016. "Organizational Environments and Bonus Payments: Rent Destruction or Rent Sharing?" *Research in Social Stratification and Mobility* 47: 7-19.

Scott, W. Richard, and Gerald F. Davis. 2015. *Organizations and Organizing: Rational, Natural and Open Systems Perspectives*. New York and London: Routledge.

Sen, Amartya. 1992. *Inequality Reexamined*. New York: Oxford University Press.

Sewell, William H., Jr. 1992. "A Theory of Structure: Duality, Agency, and Transformation." *American Journal of Sociology* 98: 1-29.

Sewell, William H., and Robert M. Hauser. 1975. *Education, Occupation, and Earnings. Achievement in the Early Career*. New York: Academic Press.

Shams, Sufi, and Donald Tomaskovic-Devey. 2017. "Trajectories of Managerial Access." Working Paper. University of Massachusetts, Amherst.

Sidel, Robin, and Dan Fitzpatrick. 2014. "J.P. Morgan's Dimon, Ex-Ally Settle Dispute." *Wall Street Journal*, January 27. http://www.wsj.com/articles/SB100014240527023 03277704579344620263063010. Retrieved 12/5/2016.

Singer, Peter. 2011. *The Expanding Circle: Ethics, Evolution, and Moral Progress*. Princeton, NJ: Princeton University Press.

Skaggs, Sheryl. 2008. "Producing Change or Bagging Opportunity? The Effects of Discrimination Litigation on Women in Supermarket Management." *American Journal of Sociology* 113: 1148–1182.

Skans, Oskar Nordström, Per-Anders Edin, and Bertil Holmlund. 2009. "Wage Dispersion Between and Within Plants: Sweden 1985–2000." In *The Structure of Wages: An International Comparison*, edited by Edward Lazear and Kathryn Shaw, 217–260. Chicago: University of Chicago Press.

Small, Mario Luis. 2009. *Unanticipated Gains: Origins of Network Inequality in Everyday Life*. New York: Oxford University Press.

Smith, Adam. 1994 (1776). *The Wealth of Nations*. New York: Modern Library.

Smith, Dorothy E. 2005. *Institutional Ethnography: A Sociology for People*. Lanham, MD: Altamira Press.

Smith-Doerr, Laurel. 2004. *Women's Work: Gender Equality vs. Hierarchy in the Life Sciences*. Boulder, CO: Lynne Rienner Publishers.

Solow, Robert M. 1957. "Technical Change and the Aggregate Production Function." *Review of Economics and Statistics* 39: 312–320.

Sommeiller, Estelle, Mark Price, and Ellis Wazeter. 2016. *Income Inequality in the U.S. by State, Metropolitan Area, and County*. Economic Policy Institute. http://www.epi.org/files/pdf/107100.pdf. Retrieved 6/22/16.

Song, Jae, David J. Price, Fatih Guvenen, Nicholas Bloom, and Till Von Wachter. 2016. "Firming up Inequality." Working Paper 21199. National Bureau of Economic Research.

Sørensen, Aage B. 1996. "The Structural Basis of Social Inequality." *American Journal of Sociology* 101: 1333–1365.

Sørensen, Aage B. 2000. "Toward a Sounder Basis for Class Analysis." *American Journal of Sociology* 105: 1523–1558.

Stack, Liam. 2016. "Light Sentence for Brock Turner in Stanford Rape Case Draws Outrage." *New York Times*, June 6. http://www.nytimes.com/2016/06/07/us/outrage-in-stanford-rape-case-over-dueling-statements-of-victim-and-attackers-father.html

Stainback, Kevin, and Donald Tomaskovic-Devey. 2012. *Documenting Desegregation: Racial and Gender Segregation in Private Sector Employment Since the Civil Rights Act*. New York: Russell Sage Press.

Starr, Evan P., J. J. Prescott, and Norman Bishara. 2016. "Noncompetes and Employee Mobility." U of Michigan Law & Econ Research Paper No. 16-032. Social Science Research Network. https://ssrn.com/abstract=2858637.

Steinberg, Ronnie J. 1990. "Social Construction of Skill: Gender, Power, and Comparable Worth." *Work and Occupations* 17: 449–482.

Stewart, Neil, Gordon D. A. Brown, and Nick Chater. 2005. "Absolute Identification by Relative Judgment." *Psychological Review* 112: 881–911.

Stiglitz, Joseph E. 2005. "More Instruments and Broader Goals: Moving Toward the Post-Washington Consensus." In *Wider Perspectives on Global Development*, edited by Tony Atkinson, 16–48. London: Palgrave Macmillan.

Stiglitz, Joseph E. 2015. *Rewriting the Rules of the American Economy: An Agenda for Growth and Shared Prosperity*. New York: W.W. Norton & Company.

Strauss, Anselm L. 1978. *Negotiations: Varieties, Contexts, Processes, and Social Order*. San Francisco: Jossey-Bass.

Sum, Andrew, Paulo Tobar, Joseph McLaughlin, and Sheila Palma. 2008. "The Great Divergence: Real-Wage Growth of all Workers versus Finance Workers." *Challenge* 51: 57–79.

Thorne, Barrie. 1993. *Gender Play: Girls and Boys in School.* New Brunswick, NJ: Rutgers University Press.

Tilcsik, András. 2011. "Pride and Prejudice: Employment Discrimination Against Openly Gay Men in the United States." *American Journal of Sociology* 117: 586–626.

Tilly, Charles. 1999. *Durable Inequality*. Berkeley: University of California Press.

Tilly, Charles. 2000. "Relational Studies of Inequality." *Contemporary Sociology* 29: 782–785.

Tomaskovic-Devey, Donald. 1993. *Gender and Racial Inequality at Work*. Ithaca, NY: Cornell University Press.

Tomaskovic-Devey, Donald. 2014. "The Relational Generation of Workplace Inequalities." *Social Currents* 1: 51–73.

Tomaskovic-Devey, Donald, and Dustin Avent-Holt. 2014. "What Is Still Missing? The Relational Context of Inequality." *Socio-Economic Review* 12: 609–636.

Tomaskovic-Devey, Donald, and Dustin Avent-Holt. 2016. "Observing Organizational Inequality Regimes." *Research in the Sociology of Work* 28: 187–212.

Tomaskovic-Devey, Donald, Dustin Avent-Holt, Catherine Zimmer, and Sandra Harding. 2009. "The Categorical Generation of Organizational Inequality: A Comparative Test of Tilly's Durable Inequality." *Research in Social Stratification and Mobility* 27: 128–142.

Tomaskovic-Devey, Donald, Dustin Avent-Holt, Catherine Zimmer, and Sandra Harding. 2016a. "Profit, Trust, and Contract: Alternative or Complimentary Logics in Market Exchange?" Social Science Research Network. https://papers.ssrn.com/sol3/papers.cfm?abstract_id=2877367.

Tomaskovic-Devey, Donald, Martin Hällsten, and Dustin Avent-Holt. 2015a. "Where Do Immigrants Fare Worse? Modeling Workplace Wage Gap Variation with Longitudinal Employer-Employee Data." *American Journal of Sociology* 120: 1095–1143.

Tomaskovic-Devey, Donald, and Ken-Hou Lin. 2011. "Income Dynamics, Economic Rents, and the Financialization of the US Economy." *American Sociological Review* 76: 538–559.

Tomaskovic-Devey, Donald, and Ken-Hou Lin. 2013. "Financialization: Causes, Inequality Consequences, and Policy Implications." *North Carolina Banking Institute* 18: 167–194.

Tomaskovic-Devey, Donald, Ken-Hou Lin, and Nathan Meyers. 2015b. "Did Financialization Reduce Economic Growth?" *Socio-Economic Review* 13: 525–548.

Tomaskovic-Devey, Donald, Silvia Melzer, and Peter Jacobebbinghaus. 2016b. "The Organizational Production of Earnings Inequalities in Germany, 1994–2010." Working Paper. University of Massachusetts, Amherst.

Tomaskovic-Devey, Donald, Anthony Rainey, Joseph King, Dustin Avent-Holt, István Boza, Olivier Godechot, Martin Hällsten, Are Skeie Hermansen, Feng Hou, Jiwook Jung, Joseph King, Naomi Kodama, Eunmi Mun, Mirna Safi, and Zaibu Tufa.

2017. "Producing Inequalities: An Examination of the Workplace Generation of Earnings Inequalities in Eight High Income Countries." Working Paper. MaxPo.

Tomaskovic-Devey, Donald, and Sheryl Skaggs. 1999. "An Establishment-Level Test of the Statistical Discrimination Hypothesis." *Work and Occupations* 26: 422-445.

Tomaskovic-Devey, Don, and Sheryl Skaggs. 2002. "Sex Segregation, Labor Process Organization, and Gender Earnings Inequality." *American Journal of Sociology* 108: 102-128.

Treiman, Donald J. 1977. *Occupational Prestige in Comparative Perspective.* New York: Academic Press.

Twohey, Megan. 2017. "Harvey Weinstein Is Fired After Sexual Reports." *New York Times*, October 8.

Uzzi, Brian. 1996. "The Sources and Consequences of Embeddedness for the Economic Performance of Organizations: The Network Effect." *American Sociological Review* 61: 674-698.

Uzzi, Brian. 1997. "Social Structure and Competition in Interfirm Networks: The Paradox of Embeddedness." *Administrative Science Quarterly* 42: 35-67.

Uzzi, Brian. 1999. "Embeddedness in the Making of Financial Capital: How Social Relations and Networks Benefit Firms Seeking Financing." *American Sociological Review* 64: 481-505.

Uzzi, Brian, and Ryon Lancaster. 2004. "Embeddedness and Price Formation in the Corporate Law Market." *American Sociological Review* 69: 319-344.

Vail, John. 2010. "Decommodification and Egalitarian Political Economy." *Politics & Society* 38: 310-346.

Vallas, Steven Peter. 1993. *Power in the Workplace: The Politics of Production at AT&T.* Albany: State University of New York Press.

Vallas, Steven Peter. 2001. "Symbolic Boundaries and the New Division of Labor: Engineers, Workers and the Restructuring of Factory Life." *Research in Social Stratification and Mobility* 18: 3-37.

Vallas, Steven Peter. 2006. "Empowerment Redux: Structure, Agency, and the Remaking of Managerial Authority." *American Journal of Sociology* 111: 1677-1717.

Vallas, Steven P., and John P. Beck. 1996. "The Transformation of Work Revisited: The Limits of Flexibility in American Manufacturing." *Social Problems* 43: 339-361.

Vallas, Steven, and Emily Cummins. 2014. "Relational Models of Organizational Inequalities Emerging Approaches and Conceptual Dilemmas." *American Behavioral Scientist* 58: 228-255.

Vallas, Steven P., and Andrea Hill. 2012. "Conceptualizing Power in Organizations." *Research in the Sociology of Organizations* 34: 165-197.

Viscelli, Steve. 2016. *The Big Rig: Trucking and the Decline of the American Dream.* Berkeley: University of California Press.

Vitali, Stefania, James B. Glattfelder, and Stefano Battiston. 2011. "The Network of Global Corporate Control." *PLoS One* 6: e25995.

Wallace, Michael, Larry J. Griffin, and Beth A. Rubin. 1989. "The Positional Power of American Labor, 1963-1977." *American Sociological Review* 54:197-214.

Wallace, Michael, Kevin T. Leicht, and Lawrence E. Raffalovich. 1999. "Unions, Strikes, and Labor's Share of Income: A Quarterly Analysis of the United States, 1949-1992." *Social Science Research* 28: 265-288.

Wallace, Michael, Bradley Wright, and Allen Hyde. 2014. "Religious Affiliation and Hiring Discrimination in the American South: A Field Experiment." *Social Currents* 1:171-189.

Weber, Max. 1947. *The Theory of Social and Economic Organization*, trans. by A. M. Henderson and Talcott Parsons. New York: Free Press.
Weeden, Kim A. 2002. "Why Do Some Occupations Pay More than Others? Social Closure and Earnings Inequality in the United States." *American Journal of Sociology* 108: 55-101.
Weick, Karl E. 1995. *Sensemaking in Organizations*. Thousand Oaks, CA: Sage.
Weil, David. 2014. *The Fissured Workplace*. Cambridge, MA: Harvard University Press.
Weitzer, Ronald. 2015. "Human Trafficking and Contemporary Slavery." *Annual Review of Sociology* 41: 223-242.
West, Candace, and Don H. Zimmerman. 1987. "Doing Gender." *Gender & Society* 1: 125-151.
Western, Bruce. 1999. *Between Class and Market: Postwar Unionization in the Capitalist Democracies*. Princeton, NJ: Princeton University Press.
Western, Bruce. 2006. *Punishment and Inequality in America*. New York: Russell Sage Press.
Western, Bruce, and Jake Rosenfeld. 2011. "Unions, Norms, and the Rise in US Wage Inequality." *American Sociological Review* 76: 513-537.
Wherry, Fred F. 2012. *The Culture of Markets*. New York: Polity Press.
White, Harrison C. 1981. "Where Do Markets Come From?" *American Journal of Sociology* 87: 517-547.
White, Harrison C. 2002. *Markets from Networks: Socioeconomic Models of Production*. Princeton, NJ: Princeton University Press.
Whitford, Josh. 2005. *The New Old Economy: Networks, Institutions, and the Organizational Transformation of American Manufacturing*. Oxford: Oxford University Press.
Williams, Bruce B. 1987. *Black Workers in an Industrial Suburb: The Struggle Against Discrimination*. New Brunswick, NJ: Rutgers University Press.
Williams, Christine L. 1992. "The Glass Escalator: Hidden Advantages for Men in the 'Female' Professions." *Social Problems* 39: 253-267.
Williamson, Oliver E. 1981. "The Economics of Organization: The Transaction Cost Approach." *American Journal of Sociology* 87: 548-577.
Wilmers, Nathan. 2017. "Wage Stagnation and Economic Governance: How Buyer-Supplier Relations Affect U.S. Workers' Wages, 1978-2014." Working Paper. Department of Sociology, Harvard University.
Wilson, George, and Vincent J. Roscigno. 2014. "The Relational Foundations of Inequality at Work II: Structure-Agency Interplay." *American Behavioral Scientist* 58: 375-378.
Wingfield, Adia Harvey. 2013. *No More Invisible Man: Race and Gender in Men's Work*. Philadelphia: Temple University Press.
Wooten, Melissa E., and Enobong H. Branch. 2012. "Defining Appropriate Labor: Race, Gender, and Idealization of Black Women in Domestic Service." *Race, Gender & Class* 19: 292-308.
Wooten, Melissa, and Andrew J. Hoffman. 2008. "Organizational Fields: Past, Present and Future." In *The SAGE Handbook of Organizational Institutionalism*, edited by Royston Greenwood, Christine Oliver, Kerstin Sahlin, and Roy Suddaby, 131-147. New York: Sage Press.
Wright, Bradley, Michael Wallace, John Bailey, and Allen Hyde. 2013. "Religious Affiliation and Hiring Discrimination in New England: A Field Experiment." *Research in Social Stratification and Mobility* 34: 111-126.

Wright, Erik Olin. 1997. *Class Counts: Comparative Studies in Class Analysis*. Cambridge: Cambridge University Press.

Wright, Erik Olin. 2000. "Reducing Income and Wealth Inequality: Real Utopian Proposals." *Contemporary Sociology* 29: 143–156.

Wright, Erik Olin. 2005. "Foundations of a Neo-Marxist Class Analysis." In *Approaches to Class Analysis*, edited by Erik Olin Wright, 4–30. Cambridge: Cambridge University Press.

Wright, Erik Olin. 2013. "Transforming Capitalism Through Real Utopias." *American Sociological Review* 78: 1–25.

Wright, Erik Olin, and Luca Perrone. 1977. "Marxist Class Categories and Income Inequality." *American Sociological Review* 42: 32–55.

Yeung, Bernice. 2017. " #MeToo Leaves Behind." https://www.revealnews.org/blog/the-people-metoo-leaves-behind/. Retrieved 7/20/2018.

Yeung, Bernice. 2016. "Why Cleaning a Hotel Room Makes You a Target for Sexual Harassment." https://www.revealnews.org/blog/why-cleaning-a-hotel-room-makes-you-a-target-for-sexual-harassment/. Retrieved 7/20/2018.

Zelizer, Viviana A. 1979. *Morals and Markets: The Development of Life Insurance in the United States*. New York: Columbia University Press.

Zelizer, Viviana A. 2007. "Pasts and Futures of Economic Sociology." *American Behavioral Scientist* 50: 1056–1069.

Zelizer, Viviana A. 2012. "How I Became a Relational Economic Sociologist and What Does That Mean?" *Politics & Society* 40: 145–174.

Zuckerman, Ezra W., and Stoyan V. Sgourev. 2006. "Peer Capitalism: Parallel Relationships in the US Economy." *American Journal of Sociology* 111: 1327–1366.

Index

Tables and figures are indicated by an italic *t* and *f* following the page number

www.ingramcontent.com/pod-product-compliance
Ingram Content Group UK Ltd.
Pitfield, Milton Keynes, MK11 3LW, UK
UKHW041644190726
13854UKWH00006B/2698

9 780190 624439